A COPTIC GNOSTIC
TREATISE

A COPTIC GNOSTIC TREATISE

CONTAINED IN THE

CODEX BRUCIANUS

[Bruce MS. 96. Bod. Lib. Oxford]

A TRANSLATION FROM THE COPTIC:
TRANSCRIPT AND COMMENTARY

BY

CHARLOTTE A. BAYNES

O.B.E., F.R.A.I.

WITH PHOTOGRAPHS OF THE TEXT

CAMBRIDGE
AT THE UNIVERSITY PRESS
1933

CAMBRIDGE UNIVERSITY PRESS
Cambridge, New York, Melbourne, Madrid, Cape Town,
Singapore, São Paulo, Delhi, Mexico City

Cambridge University Press
The Edinburgh Building, Cambridge CB2 8RU, UK

Published in the United States of America by Cambridge University Press, New York

www.cambridge.org
Information on this title: www.cambridge.org/9781107650961

First published 1933
First paperback edition 2013

A catalogue record for this publication is available from the British Library

ISBN 978-1-107-65096-1 Paperback

CONTENTS

PREFACE

It seems as well, at the outset, to define the aims and limitations of the present volume. In the first place, it is intended to make readily accessible, by means of photographic reproductions, a little-known Coptic text. Placed side by side with a transcript embodying the emendations and restorations made up to the present time, it becomes available for interested students unable to view the original at Oxford. Secondly, my aim has been to produce a translation of the Coptic text—as exact as is consistent with readable English—whilst bearing in mind the main doctrines and the technical terminology to be expected in a treatise which must rank among the best products of philosophic Gnosticism of the early centuries A.D. And thirdly, I have endeavoured to elucidate a somewhat obscure writing, by showing the relationship of its teaching to other systems of the Christian Gnosis, and by pointing out the many definite allusions to well-known Gnostic doctrines that occur in it. This has seemed to me the most helpful way of dealing with a text that owes much of its apparent obscurity to the fact that the author is neither writing an instructional or doctrinal treatise, nor defining the tenets of a particular system, but is dwelling on and expanding certain doctrines and philosophic notions already familiar to his readers. I have not discussed the question of a relationship between these doctrines and those of the non-Christian systems of the East, because, personally, I can see no convincing grounds for the theory of their Pagan derivation, although undoubtedly the effect of a certain contact with Egyptian and Alexandrian—and perhaps Iranian—notions is to be expected. My aim also excludes investigations regarding the source of this particular text or the origin of the systems to which its doctrines are allied. Finally, it should be made clear that the present work has no pretensions to be an enquiry into the subject of Gnosticism, and can only be regarded as a contribution to that study inasmuch as it deals with one of the very few original writings we possess, a writing that has hitherto been little noticed and little studied.

As regards the source of the Coptic text, or of its supposed Greek original, examination of the available evidence has been fully made by Dr Carl Schmidt, and until fresh data come to light there is nothing to add to his findings[1]. The position is much the same both as regards the origins of Christian Gnosticism generally, the sources whence the various doctrines were derived or the circumstances in which the different systems evolved and developed. These fields have been covered by many competent scholars. The traditional point of view, which has treated the Gnostics historically as Christians, has lately been re-stated, with original arguments in support of that view, by Prof. F. C. Burkitt[2]. Of the modern theory, which holds that the main tenets of Christian Gnosticism are derived directly from the Orient, or are, alternatively, a blend with Eastern philosophies or an attempt to re-state these in Christian

---

[1] Carl Schmidt, "Gnost. Schrift. in Kopt. Sprache" (*T.u.U.* Bd viii). Leipzig, 1892. "Kopt. gnost. Schriften" (*Königl. Preuss. Akad. d. Wissen.* Bd i). Leipzig, 1905. "Plotins Stellung z. Gnost. u. kirch. Christ." (*T.u.U.* N.F. Bd v). Leipzig, 1900.

[2] F. C. Burkitt, *Church and Gnosis* (Morse Lectures for 1931). Cambridge, 1932.

terms, a most able and exhaustive exposition is found in the work of Dr W. Bousset[1]. But in spite of all the careful research work done by scholars, the subject is far from having attained the status of a ranged and completed study, owing to the fact that the material for research is scanty: for which reason the value of the few original writings we possess is greatly enhanced. As observed by M. Eugène de Faye[2], the best hope of obtaining fresh light on this obscure subject, and of arriving at a true view of the beliefs of the Gnostics, is to go to the texts themselves, rather than to attempt explanations based on the records—often unintelligent and contradictory—of the anti-heresiarchs.

In the process of commenting on the text and its doctrines, I have obtained the greatest illumination from another Coptic Gnostic work to which it is closely related—*The Apocryphon of John*. This text, which has been in the care of Dr Carl Schmidt, at the Berlin University, since 1896, is part of a Coptic Gnostic Codex from which extracts only have been made accessible to the world of scholarship in the German translation that I have utilized. In view of the very limited number of such extant texts, and the great value, for research, of those that exist, all students of the subject must concur in an earnest hope that Dr Schmidt will no longer delay in giving to the world a textual transcript and full translation of the Codex Berolinensis.

In making my acknowledgments for assistance received in my work, it seems fitting, first of all, to pay a

[1] W. Bousset, *Hauptprobleme d. Gnosis*. Göttingen, 1907.
[2] Eugène de Faye, "Gnostiques et Gnosticisme" (*Bibl. d. l'École d. Hautes Études*, vol. xxvii). Paris, 1913.

tribute of grateful memory to three friends who gave me much generous help: to the late Dr J. H. Walker, who read my translation in its initial stages, and made valuable suggestions for difficult passages; to Miss F. Voisin, B.A., for her ever-ready help with obscure Greek passages and terms; and to Mr G. R. S. Mead, M.A., who by his writings and lectures inspired me with a desire to work on the subject of Christian Gnosticism.

My indebtedness to the fundamental work done on the text by Dr Carl Schmidt is not to be estimated. His emended transcript forms the basis of the present one; thus many weeks of arduous work have been saved for me. Further, the extracts, in German translation, from *The Apocryphon of John* (Codex Berolinensis), published in 1907, and kindly sent me by Dr Schmidt, have greatly served to elucidate many difficult passages in the present treatise.

I would express my great obligations to the following for help received at various times: to Miss M. A. Murray, D.Lit., my first instructor in Coptic, from whom I have continuously received most generous assistance and advice in my difficulties. To Mr W. E. Crum, M.A., unfailing in his help with linguistic and philological questions, who read the greater part of my translation, and gave critical consideration to the emendations and restorations I have made to the Coptic text.

Very special thanks are also due to the following: the Rev. W. H. Kent, O.S.C., D.D., for criticism of the Notes, and for help in the selection and translation of passages from Greek texts; the Rev. J. M. Barton, D.D., L.S.S., for information in regard to scriptural and antiquarian matters, and for general criticism of my work; Prof. F. C. Burkitt, D.D., Hon. D.Lit., from whose work *Church and Gnosis* I have derived help, as also from his kindly response to questions regarding the derivation and meaning of proper names appearing in Gnostic texts.

My acknowledgments are also due to the authorities of the Bodleian Library, Oxford, for permission to reproduce the Coptic text.

Finally, I must express sincere gratitude to the many friends who have generously helped me in various ways: critically and financially, and by their suggestive thought, their encouragement, and advice.

C. A. BAYNES

London 1933

INTRODUCTORY NOTES

I. HISTORICAL

The main historical data relative to the Coptic text here translated may be briefly summarized.

The collection of papyri known as the Codex Brucianus was bought in Upper Egypt—probably at Thebes—about the year 1769, by the Scottish traveller, James Bruce. After his return to Scotland, he sent the Codex to London, in order that the Coptic scholar, C. G. Woide, might inspect it and make a copy. In 1848, it came into the possession of the Bodleian Library (Bruce MS 96), while the copy made by Woide was also placed in the keeping of the Library (Woide MS Clar. Press, d. 13). M. G. Schwartze was the next to study the text, when in 1848 he visited England in search of Coptic MSS. He made a copy of Woide's transcript, and on comparing it with the original, found it necessary to make many corrections. Unfortunately, to the loss of Coptic scholarship, his death occurred before he had time to study, translate, and edit the text. His corrected manuscript copy then came into the possession of his collaborator, J. H. Petermann. In 1882, M. E. Amélineau drew the attention of l'Académie des Inscriptions et Belles-lettres to the papyrus. He visited Oxford and copied the text, noting also, as had done M. G. Schwartze, the numerous errors in Woide's copy. In 1891, Prof. Amélineau edited the text, giving his own transcript and a French translation[1]. But as he lacked

---

[1] M. E. Amélineau, "Notice sur le Papyrus gnostique Bruce" (*Notices et Extraits des Manuscrits de la Bibl. Nat.*). Paris, 1891.

the opportunity of comparing the original with the emended copy of Woide-Schwartze, his work has little value. In 1886, the authorities of the Bodleian Library caused the loose leaves of the Codex to be bound up in book form. Unfortunately the work was not supervised by a student of the Coptic language. There is neither order nor sequence among the leaves, while many are upside down and have the recto and verso reversed. At the same time the leaves were reduced in size, the ragged portions being trimmed off and removed. Each leaf was then enclosed between two sheets of tracing paper. And further, four leaves, in existence when Woide made his copy, disappeared, having perhaps been thrown out by the binder owing to their dilapidated condition.

By the publication, in 1882, of Amélineau's preliminary work, the attention of Prof. Harnack was directed to the Codex. In 1890, with his help and support, and that of Prof. Erman—who handed over Schwartze's copy acquired after the death of J. H. Petermann—and the assistance of the Prussian Kultusministerium, Prof. Carl Schmidt was enabled to proceed to Oxford, when he subjected the text to a lengthy and searching examination. At the same time, he compared the Woide-Schwartze copy with the original, a very arduous task, owing to the increasingly bad condition of the latter. Being, however, already acquainted with the contents of the Codex, he was fortunately able to emend many defective passages. Finding the leaves bound up in the state of confusion described above, with great skill he distinguished two MSS and some fragments in the one Codex. These are distinct as to date, contents and handwriting. Giving his own sequence to the leaves, he made a new transcript of the text, embodying the various emendations. This he published in 1892, together with a German translation and commentary[1]. This again was followed, in 1905, by a revised translation[2]. For further details relating to the history of the text, the student is referred to these works of Dr Schmidt.

The condition of the Codex has further deteriorated since the time of Dr Schmidt's examination. Much of the papyrus has perished and is full of holes. There are also mildew spots on many of the leaves, which appear to have originated in the paste used at the time of binding. It is, however, satisfactory to be able to note, that in 1928, after my work on the Codex was completed, the authorities of the Bodleian Library subjected the papyrus to treatment for the purpose of arresting the mildew, and at the same time re-numbered the pages, adopting the sequence of Dr Schmidt. The work of future students has thus been greatly simplified, and there are also good grounds for believing that the treatment has rendered the papyrus immune from further decay.

II. DESCRIPTIVE

1. THE COPTIC TEXT

As indicated by Dr Schmidt, the Bruce Codex is a collection of papyri consisting of two independent MSS and some fragments. The first of these originally comprised 43 leaves (86 pages), of which three leaves—in existence when C. G. Woide made his copy—are now missing. To this work, Dr Schmidt assigns the title: First and Second Books of Ieou. It is placed first in his

[1] Carl Schmidt, "Gnost. Schrift. in Kopt. Sprache" (*T.u.U.* Bd VIII). Leipzig, 1892.
[2] Carl Schmidt, "Kopt. gnost. Schriften" (*Königl. Preuss. Akad. a. Wissen.* Bd I). Leipzig, 1905.

1892 edition of the Codex, and is followed by the fragments. The remaining 32 leaves (61 pages), forming the second independent work, come last. It is this latter work which forms the subject of the present volume. This MS is fragmentary, and without title, beginning, or end. The papyrus on which it is written varies in colour between pale reddish, dull reddish, and a deep dull red. The material appears to be very brittle. The leaves are small folio, and originally—before they were trimmed at the time of binding—must have averaged 29 × 19 cm. The photographic reproductions are approximately half the size of the originals. The number of lines on a page ranges between 30 and 38. According to C. G. Woide, the MS was originally folded in the form of four sheets and may possibly have been bound. In any case it must always have been in book form and not a roll. In Woide's time the 32 leaves were extant, and all but one were written on both sides. Of these leaves, as has been said, four are now missing, but are preserved in his transcript. The writing of the 54 extant pages is in one hand. For the most part it is upright and fairly straight in line. The characters are uncials, and are large, square and well formed. As is usual in writing Coptic, the words are mostly run together, though there are sometimes short spaces between phrases, and longer ones when a complete change of subject-matter is introduced. What punctuation there is is the usual high point, but as with the super-lineation of certain words and consonants, so much is obliterated, and so many marks and spots have appeared owing to mildew and other causes, that I have thought it better to omit both in my transcript. The treatise is written in good normal Sahidic, the dialect of Upper Egypt, with very occasionally a possibly archaic form. As is usual with Coptic writings of a philosophic content, a very large number of Greek terms are introduced. These show the characteristic Coptic use and spelling. There are no accents, no plurals, no terminal changes other than such as are peculiar to the Coptic manner of writing Greek words. Nouns do duty for adjectives, and vice versa. Verbs are written in a form consonant with the Imperative of the Active Voice and are contracted, but active and passive voices seem, often enough, to have little, if any difference for the writer. From the Greek standpoint, it may be said that there are, apparently, no limits to the Copts' powers of misusing Greek words. One fact, however, seems clear; in the present text the writer was concerned with one thing only—the *root* meaning of the terms he adopted to express his thought; thus the grammatical form was a matter of indifference to him. There are many instances throughout the treatise, where, for the translator to adopt the usual or derived meaning of a Greek word, only results in entirely missing the writer's point.

There is a certain number of verbal errors in the text. These are indicated in the footnotes to the transcript. Simple errors in spelling—which are fairly numerous— are not dealt with, because, for economy's sake, the use of Coptic type is restricted. Further, as regards such errors, Dr Schmidt has noted them all in his printed edition of the text, to which reference can be made.

2. THE TRANSCRIPT

Dr Schmidt's printed transcript—which embodies his own emendations and restorations as well as those of

C. G. Woide and M. G. Schwartze—was used as the basis of the present one. This was compared by me with the Coptic MS at Oxford, and with the photographic reproductions, which are, in fact, more legible than is now the original text. The four leaves that were no longer to be found when Dr Schmidt made his transcript, were taken by him from the copy made by Woide, and emended. Of these I have not thought it necessary to give photographic reproductions. In one respect, my arrangement of the leaves of the MS differs from that of Dr Schmidt, in that I place his five final leaves at the beginning. This I do without hesitation, as I find the arrangement yields an orderly and more or less complete system of cosmology. With a few exceptions, I have adopted the emendations and restorations made by Dr Schmidt. To these I have been able to add a few of my own. Nearly all the emended passages are found on the first seven pages of the treatise—according to my arrangement—on the final seven—following that of Dr Schmidt. The emendations and restorations are drawn from three sources: words immediately following the point where the impaired text breaks off, are from the Woide-Schwartze transcript: those enclosed in brackets [ ], are Dr Schmidt's additions: the remainder, indicated by ⟨ ⟩, are made by myself.

3. THE TRANSLATION AND COMMENTARY

The translation is from the original Coptic, and has been kept as nearly literal as is consistent with readable English. Some change in the form and construction of the Coptic sentence is unavoidable, but I have endeavoured, wherever possible, to preserve the manner of speech of the author. Departures from a literal rendering consist principally in the occasional omission of constantly repeated or redundant pronouns and prepositions, and the substitution of the noun or proper name for the corresponding pronoun, where, in very long paragraphs, the former has not been mentioned for several sentences. When this substitution is made, the fact is indicated by enclosing the noun or proper name in brackets ( ).

The Greek words, which are numerous throughout the treatise, are introduced into the translation. As, however, it has been necessary to restrict the use of Coptic type, they are printed in the ordinary Greek alphabet instead of the uncial letters normally used by the Copts. The one Coptic letter—ϩ = *h*—which appears in some of the words, is represented by the Greek rough breathing sign ʽ, thus: αʽορατος = ⲁϩⲟⲣⲁⲧⲟⲥ. Except for this change in lettering, Greek words are reproduced exactly as they stand in the text.

The punctuation and paragraphing of the translation is according to English usage. Except for occasional wide spacing—such as occurs twice on XI—to mark a change in subject-matter, there is no paragraphing in the Coptic text, which is a continuous writing. Such parts of the treatise as embody categories, or are in the form of prayers, hymns, etc., are inset in the translation in order to mark such changes in subject-matter.

There occur in the treatise a certain number of direct quotations from Biblical texts, while other passages are plainly based on these or are paraphrastic. In quoting the originals from English versions, I have found that the anglicized Vulgate affords the closest approach to the Coptic rendering. In the case of citations from the O.T., question as to the source utilized by the writer hardly arises. The Greek of the Septuagint would be familiar to him. As regards the N.T., the source is not so certain. The following suggestions may, however, be made. The Coptic versions of the N.T.—both Sahidic and Bohairic—are assigned by modern scholarship to the family of MSS called by Westcott and Hort the Alexandrian group. This group includes the uncial Greek codices C and L, and also, according to Streeter's classification, the Westcott and Hort "Neutral" codices B and Aleph. It may be taken as well established that the Alexandrian group of MSS, both texts and versions, is Egyptian and Alexandrian, at least in general tendency, though the Sahidic version "in an important minority of readings goes over to the side of the text represented by D and the Old Latin version, especially in its African form" (Streeter, *The Four Gospels*, p. 56). In his revision of the Old Latin N.T., St Jerome is believed to have made use of a Greek text having affinities with Codices B and Aleph of the Alexandrian group. The variations in readings in the different families of texts and versions are usually slight, and there is often a considerable intermingling of types of text (e.g. the Sahidic "Western" readings mentioned above). Also it is noteworthy that "the African Latin ...in many of its readings agrees with B and Aleph against the type of Old Latin..." (Streeter, *op. cit.* p. 66). Consequently, the fact that St Jerome's Vulgate appears to confirm the readings of the Coptic text may be due to the original common use, directly or indirectly, by the Old Latin and Coptic translators, of a very ancient Greek text, or to the probability that in making his revision St Jerome used a Greek codex of the type current in Egypt.

The citations from, and references to, Patristic writers are drawn principally from the following textual editions:

IRENAEUS. *Adver. haer.* Edit. W. Wigan Harvey. Cambridge, 1857.

HIPPOLYTUS. *Ref. om. haer.* Edit. L. Düncker and F. G. Schneidewin. Göttingen, 1859.

CLEMENS (Alexandrinus). *Excerpta ex Theodoto.* [Die griech. christl. Schriftsteller d. ersten 3 Jhdte.] Bd III. Edit. O. Stählin. Leipzig, 1909.

For the "PISTIS SOPHIA" I have utilized Peter-mann's Coptic text. [Berlin, 1851.]

For *The Apocryphon of John*, the extracts in German translation, published by Dr Carl Schmidt, and re-printed from *Philotesia*. Berlin, 1907.

The source of all other references and citations is given *in situ*.

4. THE TREATISE

The treatise before us embodies the meditation of a Gnostic philosopher on the Gnosis or Science of God, of the Universe, and of Salvation. For a worthy com-parison to this treatise among Gnostic philosophies, one can look only to the profound thought and daring speculations of such thinkers as Basilides and Valentinus. As in the case of those teachers, one is arrested and enthralled as one follows the mind of the seer, soaring higher and higher, to purer and rarer conceptions, until thought itself reaches its limit and ceases, having touched the Ineffable Concept which is God.

If, however, on reaching the issue of such sublime themes, with expectations raised high by the level of the theology, one is left, finally, with a sense of something gone awry and abortive, it would seem due to the author's initial failure to perceive that his three sciences are one, and that it is only by following up the implications of the theology—truthfully conceived—that the cosmology and soteriology can be read aright. For the problems that he faced and failed to solve, find their solution only in the full realization of what is implied in an acceptance of the Divine Infinitude. Our author unmistakably conveys his innate recognition of the Absolute Simplicity, the Allness and the Infinitude of God. It is implicit in his use of such phrases and expressions as: *"the Self-alone-caused"*; *"the Unspeakable and Immeasurable One, who truly and veritably IS"*; *"the One who in Himself the Whole possesseth, whereas Himself, none doth possess"*; *"the One and Only One in the Whole, whom none doth comprehend"*. When, however, we come to consider his science of the universe, we find his thought losing touch with the high level of his earlier vision.

The purpose and aim of Gnostic philosophies was the giving to man a Gnosis of God that led to salvation. This knowledge consisted, firstly, in an understanding and acceptance of the fact that God, in His Essence, is unknowable and incomprehensible. And herein lies a resolution of contradictories—ignorance is true knowledge. Further, they taught that such truths about God as are accessible to His creatures, are obtainable only through His Only-begotten Word, which is the Utterance of all things, and the Substance of all things, and is "Light, and Life, and Grace". Such thoughts as these imply a belief that only in the Light of things Divine, can the things of man be rightly read. Thus when one is brought down from the region of these lofty conceptions to a consideration of the complex cos-

mology and soteriology of this and kindred pronounce-
ments of philosophic Gnosticism, one is puzzled and
confused by what seems a sudden failure of their thought,
and left with a sense of frustration. With their minds
equipped with sublime truths regarding the Nature of
God, and His Self-revelation in and to His Creation,
they boldly set out to seek a solution of the problems
that since time began have ever intrigued the mind of
man. Thus intently they pondered the manner of
coming into being of the universe with its multiplicity
of existences and things: the origin of evil, and the
explanation of its apparent admixture with the good:
the question as to whether or not the creation will be
restored to the Source of Perfection from whence it
came, and if so—more particularly with regard to man
—to what extent, and in what manner will this restoration be effected.

The failure of the Gnostics to resolve these problems
in a way that brings rest and satisfaction to the mind,
is not the failure of the Gnostic systems alone. It has
been the fate and failure of many a religious philosophy
and system of thought that started from the same
groundwork of Eternal Truths. What was it caused the
clouding of their vision? How was it that they failed
to see where the Light they possessed would lead? Was
it perhaps because they sought the answers to their
problems, not in the high region of thought, to which,
in their Vision of God, they undoubtedly attained—
where contradictories are resolved and seen in their
true light—but within the confines of Time and Space
and Number, where are, indeed, the problems, but no
answers? The failure of the Gnostics was their failure to
pursue to its logical term their own tremendous Con-

cept of the Infinitude of God, a concept that involves the recognition of One, Perfect, Self-existent Being, who was, is, and will be—All—and beyond All—in whose Will alone that things should be, the being of all things consists.

These men were Christians, as is plainly seen in their presentation—unorthodox though it be—of the mysteries of Redemption. Thus in the treatise we read: *"they understood the Mystery that became Man—because for this He was manifested, till they saw HIM who is indeed invisible"*. Christians they were, but heretics, and "heresy"—*"a choosing [one's opinions] for oneself"*—had then, as now, an ugly sound in the ears of the Divinely appointed Church, to whom, together with the deposit of Faith, was given the Divine promise of unfailing guidance in the way of Truth. And if, when marvelling at the beauty and truth of much that these Gnostics taught, at the earnestness of their souls, and their deep concern to proclaim the Glory of God and the miracle of His Dispensation to man, the thought arises that the treatment meted out to them was unduly harsh, it is doubtless in their failure to solve the problems before them in a manner commensurate with the worthiness of Divine Truth, that we see some measure of what the Church feared from the speculations of independent minds, removed from the restraint imposed by a defined body of Faith. And when one further considers the travesties of Christianity that arose, and the crude and unworthy developments in which some of the Gnostic systems became later involved—with their dependence upon what were little more than magical rites to the degradation of the Christian Faith and Sacraments— one sees justification for the fears and action of those who were custodians of the Faith. But such degenerate developments were for later days, and smaller minds. Profound thinkers, such as Basilides, Valentinus, and the author of our treatise, were much nearer to the Church than to the later Gnostic sects. Their thoughts were set on God; their sole aim, their whole endeavour, was directed to the enlightenment of the minds of men by "the revelation of the Mystery which was kept in silence from times eternal—which is now made manifest".

THE COPTIC TEXT
AND
TRANSCRIPT

[Originals reduced ½ in scale]

N.B.

Marginal References. E.g.

	Top numeral (I) denotes translator's sequence
I	and arrangement of leaves of the Coptic text;
MS. f. 138ᴿ	MS. f. 138ᴿ = folio number in Codex Brucianus;
C.S p. 52	C.S. p. 52 = number in Dr Schmidt's transcript.

Words following the point where impaired text breaks off are from the Woide-Schwartze transcript.

[ ] Denote emendations and restorations of the Coptic text made by Dr Schmidt supplementary to those of Woide-Schwartze.

⟨ ⟩ Denote emendations and restorations made by present translator

Ia
MS. f. 138R
C.S. p. 52

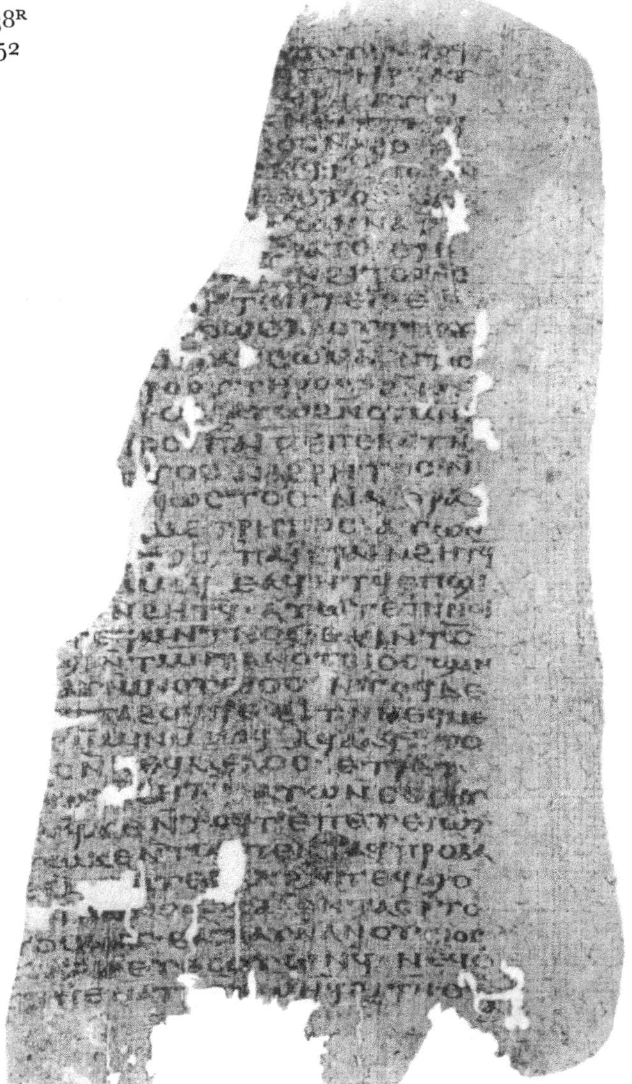

Iᵃ
MS. f. 138ᴿ
C.S. p. 52

1. ΝΑΤ]ΤΑϩΟΥ ΜΠΟΥΤΑϩΟΥ
ΜΠΕϫΙΩΤ ΝΝΙΠΤΗΡϤ ΑΥ
Ω] ⟨ΝΤΟϤ⟩ ΝΝΙΠΤΡϤ ΑΥΩ
ΝΤΟΠΟϹ⟩ ΝΝΕΙΠΤΗΡϤ
5. ΕΥΟ⟩[Ν]ΑΝΟΥϹΙΟϹ ΝΑϩΟΡΑ
ΤΟϹ ΝΑΤ]ϹΟΥΩΝϤ ΝΑΠΕΡΑΝ
ΤΟϹ ΑΥΩ] ΝΑΓΝΩϹΤΟϹ ΝΑΤ
ΤΑϩΟΥ] ΕΤΕΥϩΙΚΩΝ ΝΑΤ
ϭⲙϭⲱ]ⲙⲥ ΝΑΤΝΡΑΤϹ ΕΡΕ
10. ΠΕΥ⟩ΟΡΒ ΕϩΟΥΝ ϩΙΤΟΟΤϹ
ϹΕϹΟ⟩ΡⲘ ΝϩΗΤϹ ΝΤΕΙϩΕ Ν
ΤΟϹ] ΕΤΤΟϣ ΕΡΟΟΥ ΤΗΡΟΥ
ϩΝ ΤΕ]ϹⲘΝΤΑΤϹΩⲘΑ ΝΤΟϹ
ΕΤΤΟϣ] ΕΡΟΟΥ ΤΗΡΟΥ ϩΝ ΟΥ
15. ΑϹⲱ]ⲙΑΤΟϹ ΑΥΩ ϩΝ ΟΥⲘΝΤ
Α]Ν(Ο)ΥϹΙΟϹ ΠΑΙ ΠΕ ΠΕΙΩΤ Ν
ΑΠΟϩΡΗΤΟϹ ΝΑϩΡΗΤΟϹ Ν
ΑΚΑΤΑΓΝΩϹΤΟϹ ΝΑϩΟΡΑ
ΤΟϹ ΝΑⲙΕΤΡΗΤΟϹ ΑΥΩ Ν
20. ΑΠΕΡΑΝΤΟϹ ΠΑΙ ϩΡΑΙ ΝϩΗΤϤ
ⲙⲙΙΝ ⲙⲙΟϤ ΕΑΥΝΤϤ ΕΠϣΙ
ΝΝΕΤΝϩΗΤϤ ΑΥΩ ΤΕΠΙΝΟΙ
Α ΝΤΕΥⲙΝΤΝΟϭ ΕΑΥΝΤϹ
ΕΠϣΙ ΝΤⲘΝΤΑΝΟΥϹΙΟϹ ϢΑΝ
25. ΤΥϤΑΑΥ ΝΑΝΟΥϹΙΟϹ ΝΤΟϤ ΔΕ
ΕΥΑΤΤΑϩΟΥ ΠΕ ϩΙΤΝ ΝΕΥⲙΕ
ΛΟϹ ⲙⲙΙΝ ⲙⲙΟϤ ΑϤΑΑΥ ΝΤΟ
ΠΟϹ ΝΝΕΥⲙΕΛΟϹ ΕΤΡΕΥ
ΟΥΩϩ ΝϩΗΤϤ ΑΥΩ ΝϹΕϹΟΥ
30. ΩΝϤ ϪΕ ΝΤΟϤ ΠΕ ΠΕΥΕΙΩΤ
ΑΥΩ ϪΕ ΝΤΟϤ ΠΕΝΤΑΥΠΡΟΒΑ
ΛΕ ⲙⲙΟΟΥ ΕΒΟΛ ϩΝ ΤΕΥϢΟ
ⲣ]Π ΝΕΝΝΟΙΑ ΤΑΙ ΕΝΤΑϹⲣ ΤΟ
ΠΟϹ ΝΑΥ ΕΑϹΑΑΥ ΝΑΝΟΥϹΙΟϹ
35. (Ϫ)ΕΚΑΑϹ ΕΥΕϹΟΥΩΝϤ ΝΕϤΟ
ⲅ]ΑΡ ΠΕ ΝΑΤϹΟΥΩΝϤ ϩΙΤΝ ΟΥ

Iᵃ. The title and beginning are wanting.
3–4. Cf. lines 27–28; also X, lines 20–22 and
33–36.

II
MS. f. 138v
C.S. p. 53

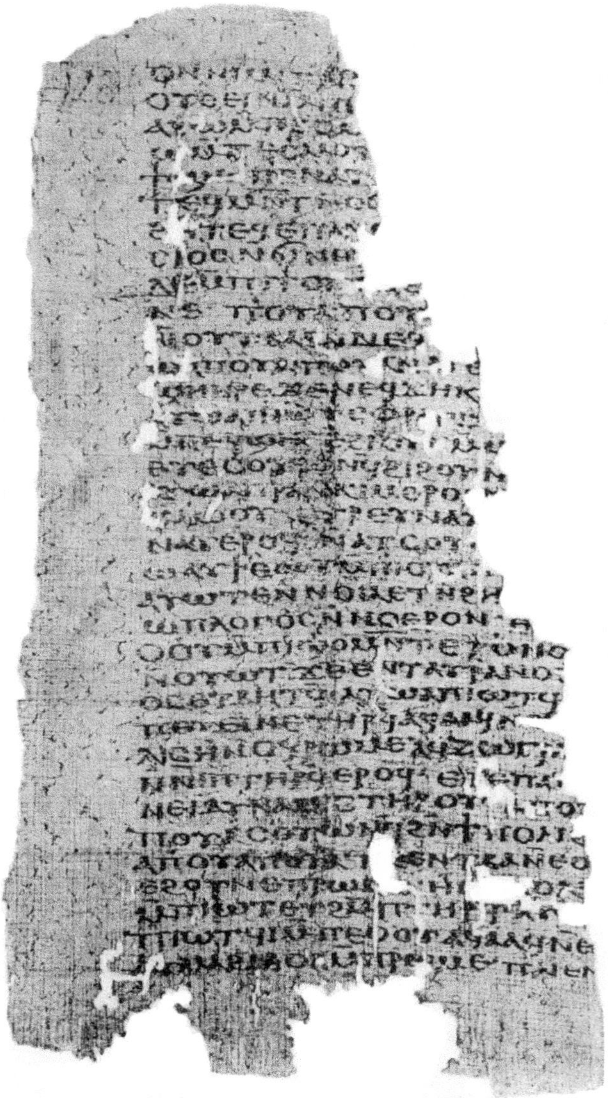

1. ON NIⲘ ⲠⲀI ⲀⲨⲢ ⲦⲈ⟨ⲨⲌIⲔⲰⲚ⟩ [Ⲛ
ⲞⲨⲞⲈⲒⲚ ⲘⲠⲈⳞⲘⲞⲦ [ⲚⲞⲨ]⟨ⲈⲚⲚⲞⲒⲀ
ⲀⲨⲰ ⲘⲠⲈⳞⲘⲞⲦ ⲚⲞ⟨ⲨⲈⲠIⲚⲞⲒⲀ⟩ [ⲀⲨ
Ⲱ ⲘⲠⲈⳞⲘⲞⲦ ⲚⲞⲨ⟨ⲦⲔ ⲚⲞⲨⲞⲈⲒⲚ ⲀⲨ

5. ⳿ⲦⳜⲰⲠⲈ ⲚⲀⲨ ⲠⲚ Ⲧ[ⲈⲠⲒⲚⲞⲒⲀ Ⲛ
ⲦⲈⳞⲘⲚⲦⲚⲞⳠ ⲀⲨⲚ[ⲦⲞⲨ ⲈⲂⲞⲖ
ⲠⲚ ⲦⲈⳞⲈⲠⲒⲚⲞⲒⲀ ⲀⲨ⟨Ⲱ⟩ [ⲀⲨⲢ ⲀⲚⲞⲨ
ⳞⲒⲞⳞ Ⲛ ⳠI ⲚⲈⳞⲘⲈⲖⲞⳞ [ⲚⲦⲞⲨ
ⲆⲈ ⲘⲠⲒⲦⲞⲠⲞⳞ ⳠⲈⲚⲀⲦ[ⲦⲀⳠⲞⲞⲨ?

10. ⲚⲈ ⲠⲞⲨⲀ ⲠⲞⲨⲀ ⲘⲘⲞ[ⲞⲨ ⲈⲒⲢⲈ
ⲚⲞⲨⲦⳘⲀ ⲠⲚ ⲚⲈⳞⲘⲈⲖⲞ[Ⳟ ⲀⲨ
Ⲱ ⲀⲠⲞⲨⲀ ⲠⲞⲨⲀ ⲚⲀⲨ ⲈⲢⲞ[Ⳝ ⟨ⳠⲘⲠ
ⳜⲎⲢⲈ ⳪Ⲉ ⲚⲈⳞ⳪ⲎⲔ᷊ ⳠⲀⲢ[ⲞⲨ? ⲠⲈ
ⲀⲨⲰ ⲀⲠⲒⲰⲦ ⳞⲪⲢⲀⲄⲒⳆⲈ ⟨ⲘⲠⲢⲀⲚ

15. ⲘⲠⲈⳞⳜⲎⲢⲈ ⳠⲒⳠⲞⲨⲚ ⲘⲘ[ⲞⲞⲨ ⳪Ⲉ
ⲈⲨⲈⲤⲞⲨⲰⲚⳜ ⳠⲒⳠⲞⲨⲚ ⲘⲘⲞⲞⲨ
ⲀⲨⲰ ⲀⲠⲢⲀⲚ ⲔⲒⲘ ⲈⲢⲞⲞⲨ ⳠⲒⳠⲞⲨⲚ
ⲘⲘⲞⲞⲨ ⲈⲦⲢⲈⲨ ⲚⲀⲨ ⲈⲠⲒⲀⲦ
ⲚⲀⲨ ⲈⲢⲞⳜ ⲚⲀⲦⳞⲞⲨⲰⲚⳝ ⲀⲨ

20. Ⲱ ⲀⲨ⳿ⲦⲈⲞⲞⲨ ⲘⲠⲒⲞⲨⲀ ⲘⲀⲨⲀⲀⲨ
ⲀⲨⲰ ⲦⲈⲚⲚⲞⲒⲀ ⲈⲦⲚⳠⲎⲦⳝ ⲀⲨ
Ⲱ ⲠⲖⲞⲄⲞⳞ ⲚⲚⲞⲈⲢⲞⲚ ⲈⲀⲨ⳿ⲦⲈ
ⲞⲞⲨ ⲘⲠⲒⳜⲞⲘⲚⲦ ⲈⲦⲞ ⲚⲞⲨⲀ
ⲚⲞⲨⲰⲦ ⳪Ⲉ ⲈⲚⲦⲀⲨⲢ ⲀⲚⲞⲨⳞⲒ

25. ⲞⳞ ⲈⲦⳘⲎⲦⳝ ⲀⲨⲰ ⲀⲠⲒⲰⲦ ⳝⲒ Ⲙ
ⲠⲈⲨⲈⲒⲚⲈ ⲦⲎⲢⳝ ⲀⳝⲀⲀⳝ ⲚⲞⲨⲠⲞ
ⲖⲒⳞ Ⲏ ⲚⲞⲨⲢⲰⲘⲈ ⲀⳝⳆⲰⲄⲢⲀⲪⲒ
ⲚⲚⲒⲠⲦⲎⲢⳝ ⲈⲢⲞⳝ ⲈⲦⲈ ⲠⲀⲒ ⲠⲈ
ⲚⲈⲒⲆⲨⲚⲀⲘⲒⳞ ⲦⲎⲢⲞⲨ ⲀⲠⲞⲨⲀ

30. ⲠⲞⲨⲀ ⳞⲞⲨⲰⲚⳝ ⳠⲚ ⳿ⲦⲠⲞⲖⲒⳞ
ⲀⲠⲞⲨⲀ ⲠⲞⲨⲀ ⳿ⲦⲚⳠⲈⲚⲦⳘⲀ ⲚⲈⲞ[ⲞⲨ
ⲈⳠⲞⲨⲚ ⲈⲠⲢⲰⲘⲈ Ⲏ ⲈⲦⲠⲞⲖⲒ[Ⳟ
ⲘⲠⲒⲰⲦ ⲈⲦⳠⲘ ⲠⲦⲎⲢⳝ ⲀⲨⲰ [Ⲁ
ⲠⲒⲰⲦ ⳝⲒ ⲘⲠⲈⲞⲞⲨ ⲀⳝⲀⲀⳝ ⲚⲈ[Ⲛ

35. ⲀⲨⲘⲀ ⳠⲒⳂⲞⲖ ⲘⲠⲢⲰⲘⲈ ⲠⲀⲒ ⲈⲚᵃ

1–4. Cf. cit. from *Apoc. of John* in note 3, I (comm.).
13 α. Dr Schmidt is doubtful about this word, but
it could well be the Egyptian _hr_ = *possessing*.
α. A folio must be missing at this point.

1. . . . .
   . . . . ⲉϨⲟⲩⲛ ⲙⲙⲟⲩ ⲁⲩⲱ ⲁⲩ
   ⲧⲁⲙⲓⲟ ⲛϨⲏⲧⲩ ⲙⲡⲧⲩⲡⲟⲥ ⲙ
   ⲯⲓⲉⲣⲟⲛ ⲙⲡⲗⲏⲣⲱⲙⲁ ⲁⲩⲱ
5. ⲁⲩⲧⲁⲙⲓⲟ ⲛⲛⲉⲩⲙⲟⲩⲧ ⲉⲟⲩ⟨ⲃⲱⲕ⟩
   ⲉⲃⲟⲗ Ϩⲛ ⲛⲉⲩⲉⲣⲏⲩ ⲙⲡⲧⲩⲡⲟⲥ
   ⲛϣⲉ ⲛⲧⲃⲁ ⲛⲁⲩⲛⲁⲙⲓⲥ ϣⲁ
   ⲧⲛ ϥⲧⲟⲟⲩ ⲛⲧⲃⲁ ⲁⲩⲱ ⲁⲩⲧⲁ
   ⲙⲓⲟ ⲙⲡⲉϪⲟⲩⲱⲧ ⲛⲧⲏⲏⲃⲉ
10. ⲙⲡⲓⲛⲉ ⲛⲧⲁⲉⲕⲁⲥ ⲥⲛⲧⲉ ⲧⲁⲉ
   ⲕⲁⲥ ⲉⲑⲏⲡ ⲙⲛ ⲧⲁⲉⲕⲁⲥ ⲉⲧⲟⲩ
   ⲟⲛϨ ⲉⲃⲟⲗ ⲁⲩⲱ ⲁⲩⲧⲁⲙⲓⲟ
   ⲛϨⲁⲡⲉ ⲛϨⲏⲧⲩ ⲙⲡⲓⲛⲉ ⲛⲧⲙⲟ
   ⲛⲁⲥ ⲉⲑⲏⲡ Ϩⲙ ⲡⲥⲛⲑⲉⲩⲥ ⲁⲩⲱ
15. ⲁⲩⲧⲁⲙⲓⲟ ⲙⲡⲛⲟϭ ⲙⲙⲁϨⲧ ⲙ
   ⲡⲓⲛⲉ ⲙⲡⲥⲛⲑⲉⲩⲥ ⲉⲧⲟ ⲛϪⲟ
   ⲉⲓⲥ ⲉϪⲙ ⲡⲉⲡⲗⲏⲣⲱⲙⲁ ⲁⲩⲱ ⲁⲩ
   ⲧⲁⲙⲓⲟ ⲛⲛⲕⲟⲩⲓ ⲙⲁϨⲧ ⲙⲡⲓⲛⲉ
   ⲛϨⲉⲛⲛⲁⲥ ⟨ⲉⲑⲏⲡ⟩? ⲙⲡⲥⲛⲑⲉⲩⲥ
20. ⲁⲩⲱ ⲁⲩⲧⲁⲙⲓⲟ ⲛⲧⲉⲩⲙⲏⲧⲣⲁ
   ⲙⲡⲧⲩⲡⲟⲥ ⲙⲡⲥⲁⲛϨⲟⲩⲛ ⲙ
   ⲯⲓⲉⲣⲟⲛ [ⲙⲡⲗⲏⲣⲱⲙⲁ . . . .
   . . . .
   . . . .
25. . . . ⲙⲙⲟⲥ ⲁⲩⲱ ⲁⲩⲧⲁⲙⲓⲟ ⲛ
   ⲛⲉⲩⲡⲁⲧ ⲙⲡⲧⲩⲡⲟⲥ ⲙⲡⲉ
   ⲣⲏⲙⲟⲥ ⲙⲛ ⲡⲁⲛⲅⲛⲱⲥⲧⲟⲥ
   ⲛⲁⲓ ⲉⲧⲇⲓⲁⲕⲟⲛⲓ ⲙⲡⲧⲏⲣϥ ⲁⲩⲱ
   ⲉⲩⲣⲁϣⲉ ⲙⲛ ⲛⲉⲧⲛⲁⲟⲩϪⲁⲓ ⲁⲩ
30. ⲱ ⲁⲩⲧⲁⲙⲓⲟ ⲛⲛⲉⲩⲙⲉⲗⲟⲥ ⲙⲡⲧⲩ
   ⲡⲟⲥ ⲙⲡⲃⲁⲑⲟⲥ ⲉⲧⲉⲣⲉ ϣⲙⲧϣⲉ
   ⲥⲉⲧⲏ ⲙⲛⲛⲧⲉ(ⲓⲱⲧ) ⲛϨⲏⲧⲩ ⲕⲁ
   ⲧⲁ ⲡⲧⲩⲡⲟⲥ ⲛⲙⲙⲛⲧⲉⲓⲱⲧ

IIIᵃ. This folio is the most fragmentary of all.
25. From this point the text is supplied from the transcript of C. G. Woide. (Woide MS. Clar. Press, d. 13.)

1. . . . .

. . . .

. . . . .ⲁⲩ

ⲱ ⲁⲩⲧⲁⲙⲓⲟ ⲛⲩⲱⲉ ⲛ̅ϩⲏⲧϥ

5. ⲙ̅ⲡⲧⲩⲡⲟⲥ ⲛⲛⲕⲟⲥⲙⲟⲥ ⲙ

ⲡⲉⲡⲗⲏⲣⲱⲙⲁ ⲁⲩⲱ ⲁⲩⲙⲁϩⲩ

ⲙ̅ⲙⲛ̅ⲧⲥⲁⲃⲉ ⲛⲑⲉ ⲙ̅ⲡⲡⲁⲛ

ⲥⲟⲫⲟⲥ ⲁⲩⲱ ⲁⲩⲙⲁϩⲩ ⲙ̅ⲙⲩⲥ

ⲧⲏⲣⲓⲟⲛ ϩⲓϩⲟⲩⲛ ⲛⲑⲉ ⲙ̅ⲡⲥⲏ

10. ⲑⲉⲩⲥ ⲁⲩⲱ ⲁⲩⲙⲁϩⲩ ϩⲓⲃⲟⲗ

ⲛⲑⲉ ⲙ̅ⲡⲁⲧⲡⲱⲱ ⲁⲩⲱ ⲁⲩ

ⲧⲁⲙⲓⲟⲩ ⲉⲩⲟ ⲛⲁⲧⲁⲙⲁϩⲧⲉ

ⲙ̅ⲙⲟⲩ ⲙ̅ⲡⲧⲩⲡⲟⲥ ⲙ̅ⲡⲁⲧⲁ

ⲙⲁϩⲧⲉ ⲙ̅ⲙⲟⲩ ⲉⲧⲛ̅ ⲙⲁ ⲛⲓⲙ

15. ⲉⲧⲟ ⲛⲟⲩⲁ ⲛⲟⲩⲱⲧ ϩⲓ ⲡⲧⲏ

ⲣϥ ⲁⲩⲱ ⲛⲥⲉⲧⲁϩⲟ ⲙ̅ⲙⲟⲩ ⲁⲛ ‾‾

ⲁⲩⲱ ⲁⲩⲧⲁⲙⲓⲟⲩ ⲉⲩⲕⲱⲧⲉ ⲉϩⲟⲩ

ⲉⲛⲉⲩⲉⲣⲏⲩ ⲙ̅ⲡⲧⲩⲡⲟⲥ ⲙⲛ̅

ⲕⲁⲗⲩⲡⲧⲟⲥ ⲉⲧϩⲱⲃⲥ ⲛⲓⲙ

20. ⲙⲩⲥⲧⲏⲣⲓⲟⲛ ⲉⲑⲏⲡ ⲁⲩⲱ

ⲁⲩⲧⲁⲙⲓⲟ ⲛ⟨ⲛ⟩ⲉⲩⲟⲩⲣⲏⲧⲉ ⲛⲟⲩ

ⲟⲉⲓⲛ⟩ⲙ̅ⲡⲧⲩⲡⲟⲥ ⲙ̅ⲡⲁⲧⲡⲱⲱ

ⲉⲩⲙⲟⲩⲧⲉ⟩ ϫⲉ ⲟⲩⲉⲣⲏⲧⲉ ⲛ

ⲟⲩⲟⲉⲓⲛ⟩ ⸂ⲁⲩⲱ ⲁⲩⲧⲁⲙⲓⲟ ⲙ̅ⲡⲉ

25. ϥⲧⲟⲟⲩ ⲛ̅ⲕⲟⲟϩ ⲙ̅ⲡⲧⲩ⸀ⲡⲟⲥ ⲛ

ⲧⲉϥⲧⲟ ⲙ̅ⲡⲩⲗⲏ ⲁⲩⲱ ⲁⲩ

ⲧⲁⲙⲓⲟ ⲙ̅ⲡⲙⲉⲣⲟⲥ ⲥⲛⲁⲩ ⲙ̅ⲡⲧⲩ

ⲡⲟⲥ ⲛ̅ⲙ̅ⲙⲩⲣⲓⲁⲣⲭⲟⲥ ⲛⲉⲧϩⲓⲧᵘ

ⲛⲁⲙ ⲙ̅ⲛ̅ ⲛⲉⲧϩⲓ ϩⲃⲟⲩⲣ ⲁⲩⲱ ⲁⲩ

30. ⲧⲁⲙⲓⲟ ⲛⲛⲉⲩⲁⲛⲁⲅⲕⲁⲓⲟⲛ ⲙ

ⲡⲧⲩⲡⲟⲥ ⲛⲛⲉⲧⲃⲏⲕ ⲉⲃⲟⲗ

ⲙ̅ⲛ̅ ⲛⲉⲧⲛⲏⲩ ⲉϩⲟⲩⲛ ⲁⲩⲱ ⲁⲩ

ⲧⲁⲙⲓⲟ ⲛ̅ⲧⲕⲉϩⲧⲉ ⲥⲛ̅ⲧⲉ ⲙ

21–24. Vide note 5, IV (comm.).

1. ⲡⲧⲩⲡⲟⲥ ⲙⲡ](ⲕ)ⲁⲣ(ⲱ)[ϥ. . . . .
   . . . .
   . . . . ⲁⲩⲧⲁ[ⲙⲓⲟ ⟨ⲛⲛⲭ
   ⲟⲉⲓⲧ⟩ ⲛⲟ[ⲏ]ⲧϥ ⲉ[ⲣⲉ ⲧⲟⲩⲉⲓ
5. ⲙⲡ]ⲧⲩⲡⲟⲥ ⲛⲁϥⲣ(ⲏⲇⲱⲛ) ⟨ⲁⲩⲱ
   ⲧ]ⲕⲉⲟⲩⲉⲓ ⲙⲡⲧⲩⲡⲟⲥ ⲙ[ⲙⲟⲩ
   ⲥ]ⲁⲛⲓⲟⲥ ⲁⲩⲱ ⲁⲩⲧⲁⲙⲓⲟ ⟨ⲛⲛ
   ϭⲱ⟩ⲡ ⲛⲛⲉⲩⲟⲩⲉⲣⲏⲧⲉ ⲧⲟⲩⲉ[ⲣ
   ⲏⲧ]ⲉ ⲛⲟⲩⲛⲁⲙ ⲙⲡⲧⲩⲡⲟⲥ
10. ⲛⲧ]ⲡⲁⲛⲇⲏⲗⲟⲥ ⲁⲩⲱ ⲧⲟⲩⲉⲣⲏ
   ⲧⲉ ⲛ]ϩⲃⲟⲩⲣ ⲙⲡⲧⲩⲡⲟⲥ ⲛⲧⲙⲁⲁⲩ
   ϩⲓⲡ]ⲉⲥⲏⲧ ⲧⲏⲣⲟⲩ ⲁⲩⲱ ⲡⲁⲓ ⲡⲉ
   ⲡⲣ]ⲱⲙⲉ ⲛⲧⲁⲩⲧⲁⲙⲓⲟⲩ ⲕⲁⲧⲁ ⲡ
   ⲁⲓ]ⲱⲛ ⲡⲁⲓⲱⲛ ⲁⲩⲱ ⲡⲁⲓ ⲡⲉⲛ
15. ⲧⲁ] ⲡⲧⲏⲣϥ ⲉⲡⲓⲑⲩⲙⲉⲓ [ⲉⲥⲟⲩⲱⲛⲩ
   ⲡⲁⲓ ⲡⲉ ⲡⲡⲁⲛⲧⲉⲗⲓⲟⲥ ⲁⲩⲱ ⲡ[ⲁⲓ
   ⲡⲉ ⲡⲣⲱⲙⲉ ⲙⲡⲛⲟⲩⲧⲉ ⲉⲩⲛⲟ[ⲩ
   ⲧⲉ ϩⲱⲱϥ ⲡⲉ ⲁⲩⲱ ⲉⲩⲁϩⲟⲣⲁ
   ⲧⲟⲥ ⲡⲉ ⲁⲩⲱ ⲉⲩⲁⲅⲛⲱⲥⲧⲟⲥ
20. ⲡⲉ ⲁⲩⲱ ⲉⲩⲡⲁⲛⲏⲣⲉⲙⲟⲥ
   ⲡⲉ ⲁⲩⲱ ⲉⲩⲁⲭⲱⲣⲏⲧⲟⲥ ⲡⲉ
   ⲁⲩⲱ ⲉⲩⲁⲥⲁⲗⲉⲩⲧⲟⲥ ⲡⲉ ⲡⲁⲓ
   ⲉϣϣⲉ ⲁⲛ ⲉⲥⲁϩⲟⲩ (ⲉⲣⲟⲩ)
   ⲉϣϣⲉ ⲉⲥⲙⲟⲩ ⲉⲣⲟⲩ ⲉⲩϫⲱ ⲙ
25. ⲙⲟⲥ ϫⲉ ϯⲥⲙⲟⲩ ⲉⲣⲟⲕ ⲡⲓⲱⲧ
   ⲛ]ⲉⲓⲱⲧ ⲛⲓⲙ ⲛⲟⲩⲟⲉⲓⲛ ϯⲥⲙⲟⲩ
   ⲉ]ⲣⲟⲕ ⲡⲁⲡⲉⲣⲁⲛⲧⲟⲥ ⲛⲟⲩⲟⲉⲓⲛ
   ⲉⲧ]ⲟⲩⲟⲧⲃ ⲉⲁⲡⲉⲣⲁⲛⲧⲟⲥ ⲛⲓⲙ
   ϯⲥⲙⲟⲩ ⲉⲣⲟⲕ ⲡⲁⲭⲱⲣⲏⲧⲟⲥ
30. ⲛ]ⲟⲩⲟⲉⲓⲛ ⲉⲧϩⲓⲧⲡⲉ ⲛⲁⲭⲱⲣⲏ
   ⲧⲟ]ⲥ ⲛⲓⲙ ϯⲥⲙⲟⲩ ⲉⲣⲟⲕ ⲡⲁ
   ϩⲣ]ⲏⲧⲟⲥ ⲛⲟⲩⲟⲉⲓⲛ ⲉⲧϩⲁⲑⲏ
   ⲛ]ⲁϩⲣⲏⲧⲟⲥ ⲛⲓⲙ ϯⲥⲙⲟⲩ ⲉⲣ(ⲟⲕ)
   ⲡⲁⲫⲑⲁⲣⲧⲟⲥ ⲛⲟⲩⲟⲉⲓⲛ [ⲉⲧⲟⲩ
35. ⲟⲧⲃ ⲉⲁⲫⲑⲁⲣⲧⲟⲥ ⲛⲓⲙ [ϯⲥⲙⲟⲩ

Vª. C. G. Woide made no attempt to copy this
page, remarking that it was illegible. Dr Schmidt
made a transcript and compared it with that of
M. G. Schwartze.

23, 24 and 25. The lineage here overlaps.

1. ЄΡΟΚ ⟨ΤΠΗΓ⟩Η Ν⟨ΟΥΟΕΙΝ ΝΤΕ⟩[ΟΥ
ΟΕΙΝ [ΝΙΜ ΤϹΜΟΥ ⟨ЄΡΟΚ⟩ [ΠΙΑΤѠϢΑ
ΧЄ ЄΡΟΥ ΝΟΥΟΕΙΝ [ΤϹΜΟΥ Є
ΡΟΚ ΠΙΑΤΜЄЄΥЄ ЄΡ[ΟΥ ΜΜΙΝ
5. ΜΜΟΥ ΝΟΥΟΕΙΝ ΤΙϹΜΟΥ Є
ΡΟΚ ΠΑΓЄΝΝΗΤΟϹ Ν[ΟΥΟΕΙΝ
ΤϹΜΟΥ ЄΡΟΚ ΠΑΥΤΟ[ΦΥΗϹ
ΝΟΥΟΕΙΝ ΤϹΜΟΥ ЄΡ[ΟΚ Π
ΠΡΟΠΑΤѠΡ ΝΟΥΟΕΙΝ [ЄΤΟΥ
10. ΟΤϤ ЄΠΡΟΠΑΤѠΡ ΝΙΜ [ΤϹΜΟΥ
ЄΡΟΚ ΠΑϨΟΡΑΤΟϹ ΝΟΥΟ[ЄΙΝ
ЄΤϨΑΘΗ ΝΑϨΟΡΑΤΟϹ Ν[ΙΜ Τ
ϹΜΟΥ ЄΡΟΚ ΤЄΠΙΝΟΙΑ [ΝΟΥ
ΟΕΙΝ ЄΤΟΥΟΤϤ ЄЄΠΙΝ[ΟΙΑ
15. ΝΙΜ ΤϹΜΟΥ ЄΡΟΚ ΠΝΟ[ΥΤΕ
ΝΟΥΟΕΙΝ ЄΤϨΑΘΗ ΝΝΟΥ[ΤЄ
ΝΙΜ ΤϹΜΟΥ ЄΡΟΚ ΤЄΓΝѠ
ϹΙϹ ЄΤΟ ΝΟΥΟΕΙΝ ЄΓΝѠϹΙϹ
ΝΙΜ ΤϹΜΟΥ ЄΡΟΚ ΠΑΓΝѠϹ
20. ΤΟϹ ΝΟΥΟΕΙΝ ЄΤϨΑΘΗ ΝΑΓ
ΝѠϹΤΟϹ ΝΙΜ ΤϹΜΟΥ ЄΡΟΚ
ΠΗΡЄΜΟϹ ΝΟΥΟΕΙΝ ЄΤϨΑΘ[Η
ΝΗΡЄΜΟϹ ΝΙΜ ΤϹΜΟΥ ЄΡ[ΟΚ
ΠΠΑΝΤΟΔΥΝΑΜΟϹ ΝΟΥΟΕΙ[Ν
25. ЄΚΟΥΟΤϤ ЄΠΑΝΤΟΔΥΝΑΜ[ΟϹ
ΝΙΜ ΤϹΜΟΥ ЄΡΟΚ ΠЄΤ[ΡΙΔΥ
ΝΑΜΟϹ ΝΟΥΟΕΙΝ ЄΚΟΥΟ[ΤϤ
ЄΤΡΙΔΥΝΑΜΟϹ ΝΙΜ ΤϹΜ[ΟΥ
ЄΡΟΚ ΠΙΑΤΔΙΑΚΡΙΝЄ ΝΟΥ[ΟΕΙΝ
30. ΝΤΟΚ ΔΕ ΠЄΤΔΙΑΚΡΙΝЄ Ν[ΟΥΟ
ЄΙ]Ν ΝΙΜ ΤϹΜΟΥ ЄΡΟΚ ΦΙΛΙ
ΚΡΙΝЄϹ ΝΟΥΟΕΙΝ ЄΚΟΥΟΤϤ
ΝϨΙΛΙΚΡΙΝЄϹ ΝΙΜ ΤϹΜΟ⟨Υ⟩

1. ЄΡΟΚ] . . . .
. . . .
. . . .
. . . . ЄΚШᴀⲬЄ ΝΤΟΚ
5. . . . . Τ]ΗΡΟΥ ϮⲤⲘΟΥ Є
ΡΟΚ ΠЄΤ]ΝΟΙ ΝΝΚᴀ ΝΙⲘ ЄⲘΝ
ⲗᴀᴀΥ ΝΟΙ] ⲘⲘΟΥ ΝΤΟΥ ϮⲤⲘΟΥ
ЄΡΟΚ ΠЄ]ΤШШΠ ⲘΠΤΗΡϤ ЄΡΟϤ
ЄⲘΝⲗᴀᴀΥ] ΝΤΟΥ ШШΠ ⲘⲘΟΥ
10. ϮⲤⲘΟΥ Є]ΡΟΚ ΠЄΤⲆΠΟ ⲘⲘΟΟΥ
ΤΗΡΟΥ Ϩ]Ν ΟΥⲘΝΤΑΓΕΝΝΗΤΟⳞ
ЄΒΟⲗ ⲬЄ] ⲘΠЄⲗᴀᴀΥ ⲬΠΟΥ Ϯ
ⲤⲘΟΥ ЄΡ]ΟΚ ΤΠΗΓΗ ⲘΠΤΗΡϤ
ᴀΥШ ⲘⲘ]ΟΟΥ ΤΗΡΟΥ ϮⲤⲘΟΥ
15. ЄΡΟΚ ΠᴀΥ]ΤΟΓΕΝΗⳞ ΝᴀⲘЄ Ν
ΟΥΟЄΙΝ] ΠЄΤϨᴀθΗ ΝᴀΥΤΟΓΕΝ
ΗⳞ ΝΙⲘ Ϯ]ⲤⲘΟΥ ЄΡΟΚ ΠᴀⳞᴀⲗЄΥ
ΤΟⳞ ΝΟΥ]ΟЄΙΝ ΝᴀⲘЄ ΝΤΟΚ
ΝΟΥΟЄΙΝ] ЄΝЄΝΤᴀΥΚΙⲘ ϨⲘΠЄΚ
20. ΟΥΟЄΙΝ] ϮⲤⲘΟΥ ЄΡΟΚ ΠΚᴀΡШϤ
ΝΚᴀ]ΡШϤ ΝΙⲘ ΝΟΥΟЄΙΝ ϮⲥⲘ
Ο]Υ ЄΡΟΚ ΠⳞШΤΗΡ ΝⳞШΤΗ
Ρ ΝΙ]Ⲙ ΝΟΥΟЄΙΝ ϮⲤⲘΟΥ
ЄΡΟ]Κ ΠᴀΤΤᴀⲘᴀⳅЄ ⲘⲘΟϤ ΝΟΥ
25. ΟЄΙΝ] ⲘᴀΥᴀᴀΥ ϮⲤⲘΟΥ ЄΡΟΚ
ΠЄΤ]Ο ΝΤΟΠΟⳞ ΝΤΟΠΟⳞ ΝΙⲘ
ⲘΠΤ]Η(Η)ΡϤ ⲘᴀΥᴀᴀΥ ϮⲤⲘΟΥ Є
ΡΟΚ] ΠⳞΟΦΟⳞ ⲘᴀΥᴀᴀΥ ᴀΥШ
ΠЄΤΟ?]ΝⳞΟΦΙᴀ ⲘᴀΥᴀᴀΥ ϮⲤⲘΟΥ
30. ЄΡΟ]Κ ΠΠᴀΝⲘΥⳞΤΗΡΙΟΝ ⲘᴀΥᴀᴀΥ
ϮⳞ]ⲘΟΥ ЄΡΟΚ ΠΠᴀΝΤЄⲗΙΟⳞ ΝΟΥ
ΟЄΙ]Ν ⲘᴀΥᴀᴀΥ ϮⲤⲘΟΥ ЄΡΟΚ ΠΙ
ᴀΤ]ϬⲘϬШⲘϤ ⲘᴀΥᴀᴀΥ ϮⲤⲘΟΥ

1. (ⲈⲢⲞⲔ) . . . .
. . . . [ⲦⲤⲘⲞⲨ
ⲈⲢⲞⲔ ⲠⲀⲄⲀⲐⲞⲤ [ⲚⲦⲞⲔ ⲈⲔⲞⲨⲰ
ⲚϨ ⲈⲂⲞⲖ ⲚⲚⲀⲄⲀⲐⲞ[Ⲥ ⲚⲒⲘ
5. ⲦⲤⲘⲞⲨ ⲈⲢⲞⲔ ⲠⲞⲨⲞ[ⲈⲒⲚ ⲚⲦⲞⲔ
ⲈⲔⲞⲨⲰⲚϨ ⲈⲂⲞⲖ ⲚⲚ[ⲞⲨⲞⲈⲒⲚ ⲦⲎ
ⲢⲞⲨ ⲘⲀⲨⲀⲀⲔ ⲦⲤⲘ[ⲞⲨ ⲈⲢⲞⲔ
ⲠⲈⲦⲦⲞⲨⲚⲞⲤ ⲚⲚⲞ[ⲨⲤ ⲚⲒⲘ ⲠⲈⲦ
ⲦⲰⲚϨ ⲘⲮⲨⲬⲎ ⲚⲒⲘ [ⲦⲤⲘⲞⲨ ⲈⲢⲞⲔ
10. ⲦⲀⲚⲀⲠⲀⲨⲤⲒⲤ ⲚⲚⲈⲦⲬⲘ ⲠⲔⲀⲢⲰⲨ [Ⲧ
ⲤⲘⲞⲨ ⲈⲢⲞⲔ ⲠⲈⲦⲞⲨ[ⲰϢ Ϩ Ⲙ
ⲘⲚⲦⲈⲒⲰⲦ ⲚⲒⲘ ϪⲒⲚ [ⲚϢⲞⲢⲠ
ϢⲀ ⲦⲈⲚⲞⲨ ⲤⲈϢⲒⲚ[Ⲉ ⲚⲤⲰⲔ
ϪⲈ ⲚⲦⲞⲔ ⲠⲈ ⲠⲈⲨϢ[ⲒⲚⲈ ϨⲀⲒⲞ?
15. ⲤⲰⲦⲘ ⲈⲠⲈϢⲖⲎⲖ ⲘⲠ[ⲢⲰⲘⲈ?
Ϩ Ⲙ ⲘⲀ ⲚⲒⲘ ⲠⲀⲒ ⲈⲦⲦ[ⲰⲂϨ Ⲙ
ϨⲎⲦ ⲦⲎⲢϤ ⲠⲀⲒⲠⲈ Ⲡ[ⲈⲒⲰⲦ Ⲛ
ⲈⲒⲰⲦ ⲚⲒⲘ ⲀⲨⲰ [ⲠⲚⲞⲨⲦⲈ
ⲚⲚⲞⲨⲦⲈ ⲚⲒⲘ ⲀⲨⲰ [ⲠϪⲞⲈⲒⲤ
20. ⲚϪⲞⲈⲒⲤ ⲚⲒⲘ ⲀⲨⲰ [ⲠϢⲎⲢⲈ
ⲚⲚϢⲎⲢⲈ ⲦⲎⲢⲞⲨ ⲠⲈ [ⲀⲨⲰ
ⲠⲤⲰⲦⲎⲢ ⲚⲚⲤⲰⲦⲎⲢ [ⲦⲎⲢⲞⲨ
ⲠⲈ ⲀⲨⲰ ⲠⲀϨⲞⲢⲀⲦⲞⲤ [ⲚⲚⲀϨⲞ
ⲢⲀⲦⲞⲤ ⲦⲎⲢⲞⲨ ⲠⲈ ⲀⲨ[Ⲱ ⲦⲤⲒⲄⲎ
25. ⲚⲚⲤⲒⲄⲎ ⲦⲎⲢⲞⲨ ⲠⲈ ⲀⲨ[Ⲱ ⲠⲀ
ⲠⲈⲢⲀⲚⲦⲞⲤ ⲚⲚⲀⲠⲈⲢⲀⲚ[ⲦⲞⲤ ⲦⲎ
ⲢⲞⲨ ⲠⲈ ⲠⲀⲬⲰⲢⲎⲦⲞⲤ Ⲛ[ⲚⲀ
ⲬⲰⲢⲎⲦⲞⲤ ⲦⲎⲢⲞⲨ ⲠⲈ Ⲁ[ⲨⲰ ⲠⲠ
ⲀⲠⲚⲞⲨⲚ ⲠⲈ ⲚⲚⲀⲠⲚⲞⲨⲚ [ⲦⲎⲢⲞⲨ
30. ⲠⲈ ⲀⲨⲰ ⲞⲨⲦⲞⲠⲞⲤ ⲠⲈ [ⲚⲚ
ⲦⲞⲠⲞⲤ ⲦⲎⲢⲞⲨ ⲠⲈ ⲠⲞⲨ[Ⲁ
ⲚⲦⲞⲨ ⲚⲞⲨⲰⲦ ⲚⲚⲞⲈⲢⲞⲚ
ⲈϤϢⲞⲞⲠ ⲚⲦⲞⲨ ϨⲀⲐⲎ ⲚⲚⲞⲨ[Ⲥ

10. Vide note 1, VIII (comm.).

ⲟⲛ ... ⲟⲛ
... ⲑⲏⲛ ... ⲛⲟⲩⲟⲛ ...
... ⲧⲁⲣⲟⲩ ⲡ ⲉ ...
ⲧ ⲟ ... ⲧⲉⲓⲛⲉ
... ⲉⲓⲛ ⲉ ⲧ ⲏ ⲣ ⲟ ⲩ ...
... ⲉ ⲩ ⲟ ⲧ ⲩ ⲟ ...
ⲛ ... ⲁ ⲩ ⲉ ...
... ⲉ ⲛ ⲁ ⲩ ⲁ ⲛ ⲟ ⲩ ...
... ⲓ ⲥ ⲉ ⲧ ⲏ ⲣ ⲟ ⲩ ⲁ ⲧ ...
ⲟ ⲫ ⲟ ⲥ ⲡ ⲁ ⲣ ⲁ ⲛ ⲥ ⲟ ⲫ ⲓ ...
... ⲉ ⲩ ⲟ ⲧ ... ⲁ ⲣ ⲁ ⲛ ⲉ
... ⲧ ⲏ ⲣ ⲟ ⲩ · ⲟ ⲩ ⲁ ⲛ ⲟ ⲥ
ⲟ ⲧ ⲟ ⲩ ⲡ ⲁ ⲣ ⲁ ⲛ ⲓ ⲁ ⲅ ⲁ ⲑ ⲟ ⲥ ⲛ
ⲧ ⲟ ⲡ ⲧ ⲉ ⲡ ⲉ ⲃ ⲣ ⲟ ⲥ ⲙ ⲛ ⲁ ⲣ
... ⲏ ⲟ ⲩ · ⲛ ⲧ ⲟ ⲟ ⲩ ⲟ ⲛ ⲡ ⲉ ⲧ ...
... ⲟ ⲩ ⲧ ⲏ ⲣ ⲟ ⲩ · ⲧ ⲙ ⲁ ⲩ ⲅ ⲟ ⲫ ⲩ ⲛ ⲥ
... ⲛ ⲧ ⲏ ⲣ ⲱ ⲙ ⲁ ⲁ ⲩ · ⲉ ⲩ ⲱ ...
... ⲁ ⲑ ⲏ ⲛ ⲛ ⲓ ⲡ ⲧ ⲏ ⲣ ⲩ ⲉ ⲛ ⲧ ...
... ⲁ ⲩ ⲁ ⲩ · ⲉ ⲩ ϣ ⲟ ⲟ ⲡ ⲛ ⲟ ⲩ ⲟ ⲃ ...
... ⲏ ⲛ · ⲟ ⲩ ⲁ ⲧ ⲧ ⲟ ⲅ ⲉ ⲛ ⲏ ...
... ⲁ ⲩ ⲱ ⲁ ⲛ ⲉ ⲥ ⲧ ⲓ ⲉ ⲉ ⲩ ⲛ ⲧ ...
ⲣ ⲁ ⲛ ... ⲁ ⲩ ⲁ ⲩ ϣ ⲉ ⲛ ⲟ ⲩ ⲧ ⲁ ⲛ ⲉ ⲛ
ⲣ ⲁ ⲛ ⲧ ⲏ ⲣ ⲥ · ⲉ ⲩ ⲱ ⲣ ⲡ ⲛ ⲥ ⲟ ⲟ ⲩ ⲛ
ⲉ ⲛ ... ⲡ ⲧ ⲏ ⲣ ⲩ · ⲉ ⲩ ⲑ ⲉ ⲱ ⲣ ⲓ ⲛ ...
ⲧ ⲏ ⲣ ⲩ ⲉ ⲩ ϭ ⲱ ϣ ⲧ ⲉ ⲣ ⲙ ⲉ ...
ⲡ ⲧ ⲏ ⲣ ⲩ · ⲉ ⲩ ⲥ ⲱ ⲧ ⲙ ⲉ ...
... ⲩ ⲉ ⲩ ϭ ⲙ ϭ ⲟ ⲙ ⲛ ϩ ⲟ ⲧ ⲟ ⲡ ⲁ ⲣ ...
... ⲟ ⲩ ⲙ ⲡ ... ⲡ ⲁ ⲓ ⲉ ⲧ ⲁ ⲛ ϩ ϭ ⲟ ⲩ ...
... ϩ ⲧ ⲏ ⲣ ⲟ ⲩ ⲛ ⲉ ϣ ⲧ ⲟ ⲩ ⲧ ⲟ ⲛ
ⲛ ⲧ ⲙ ⲁ ⲟ ⲥ · ⲡ ⲁ ⲓ ⲡ ⲉ ⲧ ⲉ ⲩ ⲱ ⲟ ...
... ⲛ ⲟ ⲩ ⲧ ⲉ ⲓ ⲛ ⲉ ⲛ ⲟ ⲩ ⲟ ⲩ ⲛ ⲁ ⲛ ⲟ ⲩ
... ⲟ ⲥ ⲛ ⲙ ⲡ ⲣ ⲉ ⲩ ⲟ ⲥ ⲙ ⲛ ⲛ ⲱ ...
... ⲛ ⲡ ⲁ ⲛ ⲙ ⲩ ⲥ ⲧ ⲏ ⲣ ⲓ ⲟ ⲛ ⲡ ⲉ

1. ⲚⲒⳘ ⲀⲨⲱ] ⲞⲚ ⲞⲨⲚⲞⲨⲤ Ⲛ
ⲦⲞⲨ? ⲠⲈⲦ] ⳠⲀⲐⲎ ⲚⲚⲞⲨⲤ ⲚⲒⳘ
ⲀⲨⲱ ⲞⲨ]ⲀⲦⲦⲀⳠⲞⲨ ⲠⲈ ⲈⲨ
ⲦⲀⳠⲞ ⳘⳘⲞⲞⲨ ⲦⲎⲢⲞⲨ ⲞⲨⲀⲦⲈⲒⲚⲈ

5. ⲠⲈ ⲈⲦⳠⲀⲐⲎ] (Ⲛ)ⲈⲒⲚⲈ ⲦⲎⲢⲞⲨ ⲈⲨ
ⲭⲞⲤⲈ ⲠⲀⲢⲀ Ⲛ⳨ⲒⲤⲈ⟩ ⲚⲒⳘ ⲈⲨⲞⲨⲞⳡⲤ
ⲠⲀⲢⲀ ⲚⲞⲨⲞⳡⲤ⟩ ⲚⲒⳘ ⲀⲨⲱ ⲈⲨⳡⲞ
ⲞⲠ]⟨ⳠⲀⲐⲎ ⲚⲞⲨⲞⳡⲤ⟩ ⲚⲒⳘ ⲀⲨⲱ ⲈⲨ
ⳡⲞⲞⲠ ⳠⲀⲐⲎ Ⲛ]⳨ⲒⲤⲈ ⲦⲎⲢⲞⲨ ⲀⲨⲱ

10. ⲚⲦⲞⲨ ⲞⲨ]ⲤⲞⲮⲞⲤ ⲠⲀⲢⲀ ⲚⲤⲞⲮⲒⲀ
ⲦⲎⲢⲞⲨ] ⲀⲨⲱ ⲈⲨⲞⲨⲀⲀⲂ ⲠⲀⲢⲀ ⲚⲈ
ⲦⲞⲨⲀⲀⲂ] ⲦⲎⲢⲞⲨ ⲞⲨⲀⲅⲀⲐⲞⲤ
ⲠⲈ Ⲛ⳨]ⲞⲨⲞ ⲠⲀⲢⲀ ⲚⲒⲀⲅⲀⲐⲞⲤ ⲦⲎ
ⲢⲞⲨ Ⲛ]ⲦⲞⲨ ⲠⲈ ⲠⲈⳢⲢⲟⳝ ⲚⲚⲀⲄⲀ

15. ⲐⲞⲚ ⲦⲎⲢⲞⲨ ⲚⲦⲞⲨ ⲞⲚ ⲠⲈⲦⲈⲈⲦ
ⳘⳘⲞⲞⲨ ⲦⲎⲢⲞⲨ ⲠⲒⲀⲨⲦⲞⲮⲨⲎⲤ
Ⲏ ⲠⲒⲢⲱⲦ ⳘⲀⲨⲀⲀⲨ ⲈⲨⳡⲞⲞⲠ
ⳠⲀⲐⲎ ⲚⲚⲒⲠⲦⲎⲢⳝ ⲈⲚⲦⲀⲨⲭⲠⲞⲨ
ⳘⲀⲨⲀⲀⲨ ⲈⲨⳡⲞⲞⲠ ⲚⲞⲨⲞⲈⲒⳡ

20. ⲚⲒⳘ ⲞⲨⲀⲨⲦⲞⲄⲈⲚⲎⲦⲞⲤ ⲠⲈ
ⲀⲨⲱ ⲞⲨⳡⲀⲈⲚⲈⳠ ⲠⲈ ⲈⳘⲚⲦⳝ
ⲢⲀⲚ ⳘⳘⲀⲨ ⲀⲨⲱ ⲈⲚⲞⲨⳝ ⲚⲈ Ⲛ
ⲢⲀⲚ ⲦⲎⲢⲞⲨ ⲈⳝⲢⲱⲢⲠ ⲚⲤⲞⲞⲨⲚ
ⲈⲚⲈⲒⲠⲦⲎⲢⳝ ⲈⲨⲐⲈⲱⲢⲒ ⲚⲚⲒ

25. ⲠⲦⲎⲢⳝ ⲈⲨⳠⲱⳡⲦ ⲈⳠⲢⲀⲒ ⲈⲭⲚ
ⲚⲒⲠⲦⲎⲢⳝ ⲈⲨⲤⲱⲦⳘ ⲈⲚⲒⲠⲦⲎ
Ⲣⳝ ⲈⳝⳠⳘⳝⳘ ⲚⳠⲞⲨⲞ ⲠⲀⲢⲀ
ⳝⲞⳘ ⲚⲒⳘ ⲠⲀⲒ ⲈⲦⲈ ⳘⲚⳡⳝⲞⳘ Ⲛ
ⳝⲱⳡⲦ ⲈⳠⲞⲨⲚ ⲈⳠⳘⲠⲈⳝⳠⲞ Ⲛ

30. ⲀⲦⲦⲀⳠⲞⳝ ⲠⲀⲒ ⲠⲈ ⲠⲈⲦⳡⲞⲞⲠ
ⳠⲚ ⲞⲨⲈⲒⲚⲈ ⲚⲞⲨⲱⲦ ⲚⲀⲚⲞⲨ
ⲤⲒⲞⲤ ⲚⲎⲢⲈⳘⲞⲤ ⲚⲀⲄⲚⲱⲤⲦⲞⲤ
ⲀⲨⲱ ⲠⲠⲀⲚⳘⲨⲤⲦⲎⲢⲒⲞⲚ ⲠⲈ

6. Cf. line 9.

7–8. Cf. line 6.

ⲁϥⲉⲓ ⲛ̄ⲧⲙⲏⲧⲉ ⲥ̄ⲟⲩ
ⲡⲁⲛ ⲁ̄ⲡⲟⲧ ⲉ
ⲡⲟⲩⲟⲉⲓⲛ ⲛ̄ⲧⲓ̈ⲛ
ⲣⲟⲥ ⲉⲧ ⲁ̄ⲥⲏⲩ
ⲙ̄ⲡⲧⲏⲣ ⲟ̄ⲩⲛ̄ⲧⲉ
ⲣⲟⲩ ⲕⲱⲃⲉ ⲧⲏⲣ
ⲉⲃⲉⲧⲁⲛⲁⲡ ⲁⲩ
ⲧⲩ ⲁⲩⲱ ⲉⲣⲉ
ⲛ̄ⲉⲛⲧⲏ ⲁⲩⲟ
ⲁⲩ ⲉⲩⲧⲱⲕϥ ⲉⲧⲟⲙ
ⲡⲁϫⲉ ⲡ̄ⲙⲁⲕⲁⲣⲓⲟⲥ ϫⲉ
ⲥⲉⲣⲣ̄ⲡⲁⲣⲁⲧⲁ̈ⲛ ⲛϭⲓ
ⲡⲧⲏⲣϥ ⲉⲧ ⲟⲩⲟⲉⲓ ⲛ
ⲉⲧⲃⲉ ⲡⲁⲓ ⲉ̄ⲛ ⲧⲥ ⲡⲉ
ⲟⲩⲛ̄ ⲛ̄ϭⲓ ⲧⲏⲣⲥ̄ ⲛ̄
ⲧⲉⲧ ⲃⲉⲉ̄ⲟ̄ⲧ ⲛⲛⲓⲧ ⲛⲛ̄ⲁⲛ
ⲁⲩⲧⲩ ⲟ̄ⲣ ⲁⲭⲱ ⲣⲏⲧⲟⲥ ⲛ̄
ⲁⲩ ϭⲉ ⲉ̄ϫⲱⲣ ⲙ̄ⲛⲓ̈ⲧⲛ̄
ⲣ ⲉϣⲱⲡ ⲁⲙ ⲟⲟⲩ ⲡⲣⲟⲥ ⲛ
ⲧ ⲁⲩ ϣⲟⲟ ⲡ ⲉ̄ⲙⲕⲟ̄ⲏ
ⲧⲁⲩ ϫⲓ ⲉ̄ⲣⲉⲛⲓ ⲧⲏ ⲣⲟⲩ
ⲉ̄ⲧ ⲙ̄ⲉⲛⲧⲏ ⲉ̄ⲩⲟⲛⲧⲟ̄ⲩⲙ ⲁⲩ
ⲧⲏⲣⲟⲩ ⲉ̄ⲱⲣ ⲁ̄ⲩⲟ ϫⲉ
ⲉⲟⲩ ⲛ̄ⲧⲏⲟⲩ ⲥⲕ ⲁϫⲟ ⲉⲣⲁⲓ
ⲛⲉ̄ ⲛⲧⲩ ⲧⲏⲣⲟⲩ ⲙⲛ̄ⲡⲉⲧⲛ
ⲉⲓⲱ ⲛ̄ⲛⲓ̈ⲱ ⲛⲉⲓ ⲉⲧⲟ̄ⲩ
ⲉ̄ⲛ ⲧⲏⲣⲟⲩ ⲉⲙ ⲛⲓ̈ⲁ
ⲡⲙⲟⲛⲟⲥ ⲁⲩ ⲁⲣ ⲕ ⲁⲣⲁ ⲓⲱ
ⲁⲩⲧⲛ ⲁ̄ⲑ ⲉⲣⲟⲛ ⲟⲩ ⲧⲉ ⲩⲉ
ⲉ̄ⲧⲡⲏⲣ ⲛ̄ ⲥⲁⲡⲓ ⲟ ⲧ ⲁⲩⲱⲓⲥ
ⲉⲩⲱ ϥⲓ ⲧⲉ ⲧ ⲉ̄ϫⲓ ⲛⲙ
ⲉⲧ ϣ ⲟ ⲟⲩ ⲛⲉ ⲛⲧ ⲉⲛ
ϫⲉ ⲩⲓ ⲧⲁ ⲃⲉ ⲣⲟϥ
ⲛ̄ⲧⲟⲟⲩ ⲣⲁ̄ⲟⲩ ⲡⲟⲟⲩ
ⲥⲉⲣⲱⲡ ⲛ̄ⲏ ⲩⲉ̄ⲩ ⲁ̄
ⲁ̄ⲣⲟ ⲟ̄ⲩⲛ ⲧ ⲏⲣⲟⲩ ⲥ̄

1. ⲁⲩⲱ ⲡⲡⲁⲛⲥⲟ[ⲫⲟⲥ ⲡⲉ ⲁⲩⲱ]⟨ⲡ
ⲡⲁⲛⲁⲣⲭⲟⲥ ⲡⲉ [ⲁⲩⲱ] ⲡⲡⲁⲛⲧⲟ
ⲡⲟⲥ ⲉⲛⲟⲩⲩ ⲛ[ⲉ⟨ⲛⲧⲟⲡⲟⲥ⟩[ⲧⲏ
ⲣⲟⲩ ⲉⲩⲛϩⲏⲧ[ⲩ ⲁⲩⲱ ⲉⲣⲉ ⲛⲟⲩⲟ
5. ⲉⲓⲛ ⲧⲏⲣⲟⲩ ⲛϩ[ⲏⲧⲩ ⲁⲩⲱ ⲉ
ⲣⲉ ⲡⲱⲛϩ ⲧⲏⲣ[ⲩ ⲛϩⲏⲧⲩ ⲁⲩⲱ
ⲉⲣⲉ ⲧⲁⲛⲁⲡⲁⲩⲥ[ⲓⲥ ⲧⲏⲣⲥ ⲛϩⲏ
ⲧⲩ ⲁⲩⲱ ⲉⲣⲉ ⲡ⟨ⲕⲁⲣⲱⲩ ⲧⲏⲣⲩ
ⲛϩⲏⲧⲩ ⲁⲩⲱ ⲡⲉⲓⲱⲧ ⲛϩⲏⲧⲩ
10. ⲁⲩⲱ ⲧⲙⲁⲁⲩ ⲁⲩⲱ ⲡϣ[ⲏⲣⲉ ⲛϩⲏⲧⲩ
ⲡⲁⲓ ⲡⲉ ⲡⲙⲁⲕⲁⲣⲓⲟⲥ ⲙⲁ[ⲅⲁⲁⲩ
ⲥⲉⲣⲭⲣⲓⲁ ⲅⲁⲣ ⲙⲡⲁⲓ ⲛϭⲓ ⟨ⲛⲓ
ⲡⲧⲏⲣⲩ ⲉⲩⲟⲛϩ ⲅⲁⲣ ⲧ[ⲏⲣⲟⲩ
ⲉⲧⲃⲉ ⲡⲁⲓ ⲉⲛⲧⲟⲩ ⲡⲉ[ⲧⲥⲟ
15. ⲟⲩⲛ ⲛⲛⲉⲓⲡⲧⲏⲣⲩ ⲛ[ϩⲏⲧⲩ
ⲡⲉⲧⲑⲉⲱⲣⲓ ⲛⲛⲓⲡⲧⲏⲣⲩ ϩⲣⲁⲓ
ⲛϩⲏⲧⲩ ⲟⲩⲁⲭⲱⲣⲏⲧⲟⲥ ⲡⲉ
ⲛⲧⲟⲩ ⲇⲉ ⲉⲩⲭⲱⲣⲓ ⲛⲛⲓⲡⲧⲏ
ⲣⲩ ⲉⲩϣⲱⲡ ⲙⲙⲟⲟⲩ ⲉⲣⲟⲩ ⲁⲩ
20. ⲱ ⲙⲛⲗⲁⲁⲩ ϣⲟⲟⲡ ⲙⲡⲃⲟⲗ ⲙ
ⲡⲁⲓ ⲁⲗⲗⲁ ⲉⲣⲉ ⲛⲓⲡⲧⲏⲣⲩ ϣⲟⲟⲡ
ϩⲣⲁⲓ ⲛϩⲏⲧⲩ ⲉⲩⲟ ⲛⲧⲟⲩ ⲛⲁⲩ
ⲧⲏⲣⲟⲩ ⲉⲩϣⲣⲃ ⲙⲙⲟⲟⲩ ⲉ
ϩⲟⲩⲛ ⲧⲏⲣⲟⲩ ⲉⲩϣⲟⲟⲡ ϩⲣⲁⲓ
25. ⲛϩⲏⲧⲩ ⲧⲏⲣⲟⲩ ⲛⲧⲟⲩ ⲡⲉ ⲡ
ⲉⲓⲱⲧ ⲛⲛⲁⲓⲱⲛ ⲉⲩϣⲟⲟⲡ ϩⲁ
ⲧⲉⲩϩⲏ ⲧⲏⲣⲟⲩ ⲙⲙⲛⲗⲁⲁⲩ
ⲛⲧⲟⲡⲟⲥ ⲙⲡⲃⲗ ⲙⲡⲁⲓ ⲙⲙⲛ
ⲗⲁⲁⲩ ⲛⲛⲟⲉⲣⲟⲛ ⲟⲩⲧⲉ ⲗⲁⲁⲩ
30. ⲉⲧⲡⲏⲣⲩ꙼ ⲛⲥⲁ ⲡⲓⲟⲩⲁ ⲙⲁⲩⲁⲁⲩ
ⲉⲩϭⲱϣⲧ ⲉⲧⲉⲩⲙⲛⲧⲁⲧⲧⲁϩⲟⲥ
ⲉⲧϣⲟⲟⲡ ⲛϩⲏⲧⲟⲩ ⲧⲏⲣⲟⲩ
ⲭⲉ ⲩⲧⲟⲩϣ ⲉⲣⲟⲟⲩ ⲧⲏⲣⲟⲩ
ⲛⲧⲟⲟⲩ ⲇⲉ ⲙⲡⲟⲩⲧⲁϩⲟⲩ
35. ⲥⲉⲣϣⲡⲏⲣⲉ ⲙⲙⲟⲩ ⲭⲉ ⲉⲩⲧⲟⲩϣ
ⲉⲣⲟⲟⲩ ⲧⲏⲣⲟⲩ ⲥⲉⲁⲅⲱⲛⲓⲍⲉ*

8. Vide note 1, VIII (comm.).

30 α. Dr Schmidt regards this as a misspelt word, but
from the sense of the passage it may well be ·the pronominal form of the Egyptian verb _pr_ = _to go forth_
through birth or _begetting_—here used reflexively.

* One or more leaves are missing between this and
the next page (XI).

XI
MS. f. 94R
C.S. p. 1

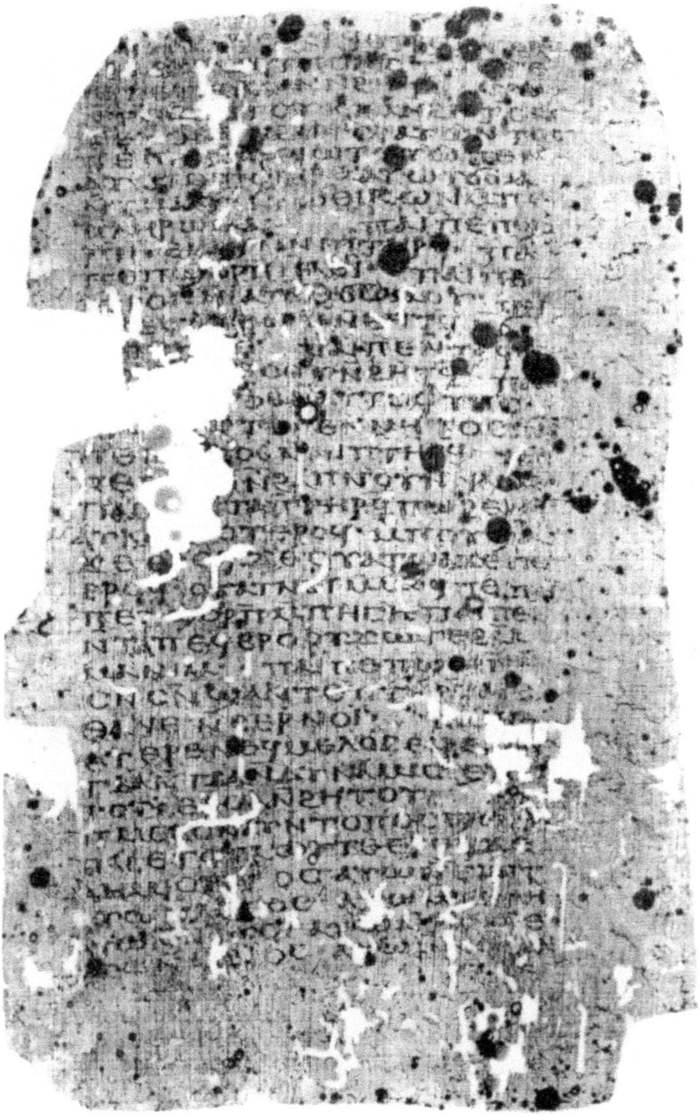

1. ⲀⲨⲦⲀϨⲞⲨ ⲈⲢⲀⲦⲨ ⲈⲦⲢⲈⲨⲀⲅⲰⲚ
ⲒⳄⲈ ⲈϨⲞⲨⲚ ⲈⲦⲠⲞⲖⲒⲤ ⲦⲀⲒ ⲈⲦⲈ
ⲢⲈ ⲦⲈⲨϨⲒⲔⲰⲚ ⲚϨⲎⲦⲤ ⲀⲨⲰ
ⲚⲦⲞⲤ ⲠⲈⲦⲞⲨⲔⲒⳘ ⲚϨⲎⲦⲤ ⲀⲨ
5. Ⲱ ⲈⲨⲞⲚϨ ⲚϨⲎⲦⲤ ⲀⲨⲰ ⲚⲦⲞⲤ
ⲠⲈ ⲠⲎⲒ ⳘⲠⲈⲒⲰⲦ ⲀⲨⲰ ⲠⲈⲚ
ⲆⲨⳘⲀ ⳘⲠϢⲎⲢⲈ ⲀⲨⲰ ⲦϬⲞⳘ
ⲚⲦⳘⲀⲀⲨ ⲀⲨⲰ ⲐⲒⲔⲰⲚ ⳘⲠⲈ
ⲠⲖⲎⲢⲰⳘⲀ   ⲠⲀⲒ ⲠⲈ ⲠϢⲞ
10. ⲢⲠ ⲚⲈⲒⲰⲦ ⲚⲚⲒⲠⲦⲎⲢⲨ ⲠⲀⲒ
ⲠⲈ ⲠϢⲞⲢⲠ ⲚⲀⲈⲒ ⲠⲀⲒ ⲠⲈ
ⲠⲢⲢⲞ ⲚⲚⲒⲀⲦ⳿Ⳙ⳿ⳁⲰⲘⲞⲨ ⲠⲀⲒ
ⲠⲈ ⲈⲦⲞⲨⲤⲞⲢⳘ ⲚϨⲎⲦⲨ ⲚϬⲒ
ⲚⲒⲠⲦⲎⲢⲨ ⲠⲀⲒ ⲠⲈ ⲚⲦⲀⲨ†
15. ⳘⲞⲢⳅⲎ ⲈⲢⲞⲞⲨ ⲚϨⲎⲦⲨ ⲠⲀⲒ
ⲠⲈ ⲠⲦⲞⲠⲞⲤ ⲚⲀⲨⲦⲞⳅⲎⲤ
ⲀⲨⲰ ⲚⲀⲨⲦⲞⲄⲈⲚⲚⲎⲦⲞⲤ ⲠⲀⲒ
ⲠⲈ ⲠⲂⲀⲐⲞⲤ ⲚⲚⲒⲠⲦⲎⲢⲨ ⲠⲀⲒ
ⲠⲈ ⲠⲚⲞϬ ⲚϨⲀⲠⲚⲞⲨⲚ ⲚⲀⳘⲈ
20. ⲠⲀⲒ ⲠⲈ ⲚⲦⲀ ⲠⲦⲎⲢⲨ ⲠⲰϨ ⲈⲢⲞⲨ
ⲀⲨⲔⲀⲢⲰⲞⲨ ⲈⲢⲞⲨ ⳘⲠⲞⲨⲰϢ
ⳄⲈ ⲈⲢⲞⲨ ⳄⲈ ⲞⲨⲀⲦϢⲀⳄⲈ ⲠⲈ
ⲈⲢⲞⲨ ⲞⲨⲀⲦⲚⲞⲒ ⳘⳘⲞⲨ ⲠⲈ ⲠⲀⲒ
ⲠⲈ ⲠϢⲞⲢⲠ ⳘⲠⲎⲄⲎ ⲠⲀⲒ ⲠⲈ
25. ⲚⲦⲀ ⲠⲈⲨϨⲢⲞⲞⲨ ⳄⲰⲦⲈ ϨⳘ
ⳘⲀ ⲚⲒⳘ ⲠⲀⲒ ⲠⲈ ⲠϢⲞⲢⲠ Ⲛ
ⲤⲚⲤⲚ ϢⲀⲚⲦⲈ ⲠⲦⲎⲢⲨ ⲀⲒⲤ
ⲐⲀⲚⲈ ⲚⲤⲈⲢⲚⲞⲒ ⲠⲀⲒ ⲠⲈ
ⲈⲦⲈⲢⲈ ⲚⲈⲨⳘⲈⲖⲞⲤ ⲈⲒⲢⲈ ⲚⲞⲨ
30. ⲦⲂⲀ ⲚⲦⲂⲀ ⲚⲀⲨⲚⲀⳘⲒⲤ ⲈⲦⲞⲨⲒ
ⲦⲞⲨⲒ ⲈⲂⲞⲖ ⲚϨⲎⲦⲞⲨ   Ⲁ
ⲠⳘⲈϨⲤⲚⲀⲨ ⲚⲦⲞⲠⲞⲤ ϢⲰⲠⲈ
ⲠⲀⲒ ⲈⲦⲞⲨⲚⲀⳘⲞⲨⲦⲈ ⲈⲢⲞⲨ ⳄⲈ
ⲆⲎⳘⲒⲞⲨⲢⲄⲞⲤ ⲀⲨⲰ ⲚⲈⲒⲰⲦ
35. ⲀⲨⲰ ⲚⲖⲞⲄⲞⲤ ⲀⲨⲰ ⳘⲠⲎⲄⲎ
ⲀⲨⲰ ⲚⲚⲞⲨⲤ ⲀⲨⲰ ⲚⲢⲰⳘⲈ
ⲀⲨⲰ ⲚⲀⲒⲆⲒⲞⲤ ⲀⲨⲰ ⲚⲀⲠⲈⲢⲀⲚ

1. ⲦⲞⲤ ⲠⲀⲒ ⲠⲈ ⲠⲈⲤⲦⲨⲖⲞⲤ ⲠⲀⲒ ⲠⲈ Ⲉ
ⲠⲒⲤⲔⲞⲠⲞⲤ ⲀⲨⲰ ⲠⲀⲒ ⲠⲈ ⲠⲒⲰⲦ (ⲙ)
ⲠⲦⲎⲢϤ ⲀⲨⲰ ⲠⲀⲒ ⲠⲈ ⲠⲈⲦⲈⲢⲈ
ⲚⲀⲒⲰⲚ Ⲟ ⲞⲨⲔⲖⲞⲙ ⲈϪⲰϤ
5. ⲈⲨⲚⲈϪ ⲀⲔⲦⲒⲚ ⲈⲂⲞⲖ ⲠⲔⲰⲦⲈ
ⲙⲠⲈϤϨⲞ ⲦⲈ ⲦⲙⲚⲦⲀⲦⲤⲞⲨⲰ
ⲚⲤ ϨⲚ ⲚⲔⲞⲤⲙⲞⲤ ⲈⲦϨⲒⲂⲞⲖ ⲚⲀⲒ
ⲈⲦϢⲒⲚⲈ ⲚⲞⲨⲞⲈⲒϢ ⲚⲒⲙ ⲚⲤⲀ
ⲠⲈϤϨⲞ ⲈⲨⲞⲨⲰϢ ⲈⲤⲞⲨⲰⲚϤ
10. ϪⲈ ⲠⲈϤϢⲀϪⲈ ⲠⲎϨ ϢⲀⲢⲞⲞⲨ
ⲀⲨⲰ ⲤⲈⲞⲨⲰϢ ⲈⲚⲀⲨ ⲈⲢⲞϤ ⲀⲨ
Ⲱ ⲠⲞⲨⲞⲈⲒⲚ ⲚⲚⲈⲨⲂⲀⲖ ϪⲰⲦⲈ
ϢⲀ ⲚⲦⲞⲠⲞⲤ ⲙⲠⲈⲠⲖⲎⲢⲰⲙⲀ
ⲙⲠⲤⲀⲚⲂⲞⲖ ⲀⲨⲰ ⲠⲖⲞⲄⲞⲤ ⲠⲈ
15. ⲦⲚⲎⲨ ⲈⲂⲞⲖ ϨⲚ ⲢⲰϤ ϤϪⲰⲦⲈ
ⲚⲚⲀⲦⲠⲈ ⲙⲚ ⲚⲀⲠⲈⲤⲎⲦ ⲀⲨⲰ
ⲠϢⲰ ⲚⲦⲈϤⲀⲠⲈ ⲠⲈ ⲦⲎⲠⲈ
ⲚⲚⲔⲞⲤⲙⲞⲤ ⲈⲐⲎⲠ ⲀⲨⲰ
ⲠⲰⲢϪ ⲈϨⲞⲨⲚ ⲙⲠⲈϤϨⲞ ⲠⲈ ⲠⲔⲀ
20. ⲐⲒⲔⲰⲚ ⲚⲚⲀⲒⲰⲚ ⲚϤϢⲱ ⲙ
ⲠⲈϤϨⲞ ⲚⲈ ⲦⲎⲠⲈ ⲚⲚⲔⲞⲤⲙⲞⲤ
ⲈⲦϨⲒ ⲠⲤⲀⲚⲂⲞⲖ ⲀⲨⲰ ⲠⲠⲰ
Ⲣϣ ⲈⲂⲞⲖ ⲚⲚⲈⲨϭⲒϪ ⲠⲈ ⲠⲞⲨⲰ
Ⲛϩ ⲈⲂⲞⲖ ⲙⲠⲈⲤⲦⲞⲤ ⲠⲠⲰⲢϣ
25. ⲈⲂⲞⲖ ⲙⲠⲈⲤⲦⲞⲤ ⲠⲈ ⲐⲈⲚⲚⲀⲤ
ⲈⲦⲤⲀⲞⲨⲚⲀⲙ ⲙⲚ ⲚⲈⲦϨⲒϨⲂⲞⲨⲢ
ⲠⲦⲞⲨⲰ ⲈϨⲢⲀⲒ ⲙⲠⲈⲤⲦⲞⲤ ⲠⲈ
ⲠⲢⲰⲙⲈ ⲚⲀⲦⲀⲙⲀϨⲦⲈ ⲙⲙⲞϤ
ⲠⲀⲒ ⲠⲈ ⲠⲒⲰⲦ ⲠⲀⲒ ⲠⲈ ⲠⲠⲎⲄⲎ
30. ⲈⲦⲂⲈ ⲈⲂⲈ ⲙⲠⲔⲀⲢⲰϤ ⲠⲀⲒ ⲠⲈ
ⲈⲦⲞⲨϢⲒⲚⲈ ⲚⲤⲰϤ Ϩⲙ ⲙⲀ ⲚⲒⲙ
ⲀⲨⲰ ⲠⲀⲒ ⲠⲈ ⲠⲒⲰⲦ ⲚⲦⲀ ⲦⲙⲞⲚⲀⲤ
ⲈⲒ ⲈⲂⲞⲖ ⲙⲙⲞϤ ⲚⲐⲈ ⲚⲞⲨⲦⲔ
ⲚⲞⲨⲞⲈⲒⲚ ⲦⲀⲒ ⲈⲦⲈⲢⲈ ⲚⲔⲞⲤ
35. ⲙⲞⲤ ⲦⲎⲢⲞⲨ Ⲟ ⲚⲐⲈ ⲚⲞⲨⲖⲀⲀⲨ

1. ΝΑϩⲢⲎⲀⲤ ⲈΝⲦⲞⲤ ⲦⲈ ΝⲦⲀⲤⲔⲓⲙ Ⲉ
ΝⲔⲀ Νⲓⲙ ϩⲙ ⲠⲈⲤⲂⲞⲨⲂⲞⲨ ⲀⲨⲰ
ⲀⲨϪⲓ ΝⲦⲈⲄΝⲰⲤⲓⲤ ⲀⲨⲰ ⲠⲰΝϩ
ⲀⲨⲰ ⲐⲈⲖⲠⲓⲤ ⲀⲨⲰ ⲦⲀΝⲀⲠⲀⲨⲤⲓⲤ

5. ⲀⲨⲰ ⲦⲀⲄⲀⲠⲎ ⲀⲨⲰ ⲦⲀΝⲀⲤⲦⲀⲤⲓⲤ
ⲀⲨⲰ ⲦⲠⲓⲤⲦⲓⲤ ⲀⲨⲰ ⲠⲈϪⲠⲞ ΝⲔⲈ
ⲤⲞⲠ ⲀⲨⲰ ⲦⲈⲤⳜⲢⲀⲄⲓⲤ ⲦⲀⲓ ⲦⲈ
ⲐⲈΝΝⲀⲤ Ⲉ́Ν́ⲦⲀ́Ⲥ ⲈΝⲦⲀⲤⲈⲓ ⲈⲂⲞⲖ
ϩⲙ ⲠⲓⲰⲦ ΝΝⲀΝⲀⲢⲬⲞⲤ ⲠⲀⲓ ⲈⲦⲞ

10. ΝⲈⲒⲰⲦ ⲈⲢⲞⲨ ⲙⲀⲨⲀⲀⲨ ϩⲓ ⲙⲀⲀⲨ
ⲠⲀⲓ ⲈⲦⲈⲢⲈ ⲠⲈⲨⲠⲖⲎⲢⲰⲙⲀ ⲔⲰⲦⲈ
ⲈⲠⲙΝⲦⲤΝⲞⲞⲨⲤ ΝⲂⲀⲐⲞⲤ ⲠⲰϢⲞ

α ⲢⲠ ΝⲂⲀⲐⲞⲤ ⲠⲈ ⲠⲠⲀΝⲠⲎⲄⲎ ⲈΝ
ⲦⲀ ⲙⲠⲎⲄⲎ ⲦⲎⲢⲞⲨ ⲈⲒ ⲈⲂⲞⲖ ΝϩⲎ

β 15. ⲦⲨ ⲠⲙⲈϩⲤΝⲀⲨ ΝⲂⲀⲐⲞⲤ ⲠⲈ ⲠⲠⲀ
ΝⲤⲞⳜⲞⲤ ⲈΝⲦⲀ ΝⲤⲞⳜⲞⲤ ⲦⲎ

γ ⲢⲞⲨ ⲈⲒ ⲈⲂⲞⲖ ⲙⲙⲞⲨ ⲠⲙⲈϩϢⲞⲨΝⲦ
ΝⲂⲀⲐⲞⲤ ⲠⲈ ⲠⲠⲀΝⲙⲨⲤⲦⲎⲢⲓⲞΝ
ⲈΝⲦⲀ ⲙⲨⲤⲦⲎⲢⲓⲞΝ Νⲓⲙ ⲈⲒ ⲈⲂⲞⲖ

δ 20. ⲙⲙⲞⲨ Ⲏ ⲈⲂⲞⲖ ΝϩⲎⲦⲨ ⲠⲙⲈϩⲨ
ⲦⲞⲞⲨ ⲆⲈ ΝⲂⲀⲐⲞⲤ ⲠⲈ ⲠⲠⲀΝⲄΝⲰ
ⲤⲓⲤ ⲈΝⲦⲀ ⲄΝⲰⲤⲓⲤ Νⲓⲙ ⲈⲒ ⲈⲂⲞⲖ

ε ΝϩⲎⲦⲨ ⲠⲙⲈϩⲦ́ⲞⲨ ΝⲂⲀⲐⲞⲤ
ⲠⲈ ⲠⲠⲀΝϩⲀⲄΝⲞΝ ⲈΝⲦⲀ ϩⲀⲄΝⲞΝ

25. Νⲓⲙ ⲈⲒ ⲈⲂⲞⲖ ΝϩⲎⲦⲨ ⲠⲙⲈϩⲤⲞⲞⲨ

(ϛ) ΝⲂⲀⲐⲞⲤ ⲠⲈ ⲦⲤⲓⲄⲎ ⲠⲀⲓ ⲠⲈ ⲈⲦⲈ
ⲢⲈ ⲔⲀⲢⲰⲨ Ν́ⲓⲙ Νⲓⲙ ΝϩⲎⲦⲨ ⲠⲙⲈϩ

(ζ) ⲤⲀϢⲨ ΝⲂⲀⲐⲞⲤ ⲠⲈ ⲠⲢⲞ ΝⲀΝⲞⲨ
ⲤⲓⲞⲤ ⲈΝⲦⲀ ⲞⲨⲤⲓⲀ Νⲓⲙ ⲈⲒ ⲈⲂⲞⲖ

(η) 30. ⲙⲙⲞⲨ ⲠⲙⲈϩϢⲙⲞⲨΝ ⲆⲈ Ν
ⲂⲀⲐⲞⲤ ⲠⲈ ⲠⲈⲠⲢⲞⲠⲀⲦⲰⲢ ⲈΝ
ⲦⲀ ⲠⲢⲞⲠⲀⲦⲰⲢ Νⲓⲙ ϢⲰⲠⲈ
ⲈⲂⲞⲖ ⲙⲙⲞⲨ Ⲏ ⲈⲂⲞⲖ ΝϩⲎⲦⲨ

(θ) ⲠⲙⲈϩⳜⲓⲤ ⲆⲈ ΝⲂⲀⲐⲞⲤ ⲞⲨⲠⲀΝ
35. ⲦⲞⲠⲀⲦⲰⲢ ⲠⲈ ΝⲀⲨⲦⲞⲠⲀⲦⲰⲢ Ⲉ

The Greek letters standing in the left-hand margin
on the recto and verso of this leaf are almost obliterated.
Dr Schmidt copied them from Woide's transcript.
8. ····· deleted word.
27. ··· deleted word.

1. ⲦⲈ ⲠⲀⲒ ⲠⲈ ⲈⲢⲈ ⲘⲚⲦⲈⲒⲰⲦ ⲚⲒⲘ [ⲚⲌⲎ
ⲦⳘ ⲈⳘⲞ ⲚⲈⲒⲰⲦ ⲈⲢⲞⲞⲨ ⲘⲀⲨⲀⲀⲨ

Ⰰ. ⲠⲘⲈⲌⲎⲦ ⲚⲂⲀⲐⲞⲤ ⲠⲈ ⲠⲠⲀⲚ
ⲦⲞⲆⲨⲚⲀⲘⲒⲤ ⲈⲚⲦⲀ ϬⲞⲘ ⲚⲒⲘ

5. ⲈⲒ ⲈⲂⲞⲖ ⲚⲎⲎⲦⳘ ⲠⲘⲈⲌⳘⲚ

ⲒⲀ. ⲦⲞⲨⲈ ⲆⲈ ⲚⲂⲀⲐⲞⲤ ⲠⲈⲦⲈⲢⲈ Ⲡ
ϢⲞⲢⲠ ⲚⲀⲌⲞⲢⲀⲦⲞⲤ ⲚⲎⲎⲦⳘ
ⲠⲀⲒ ⲈⲚⲦⲀ ⲀⲌⲞⲢⲀⲦⲞⲤ ⲚⲒⲘ ⲈⲒ Ⲉ
ⲂⲞⲖ ⲚⲎⲎⲦⳘ ⲠⲘⲈⲌⳘⲚⲦⲤⲚⲞ

ⲒⲂ. 10. ⲞⲨⲤ ⲆⲈ ⲚⲂⲀⲐⲞⲤ ⲠⲈ ⲦⲀⲖⲎⲐⲒⲀ
ⲈⲚⲦⲀ ⲘⲈ ⲚⲒⲘ ⲈⲒ ⲈⲂⲞⲖ ⲚⲎⲎⲦⳘ
ⲦⲀⲒ ⲦⲈ ⲦⲀⲖⲎⲐⲒⲀ ⲈⲦ ⲌⲰⲂⲤ Ⲙ
ⲘⲞⲞⲨ ⲦⲎⲢⲞⲨ ⲦⲀⲒ ⲦⲈ ⲐⲒⲔⲰⲚ
ⲘⲠⲈⲒⲰⲦ ⲦⲀⲒ ⲦⲈ ⲦⲀⲖ ⲘⲠⲎ

15. ⲢⳘ   ⲦⲀⲒ ⲦⲈ ⲦⲘⲀⲀⲨ ⲚⲚⲀⲒⲰⲚ
ⲦⲎⲢⲞⲨ ⲦⲀⲒ ⲦⲈ ⲈⲦⲔⲰⲦⲈ
ⲈⲚⲂⲀⲐⲞⲤ ⲦⲎⲢⲞⲨ ⲦⲀⲒ ⲦⲈ
ⲦⲘⲞⲚⲀⲤ ⲈⲦⲞ ⲚⲀⲔⲀⲦⲀⲄⲚⲰⲤ
ⲦⲞⲤ Ⲏ ⲈⲦⲞⲨⲞ ⲚⲀⲦⲤⲞⲞⲨⲚ

20. ⲘⲘⲞⲤ ⲦⲈⲒⲀⲦⲬⲀⲢⲀⲔⲦⲎⲢ
ⲦⲀⲒ ⲈⲦⲈⲢⲈ ⲚⲈⲬⲀⲢⲀⲔⲦⲎⲢ ⲦⲎ
ⲢⲞⲨ ⲚⲎⲎⲦⲤ ⲦⲀⲒ ⲈⲦⲤⲘⲀⲘⲀ
ⲀⲦ ϢⲀ ⲚⲒⲈⲚⲈⲌ ⲠⲀⲒ ⲠⲈ ⲠⲒⲰⲦ
ⲠϢⲀⲈⲚⲈⲌ ⲠⲀⲒ ⲠⲈ ⲠⲒⲰⲦ

25. ⲚⲀⲦϢⲀⲬⲈ ⲈⲢⲞⳘ ⲚⲀⲦⲚⲞⲒ
ⲘⲘⲞⳘ ⲚⲀⲦⲘⲞⲔⲘⲈⲔ ⲈⲢⲞⳘ
ⲚⲀⲦⲬⲒⲞⲞⲢ ⲘⲘⲞⳘ ⲠⲀⲒ ⲠⲈ
ⲚⲦⲀ ⲠⲦⲎⲢⳘ Ⲣ ⲈⲨⲚⲞⲨⲤⲒⲞⲤ
ⲚⲎⲎⲦⳘ ⲀⲨⲰ ⲀⲨⲢⲀϢⲈ ⲀⲨⲦⲈ

30. ⲖⲎⲖ ⲀⲨⲬⲠⲞ ⲚⲌⲈⲚⲦⲂⲀ ⲚⲦⲂⲀ
ⲚⲚⲀⲒⲰⲚ ⲌⲘ ⲠⲈⲨⲢⲀϢⲈ ⲀⲨ
ⲘⲞⲨⲦⲈ ⲈⲢⲞⲞⲨ ⲬⲈ ⲚⲈⲬⲠⲞ Ⲙ
ⲠⲢⲀϢⲈ ⲬⲈ ⲀⲨⲢⲀϢⲈ ⲘⲚ ⲠⲒⲰⲦ
ⲚⲀⲒ ⲚⲈ ⲚⲔⲞⲤⲘⲞⲤ ⲈⲚⲦⲀ ⲠⲈⲤϮⲞⲤ †

35. ⲞⲨⲰ ⲈⲂⲞⲖ ⲚⲎⲎⲦⲞⲨ ⲀⲨⲰ
ⲈⲚⲦⲀ ⲠⲢⲰⲘⲈ ϢⲰⲠⲈ ⲈⲂⲞⲖ ⲌⲚ
ⲚⲈⲒⲘⲈⲖⲞⲤ ⲚⲀⲤⲰⲘⲀⲦⲞⲤ

1. ΠΑΙ ΠΕ ΠΙѠΤ ΑΥѠ ΤΠΗΓΗ Ν
ΟΥΟΝ ΝΙΜ ΠΑΙ ΕΡΕ ΜΕΛΟC ΝΙΜ
ΝΤΑΥ ΧΗΚ ΕΒΟΛ ΑΥѠ ΕΝΤΑ ΡΑΝ
ΝΙΜ ѠѠΠΕ ΕΒΟΛ ϨΜ ΠΙѠΤ

5. ΕΙΤΕ ΑϨΡΗΤΟΝ ΕΙΤΕ ΑΦΘΑΡ
ΤΟΝ ΕΙΤΕ ΑΚΑΤΑΓΝѠCΤΟC
ΕΙΤΕ ΑϨΟΡΑΤΟC ΕΙΤΕ ϨΑΠ
ΛΟΥΝ ΕΙΤΕ ΕΡΗΜΟC ΕΙΤΕ
ΔΥΝΑΜΙC ΕΙΤΕ ΠΑΝΑΥΝΑ

10. ΜΙC ΕΙΤΕ ΡΑΝ ΝΙΜ ΕΤϨΜ ΠΚΑ
ΡѠϤ ΕΝΤΑΥѠѠΠΕ ΤΗΡΟΥ
ϨΜ ΠΕΙѠΤ ΠΑΙ ΕΤΕΡΕ Ν
ΝΚΟCΜΟC ΤΗΡΟΥ ΕΤϨΙΒΟΛ
ΝΑΥ ΕΡΟϤ ΝΘΕ ΝΝCΙΟΥ ΜΠΕ

15. CΤΕΡΕѠΜΑ ϨΝ ΤΕΥΑ̇ѠΗ Ν
ΘΕ ΕΤΕΡΕ ΝΡѠΜΕ ΕΠΙΘΥΜΕΙ
ΕΝΑΥ ΕΠΡΗ ΝΤΕΙϨΕ ϨѠѠΥ
CΕΕΠΙΘΥΜΙ ΕΝΑΥ ΕΡΟϤ ΝϭΙ
ΝΚΟCΜΟC ΕΤϨΙΒΟΛ ΕΤΒΕ

20. ΤΕϤΜΝΤΑΤΝΑΥ ΕΡΟC ΕΤΜ
ΠΕϤΚѠΤΕ ΝΤΟϤ ΝΟΥΟΙѠ
ΝΙΜ ΠΕΤ⳨ ΜΠѠΝϨ ΝΝΑΙѠΝ
ΑΥѠ ϨΙΤΜ ΠΕΥѠΑΧΕ ΕΝΤΑ
ΠΑΤΠΝѠѠ COΥΝ ΤΜΟΝΑC

25. ΕΙΜΕ ΕΡΟC ΑΥѠ ϨΙΤΜ ΠΕΥ
ѠΑΧΕ ΕΝΤΑΥѠѠΠΕ ΝϭΙ ΨΙ
ΕΡΟΝ ΜΠΛΗΡѠΜΑ ΠΑΙ ΠΕ
ΠΙѠΤ ΠΜΕϨCΝΑΥ ΝΔΗΜΙΟΥΡ
ΓΟC ΠΑΙ ϨΙΤΜ ΠΝΙϤΕ ΝΡѠϤ

30. ΑΤΕΠΡΟΝΟΙΑ ΡϨѠΒ ΕΝΕΤΕ
ΝCΕѠΟΟΠ ΑΝ ΑΥѠѠΠΕ ϨΙ
ΤΝ ΠΕΘΕΛΗΜΑ ΜΠΑΙ ΧΕ Ν
ΤΟϤ ΠΕΤΟΥΕϨCΑϨΝΕ ΜΠΤΗ
ΡϤ ΕΤΡΕϤѠѠΠΕ ΑΥΤΑΜΙΟ Μ

35. ΨΙΕΡΟΝ ΜΠΛΗΡѠΜΑ ΝΤΕΙϨΕ
ΝϤΤΟ ΜΠΥΛΗ ΕΡΕ ϤΤΟ ΜΜΟ

15. ȧ deleted.

XVI
MS. f. 98^{v}
C.S. p. 6

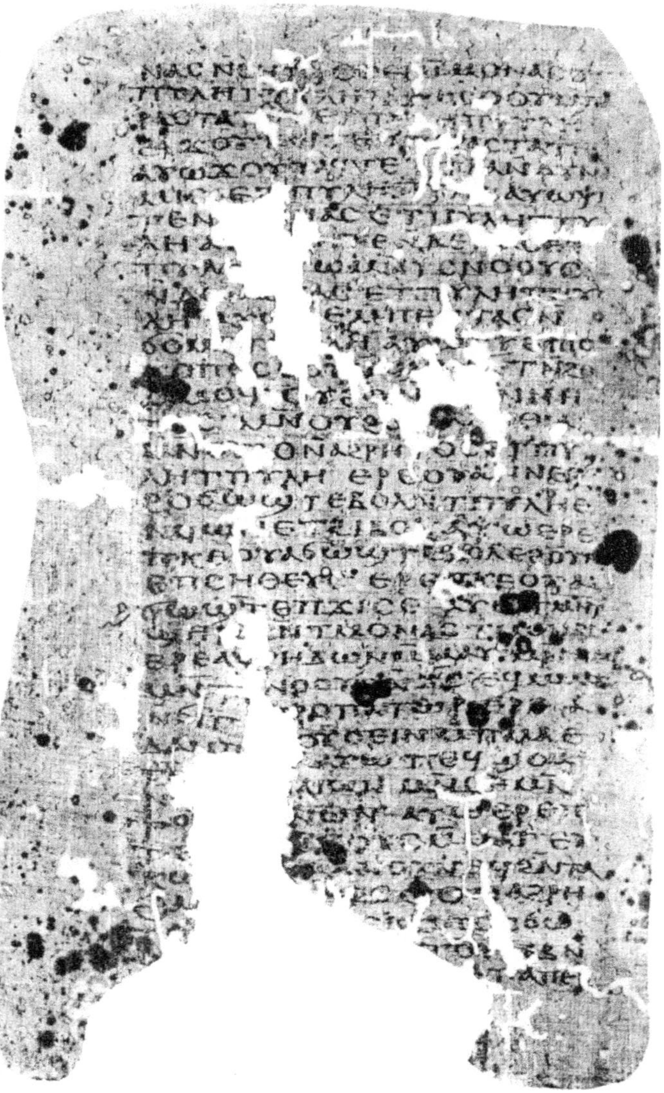

1. ⲚⲀⲤ ⲚⲈⲎⲦⳛ ⲞⳛⲈⲓ ⲘⲘⲞⲚⲀⲤ ⲈⲦ
ⲠⳛⲖⲎ ⲦⲠⳛⲖⲎ Ⲁⳛⲱ ⲤⲞⲞⳛ ⲘⲠⲀ
ⲢⲀⲤⲦⲀⲦⲎⲤ ⲈⲦⲠⳛⲖⲎ ⲦⲠⳛⲖⲎ
ⳠⲀ ⳨ⲞⳛⲦⲀⳛⲦⲈ ⲘⲠⲀⲢⲀⲤⲦⲀⲦⲎⲤ

5. Ⲁⳛⲱ ⳨ⲞⳛⲦⲀⳛⲦⲈ ⲚⲦⲂⲀ ⲚⲀⳛⲚⲀ
ⲘⲓⲤ ⲈⲦⲠⳛⲖⲎ ⲦⲠⳛⲖⲎ Ⲁⳛⲱ Ⲯⲓ
ⲦⲈ ⲚⲈⲈⲚⲚⲀⲤ ⲈⲦⲠⳛⲖⲎ ⲦⲠⳛ
ⲖⲎ Ⲁⳛⲱ ⲘⲎⲦⲈ ⲚⲀⲈⲔⲀⲤ ⲈⲦ
ⲠⳛⲖⲎ ⲠⳛⲖⲎ Ⲁⳛⲱ ⲘⲚⲦⲤⲚⲞⲞⳛⲤ

10. ⲚⲀⲱⲀⲈⲔⲀⲤ ⲈⲦⲠⳛⲖⲎ ⲦⲠⳛ
ⲖⲎ Ⲁⳛⲱ ⲦⲈ ⲘⲠⲈⲚⲦⲀⲤ Ⲛ
ⳐⲞⲘ ⲈⲦⲠⳛⲖⲎ ⲦⲠⳛⲖⲎ Ⲁⳛⲱ ⲞⳛⲈⲠⲓⲤ
ⲔⲞⲠⲞⲤ ⲈⲞⳛⲚ ⳡⲞⲘⲚⲦ ⲚⲈⲞ
ⲘⲘⲞⳛ ⲞⳛⲈⲞ ⲚⲀⲄⲈⲚⲚⲎ

15. ⲦⲞⲤ ⲘⲚ ⲞⳛⲈⲞ ⲚⲀⲖⲎⲐⲒⲀ
ⲘⲚ ⲞⳛⲈⲞ ⲚⲀⲈⲎⲦⲞⲤ ⲈⲦⲠⳛ
ⲖⲎ ⲦⲠⳛⲖⲎ ⲈⲢⲈ ⲞⳛⲀ ⲚⲚⲈⳛ
ⲈⲞ ⳐⲱⳡⲦ ⲈⲂⲞⲖ ⲚⲦⲠⳛⲖⲎ Ⲉ
ⲚⲀⲒⲱⲚ ⲈⲦⲈⲒⲂⲞⲖ Ⲁⳛⲱ ⲈⲢⲈ

20. ⲠⲔⲈⲞⳛⲀ ⳐⲱⳡⲦ ⲈⲂⲞⲖ ⲈⲈⲞⳛⲚ
ⲈⲠⲤⲎⲐⳛⲤ ⲈⲢⲈ ⲠⲔⲈⲞⳛⲀ
ⳐⲱⳡⲦ ⲈⲠ⳨ⲒⲤⲈ Ⲁⳛⲱ ⲦⲘⲚⲦ
ⳡⲎⲢⲈ ⲈⲚ ⲦⲘⲞⲚⲀⲤ ⲦⲘⲞⲚⲀⲤ
ⲈⲢⲈ ⲀⲮⲢⲎⲀⲱⲚ ⲘⲘⲀⳛ ⲘⲚ ⲠⲈⳛ

25. ⲘⲚⲦⲤⲚⲞⲞⳛⲤ Ⲛ⳨Ⲥ ⲈⳛⲘⲘⲀⳛ
ⲚⳐⲒ ⲠⲈⲠⲢⲞⲠⲀⲦⲱⲢ ⲈⲢⲈ Ⲁ
ⲀⲀⲘ ⲠⲀⲠⲞⳛⲞⲈⲒⲚ ⲘⲠⲘⲀ Ⲉ
ⲦⲘⲘⲀⳛ Ⲁⳛⲱ ⲠⲈⳛ ⳡⲞⲘⲦ
ⲚⳡⲈ ⲚⲚⲀⲒⲱⲚ ⲘⲚ ⲤⲈ ⲘⲚ

30. ⲦⲞⳛ ⲚⲚⲀⲒⲱⲚ Ⲁⳛⲱ ⲈⲢⲈ Ⲡ
ⲦⲈⲖⲒⲞⲤ ⲚⲚⲞⳛⲤ ⲘⲘⲀⳛ Ⲉⳛ
ⲔⲱⲦⲈ ⲈⳛⲔⲀⲚⲞⳛⲚ ⲈⳛⲈⲚ ⲦⲀ
ⲐⲀⲚⲀⲤⲒⲀ ⲈⲢⲈ Ⲯⲟ ⲚⲀⲈⲢⲎ
ⲦⲞⲚ ⲘⲠⲈⲠⲒⲤⲔⲞⲠⲞⲤ Ⳑⲱ

35. ⳡⲦ ⲈⲈⲞⳛⲚ ⲈⲠⲈⲦⲞⳛⲀⲀⲂ Ⲛ
ⲦⲈ ⲚⲈⳛⲞⳛⲀⲀⲂ ⲈⲦⲈ ⲠⲀⲠⲈⲢ

XVII
MS f. 100R
C.S. p. 7

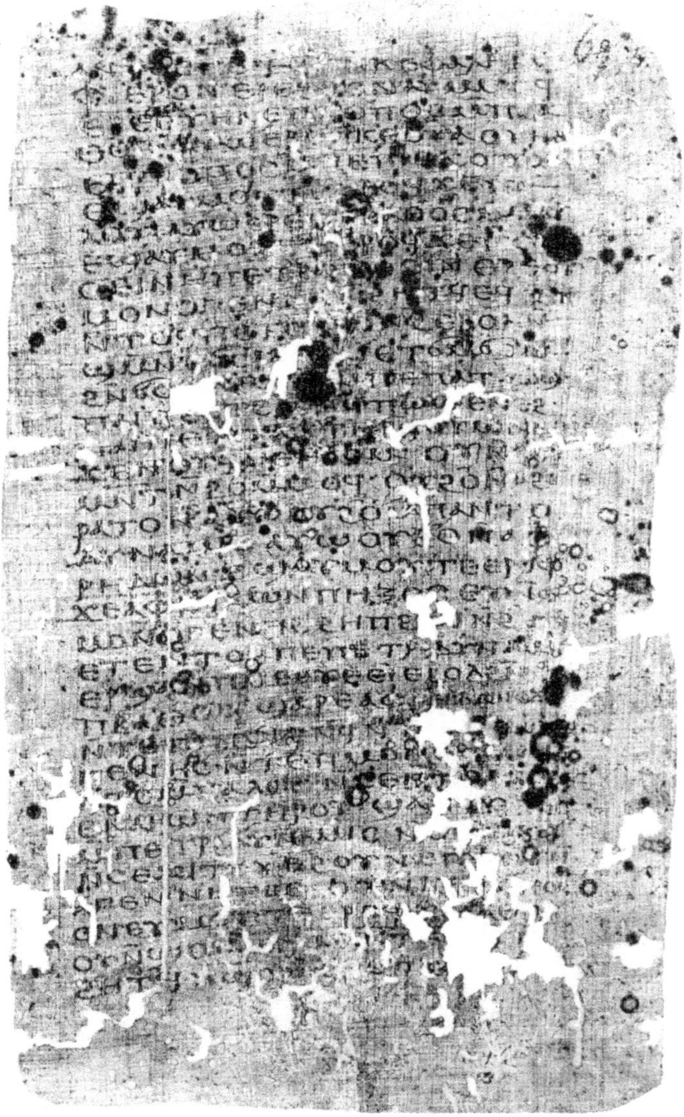

1. ⲀⲚⲦⲞⲤ ⲠⲈ ⲈⲨⲞ ⲚⲔⲈⲮⲀⲖⲎ Ⲙ
ⲮⲒⲈⲢⲞⲚ ⲈⲢⲈ � ⲞⲤⲚⲀⲨ ⲘⲘⲞⲨ
ⲈⲢⲈ ⲞⲨⲀ ⲞⲨⲎⲚ ⲈⲠⲦⲞⲠⲞⲤ ⲘⲠⲂⲀ
ⲐⲞⲤ ⲀⲨⲰ ⲈⲢⲈ ⲠⲔⲈⲞⲨⲀ ⲞⲨⲎⲚ
5. ⲈⲠⲦⲞⲠⲞⲤ ⲘⲠⲈⲠⲒⲤⲔⲞⲠⲞⲤ
ⲈϢⲀⲨⲘⲞⲨⲦⲈ ⲈⲢⲞⲨ ϪⲈ ⲠⲀ
ⲖⲞⲨ ⲀⲨⲰ ⲈⲢⲈ ⲞⲨⲂⲀⲐⲞⲤ ⲘⲘⲀⲨ
ⲈϢⲀⲨⲘⲞⲨⲦⲈ ⲈⲢⲞⲨ ϪⲈ ⲠⲞⲨ
ⲞⲈⲒⲚ Ⲏ ⲠⲈⲦⲢ ⲞⲨⲞⲈⲒⲚ ⲈⲢⲈ ⲞⲨ
10. ⲘⲞⲚⲞⲄⲈⲚⲎⲤ ⲚⲨⲢⲎⲦϤ ⲈⲨⲢⲎⲠ
ⲚⲦⲞⲨ ⲠⲈⲦⲞⲨⲰⲚⲨ ⲈⲂⲞⲖ Ⲛ
ϢⲘⲚⲦ ϬⲞⲘ ⲠⲀⲒ ⲈⲦϬⲘϬⲞⲘ
ⲨⲚ ϬⲞⲘ ⲚⲒⲘ ⲠⲀⲒ ⲠⲈ ⲠⲀⲦⲠⲰϢ
ⲠⲀⲒ ⲠⲈ ⲈⲦⲈ ⲘⲠϤⲠⲰϢ ⲈⲚⲈⲨ
ⲠⲀⲒ ⲠⲈ ⲚⲦⲀ ⲠⲦⲎⲢϤ ⲞⲨⲰⲚ ⲚⲀⲨ
15. ϪⲈ ⲚⲞⲨⲨ ⲚⲈ ⲚϬⲞⲘ ⲞⲨⲚ ϢⲞ
ⲘⲚⲦ ⲚⲨⲞ ⲘⲘⲞⲨ ⲞⲨⲨⲞ
ⲚⲀⲨⲞⲢⲀⲦⲞⲚ ⲀⲨⲰ ⲞⲨⲨⲞ ⲘⲠⲀⲚⲦⲞ
ⲆⲨⲚⲀⲘⲒⲤ ⲀⲨⲰ ⲞⲨⲨⲞ ⲚⲀⲮ
ⲢⲎⲆⲰⲚ ⲈϢⲀⲨⲘⲞⲨⲦⲈ ⲈⲢⲞⲨ
20. ϪⲈ ⲀⲮⲢⲎⲆⲰⲚ ⲠⲎϪⲞⲤ ⲈⲨⲚ ⲞⲨ
ⲘⲞⲚⲞⲄⲈⲚⲎⲤ ⲨⲎⲠ ⲨⲢⲀⲒ ⲚⲨⲎⲦϤ
ⲈⲦⲈ ⲚⲦⲞⲨ ⲠⲈ ⲠⲈⲦⲢⲒⲆⲨⲚⲀⲘⲒⲤ
ⲈⲢϢⲀⲚ ⲠⲘⲈⲈⲨⲈ ⲈⲒ ⲈⲂⲞⲖ ⲨⲚ
ⲠⲂⲀⲐⲞⲤ ϢⲀⲢⲈ ⲀⲮⲢⲎⲆⲰⲚ ϪⲒ
25. ⲚⲦⲈⲠⲒⲚⲞⲒⲀ ⲚⲨⲚⲦⲤ ⲘⲠⲘⲞⲚⲞ
ⲄⲈⲚⲎⲤ ⲚⲦⲈ ⲠⲘⲞⲚⲞⲄⲈⲚⲎⲤ
ⲚⲦⲤ ⲘⲠⲀⲖⲞⲨ ⲚⲤⲈⲚⲦⲤ ⲈⲂⲞⲖ
ⲈⲚⲀⲒⲰⲚ ⲦⲎⲢⲞⲨ ϢⲀ ⲠⲦⲞⲠⲞⲤ
ⲘⲠⲈⲦⲢⲒⲆⲨⲚⲀⲘⲒⲤ ⲚⲤⲈϪⲞⲔⲞⲨ
30. ⲚⲤⲈϪⲒⲦⲞⲨ ⲈⲨⲞⲨⲚ ⲈⲠⲦⲞⲨ Ⲛ
ⲀⲄⲈⲚⲚⲎⲦⲞⲤ ⲞⲨⲚ ⲔⲈⲦⲞⲠⲞⲤ
ⲞⲚ ⲈⲨⲘⲞⲨⲦⲈ ⲈⲢⲞⲨ ϪⲈ ⲂⲀⲐⲞⲤ
ⲞⲨⲚ ϢⲞⲘⲚⲦ ⲘⲘⲚⲦⲈⲒⲰⲦ Ⲛ
ⲨⲎⲦϤ ⲠϢⲞⲢⲠ ⲈⲢⲈ ⲠⲔⲀⲖⲨⲠⲦⲞⲤ

3. ⲞⲨⲀ written above line in original.

XVIII
MS. f. 100v
C.S. p. 8

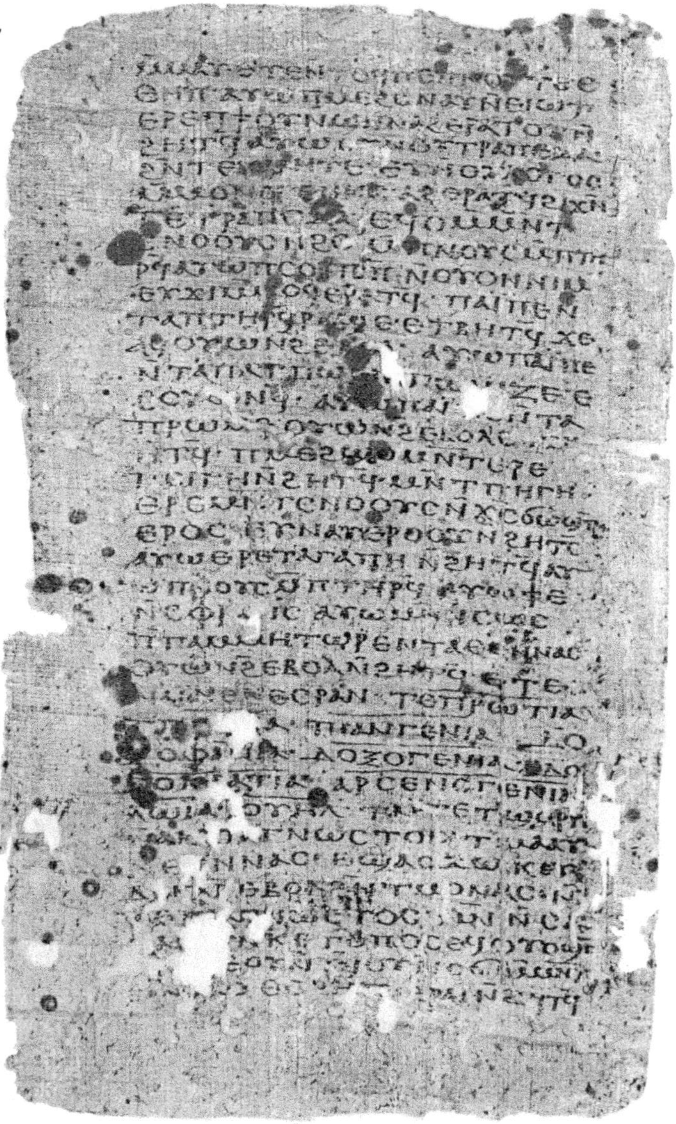

1 ⲙⲙⲁⲩ ⲉⲧⲉ ⲛⲧⲟⲩ ⲡⲉ ⲡⲛⲟⲩⲧⲉ ⲉ
ⲑⲏⲡ ⲁⲩⲱ ⲡⲙⲉϩⲥⲛⲁⲩ ⲛⲉⲓⲱⲧ
ⲉⲣⲉ ⲡⲧⲟⲩ ⲛⲱϣⲏⲛ ⲁϩⲉⲣⲁⲧⲟⲩ ⲛ
ϩⲏⲧϥ ⲁⲩⲱ ⲟⲩⲛ ⲟⲩⲧⲣⲁⲡⲉⲍⲁ
5. ϩⲛ ⲧⲉⲩⲙⲏⲧⲉ ⲉⲩⲛ ⲟⲩⲗⲟⲅⲟⲥ
ⲙⲙⲟⲛⲟⲅⲉⲛⲏⲥ ⲁϩⲉⲣⲁⲧⲩ ϩⲓϫⲛ
ⲧⲉⲧⲣⲁⲡⲉⲍⲁ ⲉϥⲟ ⲙⲙⲛⲧ
ⲥⲛⲟⲟⲩⲥ ⲛϩⲟ ⲙⲡⲛⲟⲩⲥ ⲙⲡⲧⲏ
ⲣϥ ⲁⲩⲱ ⲡⲥⲟⲡⲥⲡ ⲛⲟⲩⲟⲛ ⲛⲓⲙ
10. ⲉⲩϫⲓ ⲙⲙⲟⲩ ⲉⲣⲁⲧⲩ ⲡⲁⲓ ⲡⲉ ⲛ
ⲧⲁ ⲡⲧⲏⲣϥ ⲣⲁϣⲉ ⲉⲧⲃⲏⲧϥ ϫⲉ
ⲁϥⲟⲩⲱⲛϩ ⲉⲃⲟⲗ ⲁⲩⲱ ⲡⲁⲓ ⲡⲉ
ⲛⲧⲁ ⲡⲁⲧⲡⲱⲱϣ ⲁⲅⲱⲛⲓⲍⲉ ⲉ
ⲥⲟⲩⲱⲛϥ ⲁⲩⲱ ⲡⲁⲓ ⲡⲉ ⲛⲧⲁ
15. ⲡⲣⲱⲙⲉ ⲟⲩⲱⲛϩ ⲉⲃⲟⲗ ⲉⲧⲃⲏ
ⲛⲧϥ ⲡⲙⲉϩϣⲟⲙⲛⲧ ⲉⲣⲉ
ⲧⲥⲓⲅⲏ ⲛϩⲏⲧϥ ⲙⲛ ⲧⲡⲏⲅⲏ
ⲉⲣⲉ ⲙⲛⲧⲥⲛⲟⲟⲩⲥ ⲛⲭⲥ ϭⲱϣⲧ
ⲉⲣⲟⲥ ⲉⲩⲛⲁⲩ ⲉⲣⲟⲟⲩ ⲛϩⲏⲧⲥ
20. ⲁⲩⲱ ⲉⲣⲉ ⲧⲁⲅⲁⲡⲏ ⲛϩⲏⲧⲩ ⲁⲩ
ⲱ ⲡⲛⲟⲩⲥ ⲙⲡⲧⲏⲣϥ ⲁⲩⲱ ⲧⲉ
ⲛⲥⲫⲣⲁⲅⲓⲥ ⲁⲩⲱ ⲙⲛⲛⲥⲱⲥ
ⲡⲡⲁⲙⲙⲏⲧⲱⲣ ⲉⲛⲧⲁ ⲑⲉⲛⲛⲁⲥ
ⲟⲩⲱⲛϩ ⲉⲃⲟⲗ ⲛϩⲏⲧⲩ ⲉⲧⲉ
25. ⲛⲁⲓ ⲛⲉ ⲛⲉⲥⲣⲁⲛ ⲧⲉⲡⲣⲱⲧⲓⲁ
ⲧⲡⲁⲛⲇⲓⲁ ⲧⲡⲁⲛⲅⲉⲛⲓⲁ ⲇⲟ
ⲍⲟⲫⲁⲛⲓⲁ ⲇⲟⲍⲟⲅⲉⲛⲓⲁ ⲇⲟ
ⲍⲟⲕⲣⲁⲧⲓⲁ ⲁⲣⲥⲉⲛⲟⲅⲉⲛⲓⲁ
ⲗⲱⲓⲁ ⲓⲟⲩⲏⲗ ⲧⲁⲓ ⲧⲉ ⲧϣⲟⲣⲡ
30. ⲛⲁⲕⲁⲧⲁⲅⲛⲱⲥⲧⲟⲥ ⲧⲙⲁⲁⲩ
ⲛⲑⲉⲛⲛⲁⲥ ⲉϣⲁⲥϫⲱⲕ ⲉⲩ
ⲇⲉⲕⲁⲥ ⲉⲃⲟⲗ ϩⲛ ⲧⲙⲟⲛⲁⲥ ⲛ
ⲧⲉ ⲡⲓⲁⲅⲛⲱⲥⲧⲟⲥ ⲙⲛⲛⲥⲁ
ⲛⲁⲓ ⲟⲩⲛ ⲕⲉⲧⲟⲡⲟⲥ ⲉⲩⲟⲩⲟϣⲥ
35. ⲉⲃⲟⲗ ⲉⲟⲩⲛⲧⲩ ⲟⲩⲛⲟϭ ⲙⲙⲛⲧ
ⲣⲙⲙⲁⲟ ⲉⲥϩⲏⲡ ϩⲣⲁⲓ ⲛϩⲏⲧϥ

ⲉϭⲱϣⲧⲉⲃⲟⲗ... ...ⲏⲉⲧⲉⲧⲛ
ⲧⲉⲡⲣⲁⲃⲟⲩ... ...ⲉⲧⲏⲧⲟⲥⲉⲛ
ⲛⲟⲩⲧⲣⲁⲛ... ...ⲟⲩⲧⲉⲧⲥⲟⲟⲩ
ⲉⲣⲟⲥⲛϭⲏ... ...ⲁⲧⲉⲩⲙⲛⲧⲏⲣⲟⲥ
ⲟⲧⲏⲣⲉⲙⲉⲉⲩⲛⲟⲩⲁⲁⲧⲁⲛ
ⲛⲟⲩⲧⲟⲥⲉⲩⲛⲟⲩⲁⲁⲧⲉⲩⲙⲛⲧⲉ
ⲉⲩⲛⲟⲩⲡⲉⲛⲧⲱⲙⲏⲣⲉⲛⲧⲉⲩ
ⲟⲛⲧⲉⲧⲉⲩⲙⲉⲩⲧⲉⲉⲣⲟⲥⲙⲉⲛⲉ
ⲭⲥⲧⲉⲗⲟϭⲓⲙⲥⲧⲏⲥⲛⲧⲁⲩⲙⲉⲧ
ⲕⲟⲗⲙⲁ ⲍⲉⲛ ⲧⲟⲩⲥⲙ̅ⲟⲩ ⲁⲩ
ⲉϭⲉⲫⲣⲁⲅⲓⲍⲉⲙⲙⲟⲟⲫⲉⲛ ⲧⲉⲥ
ⲫⲣⲁⲅⲓⲥⲙⲁⲡⲟⲩⲧⲉ ⲉϭⲱⲧⲁⲙⲙⲟⲟⲩ
ⲉⲃⲟⲗ ⲛⲙⲡⲩⲟⲣⲡⲛⲁⲩⲛⲧ ⲉⲧⲣⲁ
ⲧⲧⲁⲣⲓⲁⲃⲟⲩⲧ ⲧⲁⲥⲧⲉⲃⲏ ⲛⲧⲁ
ⲉ̅ⲏ̅ⲟ̅ⲩ̅ⲉ̅ ⲧⲏⲣⲩ ϣⲱ ⲡ ⲉ ⲁ ⲟⲩ
ⲭⲛⲧⲟⲩ̅ⲧ̅ⲉⲁⲙⲧⲱⲙⲉ ⲭ̅ⲥ̅
ⲧⲣⲁⲭⲥⲩϭⲟⲣⲓϭⲙ ⲧⲉⲛⲟⲟⲧⲉ
ⲛ̅ⲥⲟ ⲟⲧ̅ ⲉⲛⲁ̅ⲡⲉⲣⲁⲛⲧⲟⲥ ⲙ̅
ⲟⲩⲉⲟⲛⲁⲩ̅ⲱ̅ⲏ̅ⲛ̅ⲧ̅ⲉⲩϣⲁⲛ
ⲛⲁⲣⲁⲉⲓ̅ⲟ̅ⲟ̅ ⲛⲙ̅ⲛⲟⲩⲧⲟⲛⲉ
ⲩ̅ⲙⲡⲟⲩⲟⲉⲓ̅ⲙ̅ⲫⲉⲓ̅ⲁ̅ⲛⲏ̅ⲥⲟⲩ̅ⲟ
ⲥⲟⲕⲏⲣⲉⲩⲙⲟⲥ ⲙ̅ⲡ̅ⲟ̅ⲩ̅ⲇ̅ⲙ̅
ⲕⲁⲧⲁⲃⲟⲥ ⲧ̅ⲥⲙⲙⲁⲧⲉ
ⲥⲟ̅ ⲧ̅ⲟⲥ ⲙ̅ⲡ̅ⲟ̅ⲩ̅ⲉ̅ⲟ̅ⲛ̅ ⲉⲥ
ⲛ̅ⲁϭⲓⲥⲙ̅ⲡⲟⲩϭⲟ̅ⲣ̅ⲓ̅ϭ̅ⲙⲉⲧ
ⲧⲟⲥ ⲙ̅ⲡ̅ⲟⲩϩⲟ̅ϭ̅ⲥ̅ⲁ̅ⲧ̅ⲣ̅ⲁ̅ⲩ
ⲧ̅ⲧ̅ⲁ̅ⲕⲟ̅ⲧⲩ̅ⲧ̅ⲉⲧⲁⲙ̅ ⲁ̅ⲧ̅ⲉ
ⲙ̅ⲡⲛⲁⲩϣⲁⲧⲉⲧⲥⲟⲟⲩⲧⲉ
ⲉⲩⲟⲟⲧ̅ ⲭⲥⲟⲩ̅ⲧⲏⲛⲓ̅ⲟ̅ⲙ̅
ⲉⲧⲩⲉⲥⲛⲱ̅ⲓ̅ⲛ̅ⲛ̅ⲧ̅ⲛⲉⲍ
ⲉ̅ⲧ̅ⲩϭⲧ̅ⲉⲉⲣⲟ̅ⲩⲧⲁⲛ̅ⲛ̅ⲁⲟ̅
ⲛⲉⲟⲁⲛ̅ⲩⲟⲙ̅ⲁ̅ⲕ̅ⲙ̅ⲡ̅ⲉ̅ⲟ̅ⲥ̅

1. ЄСХШРΗΓΙ ⲘⲠⲦⲎⲢϤ ЄⲦЄ ⲠⲀⲒ
ⲠЄ ⲠβⲀⲐⲞⲤ ⲚⲀⲘЄⲦⲢⲎⲦⲞⲤ ЄⲨ
Ⲛ ⲞⲨⲦⲢⲀⲠЄ ⲌⲀ ⲘⲘⲀⲨ ЄⲨⲤⲞⲞⲨⳞ
ЄⲢⲞⳞ ⲚϬⲒ ϢⲞⲘⲚⲦ ⲘⲘⲚⲦⲚⲞϬ
5. ⲞⲨⲎⲢЄⲘⲒⲞⳞ ⲘⲚ ⲞⲨⲀⲔⲀⲦⲀⲄ
ⲚⲰⳞⲦⲞⳞ ⲘⲚ ⲞⲨⲀⲠЄⲢⲀⲚⲦⲞⳞ
ЄⲨⲚ ⲞⲨⲘⲚⲦϢⲎⲎⲢЄ ⳞⲚ ⲦЄⲨ
ⲘⲎⲦЄ ЄⲨⲘⲞⲨⲦЄ ЄⲢⲞⳞ Ϫ Є ⲠЄ
Ⲭ Ⳟ ⲠⲆⲞϬⲒⲘⲀⳞⲦⲎⳞ ⲚⲦⲞⲨ ⲠЄⲦ
10. ⲆⲞϬⲒⲘⲀ ⳡЄ ⲘⲠⲞⲨⲀ ⲠⲞⲨⲀ ⲀⲨⲰ
ЄϤⳞⲪⲢⲀⲄⲒ ⳡЄ ⲘⲘⲞⲨ ⳞⲚ ⲦЄⳞ
ⲮⲢⲀⲄⲒ ⳡ ⲘⲠⲒⲰⲦ ЄⲨ Ϫ ⲞⲞⲨ ⲘⲘⲞⲞⲨ
Є ⳞⲞⲨⲚ ⲘⲠϢⲞⲢⲠ ⲚЄⲒⲰⲦ ЄⲦϢⲞ
ⲞⲠ ⳞⲀⲢⲒ ⳞⲀⲢⲞⲨ ⲠⲀⲒ ЄⲦβⲎⲎⲦϤ
15. ЄⲚⲦⲀ ⲠⲦⲎⲢϤ ϢⲰⲠЄ ⲀⲨⲰ Ⲁ
Ϫ ⲚⲦϤ ⲘⲠЄⲖⲀⲀⲨ ϢⲰⲠЄ ⲀⲨⲰ
ⲠЄⲒ Ⳟ ϤⲮⲞⲢⲒ ⲘⲘⲚⲦⳞⲚⲞⲞⲨⳞ
Ⲛ ⳞⲞ ⲞⲨ ⳞⲞ ⲚⲀⲠЄⲢⲀⲚⲦⲞⳞ ⲘⲚ
ⲞⲨ ⳞⲞ ⲚⲀ Ⲭ ⲰⲢⲎⲦⲞⳞ ⲘⲚ ⲞⲨ ⳞⲞ
20. ⲚⲀ ⳞⲢⲎⲦⲞⳞ ⲘⲚ ⲞⲨ ⳞⲞ Ⲛ ⳞⲀⲠⲖⲞⲨⲚ
ⲘⲚ ⲞⲨ ⳞⲞ ⲚⲀⲮⲐⲀⲢⲦⲞⲚ ⲘⲚ ⲞⲨ
ⳞⲞ ⲚⲎⲢЄⲘⲒⲞⳞ ⲘⲚ ⲞⲨ ⳞⲞ ⲚⲀ
ⲔⲀⲦⲀⲄⲚⲰⳞⲦⲞⳞ ⲘⲚ ⲞⲨ
ⳞⲞ ⲚⲀ ⳞⲞⲢⲀⲦⲞⳞ ⲘⲚ ⲞⲨ ⳞⲞ ⲚⲦⲢⲒⲀⲨ
25. ⲚⲀⲘⲒⳞ ⲘⲚ ⲞⲨ ⳞⲞ ⲚⲀⳞⲀⲖЄⲨ
ⲦⲞⳞ ⲘⲚ ⲞⲨ ⳞⲞ ⲚⲀⲄЄⲚⲚⲎ
ⲦⲞⳞ ⲘⲚ ⲞⲨ ⳞⲞ Ⲛ ⳞⲒⲖⲒⲔⲢⲒⲚЄⳞ
ⲠⲘⲀ ЄⲦⲘⲘⲀⲨ ⲞⲨⲚ ⲘⲚⲦⲒβ
ⲘⲠⲎⲄⲎ ⲘⲘⲀⲨ ЄⲨⲘⲞⲨⲦЄ
30. ЄⲢⲞⲞⲨ Ϫ Є ⲘⲠⲎⲄⲎ ⲚⲖⲞⲄⲒⲔⲞⲚ
ЄⲨⲘЄ Ⳟ ⲚⲰⲚ Ⳟ ϢⲀ ⲚⲒЄⲚЄ Ⳟ
ЄⲨⲘⲞⲨⲦЄ ЄⲢⲞⲞⲨ ⲞⲚ Ϫ Є ⲚβⲀ
ⲐⲞⳞ ⲀⲨⲰ ⲞⲚ ϢⲀⲨⲘⲞⲨⲦЄ ЄⲢⲞⲞⲨ

1. ϪⲈ ⲠⲘⲚⲦⲤⲚⲞⲞⲨⲤ ⲚⲬⲰⲢⲎⲘⲀ
ϪⲈ ⲤⲈϢⲰⲠ ⲈⲢⲞⲞⲨ ⲚⲦⲞⲠⲞⲤ
ⲚⲒⲘ ⲘⲘⲚⲦⲈⲒⲰⲦ ⲀⲨⲰ ⲠⲔⲀⲢ
ⲠⲞⲤ ⲘⲠⲦⲎⲢϤ ⲠⲀⲒ ⲈⲦⲞⲨⲢϨⲰⲂ

5. ⲈⲢⲞϤ ⲠⲀⲒ ⲠⲈ ⲠⲈⲬⲤ ⲈⲦϢⲰⲠ
ⲘⲠⲦⲎⲢϤ ⲈⲢⲞϤ ⲘⲚⲚⲤⲀ ⲚⲀⲒ
ⲦⲎⲢⲞⲨ ⲠⲂⲀⲐⲞⲤ ⲚⲤⲎⲐⲈⲨⲤ
ⲠⲈ ⲠⲀⲒ ⲈⲦϨⲒϨⲞⲨⲚ ⲘⲘⲞⲞⲨ
ⲦⲎⲢⲞⲨ ⲠⲈⲦⲈⲢⲈ ⲘⲚⲦⲤⲚⲞⲞⲨⲤ

10. ⲘⲘⲚⲦⲈⲒⲰⲦ ⲔⲰⲦⲈ ⲈⲢⲞϤ Ⲛ
ⲦⲞϤ ⲆⲈ ⲠⲈⲦϨⲚ ⲦⲈⲨⲘⲎⲦⲈ
ⲈⲢⲈ ⲠⲞⲨⲀ ⲠⲞⲨⲀ Ⲟ ⲚϢⲞⲘⲚⲦ
ⲚϨⲞ ⲠϢⲞⲢⲠ ⲚϨⲎⲦⲞⲨ ⲠⲈ
ⲠⲀⲦⲠⲰϢ ⲞⲨⲚ ϢⲞⲘⲚⲦ Ⲛ

15. ϨⲞ ⲘⲘⲞϤ ⲞⲨϨⲞ ⲚⲀⲠⲈⲢⲀⲚ
ⲦⲞⲤ ⲘⲚ ⲞⲨϨⲞ ⲚⲀϨⲞⲢⲀⲦⲞⲤ
ⲘⲚ ⲞⲨϨⲞ ⲚⲀϨⲢⲎⲦⲞⲤ ⲀⲨⲰ
ⲠⲘⲈϨⲤⲚⲀⲨ ⲚⲈⲒⲰⲦ ⲞⲨϨⲞ Ⲛ
ⲀⲬⲰⲢⲎⲦⲞⲤ ⲠⲈ ⲘⲚ ⲞⲨϨⲞ

20. ⲚⲀⲤⲀⲖⲈⲨⲦⲞⲤ ⲘⲚ ⲞⲨϨⲞ Ⲛ
ⲀⲘⲒⲀⲚⲦⲞⲤ ⲠⲘⲈϨϢⲞⲘⲚⲦ
ⲚⲈⲒⲰⲦ ⲞⲨⲚ ⲞⲨϨⲞ ⲘⲘⲞϤ
ⲚⲀⲔⲀⲦⲀⲄⲚⲰⲤⲦⲞⲤ ⲘⲚ ⲞⲨ
ϨⲞ ⲚⲀⲮⲐⲀⲢⲦⲞⲤ ⲘⲚ ⲞⲨϨⲞ

25. ⲚⲀⲮⲢⲎⲆⲰⲚ ⲠⲘⲈϤϤⲦⲞⲞⲨ
ⲚⲈⲒⲰⲦ ⲞⲨⲚ ⲞⲨϨⲞ ⲘⲘⲞϤ Ⲛ
ⲤⲒⲄⲎ ⲘⲚ ⲞⲨϨⲞ ⲘⲠⲎⲄⲎ ⲘⲚ
ⲞⲨϨⲞ ⲚⲀⲦϬⲒⲂϢⲰⲘϤ ⲠⲘⲈϨ
ϮⲞⲨ ⲚⲈⲒⲰⲦ ⲞⲨⲚ ⲞⲨϨⲞ Ⲙ

30. ⲘⲞⲨ ⲚⲎⲢⲈⲘⲒⲞⲤ ⲘⲚ ⲞⲨϨⲞ
ⲘⲠⲀⲚⲦⲞⲆⲨⲚⲀⲘⲒⲤ ⲘⲚ ⲞⲨ
ϨⲞ ⲚⲀⲄⲈⲚⲚⲎⲦⲞⲤ ⲠⲘⲈϨⲤⲞⲞⲨ
ⲚⲈⲒⲰⲦ ⲞⲨⲚ ⲞⲨϨⲞ ⲘⲘⲞϤ
ⲘⲠⲀⲚⲦⲞⲠⲀⲦⲰⲢ ⲘⲚ ⲞⲨϨⲞ

XXI
MS. f. 104[F]
C. S. p. 11

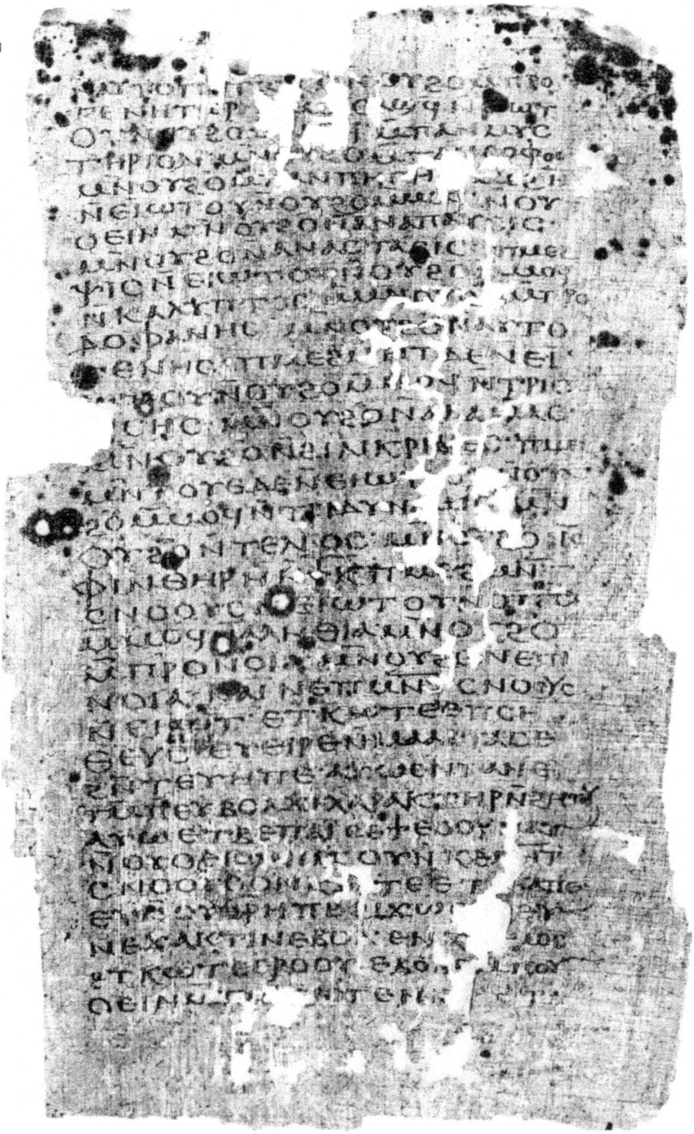

1. ⲚⲀⲨⲦⲞⲠⲀⲦⲰⲢ ⲘⲚ ⲞⲨⲌⲞ ⲘⲠⲢⲞ
ⲄⲈⲚⲎⲦⲰⲢ ⲠⲘⲈⲌⲤⲀϢϤ ⲚⲈⲒⲰⲦ
ⲞⲨⲚ ⲞⲨⲌⲞ ⲘⲘⲞⲨ ⲘⲠⲀⲚⲘⲨⲤ
ⲦⲎⲢⲒⲞⲚ ⲘⲚ ⲞⲨⲌⲞ ⲘⲠⲀⲚⲤⲞⳘⲞⲤ
5. ⲘⲚ ⲞⲨⲌⲞ ⲘⲠⲀⲚⲠⲎⲄⲎ ⲠⲘⲈⲌⲎ
ⲚⲈⲒⲰⲦ ⲞⲨⲚ ⲞⲨⲌⲞ ⲘⲘⲞⲨ ⲚⲞⲨ
ⲞⲈⲒⲚ ⲘⲚ ⲞⲨⲌⲞ ⲚⲀⲚⲀⲠⲀⲨⲤⲒⲤ
ⲘⲚ ⲞⲨⲌⲞ ⲚⲀⲚⲀⲤⲦⲀⲤⲒⲤ ⲠⲘⲈⲌ
ⲮⲒⲤ ⲚⲈⲒⲰⲦ ⲞⲨⲚ ⲞⲨⲌⲞ ⲘⲘⲞⲨ
10. ⲚⲔⲀⲖⲨⲠⲦⲞⲤ ⲘⲘⲚ ⲞⲨⲌⲞ ⲘⲠⲢⲞ
ⲆⲞⳘⲀⲚⲎⲤ ⲘⲚ ⲞⲨⲌⲞ ⲚⲀⲨⲦⲞ
ⲄⲈⲚⲎⲤ ⲠⲘⲈⲌⲘⲎⲦ ⲆⲈ ⲚⲈⲒ
ⲰⲦ ⲞⲨⲚ ⲞⲨⲌⲞ ⲘⲘⲞⲨ ⲚⲦⲢⲒⲤ
ⲀⲢⲤⲎⲤ ⲘⲚ ⲞⲨⲌⲞ ⲚⲀⲆⲀⲘⲀⲤ
15. ⲘⲚ ⲞⲨⲌⲞ ⲚⲌⲒⲖⲒⲔⲢⲒⲚⲈⲤ ⲠⲘⲈⲌ
ⲘⲚⲦⲞⲨⲈ ⲆⲈ ⲚⲈⲒⲰⲦ ⲞⲨⲚ ⲞⲨ
ⲌⲞ ⲘⲘⲞⲨ ⲚⲦⲢⲒⲆⲨⲚⲀⲘⲒⲤ ⲘⲚ
ⲞⲨⲌⲞ ⲚⲦⲈⲖⲒⲞⲤ ⲘⲚ ⲞⲨⲌⲞ ⲚⲤ
ⳘⲒⲚⲐⲎⲢ Ⲏ ⲚⲦⲔ ⲠⲘⲈⲌⲘⲚⲦ
20. ⲤⲚⲞⲞⲨⲤ ⲚⲈⲒⲰⲦ ⲞⲨⲚ ⲞⲨⲌⲞ
ⲘⲘⲞⲨ ⲚⲀⲖⲎⲐⲒⲀ ⲘⲚ ⲞⲨⲌⲞ
ⲘⲠⲢⲞⲚⲞⲒⲀ ⲘⲚ ⲞⲨⲌⲞ ⲚⲈⲠⲒ
ⲚⲞⲒⲀ ⲚⲀⲒ ⲚⲈ ⲠⲘⲚⲦⲤⲚⲞⲞⲨⲤ
ⲚⲈⲒⲰⲦ ⲈⲦⲔⲰⲦⲈ ⲈⲠⲤⲎ
25. ⲐⲈⲨⲤ ⲈⲨⲈⲒⲢⲈ ⲚⲘⲀⲀⲂⲦⲀⲤⲈ
ⲌⲚ ⲦⲈⲨⲎⲠⲈ ⲀⲨⲰ ⲈⲚⲦⲀ ⲚⲈ
ⲦⲘⲠⲈⲨⲂⲞⲖ ϪⲒ ⲬⲀⲢⲀⲔⲦⲎⲢ ⲚⲌⲎⲦⲞⲨ
ⲀⲨⲰ ⲈⲦⲂⲈ ⲠⲀⲒ ⲤⲈⲦⲈⲞⲞⲨ ⲚⲀⲨ
ⲚⲞⲨⲞⲈⲒϢ ⲚⲒⲘ ⲞⲨⲚ ⲔⲈⲘⲚⲦ
30. ⲤⲚⲞⲞⲨⲤ ⲞⲚ ⲔⲰⲦⲈ ⲈⲦⲈⲨⲀⲠⲈ
ⲈⲨⲚ ⲞⲨϬⲢⲎⲠⲈ ⲌⲒϪⲰⲞⲨ ⲈⲨ
ⲚⲈϪ ⲀⲔⲦⲒⲚ ⲈⲂⲞⲖ ⲈⲚⲔⲞⲤⲘⲞⲤ
ⲈⲦⲔⲰⲦⲈ ⲈⲢⲞⲞⲨ ⲈⲂⲞⲖ ⲌⲘ ⲠⲞⲨ
ⲞⲈⲒⲚ ⲘⲠⲘⲞⲚⲞⲄⲈⲚⲎⲤ ⲈⲦ

1. ϩⲏⲡ ⲛϩⲏⲧⲩ ⲡⲁⲓ ⲉⲧⲟⲩⲕⲱⲧⲉ
ⲛⲥⲱⲩ   ⲡϣⲁϫⲉ ⲙⲉⲛ ⲉⲧⲣⲉⲛ
ⲭⲱⲣⲓ ⲙⲙⲟⲩ ⲉⲃⲟⲗ ϩⲓⲧⲛ ⲛⲉⲧⲟⲩ
ⲟⲧⲃ ⲉϣⲁϫⲉ ⲉⲣⲟⲟⲩ ⲉⲧⲃⲏⲏⲧⲛ
5. ⲏⲇⲏ ⲙⲛ ϣⲃⲟⲙ ⲙⲙⲟⲟⲩ ⲛⲕⲉϩⲉ
ⲉⲛⲟⲓ ⲙⲙⲟⲟⲩ ⲉⲧⲉ ⲁⲛⲟⲛ ⲡⲉ
ⲉϣⲁϫⲉ ⲙⲉⲛ ⲉⲣⲟⲩ ⲉⲃⲟⲗ ϩⲓⲧⲛ
ⲟⲩⲗⲁⲥ ⲛⲥⲁⲣⳅ ⲛⲑⲉ ⲉⲧⲩϣⲟⲟⲡ
ⲙⲙⲟⲥ ⲟⲩⲁⲧϭⲟⲙ ⲡⲉ ⲡⲁⲓ ϩⲉⲛ
10. ⲛⲟϭ ⲅⲁⲣ ⲛⲉ ⲉⲩⲟⲩⲟⲧⲃ ⲉⲛⲇⲩⲛⲁ
ⲙⲓⲥ ⲉⲧⲣⲉⲩⲥⲟⲧⲙⲟⲩ ⲉⲃⲟⲗ
ϩⲓⲧⲛ ⲟⲩⲉⲛⲛⲟⲓⲁ ⲁⲩⲱ ⲉⲩⲁϩⲟⲩ
ⲛⲥⲱⲩ ⲉⲓⲙⲏⲧⲓ ⲛⲥⲉϩⲉ ⲉⲩ
ⲥⲩⲅⲅⲉⲛⲏⲥ ⲛⲧⲉ ⲛⲉⲧⲙⲙⲁⲩ
15. ϩⲣⲁⲓ ϩⲛ ⲟⲩⲁ ⲉⲩⲛ ϣⲃⲟⲙ ⲙⲙⲟⲩ
ⲉⲥⲱⲧⲙ ⲉⲧⲃⲉ ⲙⲙⲁ ⲉⲛⲧⲁⲩⲉⲓ
ⲉⲃⲟⲗ ⲛϩⲏⲧⲟⲩ Ⲫⲱⲃ ⲅⲁⲣ Ⲫⲱⲃ
ⲉϣⲁⲣⲉⲩⲟⲩⲱϩ ⲛⲥⲁ ⲧⲉⲩⲛⲟⲩ
ⲛⲉ ϩⲟⲧⲓ ⲙⲉⲛ ϫⲉ ⲟⲩⲥⲩⲅⲅⲉ
20. ⲛⲏⲥ ⲛⲧⲉ ⲙⲙⲩⲥⲧⲏⲣⲓⲟⲛ ⲡⲉ
ⲡⲣⲱⲙⲉ ⲉⲧⲃⲉ ⲡⲁⲓ ⲁⲩⲥⲱⲧⲙ
ⲉⲡⲙⲩⲥⲧⲏⲣⲓⲟⲛ ⲁⲩⲟⲩⲱϣⲧ
ⲛϭⲓ ⲛ̇ⲛⲟϭ ⲛⲇⲩⲛⲁⲙⲓⲥ ⲛⲛⲛⲟϭ
ⲛⲛⲁⲓⲱⲛ ⲧⲏⲣⲟⲩ ⲛⲧⲇⲩⲛⲁ
25. ⲙⲓⲥ ⲉⲧⲛ ⲙⲁⲣⲥⲁⲛⲏⲥ ⲡⲉϫⲁⲩ
ϫⲉ ⲛⲓⲙ ⲡⲉ ⲡⲁⲓ ⲉⲛⲧⲁⲩⲛⲁⲩ ⲉ
ⲛⲁⲓ ⲙⲡⲉⲙⲧⲟ ⲉⲃⲟⲗ ⲙⲡⲉⲩϩⲟ
ϫⲉ ⲉⲧⲃⲏⲏⲧⲩ ⲁⲩⲟⲩⲱⲛϩ ⲉⲃⲟⲗ
ⲛⲧⲉⲓϩⲉ ⲁⲛⲓⲕⲟⲑⲉⲟⲥ ϣⲁϫⲉ
30. ⲉⲧⲃⲏⲏⲧⲩ ⲁⲩⲛⲁⲩ ⲉⲣⲟⲩ ϫⲉ ⲛ
ⲧⲟⲩ ⲡⲉ ⲡⲉⲧⲙⲙⲁⲩ ⲡⲉϫⲁⲩ
ϫⲉ ⲩϣⲟⲟⲡ ⲛϭⲓ ⲡⲓⲱⲧ ⲉⲩⲟⲩ
ⲟⲧⲃ ⲉⲧⲉⲗⲓⲟⲥ ⲛⲓⲙ ⲁⲩⲟⲩ
ⲱⲛϩ ⲉⲃⲟⲗ ⲙⲡⲁϩⲟⲣⲁⲧⲟⲥ ⲛ

23. ···· deleted word.

ⲧⲣⲉⲩⲕⲁ... ⲉ̣ⲧⲡⲉⲛ̄ⲟⲑⲁⲣ...
ⲧⲙ̄ⲁⲛⲛ̣ⲧⲣ... ⲛ̄ⲧⲉⲛⲓⲟⲥⲛ̄...
ⲉⲣⲟⲩⲁⲧⲱⲡⲁ ⲣⲟⲩ ⲉⲧⲟⲩ...
ⲛⲁⲓ ⲕⲁⲧⲁⲣⲟⲟⲧ ⲡⲛ̄...
ⲛⲟⲅⲉⲛⲏⲥ ⲉⲧⲁⲡⲡⲁⲓ ⲉⲧ̣ⲥⲏ̣ⲃⲉ̣...
ⲧⲁⲓⲡⲉⲛⲧⲁⲩⲙ... ⲅⲉ ⲉⲣ̄ⲡⲩ̣ⲝⲉ̣
ⲡⲕ̄ⲁⲕⲉ ⲛⲟⲩⲟⲉⲓⲛ ⲉⲧⲉⲡⲓⲧⲉ̣
ⲍⲟⲩⲟ ⲡⲉⲟⲩⲟⲉⲓⲛ ⲙⲁⲣⲉⲕⲁⲓⲉ
ⲓⲛ̄ⲧⲟⲟⲧ ⲉⲣⲟ̣ⲩ̣... ⲧⲉ̣
ⲡⲉⲉⲧⲉⲣⲉⲧⲥⲱⲏⲥ ⲥⲱⲛ̄ⲡⲣⲁ̣
ⲉⲓⲁⲁⲓ ⲉⲓⲧⲟⲟⲧ ⲧ̄ ⲛ̄ⲛ̄ⲧⲉⲧⲣ̣
ⲱ̣ⲛ̄ⲟⲅⲉⲛⲏⲥ ⲥⲛ̄ⲁ ⲓⲉⲛⲧⲉ̣
ⲧⲛ̄ⲛ̄ⲧⲉⲓⲱⲧ ⲉⲛ̄ⲧ̣ ... ⲁ̣ⲝⲏ
ⲁⲩⲗⲁ̣ⲩⲡⲁ̣ⲧⲩⲧⲡ̣ ... ⲡⲧⲛ̄ⲧ
ⲥ̣ⲓⲟⲟⲧⲉⲛⲁⲡⲟⲥⲧ ...
ⲛ̄ⲧⲉ̣ϥ̣ϩⲣⲟⲩⲣ̣ ⲉⲟ̣ⲩ ⲛ̄... ⲉ̣
ⲉ̣ⲩ̣ⲛ̣ⲁⲙⲓⲥ ⲛⲉⲏ̣ⲧⲟ̣ⲛ̄ⲥⲉ... ⲧ̣ⲏ̣
ⲧⲟ̣ⲛ̄... ⲣⲉⲩ̣ⲙⲛ̄ⲧ... ⲥ̣ⲉ ⲟ̣...
ⲏ̣ⲥⲟⲛⲁⲩ̣ⲛ̄ⲧ̣ⲛ̄ⲧ̣ⲟ̣ⲛ̣... ⲏ̣...
ⲛ̄ⲧⲟⲉⲓ̣ⲥⲥⲏ̣ⲃⲉⲩ̣ⲙ̣ⲡⲟⲩ
ⲛ̄ϩⲟⲉϥ̣ϭⲱ̣ϣⲧⲉⲧⲙ̣ⲗⲗⲟ̣... ⲃ̣ⲣⲟ
ϩⲓⲧⲟⲁⲛⲉⲟⲩ̣ ⲧ̣ⲕ̣ϩⲟ... ⲁ̣ⲉ̣ⲛ̣ⲉ̣ⲟ̣ⲡ̣
ⲉ̣ⲧ̣ⲉⲃⲟⲗⲉ̣ⲝⲁⲡⲉ̣... ⲧ̣ⲣⲁⲩⲛⲁⲙⲓ̣ⲥ
ⲁ̣ⲩ̣ⲱ̣ⲡ̣ⲟⲧⲁ̣ⲩⲟⲩ̣ⲛ̣ⲛ̄ⲙⲛ̄ⲧ̣ ... ⲟ̣ⲟ̣...
ϩ̣ⲛ̄ⲧⲉ̣ϥϭⲓⲝⲛ̄ⲟ̣ⲩⲛ̣... ⲉ̣ⲩ̣ⲉ̣ⲣⲉⲛ
ⲱ̣ⲉⲉⲧⲏ̣ⲛ̣ⲩ̣ⲛ̣ⲁⲙⲓⲥ ⲓⲟⲟ̣ⲛⲉⲛ ⲱ̣
ϫ̣ⲉⲉⲛⲧⲁ̣ ... ⲉ̣ⲓ̣ⲙⲁ̣ⲝⲟⲟⲩⲟ̣ⲭⲟⲣ̣ⲓ̣ⲥ̣
ϫ̣ⲉⲩⲛⲁⲙⲓⲟⲧⲉⲡⲉⲕⲁⲟⲙⲛ̄ ⲉ̣ⲣⲟⲭ̣
ⲡ̣ⲉ̣ⲉⲛⲧⲣⲉⲕⲛ̄ⲙⲡⲭ̄ⲥ ⲛⲉⲏ̣ ... ⲛⲁ
ⲱ̣ⲥϭⲉⲧⲏⲣⲟⲛⲥⲁⲕⲛ̄ⲧ̣... ⲁ̣ⲧⲁⲃⲉ
... ⲣⲉⲛⲏ̣ⲥⲟⲛ ϩⲉⲛⲟⲩ̣... ⲉ̣ⲭ̣ⲗⲩ
ⲧⲟⲩⲟⲉⲓ̣ⲛⲛ̄ⲛ̄ⲏ̣ⲛ̄ϩⲟ̣... ⲟ̣ⲟ̣ⲧ̣ⲣ̣
ⲭ̣ⲙ̣ⲱⲡⲓ̣ⲱⲧⲉ̣ⲛⲏⲥ ⲭ̣ⲱ̣ⲣⲓⲥⲏⲣ̣

1. ΤΡΙΔΥΝΑΜΙC ΝΤΕΛΙΟC ΑΠΟΥΑ
   ΠΟΥΑ ΝΝΡⲰΜΕ ΝΤΕΛΙΟC ΝΑΥ
   ΕΡΟΥ ΑΥⲰΑϪΕ ΕΡΟΥ ΕΥ†ΕΟΟΥ
   ΝΑΥ ΚΑΤΑ ΡΟΟΥ ΠΑΙ ΠΕ ΠΜΟ
5. ΝΟΓΕΝΗC ΕΤϨΗΠ ϨΜ ΠCΗΘΕΥC
   ΠΑΙ ΠΕ ΝΤΑΥΜΟΥΤΕ ΕΡΟΥ Ϫε
   ΠΚΑΚΕ ΝΟΥΟΕΙΝ ΕΤΒΕ ΠΕ
   ϨΟΥΟ ⲙΠΕϤΟΥΟΕΙΝ ΑΥΡΚΑΚΕ
   ΝΤΟΟΥ ΕΡΟΟΥ ⲙΑΥΑΑΥ ΠΑΙ
10. ΠΕ ΕΤΕΡΕ ΠCΗΘΕΥC Ο ΝΡΡΟ
    ΕΒΟⲗ ϨΙΤΟΟΤΥ ΠΑΙ ΠΕ Π
    ⲙΟΝΟΓΕΝΗC ΟΥΝ ⲙΝΤΙΒ
    ⲙⲙΝΤΕΙⲰΤ ϨΝ ΤΕϤϬΙϪ Ν
    ΟΥΝΑⲙ ⲙΠΤΥΠΟC ⲙΠⲠΝⲦ
15. CΝΟΟΥC ΝΑΠΟCΤΟⲗΟC ΑΥⲰ
    ϨΝ ΤΕϤϨΒΟΥΡ ΕΟΥΝ ⲙΑΑΒΕ
    ΝΔΥΝΑⲙΙC ΝϨΗΤC ΕΡΕ ΤΟΥΙ
    ΤΟΥΙ ΕΙΡΕ ⲙⲙΝΤCΝΟΟΥC ΕΥ
    Ν ϨΟ CΝΑΥ ΝΤΟΥΙ ΤΟΥΙ ⲙΠ
20. ΤΥΠΟC ⲙΠCΗΘΕΥC ΠΟΥΑ
    ΝϨΟ ΕΥϬⲰϢΤ ΕΠΒΑΘΟC ΕΤ
    ϨΙΠCΑΝϨΟΥΝ ΠΚΕΟΥΑ ΔΕ ϬⲰ
    ϢΤ ΕΒΟⲗ ΕϪⲙ ΠΕΤΡΙΔΥΝΑⲙΙC
    ΑΥⲰ ΠΟΥΑ ΠΟΥΑ ΝΝⲙΝΤΕΙⲰΤ
25. ϨΝ ΤΕϤϬΙϪ ΝΟΥΝΑⲙ CΕΕΙΡΕ ΝϢⲙⲦ
    ϢΕ CΕΤΗ ΝΔΥΝΑⲙΙC ΚΑΤΑ ΠϢΑ
    Ϫε ΕΝΤΑ ΔΑΥΕΙΔ Ϫ ΟΟΥ ΕΥϪⲰ ⲙⲙΟC
    Ϫε †ΝΑCⲙΟΥ ΕΠΕΚⲗΟⲙ ΝΤΕΡΟⲙ
    ΠΕ ϨΝ ΤΕΚⲙΝΤΧC ΝΕΙΔΥΝΑ
30. ⲙΙC ϬΕ ΤΗΡΟΥ CΕΚⲰΤΕ ΕΠΜΟ
    ΝΟΓΕΝΗC ΝΘΕ ΝΟΥΚⲗΟⲙ ΕΥ
    †ΟΥΟΕΙΝ ΝΝΑΙⲰΝ Ϩⲙ ΠΟΥΟΕΙΝ
    ⲙΠⲙΟΝΟΓΕΝΗC ΝΘΕ ΕΤCΗϨ

ⲭⲉⲥ̅ ⲡⲉⲕⲟⲩⲟⲉⲓⲛ ⲧ̅ⲛ̅ ⲛⲁⲛⲁⲩ ⲉⲣ
ⲟⲧⲉⲓⲛ ⲁ̄ⲩⲱⲉ ⲧⲡⲟⲛⲟⲩ ⲡⲉ ⲛ̅ⲏⲥ
ⲁ̄ⲗ̅ⲡ̅ⲉϩⲣⲁⲓⲉ ⲙⲙⲟⲛ ⲛ̅ⲑⲉ ⲟⲛ
ⲧⲟⲟⲩⲧⲉ ⲉⲣⲁⲙⲓⲙⲙ ⲡⲛⲟⲩⲧⲉ
ⲟⲩⲧⲉ ⲛ̅ⲕⲱ ⲡⲡⲉ ⲁ̄ⲩⲱⲟⲛ ⲭⲉ
ⲥⲉⲛⲛⲟⲟⲉⲧ ⲣ̅ⲟⲟⲩⲧⲛⲉ ⲉⲣⲉ ⲡⲭⲟⲓⲥ
ⲛⲥ̅ⲧⲟ ⲟⲩ ⲡⲁⲓ ⲡⲉⲓ ⲡⲉⲧ ⲟⲩ ⲏ̅ⲥ
ϩⲛ̅ⲧⲭⲓⲟⲩⲁⲥ ⲉⲧⲁ ⲙ̅ⲡⲥ̅ϩⲁⲉⲓⲥ ⲧⲁ
ⲉⲓ ⲛ̅ ⲥ̅ⲉⲓ ⲉⲇⲟⲝⲁ ⲙ̅ⲡⲓⲙ̅ⲉⲛⲧⲉ
ⲗⲉⲙⲁ ⲁⲡⲟⲥⲁⲛ ⲭⲉ ⲧⲱ ⲛ̅ⲡⲉ
ⲉⲛⲧⲁ ⲥ̅ⲣⲭⲟ ⲗⲥⲉⲓ ⲧ̅ ⲁⲉ ⲏ̅
ⲛ̅ⲛⲓⲡ̅ⲡ̅ ⲛ̅ⲁⲛⲓ ⲡⲙ̅ ⲡⲓ ⲛⲟ
ⲛⲛ̅ⲧⲁⲅⲉⲛⲧⲁ ⲧⲟ ⲛ̅ⲕⲉⲓ
ⲉⲃⲟⲗ ⲙ̅ⲙ̅ⲟⲩ ⲛ̅ⲑⲉ ⲛ̅ⲟⲭⲟⲓ
ⲟⲧⲟ ⲛ̅ⲕⲁⲛⲓⲙⲓⲙ ⲉⲧⲟ
ⲁ̄ⲅ̅ ⲛ̅ⲉⲛ̅ⲟⲩⲛ ⲡ̅
ⲁ̄ⲅ̅ⲡⲉ ⲛⲟⲟⲩ ⲡ̅
ⲁ̄ⲛ̅ ⲛⲟⲉ ⲟⲛ ⲟⲩ ⲭⲟⲗⲥ ⲉ ⲙⲧ̅ⲉ
ⲛ̅ⲧ̅ⲛ̅ ⲟⲩ ⲛ̅ ⲓⲣ̅ⲣⲟⲩ ⲉⲓ ⲁⲧ
ⲛ̅ⲧⲕⲱ ⲛ̅ ⲙⲙⲛ̅ ⲣ̅ⲟϯ ⲟⲩ ⲣ̅ⲟⲉ
ⲛ̅ⲧ̅ⲧⲟⲛⲗⲉ ⲛ̅ⲧⲟⲛⲧⲉⲧ ⲁ ⲡ̅
ⲟⲩⲣ̅ⲃ̅ ⲧ̅ⲥⲛⲟⲟⲩ ⲅⲉ ⲛ̅ⲛⲁⲅ
ⲟⲛ ⲕⲁ ⲟⲩⲉ ⲭⲱⲥ ⲉⲣⲉ ⲟⲩ ⲓ̅ⲣ̅ⲩ
ⲱⲉⲓ ⲙ̅ⲙ̅ⲛ̅ ⲧ̅ⲥ̅ⲛⲟⲟⲩⲥ ⲁ̄ⲩⲟⲩⲛ
ⲗⲏ̅ⲧⲉ ⲛ̅ⲇⲉ ⲧⲁⲥ ⲙ̅ⲡⲕⲱ ⲧ̅ⲉ
ⲛⲉⲥⲛⲁⲉ̄ⲃ̅ ⲁ̄ ⲱⲟⲩ ⲛ̅ⲙⲓⲥⲉ
ⲛ̅ϩⲟⲛⲛ̅ⲥ ⲓ̅ ⲡ̅ⲕⲱ ⲧ̅ⲛ̅ⲣⲁⲛ̅
ⲁ̄ⲩⲱⲟⲧⲛⲥⲁ ⲱⲉ ⲛⲥⲉⲭ̅ⲗⲟⲙ̅ⲥ
ⲛⲉⲥⲟⲩⲣ̅ⲏ̅ⲧⲉ ⲉⲣⲉⲧⲟ ⲉ ⲓ̅
ⲁⲩ ⲉⲓ ⲉⲛⲟ ⲛⲥⲉⲭ̅ⲗⲟⲙ̅ⲥ
ⲁ̄ⲩ ⲧⲉⲥⲓ ⲕⲁⲧⲁ ⲡⲉ ⲧⲁⲥ ⲙⲁⲉⲧ
ⲕ̅ ⲥⲉⲣⲟⲥ ⲛ̅ⲑⲉ ⲙⲥ ⲙⲡ̅ ⲟ
ϩ̅ⲛ̅ⲧⲉⲛⲧ̅ ⲉⲛⲥⲟ ⲱⲉ ⲡ̅ⲛ̅ⲁⲩ ⲓ̅ⲙ̅
ⲛ̅ⲟⲩ ⲉⲧ̅ⲏ̅ ⲛⲟⲩ ⲧⲉ ⲙ̅ⲟⲟⲩ ⲉⲛ ⲧⲁ

1. ϪЄ ϨΜ ΠЄΚΟΥΟЄΙΝ ΤΝΝΑΝΑΥ ЄΥ
ΟΥΟЄΙΝ ΑΥΩ ЄΡЄ ΠΜΟΝΟΓЄΝΗС
ΤΑΛΗΥ ЄϨΡΑΙ ЄϪΩΟΥ ΝΘЄ ΟΝ
ЄΤСΗϨ ϪЄ ѰΑΡΜΑ ΜΠΝΟΥΤЄ
5. ΟΥΤΒΑ ΝΚΩΒ ΠЄ ΑΥΩ ΟΝ ϪЄ
ϨЄΝϢΟ ЄΥΡΟΟΥΤ ΝЄ ЄΡЄ ΠϪΟΙС
ΝϨΗΤΟΥ ΠΑΙ ΠЄ ΠЄΤΟΥΗϨ
ϨΝ ΤΜΟΝΑС ЄΤϨΜ ΠСΗΘЄΥС ΤΑΙ
ЄΝΤΑСЄΙ ЄΒΟΛ ϨΜ ΠΜΑ ЄΝΤЄ
10. СЄΝΑϢϪΟΟС ΑΝ ϪЄ ΤΩΝ ΠЄ
ЄΝΤΑСЄΙ ЄΒΟΛ ϨΜ ΠΑΙ ЄΤϨΑΘΗ
ΝΝΙΠΤΗΡϤ ΠΑΙ ΠЄ ΠΙΟΥΑ ΜΑΥΑΑϤ
ΠΑΙ ΠЄ ЄΝΤΑ ΤΜΟΝΑС ЄΙ
ЄΒΟΛ ΜΜΟΥ ΝΘЄ ΝΟΥϪΟΙ ЄϤ
15. ΟΤΠ ΝΝΚΑ ΝΙΜ ΝΑΓΑΘΟΝ
ΑΥΩ ΝΘЄ ΝΟΥСΩϢЄ ЄСΜЄϨ
Η ЄСΡΗΤ ΝΓЄΝΟС ΝΙΜ ΝϢΗΝ
ΑΥΩ ΝΘЄ ΝΟΥΠΟΛΙС ЄСΜЄϨ
ΝΓЄΝΟС ΝΙΜ ΝΡΩΜЄ ΑΥΩ
20. ΝϨΙΚΩΝ ΝΙΜ ΝΡΡΟ ΤΑΙ ΤЄ ΘЄ
ΝΤΜΟΝΑС ЄΥΝϨΗΤС ΤΗΡΟΥ
ΟΥΝ ΜΝΤСΝΟΟΥС ΜΜΟΝΑС
Ο ΝΚΛΟΜ ϨΙϪΩС ЄΡЄ ΤΟΥΙ ΤΟΥΙ
ЄΙΡЄ ΜΜΝΤСΝΟΟΥС ΑΥΩ ΟΥΝ
25. ΜΗΤЄ ΝΔЄΚΑС ΜΠΚΩΤЄ Ν
ΝЄСΝΑϨΒ ΑΥΩ ΟΥΝ ѰΙΤЄ
ΝϨЄΝΝΑС ΜΠΚΩΤЄ ΝϨΗΤС
ΑΥΩ ΟΥΝ СΑϢϤЄ ΝϨЄΒΔΟΜΑС
ϨΑ ΝЄСΟΥЄΡΗΤЄ ЄΡЄ ΤΟΥЄΙ
30. ΤΟΥЄΙ ЄΙΡЄ ΝΟΥϨЄΒΔΟΜΑС
ΑΥΩ ΠЄСΚΑΤΑΠЄΤΑСΜΑ ЄΤ
ΚΩΤЄ ЄΡΟС ΝΘЄ ΝΟΥΠΥΡΓΟС
ΟΥΝ ΜΝΤСΝΟΟΥС ΜΠΥΛΗ Μ
ΜΟϤ ΟΥΝ ΜΝΤСΝΟΟΥС ΝΤΒΑ

ⲛⲁⲩⲛⲁⲉⲓⲥ ⲙⲛⲉⲛⲣⲏ ⲛⲧⲏ̄ⲣ̄ⲟⲩ
ⲁⲉ̄ⲁⲁⲱⲥⲉⲙⲟⲩ ⲧⲁ̄ⲉ̄ⲓⲟⲟ ⲧⲉⲉ̄
ⲁⲣⲭⲁⲅⲅⲉⲗⲟⲥ ⲁⲧⲱⲟ̄ⲛ̄ⲭⲉⲁⲅⲅⲉ
ⲗⲟⲥ ⲧⲁ̄ⲓⲧⲉⲣⲁⲙ̄ⲛ̄ⲧⲣ̄ⲟ̄ⲡⲟⲥⲁ̄ⲡ
ⲙ̄ⲡⲓⲟⲛⲟⲅ̄ⲉ̄ⲛ̄ⲏⲥ ⲡⲁⲓⲧⲉ
ⲡⲙⲟⲛⲟⲅ̄ⲉ̄ⲛ̄ⲏⲥ ⲉⲛⲧⲁϥⲱ
ⲉ̄ⲓⲙⲁⲉ̄ⲓⲧ̄ⲏⲥ ⲟⲩ̄ⲭⲉⲃⲟⲩ̄ⲭⲉ
ⲉ̄ⲩ̄ϣⲟⲟⲡ̄ⲥ̄ⲁⲙ̄ⲛ̄ⲧⲣ̄ⲟⲩ ⲡⲁ̄ⲩ
ⲉⲛⲧⲁ̄ⲅⲧ̄ⲉ̄ⲃⲟⲗ̄ⲁⲡⲓⲟⲡⲉⲣⲁ̄ⲛ
ⲧⲟⲛ ⲁⲧ̄ⲉ̄ⲛⲁ̄ⲧⲭⲱⲣⲁⲕ̄ ⲧⲏⲣⲁⲩ
ⲟⲩⲁⲧⲉⲭⲛ̄ⲏ̄ⲛ̄ ⲁⲧⲱⲟ̄ⲛⲁ̄ⲧⲟ
ⲅⲉⲛ̄ⲏⲥ ⲟ̄ⲧⲁ̄ ⲉⲛⲧⲁ̄ⲁ̄ⲧⲓⲟⲩ
ⲓⲙ̄ⲉ̄ⲓ̄ⲛ̄ⲁ̄ⲩ̄ⲟⲧⲁ̄ⲉⲛⲁ̄ⲧⲉ̄ⲓ
ⲉ̄ⲕⲟ̄ⲗⲉⲙ̄ⲡ̄ⲓⲁ̄ⲧ̄ⲱ̄ⲁϫⲉⲥⲧ̄ⲣⲓϥ̄ⲁⲩ
ⲱ̄ⲛ̄ⲁ̄ϫⲉⲧⲣⲓ̄ⲧⲟ̄ⲥ̄ ⲧⲁ̄ϣⲟⲟⲡ̄
ⲟⲛ̄ⲧⲱⲥ̄ ⲛ̄ⲁⲓ̄ⲉ̄ ⲅⲓⲁ̄ⲛⲉⲩϥ̄ ϣⲟⲟⲡ̄
ⲛⲏ̄ⲛ̄ⲧ̄ⲩ̄ⲛ̄ϭⲓ̄ⲡ̄ⲉ̄ϥ̄ϣ̄ⲟ̄ⲣ̄ⲡ̄ⲁ̄ⲛⲟ̄ⲩ̄
ⲉ̄ϥ̄ⲉ̄ⲡⲁ̄ⲅⲅⲉ̄ⲡⲓⲥ̄ⲟ̄ⲧ̄ⲛⲁ̄ⲧⲣⲁⲉⲩϥ̄
ϥ̄ⲉ̄ϣⲟⲟⲡⲉⲓⲥ̄ⲛⲉⲩϣ̄ⲏ̄ⲏ̄ⲛ̄ⲉϫ̄ⲙⲟ̄
ⲛⲟⲅⲉⲛ̄ⲏⲥ̄ ⲉ̄ⲣⲉⲧⲓ̄ϫ̄ⲩ̄ⲁ̄ⲟ̄ⲣⲓ̄ⲥ
ⲥⲓⲙⲡ̄ⲥ̄ⲩ̄ⲁ̄ⲗⲉⲉ̄ⲣ̄ⲟⲩ̄ ⲁ̄ⲧⲟⲛⲁ̄ϩ
ⲣ̄ⲏ̄ⲧⲟⲥ̄ ⲛⲁⲧ̄ⲣ̄ⲟ̄ ⲁⲧⲟ̄ⲉ̄ⲩⲁⲧⲉ
ⲟ̄ⲛ̄ⲱⲭⲁ̄ⲛⲛⲁϥⲧⲉ ⲉⲓⲙ̄ⲙⲁⲉ̄ⲓⲧ̄ⲏ̄ⲥ
ⲩ̄ϫⲉⲉ̄ⲧⲉϥ̄ⲙ̄ⲛ̄ⲧⲛⲟ̄ⲩⲧⲉ̄ⲧ̄ⲓⲟⲩ̄ⲧⲉ̄ ⲧⲁ
ⲥ̄ⲥ̄ⲉⲛⲟⲩ̄ⲙ̄ⲛ̄ⲧⲛⲟ̄ⲩⲧⲉ̄ⲩⲛⲟ̄ⲓ̄ⲙ̄ⲉⲟϥ̄
ⲧⲉ̄ ⲁ̄ⲧⲱⲟⲛ̄ⲧⲉϥ̄ⲛⲟ̄ⲓ̄ⲱⲙ̄ⲟⲥ̄
ⲛ̄ϭⲓ̄ⲫⲱⲥ̄ⲓⲁ̄ⲙ̄ⲓⲧ̄ⲏⲥ̄ ⲡⲉⲭⲁ̄ϥ̄
ϫ̄ⲉ̄ⲉ̄ⲧⲃ̄ⲏⲏ̄ⲧ̄ⲩ̄ ⲛⲉⲧ̄ϥ̄ϣ̄ⲟ̄ⲡ̄ⲟ̄ⲛ̄
ⲧ̄ⲃⲉⲛ̄ⲙ̄ⲙ̄ⲉ̄ ⲱⲛ̄ⲛⲉⲧⲉⲛ̄ⲥ̄ⲉ̄ϣ̄ⲱ̄
ⲟⲧⲁ̄ⲛⲁⲙ̄ⲉ̄ ⲡⲁ̄ⲓ̄ⲉ̄ⲧ̄ⲟⲩϣⲟⲟⲡ̄
ⲉ̄ⲧ̄ⲃ̄ⲏ̄ⲏ̄ⲧ̄ⲥ̄ ⲛ̄ϭⲓⲛ̄ⲉ̄ⲧ̄ϣⲟⲟⲡ̄ⲛⲁ
ⲙⲉ̄ϥ̄ⲟⲏⲧ̄ ⲙⲛ̄ⲛⲉ̄ⲧ̄ⲛ̄ⲥ̄ⲉϣⲟⲟⲡ̄
ⲁ̄ⲛ̄ⲙ̄ⲙ̄ⲁ̄ⲧⲟⲩ̄ⲛⲅ̄ⲉ̄ⲗ̄ⲟⲥ̄ ⲧ̄ⲁ̄

1. ⲚⲆⲨⲚⲀⲘⲒⲤ ϩⲒⲬⲚ ⲦⲠⲨⲖⲎ ⲦⲠⲨ
ⲖⲎ ⲀⲨⲱ ⲤⲈⲘⲞⲨⲦⲈ ⲈⲢⲞⲞⲨ ⲬⲈ
ⲀⲢⲬⲀⲅⲅⲈⲖⲞⲤ ⲀⲨⲱ ⲞⲚ ⲬⲈ ⲀⲅⲅⲈ
ⲖⲞⲤ ⲦⲀⲒ ⲦⲈ ⲦⲘⲎⲦⲢⲞⲠⲞⲖⲒⲤ

5. ⲘⲠⲘⲞⲚⲞⲄⲈⲚⲎⲤ ⲠⲀⲒ ⲠⲈ
ⲠⲘⲞⲚⲞⲄⲈⲚⲎⲤ ⲈⲚⲦⲀ ⲪⲰ
ⲤⲒⲖⲀⲘⲠⲎⲤ ⲱⲀⲬⲈ ⲈⲢⲞⲨ ⲬⲈ
Ⲩⲱⲟⲟⲡ ϩⲀⲐⲎ ⲘⲠⲦⲎⲢⲨ ⲠⲀⲒ
ⲈⲚⲦⲀⲨⲈⲒ ⲈⲂⲞⲖ ϩⲘ ⲠⲀⲠⲈⲢⲀⲚ

10. ⲦⲞⲚ ⲀⲨⲱ ⲚⲀⲦⲬⲀⲢⲀⲔⲦⲎⲢ ⲀⲨ
ⲱ ⲚⲀⲦⲤⲬⲎⲘⲀ ⲀⲨⲱ ⲚⲀⲨⲦⲞ
ⲄⲈⲚⲎⲤ ⲠⲀⲒ ⲈⲚⲦⲀⲨⲬⲠⲞⲨ
ⲘⲘⲒⲚ ⲘⲘⲞⲨ ⲠⲀⲒ ⲈⲚⲦⲀⲨⲈⲒ
ⲈⲂⲞⲖ ϩⲘ ⲠⲒⲀⲦⲱⲀⲬⲈ ⲈⲢⲞⲨ ⲀⲨ

15. ⲱ ⲚⲀⲘⲈⲦⲢⲎⲦⲞⲤ ⲈⲦⲱⲟⲟⲡ
ⲞⲚⲦⲱⲤ ⲚⲀⲘⲈ ⲠⲀⲒ ⲈⲦⲨⲱⲟⲟⲡ
ⲚϩⲎⲦⲨ ⲚϬⲒ ⲠⲈⲦⲱⲟⲟⲡ ⲚⲀⲘⲈ
ⲈⲦⲈ ⲠⲀⲒ ⲠⲈ ⲠⲒⲱⲦ ⲚⲀⲦⲦⲀϩⲞⲨ
Ⲩⲱⲟⲟⲡ ϩⲘ ⲠⲈⲨⲱⲎⲢⲈ ⲘⲘⲞ

20. ⲚⲞⲄⲈⲚⲎⲤ ⲈⲢⲈ ⲠⲦⲎⲢⲨ ϩⲞⲢⲔ
ϩⲘ ⲠⲒⲀⲦⲱⲀⲬⲈ ⲈⲢⲞⲨ ⲀⲨⲱ ⲚⲀϩ
ⲢⲎⲦⲞⲤ ⲚⲀⲦⲢⲢⲞ ⲀⲨⲱ ⲈⲨⲀⲦⲈ
ⲚⲱⲬⲖⲒ ⲚⲀⲨ ⲠⲈ ⲈⲘⲚⲖⲀⲀⲨ ⲚⲀⲱ
ⲱⲀⲬⲈ ⲈⲦⲈⲨⲘⲚⲦⲚⲞⲨⲦⲈ ⲦⲀⲒ

25. ⲈⲦⲈ ⲚⲞⲨⲘⲚⲦⲚⲞⲨⲦⲈ ⲢⲰ ⲀⲚ
ⲦⲈ ⲀⲨⲱ ⲚⲦⲈⲢⲈⲨ ⲚⲞⲒ ⲘⲘⲞⲨ
ⲚϬⲒ ⲪⲰⲤⲒⲖⲀⲘⲠⲎⲤ ⲠⲈⲬⲀⲨ
ⲬⲈ ⲈⲦⲂⲎⲎⲦⲨ ⲚⲈⲦⲱⲟⲟⲡ ⲞⲚ
ⲦⲞⲤ ⲚⲀⲘⲈ ⲘⲚ ⲚⲈⲦⲈ ⲚⲤⲈⲱⲞ

30. ⲞⲠ ⲀⲚ ⲚⲀⲘⲈ ⲠⲀⲒ ⲈⲦⲞⲨⲱⲟⲟⲡ
ⲈⲦⲂⲎⲎⲦⲨ ⲚϬⲒ ⲚⲈⲦⲱⲟⲟⲡ ⲚⲀ
ⲘⲈ ⲈⲐⲎⲠ ⲘⲚ ⲚⲈⲦⲈ ⲚⲤⲈⲱⲟⲟⲡ
ⲀⲚ ⲚⲀⲘⲈ ⲈⲦⲞⲨⲞⲚϩ ⲈⲂⲞⲖ ⲠⲀⲒ

ⲡⲓⲡⲛⲟⲩⲧⲉⲉⲱⲱⲟⲛⲟⲥⲅⲉⲛⲏⲥ
ⲛⲁⲩⲃ· ⲡⲁⲓⲡⲉⲉⲛ·ⲅⲁⲧⲓⲡⲧⲏⲣϥ
ⲥⲟⲩⲱⲛⲥ ⲉⲣⲡⲛⲟⲩⲧⲉ ⲁⲩⲱ ⲛ
ⲥⲉⲉⲓⲡⲉ· ⲁⲛⲧⲉⲓⲣⲁⲛ ϫⲉⲛⲟⲩⲧⲉ
ⲡⲁⲓⲡⲉ ⲉⲛⲧⲁ·ⲓⲱⲁⲛⲛⲏⲥ ϫⲟⲟⲥ
ⲉⲧⲃⲏⲏⲧϥ ϫⲉⲥⲛ·ⲧⲉϩⲟⲩⲉⲓ
ⲡⲉⲛⲉϥϣⲟⲟⲡ ⲡⲉ ⲛⲟ...ⲗⲟⲅ...
ⲁⲩⲱ ⲡⲗⲟⲅⲟⲥ ⲛⲉϥϣⲟⲟⲡ ⲛ
ϩⲁϩ ⲣ··ⲡⲛⲟⲩⲧⲉ ⲁⲩⲱ ⲛⲉⲩ
ⲛⲟⲩⲧⲉ ⲡⲉ ⲡⲗⲟⲅⲟⲥ ⲡⲁⲓ
ϫⲛ·ⲧϥ ⲛ·ⲡⲉ··ⲁⲁⲧⲱ··· ⲡⲉ ⲁⲩ
ϣⲱⲡⲉ·· ⲁ··ϣ·ⲱ·ⲡⲉ ··ⲓ ·ⲛⲓⲙ
ⲧⲩⲡⲉ·ⲣⲱ··ⲟⲥ ⲡⲁ··ⲡⲉ·ⲛ·ⲭⲓⲟ·
ⲛⲟⲅⲉⲛⲏⲥ ⲉ·ⲣ·ⲉⲛⲧⲙⲟⲛⲁⲥⲉ
ⲧⲟⲩ···ⲉⲓ·ⲉⲛⲧⲟⲛ··ⲉⲛⲟⲩ·ⲡⲟⲗ·ⲥ
ⲁⲩⲱ·ⲧ·ⲁ·ⲉ· ·ⲙⲟⲛⲁⲥⲉ·ϥⲛ
ⲥⲓⲃⲉⲩ·ⲛ·ⲥⲉ·ⲛⲟⲩⲉⲛⲛⲟⲓⲁ
ⲡⲁⲓⲧⲉ·ⲥⲛⲟ·ⲉⲧⲉⲉ·ⲣⲟⲩ·ⲧⲉ
ⲉⲩⲫⲓ·ⲉ·ⲟⲛⲛⲉⲉⲛⲟ·ⲣⲣ·ⲁ·ⲉ·
ⲱⲉϥⲟ·ⲛⲟ·ⲧⲉⲓ·ⲡⲁⲓⲡⲉ
ⲧⲉⲗⲟⲓ··ⲉⲛⲙⲡⲓⲟⲩⲣ·ⲓⲁ·ⲟⲥ ·
ⲡⲁⲓⲡⲉ·ⲉⲧⲟⲩ·ⲉ·ⲓⲙⲁ ⲛⲉⲓⲙ
ⲡⲧⲏ·ϥ ⲉⲧⲉⲩϩⲱ···ⲡⲁⲓ·ⲡⲉ
ⲡⲛⲟⲩⲥⲛⲁⲓⲙⲓⲟⲩⲣ·ⲅⲟⲥ· ⲕⲁ
ⲧⲁⲟⲩⲉ·ⲥⲁ· ⲛⲉⲙⲡⲛⲟⲩⲧⲉ
ⲡⲉⲛⲟ·· ·ⲡⲁⲓⲡⲉⲧⲉⲣⲉⲡ·ⲉ·
ⲥⲟⲗⲟⲡⲓ·ⲙⲙⲟⲩⲱⲥⲛⲟⲩⲧⲉ·
ⲁⲩⲱⲉⲓⲥ ϫⲟⲉⲓⲥ ⲁⲩⲱ ⲁ·ⲥ
ⲥⲱⲧⲏ·ⲉ·ⲁ·ⲛ·ⲥⲱ·ⲉⲧ·ⲩⲡⲟ
ⲧⲁⲥⲥⲉⲛⲁϥ· ⲡⲛⲉⲣⲉ·ⲡⲙ·
ⲣⲟ··ⲣⲱⲧ·ⲓⲣⲉ·ⲙ·ⲟⲩ·ⲉ·ⲧⲉ·
ⲧⲉⲉ·ⲣⲁ·ⲓϩ·ⲛⲟ··ⲁ··ⲧⲁⲗⲉ
ⲧⲉ·ⲣⲉⲧⲓ·ⲓⲣ·ⲉⲓ··ⲧⲉ···ⲓ·ⲟ·
ⲛ·ⲕⲗ·ⲟ··ⲓ·ϫⲱϥ· ⲁⲩⲱ·ⲡⲁⲧⲃⲟ·
ϩⲁⲛ·ⲛⲟⲩⲉϩⲏⲧⲉ·ⲉϫⲱⲛ·ⲁⲧ
ϩⲏⲧⲉ ⲉⲧⲕⲱⲧⲉⲉⲣⲟⲟⲩⲉⲩ
ⲥⲉⲙⲩ·ⲟⲣⲟⲩⲉⲩ·ⲭⲱⲗⲉ·ⲥ·

1. ⲡⲉ ⲡⲛⲟⲩⲧⲉ ⲙⲙⲟⲛⲟⲅⲉⲛⲏⲥ
ⲛⲁⲙⲉ ⲡⲁⲓ ⲡⲉ ⲉⲛⲧⲁ ⲡⲧⲏⲣⲩ
ⲥⲟⲩⲱⲛⲩ ⲁⲩⲣⲛⲟⲩⲧⲉ ⲁⲩⲱ ⲁⲩ
ⲣⲡⲉⲧⲡⲉ ⲙⲡⲉⲓⲣⲁⲛ ϫⲉ ⲛⲟⲩⲧⲉ
5. ⲡⲁⲓ ⲡⲉ ⲉⲛⲧⲁ ⲓⲱⲁⲛⲛⲏⲥ ϫⲟⲟⲥ
ⲉⲧⲃⲏⲏⲧⲩ ϫⲉ ϩⲛ ⲧⲉϩⲟⲩⲉⲓ
ⲧⲉ ⲛⲉⲩϣⲟⲟⲡ ⲡⲉ ⲛϭⲓ ⲡⲗⲟⲅⲟⲥ
ⲁⲩⲱ ⲡⲗⲟⲅⲟⲥ ⲛⲉⲩϣⲟⲟⲡ ⲛ
ⲛⲁϩⲣⲛ ⲡⲛⲟⲩⲧⲉ ⲁⲩⲱ ⲛⲉⲩ
10. ⲛⲟⲩⲧⲉ ⲡⲉ ⲡⲗⲟⲅⲟⲥ ⲡⲁⲓ ⲁ
ϫⲛⲧⲩ ⲙⲡⲉ ⲗⲁⲁⲩ ϣⲱⲡⲉ ⲁⲩ
ⲱ ⲡⲉⲛⲧⲁⲩϣⲱⲡⲉ ϩⲣⲁⲓ ⲛϩⲏ
ⲧⲩ ⲡⲉ ⲡⲱⲛϩ ⲡⲁⲓ ⲡⲉ ⲡⲙⲟ
ⲛⲟⲅⲉⲛⲏⲥ ⲉⲧϩⲛ ⲧⲙⲟⲛⲁⲥ ⲉ
15. ⲧⲟⲩⲏϩ ⲛϩⲏⲧⲥ ⲛⲑⲉ ⲛⲟⲩⲡⲟⲗⲓⲥ
ⲁⲩⲱ ⲧⲁⲓ ⲧⲉ ⲧⲙⲟⲛⲁⲥ ⲉⲧϩⲛ
ⲥⲏⲑⲉⲩⲥ ⲛⲑⲉ ⲛⲟⲩⲉⲛⲛⲟⲓⲁ
ⲡⲁⲓ ⲡⲉ ⲥⲏⲑⲉⲩⲥ ⲉⲧⲟⲩⲏϩ
ϩⲙ ⲯⲓⲉⲣⲟⲛ ⲛⲑⲉ ⲛⲟⲩⲣⲣⲟ ⲁⲩ
20. ⲱ ⲉⲩⲟ ⲛⲛⲟⲩⲧⲉ ⲡⲁⲓ ⲡⲉ
ⲡⲗⲟⲅⲟⲥ ⲛⲇⲏⲙⲓⲟⲩⲣⲅⲟⲥ
ⲡⲁⲓ ⲡⲉ ⲉⲧⲟⲩⲉϩⲥⲁϩⲛⲉ ⲙ
ⲡⲧⲏⲣⲩ ⲉⲧⲣⲉⲩⲣϩⲱⲃ ⲡⲁⲓ ⲡⲉ
ⲡⲛⲟⲩⲥ ⲛⲇⲏⲙⲓⲟⲩⲣⲅⲟⲥ ⲕⲁ
25. ⲧⲁ ⲡⲟⲩⲉϩⲥⲁϩⲛⲉ ⲙⲡⲛⲟⲩⲧⲉ
ⲡⲉⲓⲱⲧ ⲡⲁⲓ ⲉⲧⲉⲣⲉ ⲡⲥⲱⲛⲧ
ⲥⲟⲡⲥⲡ ⲙⲙⲟⲩ ϩⲱⲥ ⲛⲟⲩⲧⲉ
ⲁⲩⲱ ϩⲱⲥ ϫⲟⲉⲓⲥ ⲁⲩⲱ ϩⲱⲥ
ⲥⲱⲧⲏⲣ ⲁⲩⲱ ϩⲱⲥ ⲉⲩϩⲩⲡⲟ
30. ⲧⲁⲥⲥⲉ ⲛⲁⲩ ⲡⲁⲓ ⲉⲣⲉ ⲡⲧⲏ
ⲣⲩ ⲣϣⲡⲏⲣⲉ ⲙⲙⲟⲩ ⲉⲧⲃⲉ
ⲡⲉⲩⲥⲁ ⲙⲛ ⲡⲉⲩⲁⲛⲁⲓ ⲡⲁⲓ ⲉ
ⲧⲉⲣⲉ ⲡⲧⲏⲣⲩ ⲛⲁⲡϩⲟⲩⲛ ⲟ
ⲛⲕⲗⲟⲙ ϩⲓϫⲱⲩ ⲁⲩⲱ ⲛⲁⲡⲃⲟⲗ
35. ϩⲁ ⲛⲉⲩⲟⲩⲉⲣⲏⲧⲉ ⲁⲩⲱ ⲛⲁⲧ
ⲙⲏⲧⲉ ⲉⲩⲕⲱⲧⲉ ⲉⲣⲟⲩ ⲉⲩ
ⲥⲙⲟⲩ ⲉⲣⲟⲩ ⲉⲩϫⲱ ⲙⲙⲟⲥ

ϫⲉ ⲟ ⲇⲁⲉ ϭⲟⲩⲇⲉ ϭⲟⲩⲇⲉ
ⲡⲉⲓⲁⲗⲗⲏⲏ ⲉⲃⲃ ⲟⲟⲩ
ϭⲟⲩⲱ ⲉⲧⲉⲛⲁⲡⲉϫⲉⲕⲁ
ⲁⲧ ⲛⲉⲧⲟⲛⲉ ⲧⲩⲕⲇⲉϭⲩⲇⲁ
ⲧⲟⲩⲁⲁⲃ ⲁⲩⲱ ⲕⲱ ⲟⲩⲟⲉⲓⲛ
ⲛⲉⲧϣⲟⲟⲡ ⲁⲩⲱ ⲕⲟ ⲛ ⲉⲡⲁⲩ
ⲁⲛ ⲛⲉⲓⲟⲧⲉ ⲁⲩⲱ ⲕⲱ ⲛ ⲟⲩ
ⲡⲉϫⲓ ⲛ ⲛⲟⲩⲧⲉ ⲁⲩⲱ ⲕⲟ
ⲭⲟⲉⲓⲥ ⲉⲛ ⲛϫⲟⲉⲓⲥ ⲁⲩⲱ ⲕⲟ
ⲛ ⲉ ⲡⲣⲟⲥ ⲉⲛ ⲡ ⲧⲟⲡⲟⲥ ⲁⲩ
ⲥⲁ ⲉ ⲉⲣⲟⲩ ⲉⲩϫⲱ ⲙ
ϫⲉ ⲟ ⲟⲕ ⲡⲉⲧ ϩⲓ ⲁⲩⲱ ⲡⲉϫⲕ
ⲡⲉⲣ ⲟⲩ ⲛ ⲡⲓ ⲡ ⲡⲓⲕⲁ ⲁⲱⲟⲛ
ⲉⲧⲉ ⲙⲟⲟⲩ ⲉⲧⲭⲱ ⲙⲙⲟⲥ ⲉ ⲛⲟⲛ
ϫⲉ ⲛ ⲓ ⲥⲛ ⲟⲩ ⲉ ⲧ ⲡⲁⲣⲉⲛⲏ ϫⲉ
ⲕ ⲱ ⲟⲟⲡ ⲕ ⲱ ⲟⲟⲡ ⲧ ⲡ ⲧ ⲟⲡⲟⲡ ⲉ
ⲛⲏⲥ ⲡ ⲟⲩⲟⲉⲓⲛ ⲛ ⲟⲩ ⲛ ⲟ ⲛ
ⲁⲩⲱ ⲧ ⲉ ⲭⲣ ⲓ ⲥ ⲓ ⲟⲧⲉ ⲉⲛⲉ ⲉ
ⲁⲩⲡⲓ ⲛ ⲟⲟⲩ ⲡⲡⲉⲥ ⲧⲓ ⲛⲟⲩ ⲛ
ⲉ ⲉⲣ ⲡⲁ ⲉ ⲉ ⲓⲱ ϯ ⲁ ⲧ
ⲗⲟⲩ ⲗⲟⲩ ⲁ ϫⲓ ⲟⲩ ⲟⲉⲓⲛ ⲉⲡⲧⲟ
ⲧⲟⲟⲥ ⲧ ⲏ ⲓ ⲩ ⲱ ⲡⲓⲉⲣⲟⲛ ⲩ
ⲱ ⲧⲁⲏⲉ ⲱ ⲱ ⲁⲩ ⲱ ⲩ ⲓ ⲙ ⲉ
ⲟ ⲡ ⲟ ⲩ ⲟⲉⲓⲛ ⲉ ⲧ ⲡⲉⲥ ⲓ ⲛ ⲉ
ⲁⲉ ⲓⲁ ⲁ ⲉ ⲁⲩ ⲱ ⲇ ϯ ⲛ ⲛⲧⲃ
ⲁ ⲩ ⲣⲁⲛ ⲃⲟⲟⲩ ⲩ ϭ ⲟ ⲩ ⲛ ⲉ ⲡⲉ ⲉ ⲙ
ⲥ ⲩ ⲥ ⲙ ⲡⲉⲥⲟⲩ ⲛ ⲉ ⲡ ⲉ ⲥ ⲧ ⲓ ⲛ
ⲑ ⲏ ⲡ ⲟ ⲩⲟⲉⲓⲛ ⲧ ⲏ ⲓ ⲉ ⲛ ⲧ ϥ
ⲟⲩⲱ ⲡ ⲡ ⲉ ⲣ ⲟ ⲛ ⲉ ⲁ ⲛ ⲟ ⲧ ⲉ ⲣ ⲟ ϥ
ϫⲉ ⲓ ⲧ ⲉ ⲩ ⲱ ⲓ ⲛ ⲉ ⲧ ⲉ ⲣ ⲟ ⲩ ⲛ ϩ ⲏ ⲧ
ⲁ ⲩ ⲇ ⲓ ⲓ ϫ ⲱ ⲧ ⲣ ⲁ ⲫ ⲓ ⲱ ⲧ ⲉⲥ ⲧ ⲓ
ⲥ ⲛ ⲧ ⲉ ⲩ ϭ ⲓ ⲛ ⲉ ⲛ ⲧ ⲟ ⲩ ⲧ ⲟ ⲩ ⲱ ⲥ
ⲱ ⲓ ⲙ ⲙ ⲉ ⲛ ⲁ ⲟ ⲩ

XXVII
MS. f. 110^{R}
C.S. p. 17

ϪΕ ϤΟΥΑΑΒ ϤΟΥΑΑΒ ϤΟΥΑΑΒ
ΠΕΙ ΑΑΑ ΗΗΗ ΕΕΕ ΟΟΟ ΥΥΥ
ΩΩΩ ΕΤΕ ΠΑΙ ΠΕ ϪΕ ΚΟΝϨ
ϨΝ ΝΕΤΟΝϨ ΑΥΩ ΚΟΥΑΑΒ ϨΝ
ΝΕΤΟΥΑΑΒ ΑΥΩ ΚϢΟΟΠ ϨΝ
ΝΕΤϢΟΟΠ ΑΥΩ ΚΟ ΝΕΙΩΤ
ϨΝ ΝΕΙΟΤΕ ΑΥΩ ΚΟ ΝΝΟΥ
ΤΕ ϨΝ ΝΝΟΥΤΕ ΑΥΩ ΚΟ Ν
ϪΟΕΙϹ ϨΝ ΝϪΟΕΙϹ ΑΥΩ ΚΟ
ΝΤΟΠΟϹ ϨΝ ΝΤΟΠΟϹ ΑΥΩ
ϹΕϹΜΟΥ ΕΡΟϤ ΕΥϪΩ ΜΜΟϹ
ϪΕ ΝΤΟΚ ΠΕ ΠΗΙ ΑΥΩ ΝΤΟΚ
ΠΕ ΕΤΟΥΗϨ ϨΜ ΠΗΙ ΑΥΩ ΟΝ
ΕΥϹΜΟΥ ΕΥϪΩ ΜΜΟϹ ΕΠϢΗ
ΡΕ ΕΤϨΗΠ ϨΡΑΙ ΝϨΗΤϤ ϪΕ
ΚϢΟΟΠ ΚϢΟΟΠ ΠΜΟΝΟΓΕ
ΝΗϹ ΠΟΥΟΕΙΝ ΑΥΩ ΠΩΝϨ
ΑΥΩ ΤΕΧΑΡΙϹ ΤΟΤΕ ϹΗΘΕΥϹ
ΑϤΤΝΝΟΟΥ ΜΠΕϹΠΙΝΘΗΡ
ΕϨΡΑΙ ΕΠΑΤΠΩϢ ΑΥΩ ΑϤ
ΒΟΥΒΟΥ ΑϤΡ ΟΥΟΕΙΝ ΕΠΤΟ
ΠΟϹ ΤΗΡϤ ΜΨΙΕΡΟΝ Μ
ΠΛΗΡΩΜΑ ΑΥΩ ΑΥΝΑΥ Ε
ΠΟΥΟΕΙΝ ΜΠΕϹΠΙΝΘΗΡ
ΑΥΡΑϢΕ ΑΥΩ ΑΥϮ ΝϨΕΝΤΒΑ
ΝΤΒΑ ΝΕΟΟΥ ΕϨΟΥΝ ΕΠϹΗ
ΘΕΥϹ ΑΥΩ ΕϨΟΥΝ ΕΠΕϹΠΙΝ
ΘΗΡ ΝΟΥΟΕΙΝ ΠΑΙ ΕΝΤΑϤ
ΟΥΩΝϨ ΕΒΟΛ ΕΑΥΝΑΥ ΕΡΟϤ
ϪΕ ΠΕϤΕΙΝΕ ΤΗΡΟΥ ΝϨΗΤϤ
ΑΥΩ ΑΥΖΩΓΡΑΨΙ ΜΠΕϹΠΙΝ
ΘΗΡ ϨΡΑΙ ΝϨΗΤΟΥ ΝΟΥΡΩΜΕ
ΝΟΥΟΕΙΝ ΑΥΩ ΜΜΕ ΑΥΜΟΥ

XXVIII
MS. f. 110v
C.S. p. 18

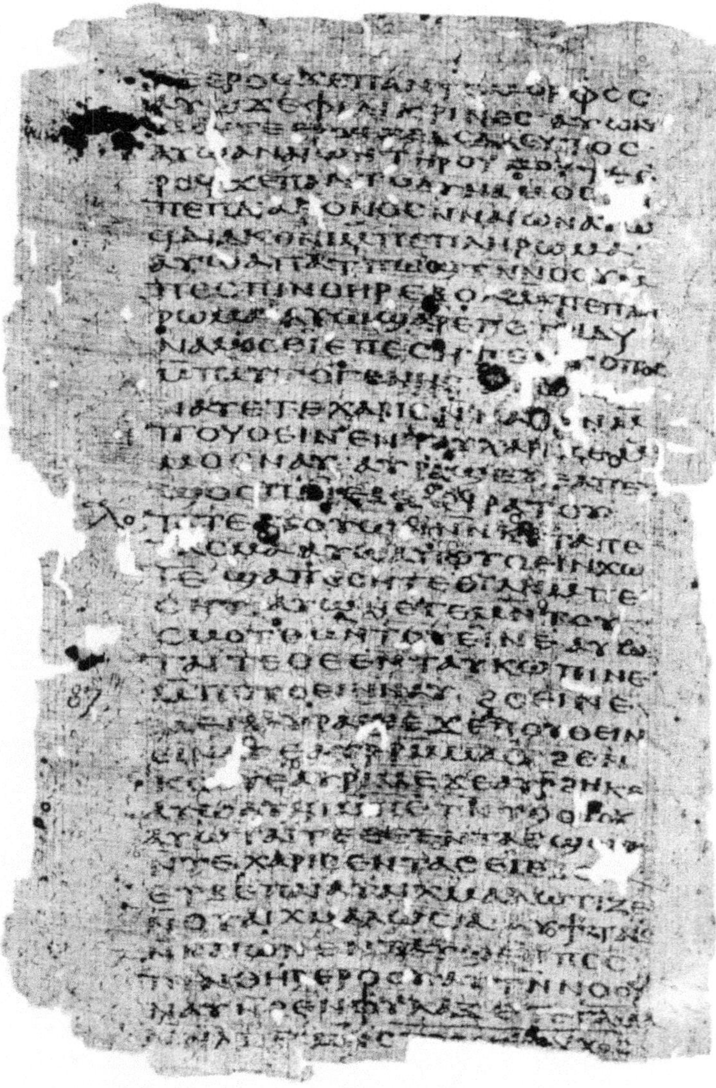

1. ⲧⲉ ⲉⲣⲟⲩ ϫⲉ ⲡⲁⲛⲧⲟⲙⲟⲣⲫⲟⲥ
ⲁⲩⲱ ϫⲉ ⲯⲓⲗⲓⲕⲣⲓⲛⲉⲥ ⲁⲩⲱ ⲁⲩ
ⲙⲟⲩⲧⲉ ⲉⲣⲟⲩ ϫⲉ ⲁⲥⲁⲗⲉⲩⲧⲟⲥ
ⲁⲩⲱ ⲁⲛⲁⲓⲱⲛ ⲧⲏⲣⲟⲩ ⲙⲟⲩⲧⲉ ⲉ
5. ⲣⲟⲩ ϫⲉ ⲡⲁⲛⲧⲟⲇⲩⲛⲁⲙⲟⲥ ⲡⲁⲓ
ⲡⲉ ⲡⲇⲓⲁⲕⲟⲛⲟⲥ ⲛⲛⲁⲓⲱⲛ ⲁⲩⲱ
ⲩⲇⲓⲁⲕⲟⲛⲓ ⲙⲡⲉⲡⲗⲏⲣⲱⲙⲁ
ⲁⲩⲱ ⲁⲡⲁⲧⲡⲱϣ ⲧⲛⲛⲟⲟⲩ ⲙ
ⲡⲉⲥⲡⲓⲛⲑⲏⲣ ⲉⲃⲟⲗ ϧⲙ ⲡⲉⲡⲗⲏ
10. ⲣⲱⲙⲁ ⲁⲩⲱ ϣⲁⲣⲉ ⲡⲉⲧⲣⲓⲇⲩ
ⲛⲁⲙⲟⲥ ⲉⲓ ⲉⲡⲉⲥⲏⲧ ⲉⲛⲧⲟⲡⲟⲥ
ⲙⲡⲁⲩⲧⲟⲅⲉⲛⲏⲥ ⲁⲩⲱ ⲁⲩ
ⲛⲁⲩ ⲉⲧⲉⲭⲁⲣⲓⲥ ⲛⲛⲁⲓⲱⲛ ⲙ
ⲡⲟⲩⲟⲉⲓⲛ ⲉⲛⲧⲁⲩⲭⲁⲣⲓⲍⲉ ⲙ
15. ⲙⲟⲥ ⲛⲁⲩ ⲁⲩⲣⲁϣⲉ ϫⲉ ⲁⲡⲉⲧ
ϣⲟⲟⲡ ⲉⲓ ⲉⲃⲟⲗ ϩⲓⲣⲁⲧⲟⲩ
ⲧⲟⲧⲉ ⲁⲩⲟⲩⲱⲛ ⲛⲛⲕⲁⲧⲁⲡⲉ
ⲧⲁⲥⲙⲁ ⲁⲩⲱ ⲁⲡⲟⲩⲟⲉⲓⲛ ϫⲱ
ⲧⲉ ϣⲁⲡⲉⲥⲏⲧ ⲉⲑⲩⲗⲏ ⲙⲡⲉ
20. ⲥⲏⲧ ⲁⲩⲱ ⲛⲉⲧⲉ ⲙⲛⲧⲟⲩ
ⲥⲙⲟⲧ ⲉⲙⲛⲧⲟⲩ ⲉⲓⲛⲉ ⲁⲩⲱ
ⲧⲁⲓ ⲧⲉ ⲑⲉ ⲉⲛⲧⲁⲩⲕⲱ ⲡⲓⲛⲉ
ⲙⲡⲟⲩⲟⲉⲓⲛ ⲛⲁⲩ ϩⲟⲉⲓⲛⲉ
ⲙⲉⲛ ⲁⲩⲣⲁϣⲉ ϫⲉ ⲁⲡⲟⲩⲟⲉⲓⲛ
25. ⲉⲓ ⲛⲁⲩ ⲉⲁⲩⲣⲣⲙⲙⲁⲟ ϩⲉⲛ
ⲕⲟⲟⲩⲉ ⲁⲩⲣⲓⲙⲉ ϫⲉ ⲁⲩⲣϩⲏⲕⲉ
ⲁⲩⲱ ⲁⲩϥⲓ ⲙⲡⲉⲧⲛⲧⲟⲟⲧⲟⲩ
ⲁⲩⲱ ⲧⲁⲓ ⲧⲉ ⲑⲉ ⲉⲛⲧⲁⲥϣⲱⲡⲉ
ⲛⲧⲉⲭⲁⲣⲓⲥ ⲉⲛⲧⲁⲥⲉⲓ ⲉⲃⲟⲗ
30. ⲉⲧⲃⲉ ⲡⲁⲓ ⲁⲩⲁⲓⲭⲙⲁⲗⲱⲧⲓⲍⲉ
ⲛⲟⲩⲭⲙⲁⲗⲱⲥⲓⲁ ⲁⲩⲧ ⲧⲁⲓⲟ
ⲛⲛⲁⲓⲱⲛ ⲉⲛⲧⲁⲩϣⲉⲡ ⲡⲉⲥ
ⲡⲓⲛⲑⲏⲣ ⲉⲣⲟⲟⲩ ⲁⲩⲧⲛⲛⲟⲟⲩ
ⲛⲁⲩ ⲛϩⲉⲛⲯⲩⲗⲁⲍ ⲉⲧⲉ ⲅⲁⲙⲁ
35. ⲗⲓⲏⲗ ⲡⲉ ⲙⲛ ⲥⲧⲣⲉⲙⲯⲟⲩⲭⲟⲥ

24. The ⲁ in the last word is written above the
line in the original.

1. ⲙⲛ ⲁⲅⲣⲁⲙⲁⲥ ⲙⲛ ⲛⲉⲧⲛⲙⲙⲁϥ
ⲁⲩⲣⲃⲟⲏⲑⲟⲥ ⲛⲛⲉⲛⲧⲁⲩⲡⲓⲥ
ⲧⲉⲩⲉ ⲉⲡⲉⲥⲡⲓⲛⲑⲏⲣ ⲙⲡⲟⲩⲟⲉⲓⲛ
ⲁⲩⲱ ϩⲣⲁⲓ ϩⲙ ⲡⲧⲟⲡⲟⲥ ⲙⲡⲁⲧ
5. ⲡⲱϣ ⲟⲩⲛ ⲙⲛⲧⲥⲛⲟⲟⲩⲥ ⲙⲡⲏ
ⲅⲏ ⲛϩⲏⲧϥ ⲉⲣⲉ ⲙⲛⲧⲥⲛⲟⲟⲩⲥ
ⲙⲙⲛⲧⲉⲓⲱⲧ ϩⲓϫⲱⲟⲩ ⲉⲩⲕⲱ
ⲧⲉ ⲉⲡⲁⲧⲡⲱϣ ⲛⲑⲉ ⲛⲛⲉⲓⲃⲁ
ⲑⲟⲥ ⲏ ⲛⲑⲉ ⲛⲛⲉⲓⲕⲁⲧⲁⲡⲉⲧⲁⲥ
10. ⲙⲁ ⲁⲩⲱ ⲟⲩⲛ ⲟⲩⲕⲗⲟⲙ ϩⲓϫⲙ
ⲡⲁⲧⲡⲱϣ ⲉⲟⲩⲛ ⲅⲉⲛⲟⲥ ⲛⲓⲙ
ⲛⲱⲛϩ ⲛϩⲏⲧϥ ⲁⲩⲱ ⲅⲉ ⲛⲓⲙ ⲛ
ⲧⲣⲓⲇⲩⲛⲁⲙⲟⲥ ⲁⲩⲱ ⲅⲉⲛⲟⲥ ⲛⲓⲙ
ⲛⲁⲭⲱⲣⲏⲧⲟⲥ ⲁⲩⲱ ⲅⲉⲛⲟⲥ
15. ⲛⲓⲙ ⲛⲁⲡⲉⲣⲁⲛⲧⲟⲥ ⲁⲩⲱ ⲅⲉ
ⲛⲟⲥ ⲛⲓⲙ ⲛⲁϩⲣⲏⲧⲟⲥ ⲁⲩⲱ ⲅⲉ
ⲛⲟⲥ ⲛⲓⲙ ⲛⲥⲓⲅⲏ ⲁⲩⲱ ⲅⲉⲛⲟⲥ
ⲛⲓⲙ ⲛⲁⲅⲛⲱⲥⲧⲟⲥ ⲁⲩⲱ ⲅⲉⲛⲟⲥ
ⲛⲓⲙ ⲛⲏⲣⲉⲙⲓⲟⲥ ⲁⲩⲱ ⲅⲉⲛⲟⲥ
20. ⲛⲓⲙ ⲛⲁⲥⲁⲗⲉⲩⲧⲟⲥ ⲁⲩⲱ ⲅⲉⲛⲟⲥ
ⲛⲓⲙ ⲙⲡⲣⲟⲇⲟⲫⲁⲛⲏⲥ ⲁⲩⲱ ⲅⲉⲛⲟⲥ
ⲛⲓⲙ ⲛⲁⲩⲧⲟⲅⲉⲛⲏⲥ ⲁⲩⲱ ⲅⲉⲛⲟⲥ
ⲛⲓⲙ ⲛⲁⲗⲏⲑⲓⲁ ⲉⲩⲛ ϩⲣⲁⲓ ⲛϩⲏ
ⲧⲩ ⲧⲏⲣⲟⲩ ⲁⲩⲱ ⲡⲁⲓ ⲡⲉ ⲉⲧⲉⲣⲉ
25. ⲅⲉⲛⲟⲥ ⲛⲓⲙ ⲛϩⲏⲧⲩ ⲁⲩⲱ ⲅⲛⲱⲥⲓⲥ
ⲛⲓⲙ ⲁⲩⲱ ⲉⲣⲉ ϭⲟⲙ ⲛⲓⲙ ϫⲓ ⲟⲩ
ⲟⲉⲓⲛ ⲉⲃⲟⲗ ⲛϩⲏⲧⲩ ⲁⲩⲱ ⲛⲧⲁ
ⲛⲟⲩⲥ ⲛⲓⲙ ⲟⲩⲱⲛϩ ⲉⲃⲟⲗ ⲛϩⲏ
ⲧⲩ ⲡⲁⲓ ⲡⲉ ⲡⲉⲕⲗⲟⲙ ⲉⲛⲧⲁ
30. ⲡⲓⲱⲧ ⲛⲛⲓⲡⲧⲏⲣⲩ ⲧⲁⲁⲩ ⲙ
ⲡⲁⲧⲡⲱϣ ⲡⲁⲓ ⲉⲣⲉ ϣⲙⲧϣⲉ
ⲥⲉⲧⲏ ⲛⲅⲉⲛⲟⲥ ⲛϩⲏⲧⲩ ⲁⲩⲱ
ⲉⲩⲃⲟⲩⲃⲟⲩ ⲉⲩⲙⲟⲩϩ ⲙⲡⲧⲏⲣⲩ

1. ⲚⲞⲨⲞⲈⲒⲚ ⲚⲀⲦⲦⲀⲔⲞ ⲀⲨⲱ ⲚⲀⲦⲢⲱ
ⲤⲂ ⲠⲀⲒ ⲠⲈⲔⲖⲞⲙ ⲈⲦⲦ̄ϬⲞⲙ ⲚⲀⲨ
ⲚⲀⲙⲒⲤ ⲚⲒⲙ ⲀⲨⲱ ⲠⲀⲒ ⲠⲈ ⲠⲈⲔⲖⲞⲙ
ⲈⲦⲞⲨⲱⲖⲏⲖ ⲈⲦⲂⲎⲎⲦⲨ ⲚϬⲒ ⲚⲀ
5. ⲐⲀⲚⲀⲦⲞⲤ ⲦⲎⲢⲞⲨ ⲀⲨⲱ ⲈⲂⲞⲖ Ϩⲙ
ⲠⲀⲒ ⲈⲨⲚⲀⲦ̄ ⲙⲠⲀϨⲞⲢⲀⲦⲞⲤ Ⲛ
ϨⲎⲦⲨᵃ ⲙⲠⲈϨⲞⲞⲨ ⲙⲠⲢⲀⲱϢⲈ
ⲚϬⲒ ⲚⲈⲚⲦⲀⲨⲞⲨⲱⲚϨ ⲈⲂⲞⲖ Ⲛ
ϢⲞⲢⲠ ϨⲢⲀⲒ Ϩⲙ ⲠⲈⲐⲈⲖⲏⲙⲀ
10. ⲙⲠⲒⲀⲦⲤⲞⲨⲱⲚⲨ ⲈⲦⲈ ⲦⲀⲒ ⲦⲈ
ⲦⲈⲠⲢⲞⲦⲒⲀ ⲦⲠⲀⲚⲆⲒⲀ ⲦⲠⲀⲚ
ⲄⲈⲚⲒⲀ ⲚⲦⲞⲞⲨ ⲙⲚ ⲚⲈⲦⲚⲙ
ⲙⲀⲨ ⲀⲨⲱ ⲙⲚⲚⲤⲀ ⲠⲀϨⲞⲢⲀⲦⲞⲤ
ⲚⲀⲒⲱⲚ ⲦⲎⲢⲞⲨ ⲚⲀϪ̄Ⲓ ⲠⲈⲨⲔⲖⲞⲙ
15. ⲈⲂⲞⲖ ⲚϨⲎⲦⲨ ⲚⲤⲈⲠⲱⲦ Ⲉ
ϨⲢⲀⲒ ⲙⲚ ⲠⲀϨⲞⲢⲀⲦⲞⲤ ⲈⲨϪⲒ
ⲔⲖⲞⲙ ⲦⲎⲢⲞⲨ ⲙⲙⲀⲨ Ϩⲙ ⲠⲈⲔ
ⲖⲞⲙ ⲙⲠⲀⲦⲠⲱϢ ⲀⲨⲱ ⲠⲦⲎ
ⲢⲨ ⲚⲀϪⲒ ⲙⲠⲈⲨϪⲱⲔ ⲈⲂⲞⲖ Ϩⲙ
20. ⲠⲒⲀⲦⲦⲀⲔⲞ ⲀⲨⲱ ⲈⲦⲂⲈ ⲠⲀⲒ
ⲤⲈⲱϢⲖⲎⲖ ⲚϬⲒ ⲚⲈⲚⲦⲀⲨϪⲒⲤⲱ
ⲙⲀ ⲈⲨⲞⲨⲱϢ ⲈⲔⲀ ⲠⲤⲱⲙⲀ
ⲚⲤⲱⲞⲨ ⲚⲤⲈϪⲒ ⲙⲠⲈⲔⲖⲞⲙ
ⲠⲀⲒ ⲈⲦⲔⲎ ⲚⲀⲨ ⲈϨⲢⲀⲒ Ϩⲙ ⲠⲀⲒ
25. ⲱⲚ ⲚⲀⲦⲦⲀⲔⲞ ⲀⲨⲱ ⲠⲀⲒ ⲠⲈ
ⲠⲀⲦⲠⲱϢ ⲈⲚⲦⲀⲨⲢ ⲠⲀⲄⲱⲚ
ϨⲀ ⲠⲦⲎⲢⲨ ⲀⲨⲱ ⲀⲨⲭⲀⲢⲒⲌⲈ ⲚⲀⲨ
ⲚⲚⲔⲀ ⲚⲒⲙ ϨⲒⲦⲙ ⲠⲈⲦⲞⲦⲂ Ⲉ
ⲚⲔⲀ ⲚⲒⲙ ⲀⲨⲱ ⲀⲨⲭⲀⲢⲒⲌⲈ ⲚⲀⲨ
30. ⲙⲠⲂⲀⲐⲞⲤ ⲚⲀⲙⲈⲦⲢⲎⲦⲞⲚ
ⲠⲀⲒ ⲈⲙⲠⲞⲨϪⲒ ⲎⲠⲈ ⲚⲙⲙⲚⲦ
ⲈⲒⲱⲦ ⲈⲦⲚϨⲎⲦⲨ ⲀⲨⲱ ⲠⲀⲒ Ⲉ
ⲦⲈⲢⲈ ⲦⲈⲨϨⲈⲚⲚⲀⲤ Ⲟ ⲚⲀⲦⲭⲀ
ⲢⲀⲔⲦⲎⲢ ⲀⲨⲱ ⲈⲢⲈ ⲚⲈⲭⲀⲢⲀⲔ
35. ⲦⲎⲢ ⲙⲠⲤⲱⲚⲦ ⲦⲎⲢⲨ ⲚϨⲎⲦⲤ
ⲠⲀⲒ ⲈⲢⲈ ⲦⲈⲨϨⲈⲚⲚⲀⲤ Ⲟ ⲙⲙⲚⲦ

7 α. 3rd pers. sing. pron. in error for 3rd pers. plur.

XXXI
MS. f. 114[R]
C.S. p. 21

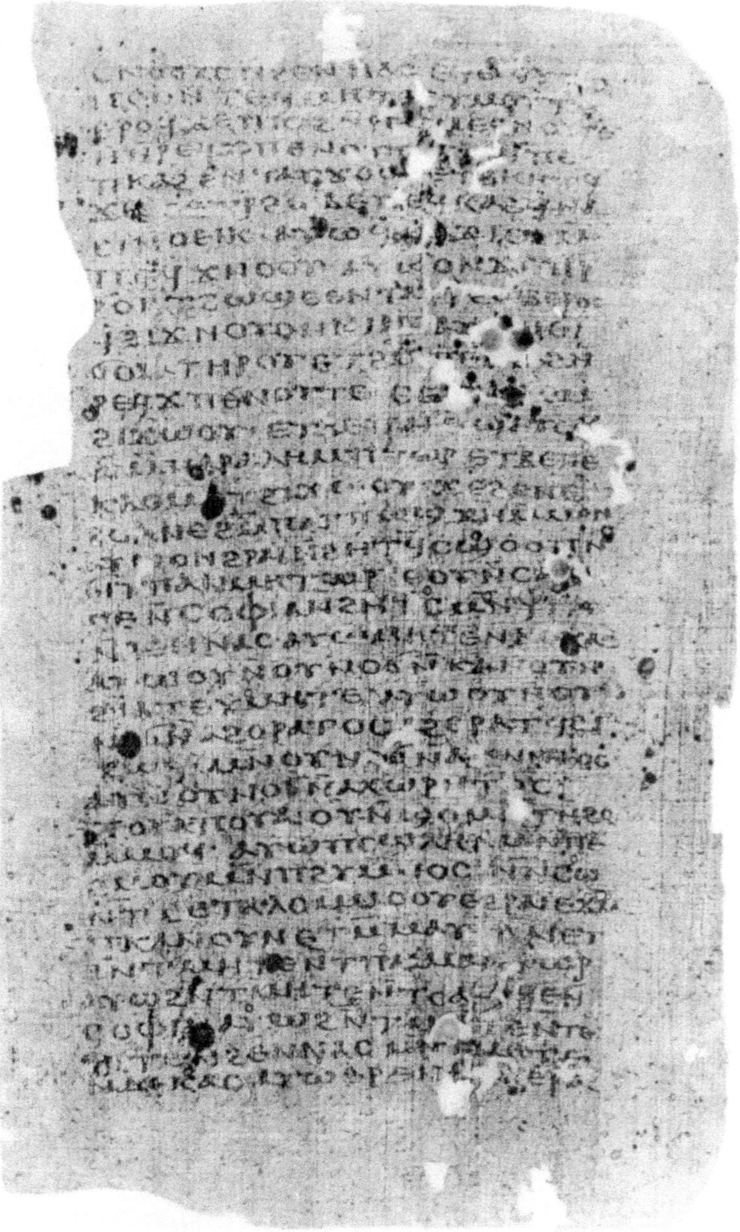

1. ⲤⲚⲞⲞⲨⲤ ⲚϨⲈⲚⲚⲀⲤ ⲈⲢⲈ ⲞⲨⲦⲞ
ⲠⲞⲤ ⲚⲦⲈⳛⲘⲎⲦⲈ ⲈⲨⲘⲞⲨⲦⲈ
ⲈⲢⲞⳙ ⲬⲈ ⲠⲔⲀϨ ⲚⲢⲈⳙⲘⲈⲤ ⲚⲞⲨⲦⲈ
Ⲏ ⲚⲢⲈⳙⲬⲠⲈ ⲚⲞⲨⲦⲈ ⲠⲀⲒ ⲠⲈ

5. ⲠⲔⲀϨ ⲈⲚⲦⲀⲨⳘⲞⲞⲤ ⲈⲦⲂⲎⲎⲦⳙ
ⲬⲈ ⲠⲈⲦⲢϨⲱⲂ ⲈⲠⲈⳙⲔⲀϨ ⳙⲚⲀ
ⲤⲒ ⲚⲞⲈⲒⲔ ⲀⲨⲱ ⳙⲚⲀⳘⲒⲤⲈ Ⲙ
ⲠⲈⳙⳘⲚⲞⲞⲨ ⲀⲨⲱ ⲞⲚ ⲬⲈ ⲠⲢ
ⲢⲞ ⲚⲦⲤⲱ ⲈⲚⲦⲀⲨⲢϨⲱⲂ ⲈⲢⲞⲤ

10. ⳙϨⲒⳘⲚ ⲞⲨⲞⲚ ⲚⲒⳘ ⲀⲨⲱ ⲚⲈⲒ
ϬⲞⳘ ⲦⲎⲢⲞⲨ ⲈⲦϨⳘ ⲠⲈⲒⲔⲀϨ Ⲛ
ⲢⲈⳙⳘⲠⲈ ⲚⲞⲨⲦⲈ ⲤⲈⳘⲒ ⲔⲖⲞⳘ
ϨⲒⳘⲰⲞⲨ ⲈⲦⲂⲈ ⲠⲀⲒ ⲈⳛⲀⲨⲤⲞⲨ
Ⲛ ⳘⲠⲀⲢⲀⲖⲎⳘⲠⲦⲰⲢ ⲈⲦⲂⲈ ⲠⲈ

15. ⲔⲖⲞⳘ ⲈⲦϨⲒⳘⲰⲞⲨ ⲬⲈ ϨⲈⲚⲈ
ⲂⲞⲖ ⲚⲈ ϨⳘ ⲠⲀⲦⲠⲰ ⳘⲚ ⳘⳘⲞⲚ
ⲀⲨⲱ ⲞⲚ ϨⲢⲀⲒ ⲚϨⲎⲦⳙ ⲤⳛⲞⲞⲠ Ⲛ
ϬⲒ ⲦⲠⲀⳘⳘⲎⲦⲰⲢ ⲈⲞⲨⲚ ⲤⲀⳛ
ⳙⲈ ⲚⲤⲞⳎⲒⲀ ⲚϨⲎⲦⲤ ⳘⲚ ⲯⲒⲦⲈ

20. ⲚϨⲈⲚⲚⲀⲤ ⲀⲨⲱ ⳘⲎⲦⲈ ⲚⲆⲈⲔⲀⲤ
ⲀⲨⲱ ⲞⲨⲚ ⲞⲨⲚⲞϬ ⲚⲔⲀⲚⲞⲨⲚ
ϨⲚ ⲦⲈⳙⳘⲎⲦⲈ ⲀⲨⲱ ⲞⲨⲚ ⲞⲨ
ⲚⲞϬ ⲚⲀϨⲞⲢⲀⲦⲞⲤ ⲀϨⲈⲢⲀⲦⳙ ϨⲒ
ⳘⲰⳙ ⳘⲚ ⲞⲨⲚⲞϬ ⲚⲀⲄⲈⲚⲚⲎⲦⲞⲤ

25. ⲀⲨⲱ ⲞⲨⲚⲞϬ ⲚⲀⳘⲰⲢⲎⲦⲞⲤ
ⲠⲞⲨⲀ ⲠⲞⲨⲀ ⲞⲨⲚ ⳛⲞⳘⲚⲦ ⲚϨⲞ
ⳘⲘⲞⲨ ⲀⲨⲱ ⲠⲈⳛⳛⲖⲎⲖ ⳘⲚ ⲠⲈ
ⲤⳘⲞⲨ ⳘⲚ ⲠϨⲨⳘⲚⲞⲤ ⲚⲚⲤⲰ
ⲚⲦ ⲤⲈⲦⲀⲖⲞ ⳘⳘⲞⲞⲨ ⲈϨⲢⲀⲒ ⲈⳘⳘ

30. ⲠⲔⲀⲚⲞⲨⲚ ⲈⲦⳘⳘⲀⲨ ⲠⲀⲒ ⲈⲦ
ϨⲚ ⲦⳘⲎⲦⲈ ⲚⲦⲠⲀⳘⳘⲎⲦⲰⲢ
ⲀⲨⲱ ϨⲚ ⲦⳘⲎⲦⲈ ⲚⲦⲤⲀⳛⳛⲈ Ⲛ
ⲤⲞⳎⲒⲀ ⲀⲨⲱ ϨⲚ ⲦⳘⲎⲦⲈ ⲚⲦⲈ
ⲯⲒⲦⲈ ⲚϨⲈⲚⲚⲀⲤ ⳘⲚ ⲦⳘⲎⲦⲈ

35. ⲚⲆⲈⲔⲀⲤ ⲀⲨⲱ ⲈⲢⲈ ⲚⲀⲒ ⲀϨⲈⲢⲀ

ⲡⲁⲉⲓⲱⲧ ⲉⲓⲭⲁⲡⲓⲙⲟⲩⲱ...
ⲉⲩⲟⲩⲱϣ ⲛ̄ϩⲓⲧⲕ̄...
ⲛ̄ⲙⲟⲟⲩ ⲁⲩⲱ ⲛⲉⲧϩⲟⲣ...
ⲛⲉⲥ...ϯ ⲡⲉⲛⲇⲓ ⲟⲛ ⲟⲩ...
ⲛⲏ ⲣⲟⲥ ⲉ̄ⲧⲁⲡ ⲓⲕ...
ⲡⲁⲓ ⲉ̄ⲩⲟⲩⲟ ⲓ ⲡ̄ϩⲁ...
ⲉ̄ⲟⲧⲁⲙ ⲉⲧⲥ ⲙⲟⲟⲩ ⲥⲛ ⲁⲩ...
ⲧⲉ ⲣⲟⲥ ⲁⲩⲱ ⲉ̄ⲟⲩ ⲛ̄ ⲟⲩⲕ...
ϩⲓ ⲭⲛ̄ ⲡⲉⲓⲙⲁ ⲟⲩⲁ ⲟⲩ...
ⲉⲩ... ...ⲉⲩⲛ ⲟⲟⲩ ⲉ̄ⲛⲁ ⲛⲓ
ⲉ... ...ⲟ̄ϥ ⲉⲩⲕⲱ ⲣⲉⲉⲥ
ⲉⲣⲁ̄ ...ⲁ̄ⲉⲧ ⲟ ⲙⲟⲟ ⲡⲛ̄ ϩⲟⲩ
ⲁ̄ⲓⲱⲛ ⲟ̄ⲅⲉⲛ ⲓⲥ ⲉ̄ⲩⲭⲱ ⲛ̄ⲁ...
ϫⲉ ⲉ̄ⲧⲃ ⲏ ⲏⲧ ⲕ̄ ⲁ̄ ⲛ̄ ⲟⲥ ⲡⲓ ⲁⲩ...
ⲉ̄ⲟⲟⲩ ⲁⲓ ⲱⲉⲣ ⲟⲗ ⲛ̄ ⲡⲟⲓ...
ⲁ̄ⲛ ⲙ̄ⲁⲧⲉ ⲡⲓⲱⲧ ⲁⲓⲧ ⲟⲧ ⲟⲩ ⲣ̄...
ⲓⲱⲥ ⲓⲟ ⲁⲧⲟⲟⲩⲱ̄ⲉⲣ ⲁ̄ϥ ...ⲟ̄ ⲟⲛ
ⲱ̄ ⲓⲁ ...ⲧ ⲁⲓⲉⲧⲟ ⲡⲉ ⲁ ⲙⲱⲛ...
ⲉ̄ⲧⲉ̄ ⲛ̄ⲙ ⲟⲥ ⲧⲉ̄ ⲧⲉ̄ ⲡ̄ ⲛ̄ⲟⲩ
ⲛ̄ⲁⲓⲱ ⲛ̄ ⲛⲓ ⲕ̄ ⲁⲧ ⲟⲛ ⲛⲟⲥ...
ⲧⲉ̄ⲛ ⲛⲟⲓ ⲁⲛ ⲛ̄ⲟⲩ ⲧ ⲉⲛⲓⲥ...
ϫⲉ ⲉ̄ⲃⲟⲗ ϩⲛ̄ ⲓⲁ̄ ⲉ̄ⲱⲛ ⲧⲟⲥ ⲧ
ⲧⲉ̄ ⲣ̄ ⲛⲱⲥⲓⲥ ⲛ̄ⲁ̄ ⲣⲟ ⲣⲁ ⲧ...
ⲁⲓ ...ⲏ ⲗ̄ⲩ ⲛ̄ⲧ ⲉ̄ ⲕ̄ⲉ ⲓ ⲕ̄ ⲱ ⲛ̄ ⲧ
ⲏ̄ⲁⲣ ⲧⲁ ⲁ̄ ⲕ̄ⲩ ⲣⲏ ⲧⲟⲥ ⲛ̄ ⲓⲁ...
ⲉ̄ⲓ ⲡ̄ⲣⲟⲥ ⲉ̄ⲧ ⲟⲟ ⲟⲩ ⲁ ⲧⲉ̄ ⲧⲁ
ⲏ̄ ⲧⲁⲉⲛ ⲓ̄ⲁⲡ ⲁ̄ ⲛ̄ ⲟ̄ ⲱ̄ ⲉⲩ ⲁⲩ ⲧ ⲉ̄
ⲛⲟⲥ ...ⲥⲉⲃ ⲏ̄ ⲥ ⲉⲩ ⲁ̄ⲱ ...ⲧ ⲟⲛ
ϫⲉ ⲉ̄ⲛⲁ ⲣⲉⲓ ⲉ̄ⲓ ⲕ̄ ⲓ̄ ⲱ ⲛ̄ ⲁ̄ ⲛ̄ ⲏ̄
ⲉ̄ ⲟ̄ ⲕ̄ ⲁⲛ ⲧ ⲟⲥ ⲧⲉ̄ ⲣ ⲙ̄ⲓ ⲁⲛ ⲁ̄
ⲣⲁ̄ ⲛ̄ ⲏⲉⲓⲧⲕ̄ ⲁⲧⲟⲟ ⲩ ⲁⲓⲭⲓⲛⲓ...
ⲛ̄ⲁ ⲓ̄ ⲟ ⲟ̄ ⲓ̄ⲧⲕ̄ ⲁ̄
ⲧⲁⲥ ⲟⲩ... ⲛ̄ ⲩ̄ ⲉ̄ ⲟ̄ ⲗ̄ ⲁ ⲟⲟⲩ...
ⲩ̄ⲉⲥ ⲓⲱ ...ⲛ̄ ⲧⲁ ϣ̄ ⲓ ⲏ̄ ...
ⲣⲟⲥ ...ϩ̄ ...ⲕ̄ ⲥ ⲓ̄ⲟ ⲓ̄ⲥ ⲟ̄ ⲧ ⲟⲩ̄...

1. ⲧⲟⲩ ⲧⲏⲣⲟⲩ ϩⲓⲭⲙ ⲡⲕⲁⲛⲟⲩⲛ
   ⲉⲩϫⲱⲕ ⲉⲃⲟⲗ ϩⲙ ⲡⲕⲁⲣⲡⲟⲥ
   ⲛⲛⲁⲓⲱⲛ ⲡⲁⲓ ⲉⲧⲩⲟⲩⲉϩⲥⲁϩ
   ⲛⲉ ⲙⲙⲟⲩ ⲛⲁⲩ ⲛϭⲓ ⲡⲙⲟⲛⲟⲅⲉ
5. ⲛⲏⲥ ⲉⲑⲏⲡ ϩⲙ ⲡⲁⲧⲡⲱϣ
   ⲡⲁⲓ ⲉⲟⲩⲛ ⲟⲩⲡⲏⲅⲏ ϩⲓϩⲏ ⲙⲙⲟⲩ
   ⲉⲟⲩⲛ ⲙⲛⲧⲥⲛⲟⲟⲩⲥ ⲛⲭⲣ̅ⲥ̅ ⲕⲱ
   ⲧⲉ ⲉⲣⲟⲥ ⲁⲩⲱ ⲉⲟⲩⲛ ⲟⲩⲕⲗⲟⲙ
   ϩⲓϫⲛ ⲧⲁⲡⲉ ⲙⲡⲟⲩⲁ ⲡⲟⲩⲁ
10. ⲉⲩⲛ ⲙⲛⲧⲥⲛⲟⲟⲩⲥ ⲛⲁⲩⲛⲁ
    ⲙⲓⲥ ⲙⲙⲟⲩ ⲉⲩⲕⲱⲧⲉ ⲉϩⲟⲩⲛ
    ⲉⲣⲟⲩ ⲁⲩⲱ ⲉⲩⲥⲙⲟⲩ ⲉⲡⲣⲣⲟ
    ⲡⲙⲟⲛⲟⲅⲉⲛⲏⲥ ⲉⲩϫⲱ ⲙⲙⲟⲥ
    ϫⲉ ⲉⲧⲃⲏⲏⲧⲕ ⲁⲛⲯⲟⲣⲓ ⲙⲡⲓ
15. ⲉⲟⲟⲩ ⲁⲩⲱ ⲉⲃⲟⲗ ϩⲓⲧⲟⲟⲧⲕ
    ⲁⲛⲛⲁⲩ ⲉⲡⲓⲱⲧ ⲙⲡⲧⲏⲣϥ ⲁⲗⲗ
    ⲱ ⲱ ⲱ ⲁⲩⲱ ⲧⲙⲁⲁⲩ ⲛⲛⲕⲁ
    ⲛⲓⲙ ⲧⲁⲓ ⲉⲧϩⲏⲡ ϩⲙ ⲙⲁ ⲛⲓⲙ
    ⲉⲧⲉ ⲛⲧⲟⲥ ⲧⲉ ⲧⲉⲡⲓⲛⲟⲓⲁ ⲛ
20. ⲛⲁⲓⲱⲛ ⲛⲓⲙ ⲁⲩⲱ ⲛⲧⲟⲥ ⲧⲉ
    ⲧⲉⲛⲛⲟⲓⲁ ⲛⲛⲟⲩⲧⲉ ⲛⲓⲙ ⲙⲛ
    ϫⲟⲉⲓⲥ ⲛⲓⲙ ⲁⲩⲱ ⲛⲧⲟⲥ ⲧⲉ
    ⲧⲉⲅⲛⲱⲥⲓⲥ ⲛⲁϩⲟⲣⲁⲧⲟⲥ
    ⲛⲓⲙ ⲁⲩⲱ ⲧⲉⲕϩⲓⲕⲱⲛ ⲧⲉ ⲧ
25. ⲙⲁⲁⲩ ⲛⲁⲭⲱⲣⲏⲧⲟⲥ ⲛⲓⲙ ⲁⲩ
    ⲱ ⲛⲧⲟⲥ ⲧⲉ ⲧϭⲟⲙ ⲛⲁⲡⲉⲣⲁⲛ
    ⲧⲟⲥ ⲛⲓⲙ ⲁⲩⲱ ⲉⲩⲥⲙⲟⲩ ⲉⲡ
    ⲙⲟⲛⲟⲅⲉⲛⲏⲥ ⲉⲩϫⲱ ⲙⲙⲟⲥ
    ϫⲉ ⲉⲧⲃⲉ ⲧⲉⲕϩⲓⲕⲱⲛ ⲁⲛⲛⲁⲩ
30. ⲉⲣⲟⲕ ⲁⲛⲡⲱⲧ ⲉⲣⲁⲧⲕ ⲁⲛⲁϩⲉ
    ⲣⲁⲧⲛ ⲛϩⲏⲧⲕ ⲁⲩⲱ ⲁⲛϫⲓ ⲙ
    ⲡⲉⲕⲗⲟⲙ ⲛⲁⲧϩⲱϭⲃ ⲡⲁⲓ ⲉⲛ
    ⲧⲁⲩⲥⲟⲩⲱⲛϥ ⲉⲃⲟⲗ ϩⲓⲧⲟⲟⲧⲕ
    ⲡⲉⲟⲟⲩ ⲛⲁⲕ ⲡⲙⲟⲛⲟⲅⲉⲛⲏⲥ
35. ⲛϣⲁⲉⲛⲉϩ ⲁⲩⲱ ⲁⲩϫⲱ ⲧⲏ
    ⲣⲟⲩ ⲙⲯⲁⲙⲏⲛ ϩⲓ ⲟⲩⲥⲟⲡ

1. ⲀⲨⲰ ⲀⲨⲢ ⲞⲨⲤⲰⲘⲀ ⲚⲞⲨⲞⲈⲒⲚ ⲀⲨ
ⲬⲰⲦⲈ ⳩Ⲛ ⲚⲀⲒⲰⲚ ⲘⲠⲀⲦⲠⲰⳡ
ⳡⲀⲚⲦⲨⲠⲰ⳩ Ⲉ⳩ⲞⲨⲚ ⲈⲠⲘⲞⲚⲞ
ⲄⲈⲚⲎⲤ ⲈⲦ⳩Ⲛ ⲦⲘⲞⲚⲀⲤ ⲠⲀⲒ

5. ⲈⲦ6ⲈⲈⲦ ⳩Ⲛ ⲞⲨ⳩ⲨⲤⲨⲬⲒⲀ Ⲏ
⳩Ⲛ ⲞⲨⲎⲢⲈⲘⲞⲤ ⲀⲨⲰ ͣⲀⲨⲬⲒ Ⲛ
ⲦⲈⲬⲀⲢⲒⲤ ⲘⲠⲘⲞⲚⲞⲄⲈⲚⲎⲤ
ⲈⲦⲈ ⲠⲀⲒ ⲠⲈ ⲚⲦⲈⲨⲘⲚⲦⲬⲢⲤ
ⲀⲨⲰ ⲀⲨⲬⲒ ⲘⲠⲈⲔⲖⲞⲘ ⲚⳡⲀⲈⲚⲈ⳩

10. ⲠⲀⲒ ⲠⲈ ⲠⲒⲰⲦ ⲚⲚⲈⲤⲠⲒⲚⲐⲎⲢ
ⲦⲎⲢⲞⲨ ⲀⲨⲰ ⲠⲀⲒ ⲠⲈ ⲦⲀⲠⲈ Ⲛ
ⲤⲰⲘⲀ ⲚⲒⲘ ⲚⲀⲐⲀⲚⲀⲦⲞⲤ ⲀⲨ
Ⲱ ⲠⲀⲒ ⲠⲈ ⲈⲚⲦⲀⲨ†ⲀⲚⲀⲤⲦⲀⲤⲒⲤ
ⲚⲚⲤⲰⲘⲀ ⲈⲦⲂⲎⲎⲦⲨ ⳩ⲒⲂⲞⲖ

15. ⲆⲈ ⲘⲠⲀⲦⲠⲰⳡ ⲀⲨⲰ ⳩ⲒⲂⲞⲖ Ⲛ
ⲦⲈⲨ⳩ⲈⲚⲚⲀⲤ ⲚⲀⲦⲬⲀⲢⲀⲔⲦⲎⲢ
ⲦⲀⲒ ⲈⲦⲈⲢⲈ ⲚⲈⲬⲀⲢⲀⲔⲦⲎⲢ ⲦⲎ
ⲢⲞⲨ Ⲛ⳩ⲎⲦⲤ ⲞⲨⲚ ⲔⲈⳡⲞⲘⲦⲈ
Ⲛ⳩ⲈⲚⲚⲀⲤ ⲈⲢⲈ ⲦⲞⲨⲈⲒ ⲦⲞⲨⲈⲒ

20. ⲈⲒⲢⲈ Ⲙⳡ̈ⲒⲦⲈ Ⲛ⳩ⲈⲚⲚⲀⲤ ⲀⲨⲰ
ⲦⲞⲨⲈⲒ ⲦⲞⲨⲈⲒ ⲞⲨⲚ ⲞⲨⲔⲀⲚⲞⲨⲚ
Ⲛ⳩ⲎⲦⲤ ⲈⲨⲤⲞⲞⲨ⳩ ⲈⲢⲞⲨ Ⲛ6Ⲓ
ⳡⲞⲘⲚⲦ ⲚⲈⲒⲰⲦ ⲞⲨⲀⲠⲈⲢⲀⲚ
ⲦⲞⲤ ⲘⲚ ⲞⲨⲀ⳩ⲢⲎⲦⲞⲤ ⲘⲚ ⲞⲨ

25. ⲀⲬⲰⲢⲎⲦⲞⲤ ⲀⲨⲰ ⳩ⲢⲀⲒ ⳩Ⲛ ⲦⲘⲈ⳩
ⲤⲚⲦⲈ ⲞⲨⲚ ⲞⲨⲔⲀⲚⲞⲨⲚ ⳩Ⲛ ⲦⲈⲤ
ⲘⲎⲦⲈ ⲈⲨⲚ ⳡⲞⲘⲦⲈ ⲘⲘⲚⲦⲈⲒ
ⲰⲦ Ⲛ⳩ⲎⲦⲤ ⲞⲨⲀ⳩ⲞⲢⲀⲦⲞⲤ ⲘⲚ
ⲞⲨⲀⲄⲈ́ⲚⲚⲎⲦⲞⲤ ⲘⲚ ⲞⲨⲀⲤⲀ

30. ⲖⲈⲨⲦⲞⲤ ⳩ⲢⲀⲒ ⲞⲚ ⳩Ⲛ ⲦⲘⲈ⳩ⳡⲞⲘ
ⲦⲈ ⲞⲨⲚ ⲞⲨⲔⲀⲚⲞⲨⲚ Ⲛ⳩ⲎⲦⲤ
ⲞⲨⲚ ⳡⲞⲘⲦⲈ ⲘⲘⲚⲦⲈⲒⲰⲦ Ⲛ
⳩ⲎⲦⲤ ⲞⲨⲎⲢⲈⲘⲞⲤ ⲘⲚ ⲞⲨⲀⲄ
ⲚⲰⲤⲦⲞⲤ ⲘⲚ ⲞⲨⲦⲢⲒⲆⲨⲚⲀ

35. ⲘⲞⲤ ⲀⲨⲰ ⲈⲂⲞⲖ ⳩ⲒⲦⲚ ⲚⲀⲒ ⲈⲚ
ⲦⲀ ⲠⲦⲎⲢⲨ ⲤⲞⲨⲚ ⲠⲚⲞⲨⲦⲈ

---

6 α. 3rd pers. plur. pron. in error for 3rd pers. sing.

1. ⲁⲩⲱ ⲁⲩⲡⲱⲧ ⲉⲣⲁⲧⲩ ⲁⲩⲱ ⲁⲩⲭⲡⲟ
ⲛⲟⲩⲙⲏⲏϣⲉ ⲛⲛⲁⲓⲱⲛ ⲛⲁⲧ⳨(ⲏ)
ⲡⲉ ⲉⲣⲟⲟⲩ ⲁⲩⲱ ⲕⲁⲧⲁ ⲑⲉⲛⲛⲁⲥ
ⲑⲉⲛⲛⲁⲥ ⲥⲉⲉⲓⲣⲉ ⲛϩⲉⲛⲧⲃⲁ ⲛ[ⲧ]ⲃⲁ

5. ⲛⲉⲟⲟⲩ ⲁⲩⲱ ⲟⲩⲛⲧⲉ ⲧⲟⲩⲉⲓ ⲧⲟⲩⲓ
ⲛⲛⲉⲓϩⲉⲛⲛⲁⲥ ⲟⲩⲙⲟⲛⲁⲥ ϩⲣⲁⲓ
ⲛϩⲏⲧⲥ ⲁⲩⲱ ⲟⲩⲛ ⲟⲩⲧⲟⲡⲟⲥ
ϩⲛ ⲧⲙⲟⲛⲁⲥ ⲧⲙⲟⲛⲁⲥ ⲉⲩⲙⲟⲩ
ⲧⲉ ⲉⲣⲟⲩ ϫⲉ ⲁⲫⲑⲁⲣⲧⲟⲥ ⲉⲧⲉ

10. ⲡⲁⲓ ⲡⲉ ⲡⲕⲁϩ ⲉⲧⲟⲩⲁⲁⲃ ⲟⲩⲛ ⲟⲩ
ⲡⲏⲅⲏ ϩⲙ ⲡⲕⲁϩ ⲛⲧⲟⲩⲓ ⲧⲟⲩⲓ
ⲛⲛⲉⲓⲙⲟⲛⲁⲥ ⲉⲟⲩⲛ ϩⲉⲛⲧⲃⲁ
ⲛⲧⲃⲁ ⲛⲁⲩⲛⲁⲙⲓⲥ ⲉⲩϫⲓ ⲕⲗⲟⲙ
ϩⲓϫⲱⲥ ϩⲙ ⲡⲉⲕⲗⲟⲙ ⲙⲡⲉⲧⲣⲓ

15. ⲇⲩⲛⲁⲙⲟⲥ ⲁⲩⲱ ϩⲛ ⲧⲙⲏⲧⲉ
ⲛⲛϩⲉⲛⲛⲁⲥ ⲁⲩⲱ ϩⲛ ⲧⲙⲏⲧⲉ
ⲛⲙⲙⲟⲛⲁⲥ ϥϣⲟⲟⲡ ⲛϭⲓ ⲡⲃⲁ
ⲑⲟⲥ ⲛⲁⲙⲉⲧⲣⲏⲧⲟⲛ ⲉⲣⲉ ⲡⲓ
ⲡⲧⲏⲣϥ ϭⲱϣⲧ ⲉϩⲣⲁⲓ ⲉϫⲱⲩ

20. ⲛⲁⲡϩⲟⲩⲛ ⲙⲛⲛⲁⲡⲃⲟⲗ ⲉⲩⲛ
ⲙⲛⲧⲥⲛⲟⲟⲩⲥ ⲙⲙⲛⲧⲉⲓⲱⲧ
ϩⲓϫⲱⲩ ⲉⲩⲛⲙⲁⲁⲃⲉ ⲛⲁⲩⲛⲁ
ⲙⲓⲥ ⲕⲱⲧⲉ ⲉⲡⲟⲩⲁ ⲡⲟⲩⲁ

ⲁ ⲧϣⲟⲣⲡ ⲙⲙⲛⲧⲉⲓⲱⲧ ⲟⲩϩⲟ

25. ⲛⲁⲡⲉⲣⲁⲛⲧⲟⲥ ⲡⲉ ⲉⲟⲩⲛ ⲙⲁ
ⲁⲃⲉ ⲛⲁⲩⲛⲁⲙⲓⲥ ⲕⲱⲧⲉ ⲉⲣⲟⲩ

ⲃ ⲉⲩⲟ ⲛⲁⲡⲉⲣⲁⲛⲧⲟⲥ ⲧⲙⲉϩⲥⲛ
ⲧⲉ ⲙⲙⲛⲧⲉⲓⲱⲧ ⲟⲩϩⲟ ⲛⲁ
ϩⲟⲣⲁⲧⲟⲥ ⲡⲉ ⲁⲩⲱ ⲟⲩⲛ ⲙⲁⲁⲃ

ⲅ 30. ⲛⲁϩⲟⲣⲁⲧⲟⲥ ⲕⲱⲧⲉ ⲉⲣⲟⲩ ⲧ
ⲙⲉϩϣⲟⲙⲧⲉ ⲙⲙⲛⲧⲉⲓⲱⲧ
ⲟⲩϩⲟ ⲛⲁⲭⲱⲣⲏⲧⲟⲥ ⲡⲉ ⲁⲩ
ⲱ ⲟⲩⲛ ⲙⲁⲁⲃ ⲛⲁⲭⲱⲣⲏⲧⲟⲥ

ⲇ ⲕⲱⲧⲉ ⲉⲣⲟⲩ ⲁⲩⲱ ⲧⲙⲉϩ

35. ϥⲧⲟ ⲙⲙⲛⲧⲉⲓⲱⲧ ⲟⲩϩⲟ ⲛ
ⲁϩⲟⲣⲁⲧⲟⲥˢ ⲡⲉ ⲟⲩⲛ ⲙⲁⲁⲃ ⲛ
ⲇⲩⲛⲁⲙⲓⲥ ⲛⲁϩⲟⲣⲁⲧⲟⲥ ⲕⲱⲧⲉ

ⲉ ⲉⲣⲟⲩ ⲧⲙⲉϩϯⲉ ⲙⲙⲛⲧⲉⲓⲱⲧ

14 α. 3rd pers. sing. pron. in error for 3rd pers. plur.
36 α. ⲁϩⲟⲣⲁⲧⲟⲥ having been already used in the
category (line 29), it is probable that ⲁϩⲣⲏⲧⲟⲥ is intended.

N.B.

The originals of the next seven pages were no longer to be found when Dr Schmidt copied the text in 1890. He therefore compared and emended the transcripts of C. G. Woide and M. G. Schwartze. The resultant text is reproduced here. The marginal letter and numerals, e.g. W. p. 97—have reference to hand-written numbers on the pages of Woide's copy (Woide MS. Clar. Press, d. 13). Fortunately there is no break in the continuity of the discourse.

1. ОΥ2О ΜΠΑΝΤΟΔΥΝΑΜΟС ΠЄ
ΑΥШ ОΥΝ ΜΑΑΒ ΜΠΑΝΤΟΔΥΝΑ
Ꞓ ΜОС ΚШΤЄ ЄРОΥ ΤΜЄ2СО Μ
ΜΝΤЄΙШΤ ОΥ2О ΝΠΑΝСОФОС
5. ΠЄ ЄΥΝ ΜΑΑΒ ΝΠΑΝСОФОС
Ʒ̄ ΚШΤЄ ЄРОΥ ΤΜЄ2САШЧЄ
ΜΝΤЄΙШΤ ОΥ2О ΝΑΓΝШСТОС
ΠЄ ЄΥΝ ΜΑΑΒ ΝΔΥΝΑΜΙС Ν
H̄ ΑΓΝШСТОС ΚШΤЄ ЄРОΥ ΤΜЄ2
10. ШΜОΥΝЄ ΜΜΝΤЄΙШΤ ОΥ2О Ν
ΗΡЄΜΙО ΠЄ ΑΥШ ОΥΝ ΜΑΑΒ Ν
ΔΥΝΑΜΙС ΝΗΡЄΜΙОС ΚШΤЄ Є
Θ̄ РОΥ ΤΜЄΨΙΤЄ ΜΜΝΤЄΙШΤ
ОΥ2О ΝΑΓЄΝΝΗΤОС ΠЄ ΑΥШ
15. ОΥΝ ΜΑΑΒ ΝΔΥΝΑΜΙС ΝΑΓЄΝ
Ⲧ̄ ΝΗΤОС ΚШΤЄ ЄРОΥ ΤΜЄ2ΜΗΤЄ
ΜΜΝΤЄΙШΤ ОΥ2О ΝΑСΑΛЄΥΤОС
ΠЄ ЄΥΝ ΜΑΑΒ ΝΔΥΝΑΜΙС
ΝΑСΑΛЄΥΤОС ΚШΤЄ ЄРОΥ
Ⲓ̄Ⲁ 20. ΤΜЄ2ΜΝΤОΥЄ ΜΜΝΤЄΙШΤ
ОΥ2О ΜΠΑΝΜΥСΤΗΡΙОΝ ΠЄ
ΑΥШ ОΥΝ ΜΑΑΒ ΝΔΥΝΑΜΙС Μ
ΠΑΝΜΥСΤΗΡΙОΝ ΚШΤЄ ЄРОΥ
Ⲓ̄Ⲃ ΤΜЄ2ΜΝΤ СΝООΥС ΜΜΝΤ
25. ЄΙШΤ ОΥ2О ΝΤΡΙΔΥΝΑΜОС
ΠЄ ΑΥШ ОΥΝ ΜΑΑΒ ΝΔΥΝΑ
ΜΙС ΝΤΡΙΔΥΝΑΜОС ΚШΤЄ
ЄРОΥ ΑΥШ 2Ν ΤΜΗΤЄ ΜΠΒΑ
Ⲉ̄ ΘОС ΝΑΜЄΤΡΗΤОС ОΥΝ Ⲧ̄(Є)
30. ΝΔΥΝΑΜΙС ЄΥΜОΥΤЄ ЄРОС
[Ⲁ̄] ΝΝЄΙΡΑΝ ΝΑ2РΗΤОΝ ΤШОРΠ
ЄΥΜОΥΤЄ ЄРОС ХЄ ΤΑΓΑΠΗ
ЄΝΤΑ ΑΓΑΠΗ ΝΙΜ ЄΙ ЄΒОΛ Ν2Η
Ⲃ̄ ΤС ΤΜЄ2СΝΤЄ ХЄ ΘЄΛΠΙС
35. ЄΒОΛ 2ΙΤООΤС ЄΝΤΑΥ2ЄΛΠΙZЄ

Γ̄ 1 ⲉⲡⲙⲟⲛⲟⲅⲉⲛⲏⲥ ⲛ̄ϣⲏⲣⲉ ⲛ̄
ⲧⲉ ⲡⲛⲟⲩⲧⲉ ⲧⲙⲉϩϣⲟⲩⲧⲉ
ⲥⲉⲙⲟⲩⲧⲉ ⲉⲣⲟⲥ ϫⲉ ⲡⲓⲥⲧⲓⲥ
ⲧⲁⲓ ⲉⲃⲟⲗ ϩⲓⲧⲟⲟⲧⲥ ⲉⲛⲧⲁⲩⲡⲓⲥ

Δ̄ 5. ⲧⲉⲩⲉ ⲉⲙⲙⲩⲥⲧⲏⲣⲓⲟⲛ ⲙ̄ⲡⲓⲁⲧ
ϣⲁϫⲉ ⲉⲣⲟⲩ ⲧⲙⲉϩⲩⲧⲟ ⲉⲩⲙⲟⲩ
ⲧⲉ ⲉⲣⲟⲥ ϫⲉ ⲧⲉⲅⲛⲱⲥⲓⲥ ⲉⲃⲟⲗ
ϩⲓⲧⲟⲟⲧⲥ ⲁⲩⲥⲟⲩⲛ ⲡϣⲟⲣⲡ ⲛⲉⲓ
ⲱⲧ ⲡⲁⲓ ⲉⲧⲟⲩϣⲟⲟⲡ ⲉⲧⲃⲏⲧⲩ

10. ⲁⲩⲱ ⲁⲩⲥⲟⲩⲛ ⲡⲙⲩⲥⲧⲏⲣⲓⲟⲛ
ⲙ̄ⲡⲕⲁⲣⲱⲩ ⲡⲁⲓ ⲉⲧϣⲁϫⲉ ϩⲁ
ϩⲱⲃ ⲛⲓⲙ ⲡⲁⲓ ⲉⲑⲏⲡ ⲧⲙⲟ
ⲛⲁⲥ ⲛ̄ϩⲟⲩⲉⲓⲧⲉ ⲧⲁⲓ ⲉⲛⲧⲁ
ⲡⲧⲏⲣⲩ ⲣ ⲁⲛⲟⲩⲥⲓⲟⲥ ⲉⲧⲃⲏⲧⲥ

ⲦϪⲈ 15. ⲡⲁⲓ ⲡⲉ ⲡⲙⲩⲥⲧⲏⲣⲓⲟⲛ ⲉⲧⲉⲣⲉ
ⲡϣⲙⲧϣⲉ ⲥⲉⲧⲏ ⲛⲟⲩⲥⲓⲁ ⲟ ⲛ̄
ⲕⲗⲟⲙ ϩⲓϫⲛ ⲧⲉⲩⲁⲡⲉ ⲛⲑⲉ ⲙ̄
ⲡ̄ϣⲱ ⲛⲟⲩⲣⲱⲙⲉ ⲁⲩⲱ ⲉⲣⲉ ⲫⲓ
ⲉⲣⲟⲛ ⲙ̄ⲡⲗⲏⲣⲱⲙⲁ ⲟ ⲛⲑⲉ ⲛ̄

20. ⲛⲉⲓϩⲩⲡⲟⲡⲟⲇⲓⲟⲛ ϩⲁ ⲛⲉⲩⲟⲩⲉ
ⲣⲏⲧⲉ ⲡⲁⲓ ⲡⲉ ⲡⲣⲟ ⲙ̄ⲡⲛⲟⲩⲧⲉ·
Ē ⲧⲙⲉϩⲧⲉ ⲥⲉⲙⲟⲩⲧⲉ ⲉⲣⲟⲥ ϫⲉ
ϯⲣⲏⲛⲏ ⲉⲃⲟⲗ ϩⲓⲧⲟⲟⲧⲥ ⲁⲩϯ ⲛ̄
ϯⲣⲏⲛⲏ ⲛⲟⲩⲟⲛ ⲛⲓⲙ ⲛ̄ⲛⲁⲡϩⲟⲩⲛ

25. ⲙⲛ ⲛⲁⲡⲃⲟⲗ ϫⲉ ϩⲣⲁⲓ ⲛ̄ϩⲏⲧⲥ
ⲁⲩⲥⲱⲛⲧ ⲙ̄ⲡⲧⲏⲣⲩ ⲡⲁⲓ ⲡⲉ
ⲡⲃⲁⲑⲟⲥ ⲛⲁⲙⲉⲧⲣⲏⲧⲟⲛ ⲡⲁⲓ ⲡⲉ
ⲉⲧⲉⲣⲉ ⲡϣⲙⲧϣⲉ ⲥⲉⲧⲏ ⲙ̄
ⲙⲛ̄ⲧⲉⲓⲱⲧ ⲛ̄ϩⲏⲧⲩ ⲁⲩⲱ ⲉⲛⲧⲁⲩ

30. ⲡⲱϣ ⲛ̄ⲧⲉⲣⲟⲩⲡⲉ ϩⲓⲧⲛ ⲛⲁⲓ
ⲡⲁⲓ ⲡⲉ ⲡⲃⲁⲑⲟⲥ ⲉⲧⲕⲱⲧⲉ ϩⲓⲃⲟⲗ
ⲙ̄ⲫⲓⲉⲣⲟⲛ ⲙ̄ⲡⲗⲏⲣⲱⲙⲁ ⲡⲁⲓ ⲡⲉ
ⲉⲧⲉⲣⲉ ⲡⲉⲧⲣⲓⲇⲩⲛⲁⲙⲟⲥ ϩⲓϫⲱⲩ
ⲙⲛ ⲛⲉⲩⲕⲗⲁⲇⲟⲥ ⲛⲑⲉ ⲛ̄ⲛⲉⲓ

35. ϣⲏⲛ ⲁⲩⲱ ⲡⲁⲓ ⲡⲉ ⲉⲧⲉⲣⲉ ⲡⲙⲟⲩ
ⲥⲁⲛⲓⲟⲥ ϩⲓϫⲱⲩ ⲙⲛ ⲛⲉⲧⲉ ⲛⲟⲩⲩ
ⲧⲏⲣⲟⲩ ⲛⲉ ⲁⲩⲱ ⲉⲣⲉ ⲁⲯⲣⲏⲇⲱⲛ

1. ⲙⲙⲁⲩ ⲙⲛ ⲡⲉϥⲙⲛⲧⲥⲛⲟⲟⲩⲥ
ⲛⲭⲣⲥ ⲉⲣⲉ ⲟⲩⲕⲁⲛⲟⲩⲛ ϩⲛ ⲧⲉⲩ
ⲙⲏⲏⲧⲉ ⲉⲩⲉⲓⲛⲉ ⲉϩⲟⲩⲛ ⲛⲛⲉⲥ
ⲙⲟⲩ ⲙⲛ ⲛϩⲩⲙⲛⲟⲥ ⲁⲩⲱ ⲛⲥⲟ

5. ⲡⲥ ⲙⲛ ⲛⲉϣⲗⲏⲗ ⲛⲧⲙⲁⲁⲩ ⲛ
ⲛϩⲟⲗⲟⲛ ⲏ ⲧⲙⲁⲁⲩ ⲙⲡⲧⲏⲣϥ
ⲉⲧⲉ ⲧⲁⲓ ⲧⲉ ⲉⲧⲟⲩⲙⲟⲩⲧⲉ ⲉⲣⲟⲥ
ⲭⲉ ⲫⲁⲛⲉⲣⲓⲟⲥ ⲁⲩⲱ ⲛⲥⲉⲧⲙⲟⲣ
ⲫⲏ ⲉⲣⲟⲟⲩ ϩⲓⲧⲙ ⲡⲙⲛⲧⲥⲛⲟⲟⲩⲥ

10. ⲛⲭⲣⲏⲥⲧⲟⲥ ⲥⲉⲭⲟⲟⲩ ⲙⲙⲟⲟⲩ
ⲉϩⲣⲁⲓ ⲉⲡⲉⲡⲗⲏⲣⲱⲙⲁ ⲛⲥⲏⲑⲉⲩⲥ
ⲉⲃⲟⲗ ϩⲓⲧⲟⲟⲧϥ ⲥⲉⲉⲓⲣⲉ ⲙⲡⲙⲉ
ⲉⲩⲉ ⲛⲛⲁⲓ ϩⲙ ⲡⲁⲓⲱⲛ ⲉⲧϩⲓⲃⲟⲗ
ⲡⲁⲓ ⲉⲧⲉ ⲧϩⲩⲗⲏ ⲛϩⲏⲧϥ ⲡⲁⲓ

15. ⲡⲉ ⲡⲃⲁⲑⲟⲥ ⲉⲛⲧⲁ ⲡⲉⲧⲣⲓⲇⲩⲛⲁ
ⲙⲟⲥ ⲭⲓ ⲉⲟⲟⲩ ⲙⲙⲟϥ ϣⲁⲛⲧϥ
ⲡⲱϩ ⲉⲡⲁⲧⲡⲱϣ ⲁⲩⲱ ⲁϥⲭⲓ
ⲛⲧⲉⲭⲁⲣⲓⲥ ⲙⲡⲓⲁⲧⲥⲟⲩⲱⲛϥ
ⲧⲁⲓ ⲉⲃⲟⲗ ϩⲓⲧⲟⲟⲧⲥ ⲁⲩⲭⲓ ⲛϯ

20. ⲙⲛⲧϣⲏⲣⲉ ⲛⲧⲉⲓϭⲟⲧ ⲧⲁⲓ ⲉ
ⲧⲉ ⲙⲡⲉ ⲡⲉⲡⲗⲏⲣⲱⲙⲁ ⲉϣ
ϭⲙϭⲟⲙ ⲉⲧⲱⲟⲩⲛ ϩⲁⲣⲟⲥ ⲉⲧⲃⲉ
ⲡⲉϩⲟⲩⲟ ⲙⲡⲉⲥⲟⲩⲟⲉⲓⲛ ⲁⲩⲱ
ⲡⲃⲟⲩⲃⲟⲩ ⲉⲧⲛϩⲏⲧⲩ ⲁⲩⲱ ⲁ

25. ⲡⲉⲡⲗⲏⲣⲱⲙⲁ ⲧⲏⲣϥ ϣⲧⲟⲣⲧⲣ
ⲁⲩⲱ ⲡⲃⲁⲑⲟⲥ ⲕⲓⲙ ⲙⲛ ⲛⲉ
ⲧⲛϩⲏⲧϥ ⲧⲏⲣⲟⲩ ⲁⲩⲱ ⲁⲩ
ⲡⲱⲧ ⲉⲃⲟⲗ ⲉⲡⲁⲓⲱⲛ ⲛⲧⲙⲁⲩ
ⲁⲩⲱ ⲁϥⲕⲉⲗⲉⲩⲉ ⲛϭⲓ ⲡⲙⲩⲥ

30. ⲧⲏⲣⲓⲟⲛ ⲉⲧⲣⲉⲩⲥⲱⲕ ⲛⲛ
ⲕⲁⲧⲁⲡⲉⲧⲁⲥⲙⲁ ⲛⲛⲁⲓⲱⲛ
ϣⲁⲛⲧⲉ ⲡⲉⲡⲓⲥⲕⲟⲡⲟⲥ ⲧⲁⲭⲣⲉ
ⲛⲁⲓⲱⲛ ⲛⲕⲉⲥⲟⲡ ⲁⲩⲱ ⲁⲡⲉ
ⲡⲓⲥⲕⲟⲡⲟⲥ ⲧⲁⲭⲣⲉ ⲛⲁⲓⲱⲛ

1. ⲚⲔⲈⲤⲞⲠ ⲔⲀⲦⲀ ⲐⲈ ⲈⲦⲤⲎⲢ ϪⲈ
ⲀⲨⲦⲀⲬⲢⲞ ⲚⲦⲞⲒⲔⲞⲨⲘⲈⲚⲎ ⲀⲨ
ⲱ ⲚⲤⲚⲀⲔⲒⲘ ⲀⲚ ⲀⲨⲱ ⲞⲚ ϪⲈ
ⲀⲠⲔⲀϨ Ⲃⲱⲗ ⲈⲂⲞⲗ ⲘⲚ ⲚⲈⲦϢⲞ
5. ⲞⲠ ⲦⲎⲢⲞⲨ ϨⲒϪⲱⲨ ⲀⲨⲱ ⲦⲞⲦⲈ
ⲀⲠⲈⲦⲢⲒⲆⲨⲚⲀⲘⲞⲤ ⲈⲒ ⲈⲂⲞⲗ Ⲉ
ⲢⲈ ⲠϢⲎⲢⲈ ϨⲎⲠ ϨⲢⲀⲒ ⲚϨⲎⲦⲨ
ⲀⲨⲱ ⲈⲢⲈ ⲠⲈⲔⲗⲞⲘ ⲚⲦⲀⲬⲢⲞ ϨⲒ
ϪⲚ ⲦⲈⲨⲀⲠⲈ ⲈⲨⲈⲒⲢⲈ ⲚϨⲈⲚ
10. ⲦⲂⲀ ⲚⲦⲂⲀ ⲚⲈⲞⲞⲨ ⲀⲨⲱ ⲚⲈⲦ
ⲱϢ ⲈⲂⲞⲗ ϪⲈ ⲤⲞⲞⲨⲦⲚ ⲚⲦⲈϨⲒⲎ
ⲘⲠϪⲞⲈⲒⲤ ⲀⲨⲱ ϢⲱⲠⲈ ϪⲱⲦⲚ
ⲚⲦⲈⲬⲀⲢⲒⲤ ⲘⲠⲚⲞⲨⲦⲈ ⲀⲨⲱ
ⲀⲒⲱⲚ ⲚⲒⲘ ⲈⲠⲱⲦⲚ ⲠⲈ ⲨⲚⲀⲘⲞⲨϨ
15. ϨⲚ ⲦⲈⲬⲀⲢⲒⲤ ⲘⲠϢⲎⲢⲈ ⲘⲘⲞ
ⲚⲞⲄⲈⲚⲎⲤ ⲀⲨⲱ ⲀⲨⲀϨⲈⲈⲢⲀ
ⲦⲨ ϨⲒϪⲚ ⲠⲂⲀⲐⲞⲤ ⲚⲀⲘⲈⲦⲢⲎ
ⲦⲞⲤ ⲚϬⲒ ⲠⲒⲱⲦ ⲈⲦⲞⲨⲀⲀⲂ ⲀⲨⲱ
ⲠⲠⲀⲚⲦⲈⲗⲒⲞⲤ ⲀⲨⲱ ⲠⲀⲒ ⲈⲢⲈ
20. ⲠϪⲱⲔ ⲦⲎⲢⲨ ⲚⲦⲞⲞⲦⲨ Ⲉ
ⲂⲞⲗ ϨⲘ ⲠⲈⲨϪⲱⲔ ⲀⲚϪⲒ Ⲛ
ⲦⲈⲬⲀⲢⲒⲤ ⲦⲞⲦⲈ ⲀⲠⲀⲒⲱⲚ
ⲦⲀⲬⲢⲞ ⲀⲨⲗⲞ ⲈⲨⲔⲒⲘ ⲀⲠⲒⲱⲦ
ⲦⲀⲬⲢⲞⲨ ϪⲈ ⲈⲚⲈⲨⲔⲒⲘ ⲚϢⲀ
25. ⲈⲚⲈϨ ⲀⲨⲱ ⲀⲠⲀⲒⲱⲚ ⲚⲦⲘⲀⲀⲨ
Ϭⲱ ⲈⲨⲘⲈϨ ⲈⲂⲞⲗ ϨⲚ ⲚⲈⲦⲚ
ϨⲎⲦⲨ ϢⲀⲚⲦⲈ ⲦⲔⲈⲗⲈⲨⲤⲒⲤ
ⲈⲒ ⲈⲂⲞⲗ ϨⲒⲦⲘ ⲠⲘⲨⲤⲦⲎⲢⲒⲞⲚ
ⲈⲐⲎⲠ ϨⲘ ⲠϢⲞⲢⲠ ⲚⲈⲒⲱⲦ
30. ⲠⲀⲒ ⲈⲚⲦⲀ ⲠⲘⲨⲤⲦⲈⲢⲒⲞⲚ ⲈⲒ
ⲈⲂⲞⲗ ⲘⲘⲞⲨ ϪⲈⲔⲀⲀⲤ ⲞⲚ Ⲉ
ⲢⲈ ⲠⲈⲨϢⲎⲢⲈ ⲦⲀϨⲈ ⲠⲦⲎⲢⲨ
ⲈⲢⲀⲦⲨ ⲚⲔⲈⲤⲞⲠ ϨⲚ ⲦⲈⲨ
ⲄⲚⲰⲤⲒⲤ ⲦⲀⲒ ⲈⲦⲈⲢⲈ ⲠⲦⲎⲢⲨ
35. ⲚϨⲎⲦⲤ ⲦⲞⲦⲈ ⲀⲠⲤⲎⲐⲈⲨⲤ
ⲦⲚⲚⲞⲞⲨ ⲚⲞⲨⲗⲞⲄⲞⲤ ⲚⲀⲎⲘⲒ

ⲟⲩⲣⲅⲟⲥ ⲡⲁⲓ ⲉⲟⲩⲛ ⲟⲩⲙⲏⲏϣⲉ
ⲛⲇⲩⲛⲁⲙⲓⲥ ⲛⲙⲙⲁⲩ ⲉⲩϫⲓ ⲕⲗⲟⲙ
ϩⲓϫⲱⲟⲩ ⲉⲣⲉ ⲛⲉⲩⲕⲗⲟⲙ ⲛⲉⲝ ⲁⲕ
ⲧⲓⲛ ⲉⲃⲟⲗ ⲁⲩⲱ ⲉⲣⲉ ⲡⲃⲟⲩⲃⲟⲩ ⲛ
5. ⲛⲉⲩⲥⲱⲙⲁ ⲟⲛϩ ϩⲙ ⲡⲧⲟⲡⲟⲥ
ⲉⲛⲧⲁⲩⲉⲓ ⲉⲣⲟϥ ⲁⲩⲱ ⲡⲗⲟⲅⲟⲥ ⲉⲧ
ⲛⲏⲩ ⲉⲃⲟⲗ ϩⲛ ⲧⲉⲩⲧⲁⲡⲣⲟ ⲟⲩⲱ
ⲛϩ ⲡⲉ ⲛϣⲁⲉⲛⲉϩ ⲁⲩⲱ ⲡⲟⲩⲟ
ⲉⲓⲛ ⲉⲧⲛⲏⲩ ⲉⲃⲟⲗ ϩⲛ ⲛⲉⲩⲃⲁⲗ
10. ⲟⲩⲁⲛⲁⲡⲁⲩⲥⲓⲥ ⲛⲁⲩ ⲧⲉ ⲁⲩⲱ
ⲡϭⲓⲙ ⲛⲧⲉⲩϭⲓϫ ⲡⲉ ⲧⲉⲩϭⲛⲡⲱⲧ
ⲉϩⲟⲩⲛ ⲉⲡⲧⲟⲡⲟⲥ ⲉⲛⲧⲁⲩⲉⲓ
ⲉⲃⲟⲗ ⲛϩⲏⲧϥ ⲁⲩⲱ ⲧⲉⲩϭⲛ
ϭⲱϣⲧ ⲉϩⲟⲩⲛ ⲉϩⲣⲁⲩⲡⲉ ⲧⲉ
15. ⲅⲛⲱⲥⲓⲥ ⲉϩⲟⲩⲛ ⲉⲣⲟⲟⲩ ⲁⲩⲱ
ⲧⲉⲩϭⲓⲙⲙⲟⲟϣⲉ ϣⲁⲣⲟⲟⲩ ⲡⲉ
ⲡⲉⲩⲕⲧⲟ ⲉϩⲟⲩⲛ ⲛⲕⲉⲥⲟⲡ ⲁⲩⲱ
ⲡⲡⲱⲣϣ ⲉⲃⲟⲗ ⲛⲛⲉⲩϭⲓϫ ⲡⲉ
ⲧⲉⲩϭⲓⲛⲧⲁϩⲟⲟⲩ ⲉⲣⲁⲧⲟⲩ ⲁⲩⲱ
20. ⲡⲥⲱⲧⲙ ⲛⲛⲉⲩⲙⲁⲁϫⲉ ⲡⲉ ⲧⲁⲓⲥ
ⲑⲏⲥⲓⲥ ⲉⲧϩⲙ ⲡⲉⲩϩⲏⲧ ⲁⲩⲱ
ⲡϣⲱⲛⲃ ⲛⲛⲉⲩⲙⲉⲗⲟⲥ ⲡⲉ
ⲡⲥⲱⲟⲩϩ ⲉϩⲟⲩⲛ ⲙⲡⲗⲱⲱⲣⲉ
ⲉⲃⲟⲗ ⲙⲡⲓⲏⲗ ⲁⲩⲱ ⲧϭⲓⲛⲁⲙⲁϩ
25. ⲧⲉ ⲙⲙⲟⲟⲩ ⲡⲉ ⲡⲉⲩϣⲱⲧ ⲉϩⲟⲩⲛ
ⲉⲡⲗⲟⲅⲟⲥ ⲁⲩⲱ ⲧⲉⲯⲏⲫⲟⲥ
ⲉⲧϩⲛ ⲛⲉⲩⲧⲏⲏⲃⲉ ⲡⲉ ⲡⲁⲣⲓ
ⲑⲙⲟⲥ ⲏ ⲡⲱⲡ ⲛⲧⲁⲩⲉⲓ ⲉⲃⲟⲗ
ⲕⲁⲧⲁ ⲡⲉⲧⲥⲏϩ ϫⲉ ⲡⲉⲧⲱⲡ ⲛ
30. ⲛⲓⲙⲏⲏϣⲉ ⲛⲥⲓⲟⲩ ⲉⲧϯ ⲣⲁⲛ
ⲉⲣⲟⲟⲩ ⲧⲏⲣⲟⲩ ⲁⲩⲱ ⲡϣⲱⲛⲃ
ⲧⲏⲣϥ ⲙⲡⲗⲟⲅⲟⲥ ⲛⲇⲏⲙⲓⲟⲩ
ⲅⲟⲥ ⲁϥϣⲱⲡⲉ ⲙⲛ ⲛⲉⲛⲧⲁⲩ
ⲉⲓ ϩⲙ ⲡⲕⲓⲙ ⲉⲛⲧⲁⲩϣⲱⲡⲉ
35. ⲁⲩⲱ ⲁⲩⲣⲟⲩⲁ ⲛⲟⲩⲱⲧ ⲧⲏ

1. ⲣⲟⲩ ⲕⲁⲧⲁ ⲑⲉ ⲉⲧⲥⲏ ϩ ϫⲉ ⲁⲩⲣ ⲟⲩⲁ
ⲛⲟⲩⲱⲧ ⲧⲏⲣⲟⲩ ϩⲙ ⲡⲓⲟⲩⲁ ⲛ
ⲟⲩⲱⲧ ⲙⲁⲩⲁⲁⲩ ⲁⲩⲱ ⲧⲟⲧⲉ
ⲁⲡⲓⲗⲟⲅⲟⲥ ⲛⲇⲏⲙⲓⲟⲩⲣⲅⲟⲥ ⲁⲩ
5. ϣⲱⲡⲉ ⲛϭⲟⲙ ⲛⲛⲟⲩⲧⲉ ⲁⲩⲱ
ⲛϫⲟⲉⲓⲥ ⲁⲩⲱ ⲛⲥⲱⲧⲏⲣ ⲁⲩⲱ
ⲛⲭⲣⲥ ⲁⲩⲱ ⲛⲣⲣⲟ ⲁⲩⲱ ⲛⲁ
ⲅⲁⲑⲟⲥ ⲁⲩⲱ ⲛⲉⲓⲱⲧ ⲁⲩⲱ
ⲙⲙⲁⲁⲩ ⲡⲁⲓ ⲡⲉ ⲉⲛⲧⲁ ⲡⲉϥ
10. ϩⲱⲃ ⲣϣⲁⲩ ⲁⲩϫⲓ ⲧⲁⲓⲟ ⲁⲩⲱ
ⲁⲩϣⲱⲡⲉ ⲛⲉⲓⲱⲧ ⲛⲛⲉⲛⲧⲁⲩ
ⲡⲓⲥⲧⲉⲩⲉ ⲁⲡⲁⲓ ϣⲱⲡⲉ ⲛⲛⲟ
ⲙⲟⲥ ϩⲛ ⲧⲁⲯⲏⲇⲱⲛⲓⲁ ⲁⲩⲱ
ⲛⲇⲩⲛⲁⲧⲟⲥ ⲁⲩⲱ ⲁⲧⲡⲁⲛⲇⲏ
15. ⲗⲟⲥ ⲉⲓ ⲉⲃⲟⲗ ⲉⲣⲉ ⲡⲉⲕⲗⲟⲙ ϩⲓ
ϫⲱⲥ ⲁⲥⲧⲁⲁⲩ ⲉϫⲛ ⲛⲉⲛⲧⲁⲩ
ⲡⲓⲥⲧⲉⲩⲉ ⲁⲩⲱ ⲁⲧⲙⲁⲁⲩ
ⲧⲡⲁⲣⲑⲉⲛⲟⲥ ⟨ⲁⲥ ⲱ̂ ⲛ⟩ ⲧϭⲟⲙ
ⲛⲛⲁⲓⲱⲛ ⲁⲩⲱ ⲁⲥ ⲧ ⲧⲁⲝⲓⲥ
20. ⲛⲛⲉⲥⲕⲟⲥⲙⲟⲥ ⲕⲁⲧⲁ ⲡⲧⲱϣ
ⲙⲡⲥⲁⲛϩⲟⲩⲛ ⲁⲩⲱ ⲁⲥⲕⲱ
ⲛϩⲣⲁⲓ ⲛϩⲏⲧⲥ ⲙⲡⲉⲥⲡⲓⲛ
ⲑⲏⲣ ⲛⲟⲩⲟⲉⲓⲛ ⲕⲁⲧⲁ ⲡⲧⲩⲡⲟⲥ
ⲛⲧⲙⲟⲛⲁⲥ ⲁⲩⲱ ⲁⲥⲕⲱ ⲙⲡ
25. ⲕⲁⲗⲩⲡⲧⲟⲥ ⲉⲩⲕⲱⲧⲉ ⲉⲣⲟⲥ
ⲁⲩⲱ ⲁⲥⲕⲱ ⲙⲡⲉⲡⲣⲟⲡⲁⲧⲱⲣ
ⲙⲡⲧⲩⲡⲟⲥ ⲙⲡⲁⲧⲡⲱϣ ⲁⲩⲱ
ⲡⲙⲛⲧⲥⲛⲟⲟⲩⲥ ⲛⲭⲣⲥ ⲉⲩⲕⲱ
ⲧⲉ ⲉⲣⲟⲩ ⲉⲣⲉ ϩⲉⲛⲕⲗⲟⲙ ϩⲓϫⲱ
30. ⲟⲩ ⲁⲩⲱ ⲟⲩⲥⲫⲣⲁⲅⲓⲥ ⲛⲉⲟⲟⲩ

18 α. The word standing in Woide's transcript
is ⲁⲩⲱ. Vide note 3, XL (comm.).

1 ϩΝ ΤΕΥΟΥΝΑϻ ΑΥѠ ΟΥΑΓΑΠΗ°
ϩΝ ΤΕΥϻΗΤΕ ΑΥѠ ΟΥϩΟ ΝΤΡΙ
ΔΥΝΑϻΟC ϩΝ ΤΠΥΓΗ ΑΥѠ
ΟΥΚΑΝΟΥΝ ΕΥΚѠΤΕ ΕΡΟΥ

5. ΝϬΙ ΠϻΝΤCΝΟΟΥC ΝΕΙѠΤ
ΑΥѠ ΟΥϻΝΤѠϪΗΡΕ ΕCϩΗΠ
ΝϩΗΤΟΥ ΑΥѠ ΑCΤΑϩΟ ΕΡΑ
ΤΥ ϻΠΑΥΤΟΠΑΤѠΡ ϻΠΤΥ
ΠΟC ΝΤϩΕΝΝΑC ΝΑΤΧΑΡΑ

10. ΚΤΗΡ ΑΥѠ ΑCΤ ΝΑΥ ΝΤΕ
ϪΟΥCΙΑ ΕϪΝ ΟΥΟΝ ΝΙϻ ΕΤΟ
ΝΕΙѠΤ ΕΡΟΥ ϻΑΥΑΑΥ ΑΥѠ
ΑCCΤΕϢΑΝΟΥ ϻϻΟΥ ϩΝ Ε
ΟΟΥ ΝΙϻ ΑΥѠ ΑCΤ ΝΑΥ ΝΤΑ

15. ΓΑΠΗ ϻΝ ΤΡΗΝΗ ΑΥѠ ΤΑ
ΛΗΘΙΑ ΑΥѠ ϩΕΝΤΒΑ ΝΑΥ
ΝΑϻΙC ϪΕΚΑΑC ΕΥΝΑCѠΟΥϩ
ΕϩΟΥΝ ΝΝΕΝΤΑΥΔѠѠΡΕ Ε
ΒΟλ ϩϻ ΠΕϢΤΟΡΤΡ ΕΝΤΑΥ

20. ѠѠΠΕ ϻΠΝΑΥ ΕΝΤΑ ΠΕ
ΤΡΙΔΥΝΑϻΟC ΕΙ ΕΒΟλ ϻΝ
ΠΡΑϢΕ ΑΥѠ ΠϪΟΕΙC ϻΠ
ΤΗΡΥ ΠΑΙ ΕΤΟΥΝ ϬΟϻ ϻ
ϻΟΥ ΕΤΑΝϩΟ ΑΥѠ ΕΤΑΚΟ

25. ΑΥѠ ΑCΤΑϩΟ ΕΡΑΤΥ ϻΠΕ
ΠΡΟΤΟΓΕΝΝΗΤѠΡ ΝϢΗΡΕ ϻΠ
ΤΥΠΟC ϻΠΕΤΡΙΔΥΝΑϻΙC
ΑΥѠ ΑCΤ ΝΑΥ ΝΟΥϩΕΝΝΑC
ϻΨΙC ΝCΟΠ ΑΥѠ ΑCΤ Τ̅ΟΥ

30. ΝΔΕΚΑC ϻϻΗΤ ΝCΟΠ ϪΕ
ΚΑΑC ΕΥΝΑϢϬϻϬΟϻ ΕϪѠΚ
ΕΒΟλ ϻΠΑΓѠΝ ΕΝΤΑΥΤΑΑΥ

---

1 α. This should be πηгн; vide line 3, where the word is again, though differently, misspelt.

The Coptic originals are once more available.

1. ναυ αγω αϲϯ ναυ νταπαρχη
ντμντϣηρε ται ϩραι νϩητϲ
αυϭμϭομ εϣωπε ντριαγνα
μοϲ αγω αγϫι μπερητ ντμ
5. ντϣηρε παι ενταγϯ μπτη
ργ εβολ νϩητγ αγω αγϫι μπα
γων ενταγτανϩογτγ εрог
αγω αγτογνοϲ μϥιλικρινεϲ
τηργ νθηλη αγω αγααγ νογ
10. κοϲμοϲ αγω νογαιων αγω
νογπολιϲ παι ετογμογτε
ερογ ϫε αϥθαρϲια αγω ϫε ϩι
ερογϲαλημ αγω ον ϲεμογτε
ερογ ϫε πκαϩ νβρρε αγω ον
15. ϲεμογτε ερογ ϫε αγτοτελнϲ
αγω ον ϲεμογτε ερογ ϫε αβα
ϲιλεγτοϲ αγω ον πεικαϩ
ετμμαγ ογρεγμεϲ νογτε πε
αγω ογρεγτανϩο πε παι πε
20. εντα τμααγ αιτι μμογ εταϩογ
εратγ ετβε παι αϲκα τωϣ ϩι
ταξιϲ αγω αϲκα προνοια ϩι
αγαπη ϩμ πεικαϩ παι πε
πκαϩ ενταγϲϩαι ετβηнтγ ϫε
25. πκαϩ ετϲω μπμογ νϩωογ
νϩαϩ νϲοπ ετε παι πε πετ
ταϣε ογοειν νϩητγ νϩαϩ ν
ϩαϩ νϲοπ ϫιν μπεγει εβολ
ϣα πεγει εϩογν παι πε ενταγ
30. ϲϩαι πρωμε ναιϲθητοϲ ε
τβηнтγ αγω αγτγπογ μμογ
αγταμιογ μπτγποϲ μπικαϩ
παι πε εντα πεπρωτογενη
τωρ τογϫοογ εβολ ϩν τεγ

1. ⲙ̄ⲛⲧⲭⲱⲱⲣⲉ ⲙ̄ⲙⲓⲛ ⲙ̄ⲙⲟⲩ ⲉⲧ
ⲃⲉ ⲡⲉⲓϩⲱⲃ ⲁⲡⲓⲱⲧ ⲛ̄ⲛⲓⲡⲧⲏⲣϥ
ⲡⲓⲁⲗⲉⲕⲧⲟⲥ ⲁⲩⲧⲛ̄ⲛⲟⲟⲩ ⲛⲟⲩ
ⲕⲗⲟⲙ ⲉⲣⲉ ⲡⲣⲁⲛ ⲛ̄ⲛⲉⲓⲡⲧⲏⲣϥ

5. ⲛ̄ϩⲏⲧϥ ⲉⲓⲧⲉ ⲁⲡⲉⲣⲁⲛⲧⲟⲥ ⲉⲓ
ⲧⲉ ⲁϩⲣⲏⲧⲟⲥ ⲉⲓⲧⲉ ⲁⲭⲱⲣⲏⲧⲟⲥ
ⲉⲓⲧⲉ ⲁⲫⲑⲁⲣⲧⲟⲥ ⲉⲓⲧⲉ ⲁⲅⲛⲱⲥ
ⲧⲟⲥ ⲉⲓⲧⲉ ⲏ̄ⲣⲉⲙⲟⲥ ⲉⲓⲧⲉ ⲡⲁⲛ
ⲧⲟⲇⲩⲛⲁⲙⲟⲥ ⲉⲓⲧⲉ ⲡⲁⲧⲡⲱϣ

10. ⲡⲁⲓ ⲡⲉ ⲡⲉⲕⲗⲟⲙ ⲉⲛⲧⲁⲩⲥϩⲁⲓ
ⲉⲧⲃⲏⲏⲧϥ ⲇⲉ ⲁⲩⲧⲁⲁⲩ ⲛ̄ⲥⲟⲗⲟⲙⲱⲛ
ⲙ̄ⲡⲉϩⲟⲟⲩ ⲙ̄ⲡⲉϥⲟⲩⲛⲟⲩ ⲛ̄ϩⲏⲧ
ⲁⲩⲱ ⲟⲛ ⲁⲧⲙⲟⲛⲁⲥ ⲛ̄ϩⲟⲩⲉⲓⲧⲉ
ⲁⲥⲧⲛ̄ⲛⲟⲟⲩ ⲛⲁϥ ⲛⲟⲩϩⲃⲥⲱ ⲛ̄

15. ⲁⲧϣⲁϫⲉ ⲉⲣⲟⲥ ⲉⲩⲟⲩⲟⲉⲓⲛ ⲧⲏⲣⲥ̄
ⲧⲉ ⲁⲩⲱ ⲉⲩⲱⲛϩ ⲧⲏⲣⲥ ⲧⲉ ⲁⲩ̄
ⲱ ⲉⲩⲁⲛⲁⲥⲧⲁⲥⲓⲥ ⲧⲏⲣⲥ ⲧⲉ ⲁⲩ
ⲱ ⲉⲩⲁⲅⲁⲡⲏ ⲧⲏⲣⲥ ⲧⲉ ⲁⲩⲱ
ⲉⲩϩⲉⲗⲡⲓⲥ ⲧⲏⲣⲥ ⲧⲉ ⲁⲩⲱ ⲉⲩ

20. ⲡⲓⲥⲧⲓⲥ ⲧⲏⲣⲥ ⲧⲉ ⲁⲩⲱ ⲉⲩⲥⲟ
ⲫⲓⲁ ⲧⲏⲣⲥ ⲧⲏⲣⲥ ⲧⲉ ⲁⲩⲱ ⲟⲩ
ⲅⲛⲱⲥⲓⲥ ⲧⲏⲣⲥ ⲧⲉ ⲁⲩⲱ ⲟⲩⲁ
ⲗⲏⲑⲓⲁ ⲧⲏⲣⲥ ⲧⲉ ⲁⲩⲱ ⲟⲩⲉⲓⲣⲏ
ⲛⲏ ⲧⲏⲣⲥ ⲧⲉ ⲁⲩⲱ ⲟⲩⲡⲁⲛⲧⲏ

25. ⲗⲱⲥ ⲧⲏⲣⲥ ⲧⲉ ⲁⲩⲱ ⲟⲩⲡⲁⲛ
ⲙⲏⲧⲱⲣ ⲧⲏⲣⲥ ⲧⲉ ⲁⲩⲱ ⲟⲩⲡⲁⲛ
ⲙⲩⲥⲧⲏⲣⲓⲟⲛ ⲧⲏⲣⲥ ⲧⲉ ⲁⲩⲱ ⲟⲩ
ⲡⲁⲛⲡⲏⲅⲏ ⲧⲏⲣⲥ ⲧⲉ ⲁⲩⲱ ⲟⲩ
ⲡⲁⲛⲧⲉⲗⲓⲟⲥ ⲧⲏⲣⲥ ⲧⲉ ⲁⲩⲱ ⲟⲩ

30. ⲁϩⲟⲣⲁⲧⲟⲥ ⲧⲏⲣⲥ ⲧⲉ ⲁⲩⲱ ⲟⲩⲁ
ⲅⲛⲱⲥⲧⲟⲥ ⲧⲏⲣⲥ ⲧⲉ ⲁⲩⲱ ⲟⲩⲁ
ⲡⲉⲣⲁⲛⲧⲟⲥ ⲧⲏⲣⲥ ⲧⲉ ⲁⲩⲱ ⲟⲩⲁ
ϩⲣⲏⲧⲟⲥ ⲧⲏⲣⲥ ⲧⲉ ⲁⲩⲱ ⲟⲩⲃⲁ
ⲑⲟⲥ ⲧⲏⲣⲥ ⲧⲉ ⲁⲩⲱ ⲟⲩⲁⲭⲱⲣⲏ

35. ⲧⲟⲥ ⲧⲏⲣⲥ ⲧⲉ ⲁⲩⲱ ⲟⲩⲡⲗⲏ

15α. The ⲩ is written above the line.

1. ρωμα τηρс τε αγω ογсιгη τη
ρс τε αγω ογасαλεγτος τηρс
τε αγω ογαгεννητος τηρс
τε αγω ογπανηρεμος τηρс τη
5. ρс τε αγω ογμονας τηρс τε
αγω ογϩεννας τηρс τε αγω
ογ ↓ωλεκας τηρс τε αγω ογ
ϩογλολς τηρс τε αγω ογλε
κας τηρс τε αγω ογϩεβλομας
10. τηρс τε αγω ογεϩας τηρс τε
αγω ογπεντας τηρс τε αγω
ογ τετρας τηρс τε αγω ογτρι
ας τηρс τε αγω ογλγας τηρс
τε αγω ογμονας τηρс τε
15. αγω ερε πτηργ ⲛϩητϥ αγω
εντα πτηργ ον ϩε εροογ ϩν
ται αγω αγсογωνογ ⲛϩητс
αγω αсϯ ογοειν ναγ τηρογ
ϩμ πεсογοειν νατϣαχε
20. εροϥ αγϯ νας ⲛϩεⲛⲧⲃⲁ ⲛⲧⲃⲁ
ναγναμις ⲭεκαас εснατα
ϩε πτηργ ερατϥ νογсοπ ν
ογωτ αγω αссωογϩ ннεс
εναγμα ερος εасλλγ μπε
25. сμοτ νογκαταπεταсμα
εγκωτε ερος νса са νιμ μ
μος αγω аспаϩτс εβολ ε
ⲭωογ τηρογ αστογνοсογ
τηρογ αγω асλιακρινε μ
30. μοογ τηρογ κατα ταϩιс αγω
κατα τωϣ αγω κατα προ
νοια αγω τοτε απετϣοοπ
πωρⲭ εβολ μπετε νϥϣοοπ
αν αγω πετε νϥϣοοπ αν πε
35. τκακια ται ενταсογωνϩ εβολ

4. · · · · deleted word.
9. ⲧⲉ written above the line.
15 α. The masc. pron. in error for the fem.; the word
should be ⲛϩⲏⲧⲥ.

1. ϨΝ ΘΥΛΗ ΑΥω ΑΤΔΥΝΑΜΙС ΝϨΒ
Сω ΠωΡϪ ΕΒΟΛ ΝΝΕΤϢΟΟΠ Ν
ΝΕΤΕ ΝСΕϢΟΟΠ ΑΝ ΑΥω ΑСΜΟΥ
ΤΕ ΕΝΕΤϢΟΟΠ ϪΕ ΝΑΙωΝΙΟС

5. ΑΥω ΑСΜΟΥΤΕ ΕΝΕΤΕ ΝСΕϢΟΟΠ
ΑΝ ϪΕ ϨΥΛΗ ΑΥω ΑСΠωΡϪ Ε
ΒΟΛ ϨΝ ΤΜΗΤΕ ΝΝΕΤϢΟΟΠ
ΜΝ ΝΕΤΕ ΝСΕϢΟΟΠ ΑΝ ΑΥω
ΑСΚω ΝϨΕΝΚΑΤΑΠΕΤΑСΜΑ

10. ΟΥΤωΟΥ ΑΥω ΑСΚω ΝϨΕΝ
ϬΟΜ ΝΡΕΥСωΤΥ ϪΕΚΛΑС ΕΥ
ΕСΟΤΥΟΥ ΑΥω ΝСΕΚΑΘΑΡΙ
ϪΕ ΜΜΟΟΥ ΑΥω ΑСϮΤωϢ Ε
ΝΕΤϢΟΟΠ ΝΤΕΙϨΕ ΑΥω ΑС

15. Κω ΝΤΜΑΑΥ ΝΑΠΕ ΑΥω ΑС
Ϯ ΝΑС ΜΜΗΤ ΝΝΑΙωΝ ΕΟΥΝ
ΟΥΤΒΑ ΝΔΥΝΑΜΙС ϨΜ ΠΑΙωΝ
ΠΑΙωΝ ΑΥω ΟΥΜΟΝΑС ΜΝ
ΟΥϨΕΝΝΑС ϨΜ ΠΑΙωΝ ΠΑΙωΝ

20. ΑΥω ΑСΚω ϨΡΑΙ ΝϨΗΤС ΝΟΥ
ΠΑΝΜΗΤωΡ ΑΥω ΑСϮ ΝΑС
ΝΟΥϬΟΜ ϪΕΚΛΑС ΕСΕΚΛΑС
ΕСϨΗΠ ϨΡΑΙ ΝϨΗΤС ϪΕ ΕΝΕ
ΛΑΑΥ СΟΥωΝС ΑΥω ΑСΚω Ν

25. ϨΗΤС ΝΟΥΝΟϬ ΝΚΑΝΟΥΝ ΕΥΝ
ϢΟΜΤΕ ΝΔΥΝΑΜΙС ΑϨΕΡΑΤΟΥ
ΕΡΟΥ ΟΥΑΓΕΝΝΗΤΟС ΜΝ ΟΥ
ΑСΑΛΕΥΤΟС ΜΝ ΠΝΟϬ ΝϨΙΛΙ
ΚΡΙΝΕС ΑΥω ΑСϮ ΝΑΥ ΝΚΕΙΒ

30. ΕΥϪΙ ΚΛΟΜ ΕΥΚωΤΕ ΕΡΟΥ ΑΥω
ΑСϮ ΝΑΥ ΝΚΕСΑϢΥ ΝСΤΡΑΤΗ
ΛΑΤΗС ΕΥΝΤΑΥ ΜΜΑΥ ΝΤΕС
ΦΡΑΓΙС ΜΠΑΝΤΕΛΙΟС ΑΥω

ⲉⲩⲛⲟⲩⲕⲁⲟⲗⲉⲓⲭⲛⲧⲉⲩⲙⲁⲅⲓⲉⲉⲙⲛ
ⲙⲡⲉⲥⲛⲟⲥⲧⲉⲛⲱⲧⲉⲛϩⲏⲧϥ
ⲛⲁⲛⲁⲙⲱⲛⲧⲟⲥⲉⲍⲉⲙⲉⲕⲟⲗ·
ⲉⲛⲁⲗⲁⲙⲁⲥⲧⲓⲣⲟⲙⲉⲛⲟⲩⲟⲉⲓⲏ
ⲁⲧⲱⲱⲁⲥⲧⲁϩⲟⲉⲓⲣⲁⲩⲙⲡⲉⲡⲣⲟ
ⲡⲓⲥⲧⲱⲣⲉⲛⲛⲁⲓⲱⲛⲛⲧⲱⲁⲩ
ⲓⲏⲁⲩⲁⲁⲥⲧⲏⲛⲧⲉⲍⲟⲩⲥⲓⲁ
ⲧⲏⲣⲥⲛⲧⲱⲧⲉⲓⲱⲧⲛⲁⲩⲁⲱ
ⲁⲥ·ϩⲏⲙⲉⲣⲟⲛⲕⲟⲕⲉⲧⲕⲉⲣ
ⲥⲁⲧⲉⲓⲛⲧⲉⲱϥⲁⲁϥⲉⲓⲛ
ⲁⲧⲱⲉⲩⲥⲱⲧⲣⲛⲉϥⲟⲧⲛⲏⲉⲁ
ⲉⲁⲩⲟⲩⲱⲧⲉⲧⲏⲣⲟⲩⲁⲩⲱⲉ
ϯⲛⲁϥⲛⲟⲩⲕⲁⲟⲗⲉⲭⲱⲩⲧⲉⲓⲛⲏ
ⲉⲛⲟⲟⲩⲥⲉⲛⲡⲉⲛⲟⲥⲁⲩⲱⲁⲥⲧ
ⲛⲉⲛⲟⲩⲁⲛⲁⲟⲕⲉⲥⲱⲓⲛⲧⲉ
ⲁⲩⲛⲁⲙⲟⲥⲁⲩⲱⲥⲉⲟⲩⲧⲱⲛ
ⲧⲟⲁⲧⲏⲁⲁⲟⲩⲁⲩⲱⲥϯⲛⲁⲣⲱ
ⲕⲉⲓⲛⲓϣⲟⲩⲡⲣⲉⲁⲩⲱⲉⲛ
ⲧⲱⲁⲛⲡⲩⲭⲉⲟⲁⲟ·ⲥⲉⲥⲧⲁⲱ·
ⲛⲁⲁ·ⲁⲩⲱⲭⲁⲧⲟⲉⲣⲟⲥⲁⲡⲛ
ⲡⲗⲏⲣⲱⲙⲁⲕⲩⲱⲁⲥϩⲱⲉⲛ
ⲉⲓⲛⲁⲩⲉⲣⲟϣⲁⲓⲁⲥⲧⲁⲛ
ⲁϫⲉⲡⲕⲟ·ⲥⲉⲱⲩ·ⲁⲩⲏ
ⲟⲁⲩⲛⲁⲙⲓⲟⲥ·ⲉⲓⲟⲛⲉⲥⲧⲛ
ⲛⲙⲉⲧⲟⲩⲧⲁⲁⲩⲉⲧⲟⲩ
ⲛⲉⲟⲟⲗⲛⲉⲥⲧⲟⲟⲩⲁⲉⲧⲟⲩ
ⲛⲉⲛⲉⲛⲥⲱⲉ·ⲁⲩⲁⲩⲛⲁ·ⲛⲏϩ
ⲁⲟⲛⲭⲉⲁⲁⲩⲁⲩⲛⲉⲉⲛⲧⲕⲁ
ⲁⲓⲧⲉⲁⲉⲉⲟⲁ·ⲟⲩⲃⲁⲗⲓⲱⲛ
ⲉϯⲛⲏϫⲩⲩ·ⲥⲉⲥⲟⲩ·ⲧⲉⲙⲉⲛ
ⲉⲧⲁⲩⲓⲛⲉⲁⲉⲟⲛ·ϫⲩⲧⲱⲗ·ⲥ
ⲧⲉⲥⲩ·ⲁⲓⲉⲛⲧⲟⲃⲭⲉⲡⲣⲟⲧⲟⲅⲟⲛ
ⲏⲡⲉⲥⲁⲕⲟⲟⲭⲉⲛⲧⲣϥⲕⲟⲙⲉ

ⲉⲛⲧⲓϥⲧⲱⲛⲍⲉϩⲁⲟⲩⲱⲕⲁⲱ·

1. ⲉⲩⲛ ⲟⲩⲕⲗⲟⲙ ⳩ⲓⲭⲛ ⲧⲉⲩⲁⲡⲉ ⲉⲩⲛ
ⲙⲛⲧⲥⲛⲟⲟⲩⲥ ⲛ̄ⲱⲛⲉ ⲛ⳩ⲏⲧϥ
ⲛⲁⲇⲁⲙⲁⲛⲧⲟⲥ ⲉ⳩ⲉⲛⲉⲃⲟⲗ ⲛⲉ
⳩ⲛ ⲁⲇⲁⲙⲁⲥ ⲡⲣⲱⲙⲉ ⲛⲟⲩⲟⲉⲓⲛ
5. ⲁⲩⲱ ⲁⲥⲧⲁ⳩ⲟ ⲉⲣⲁⲧϥ ⲙ̄ⲡⲉⲡⲣⲟ
ⲡⲁⲧⲱⲣ ⳩ⲛ ⲛⲁⲓⲱⲛ ⲛ̄ⲧⲙⲁⲁⲩ
ⲛⲛ⳩ⲟⲗⲱⲛ ⲁⲥϯ ⲛⲧⲉ⳨ⲟⲩⲥⲓⲁ
ⲧⲏⲣⲥ ⲛ̄ⲧⲙⲛⲧⲉⲓⲱⲧ ⲛⲁⲩ ⲁⲩⲱ
ⲁⲥϯ ⲛⲁⲩ ⲛ⳩ⲉⲛϭⲟⲙ ⲉⲧⲣⲉⲩ
10. ⲥⲱⲧⲙ ⲛⲥⲱϥ ⳩ⲱⲥ ⲉⲓⲱⲧ
ⲁⲩⲱ ⳩ⲱⲥ ϣⲟⲣⲡ ⲛⲉⲓⲱⲧ ⲛ̄ⲛⲉⲛ
ⲧⲁⲩ ϣⲱⲡⲉ ⲧⲏⲣⲟⲩ ⲁⲩⲱ ⲁⲥ
ϯ ⲛⲁⲩ ⲛⲟⲩⲕⲗⲟⲙ ⲉ⳨ⲱϥ ⲙ̄ⲙⲛⲧ
ⲥⲛⲟⲟⲩⲥ ⲛ̄ⲅⲉⲛⲟⲥ ⲁⲩⲱ ⲁⲥϯ
15. ⲛⲁⲩ ⲛⲟⲩⲇⲩⲛⲁⲙⲓⲥ ⲉⲥⲟ ⲛ̄ⲧⲣⲓ
ⲇⲩⲛⲁⲙⲟⲥ ⲁⲩⲱ ⲉⲥⲟ ⲙ̄ⲡⲁⲛ
ⲧⲟⲇⲩⲛⲁⲙⲟⲥ ⲁⲩⲱ ⲁⲥϯ ⲛⲁⲩ
ⲛ̄ⲧⲙⲛⲧϣⲏⲣⲉ ⲁⲩⲱ ⳩ⲉⲛ
ⲧⲃⲁ ⲛ̄ⲧⲃⲁ ⲛⲉⲟⲟⲩ ⲉⲁⲥⲧⲁⲁⲩ
20. ⲛⲁⲩ ⲁⲩⲱ ⲁⲥⲕⲧⲟ ⲉⲣⲟⲩ ⲙ̄ⲡⲉ
ⲡⲗⲏⲣⲱⲙⲁ ⲁⲩⲱ ⲁⲥϯ ⲧⲉ⳨ⲟⲩ
ⲥⲓⲁ ⲛⲁⲩ ⲉⲣ⳩ ⲱⲃ ⲛⲓⲙ ⲉⲧⲁⲛ⳩ⲟ
ⲁⲩⲱ ⲉⲧⲁⲕⲟ ⲁⲩⲱ ⲁⲥϯ ⲛⲁⲩ ⲛ
ⲟⲩⲇⲩⲛⲁⲙⲓⲥ ⲉⲃⲟⲗ ⳩ⲙ ⲡⲁⲓ
25. ⲱⲛ ⲉⲧⲟⲩⲙⲟⲩⲧⲉ ⲉⲣⲟⲩ
⳨ⲉ ⲥⲟⲗⲙⲓⲥⲧⲟⲥ ⲡⲁⲓ ⲉⲧⲟⲩ
ϣⲓⲛⲉ ⲛⲥⲱⲟⲩ ⲧⲏⲣⲟⲩ ⲛϭⲓ ⲛⲁⲓ
ⲱⲛ ⳨ⲉ ᵃⲁⲩϯ ⲛⲁⲩ ⲛ⳩ⲉⲛⲧⲃⲁ
ⲛⲧⲃⲁ ⲛⲉⲟⲟⲩ ⲙⲛ ⲛⲁⲓⲱⲛ
30. ⲉⲧⲛⲙⲙⲁⲩ ⲥⲉⲙⲟⲩⲧⲉ ⲙⲉⲛ
ⲉⲧⲇⲩⲛⲁⲙⲓⲥ ⲉⲛⲧⲁⲩⲧⲁⲁⲥ ⲙ
ⲡⲉⲡⲣⲟⲡⲁⲧⲱⲣ ⳨ⲉ ⲡⲣⲟⲧⲟⲫⲁ
ⲛⲏⲥ ⲉⲃⲟⲗ ⳨ⲉ ⲛⲧⲟⲩ ⲡⲉⲛⲧⲁⲩ

ⲉⲛⲧⲁⲩⲟⲩⲱⲛ⳩ ⲉⲃⲟⲗ ⲧⲱⲛ ⲁⲩⲱ

The phrase written below the text (vide original),
should be read in at ᵃ/, line 28.

1 ογωₙϩ εβολ ⲛⲱⲟⲣⲡ ⲁⲩⲱ ⲁⲩⲙⲟⲩ
ⲧⲉ ⲉⲣⲟⲩ ϫⲉ ⲁⲅⲉⲛⲛⲏⲧⲟⲥ ⲉⲃⲟⲗ ϫⲉ
ⲙⲡⲉ ⲗⲁⲁⲩ ⲧⲁⲙⲓⲟⲩ ⲁⲩⲱ ⲟⲛ ⲁⲩ
ⲙⲟⲩⲧⲉ ⲉⲣⲟⲩ ϫⲉ ⲡⲓⲁⲧⲱⲁϫⲉ ⲉⲣⲟⲩ

5. ⲁⲩⲱ ⲡⲓⲁⲧⲧⲣⲁⲛ ⲉⲣⲟⲩ ⲁⲩⲱ ⲟⲛ
ⲁⲩⲙⲟⲩⲧⲉ ⲉⲣⲟⲩ ϫⲉ ⲁⲩⲧⲟⲅⲉⲛⲏⲥ
ⲁⲩⲱ ⲟⲛ ⲛⲁⲩⲧⲟⲑⲉⲗⲏⲧⲟⲥ ⲉ
ⲃⲟⲗ ϫⲉ ϩⲣⲁⲓ ϩⲙ ⲡⲉϥⲟⲩⲱⲱ ⲁⲩ
ⲟⲩⲱⲛϩ ⲉⲃⲟⲗ ⲁⲩⲱ ⲁⲩⲙⲟⲩⲧⲉ

10. ⲉⲣⲟⲩ ϫⲉ ⲁⲩⲧⲟⲇⲟⲝⲁⲥⲧⲟⲥ
ⲉⲃⲟⲗ ϫⲉ ⲁⲩⲟⲩⲱⲛϩ ⲉⲃⲟⲗ ⲙⲛ
ⲛⲁ ⲟⲟⲩ ⲉⲧⲉ ⲟⲩⲛⲧⲁⲩⲥⲟⲩ ⲁⲩ
ⲙⲟⲩⲧⲉ ⲉⲣⲟⲩ ⲟⲛ ϫⲉ ⲁⲟⲣⲁⲧⲟⲥ
ⲉⲃⲟⲗ ϫⲉ ϥϩⲏⲡ ⲉⲛⲥⲉⲛⲁⲩ ⲉ

15. ⲣⲟⲩ ⲁⲛ ⲁⲩⲱ ⲁⲥϯ ⲛⲁⲩ ⲛⲕⲉ
ϭⲟⲙ ⲧⲁⲓ ⲉⲛⲧⲁⲥⲟⲩⲱⲛϩ ⲉⲃⲟⲗ
ⲙⲡⲧⲕ ϫⲓⲛ ⲛⲱⲟⲣⲡ ϩⲙ ⲡⲓⲙⲁ
ⲛⲟⲩⲱⲧ ⲧⲁⲓ ⲉⲧⲟⲩⲙⲟⲩⲧⲉ
ⲉⲣⲟⲥ ⲛⲛⲣⲁⲛ ⲉⲧⲟⲩⲁⲁⲃ ⲁⲩⲱ

20. ⲛⲣⲁⲛ ⲙⲡⲁⲛⲧⲉⲗⲉⲓⲟⲥ ⲉⲧⲉ
ⲛⲧⲟⲥ ⲧⲉ ⲧⲉⲡⲣⲱⲧⲓⲁ ⲉⲧⲉ ⲧ
ⲱⲟⲣⲡ ⲧⲉ ⲥⲉⲙⲟⲩⲧⲉ ⲉⲣⲟⲥ
ϫⲉ ⲡⲁⲛⲇⲓⲁ ⲉⲧⲉ ⲧⲉⲧϣⲟⲟⲡ
ⲛϩⲏⲧⲟⲩ ⲧⲏⲣⲟⲩ ⲧⲉ ⲥⲉⲙⲟⲩ

25. ⲧⲉ ⲟⲛ ⲉⲣⲟⲥ ϫⲉ ⲡⲁⲅⲅⲉⲛⲓⲁ
ⲉⲧⲉ ⲧⲉⲛⲧⲁⲥϫⲡⲟⲟⲩ ⲧⲏⲣⲟⲩ
ⲧⲉ ⲥⲉⲙⲟⲩⲧⲉ ⲟⲛ ⲉⲣⲟⲥ ϫⲉ ⲇⲟ
ⲝⲟⲅⲉⲛⲓⲁ ϫⲉ ⲛⲧⲟⲥ ⲧⲉ ⲧⲣⲉϥ
ϫⲡⲟ ⲙⲡⲉⲟⲟⲩ ⲥⲉⲙⲟⲩⲧⲉ ⲟⲛ

30. ⲉⲣⲟⲥ ϫⲉ ⲇⲟⲝⲟⲫⲁⲛⲓⲁ ϫⲉ ⲛ
ⲧⲟⲥ ⲧⲉ ⲧⲣⲉϥⲟⲩⲱⲛϩ ⲉⲃⲟⲗ ⲙ
ⲡⲉⲟⲟⲩ ⲥⲉⲙⲟⲩⲧⲉ ⲟⲛ ⲉⲣⲟⲥ
ϫⲉ ⲁⲣⲧⲟⲕⲣⲁⲧⲓⲁ ϫⲉ ⲥⲁⲙⲁϩ
ⲧⲉ ⲉϫⲙ ⲡⲉⲟⲟⲩ ⲥⲉⲙⲟⲩⲧⲉ

35. ⲟⲛ ⲉⲣⲟⲥ ϫⲉ ⲁⲣⲥⲟⲅⲉⲛⲓⲁ ⲉⲧⲉ
ⲧⲣⲉϥϫⲡⲉ ϩⲟⲟⲩⲧ ⲧⲉ ⲥⲉⲙⲟⲩ

33 α. The word should be ⲇⲟⲝⲟⲕⲣⲁⲧⲓⲁ, vide XVIII,
lines 27–28.

XLVIII
MS. f. 124R
C.S. p. 38

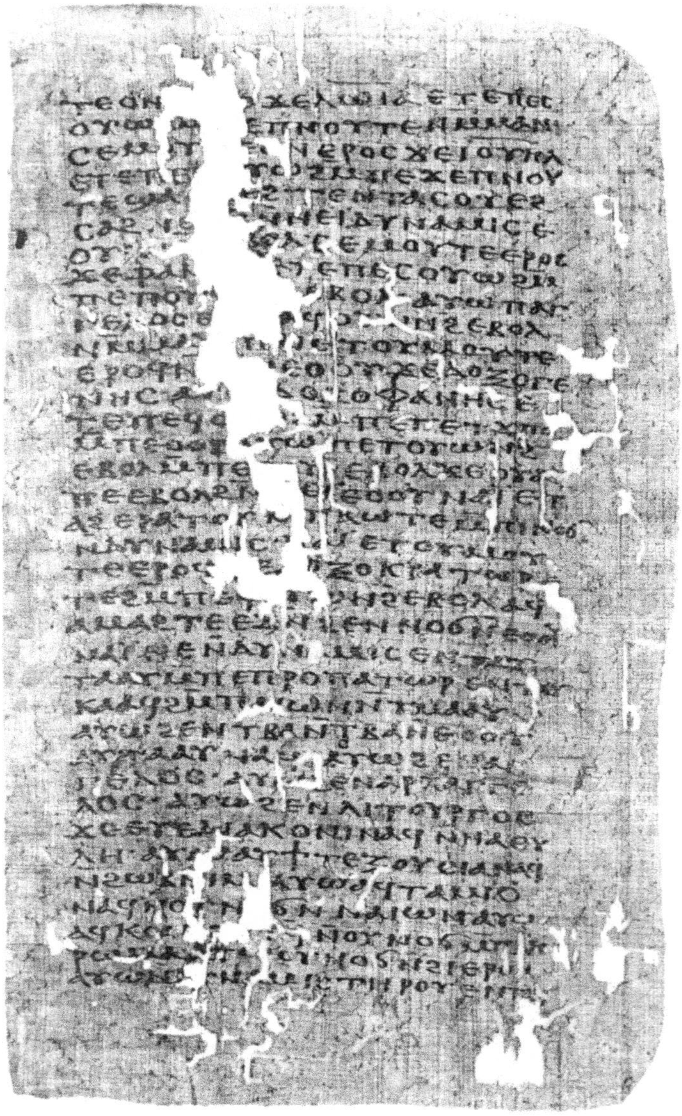

1. ⲦⲈ ⲞⲚ ⲈⲢⲞⲤ ⲬⲈ ⲖⲰⲒⲀ ⲈⲦⲈ ⲠⲈⲤ
ⲞⲨⲰϨⲘ ⲠⲈ ⲠⲚⲞⲨⲦⲈ ⲚⲘⲘⲀⲚ
ⲤⲈⲘⲞⲨⲦⲈ ⲞⲚ ⲈⲢⲞⲤ ⲬⲈ ⲒⲞⲨⲎⲖ
ⲈⲦⲈ ⲠⲈⲤⲞⲨⲰϨⲘ ⲠⲈ ⲬⲈ ⲠⲚⲞⲨ

5. ⲦⲈ ϢⲀ ⲈⲚⲈϨ ⲦⲈⲚⲦⲀⲤⲞⲨⲈϨ
ⲤⲀϨⲚⲈ ⲆⲈ ⲚⲚⲈⲒⲆⲨⲚⲀⲘⲒⲤ Ⲉ
ⲞⲨⲰⲚϨ ⲈⲂⲞⲖ ⲤⲈⲘⲞⲨⲦⲈ ⲈⲢⲞⲤ
ⲬⲈ ⲮⲀⲚⲒⲀ ⲈⲦⲈ ⲠⲈⲤⲞⲨⲰϨⲘ
ⲠⲈ ⲠⲞⲨⲰⲚϨ ⲈⲂⲞⲖ ⲀⲨⲰ ⲠⲀⲄ

10. ⲄⲈⲖⲞⲤ ⲈⲚⲦⲀⲨⲞⲨⲰⲚϨ ⲈⲂⲞⲖ
ⲚⲘⲘⲀⲨ ⲠⲀⲒ ⲈⲦⲞⲨⲘⲞⲨⲦⲈ
ⲈⲢⲞⲨ ⲚϬⲒ ⲚⲈⲞⲞⲨ ⲬⲈ ⲆⲞⲌⲞⲄⲈ
ⲚⲎⲤ ⲀⲨⲰ ⲆⲞⲌⲞⲮⲀⲚⲎⲤ Ⲉ
ⲦⲈ ⲠⲈⲨⲞⲨⲰϨⲘ ⲠⲈ ⲠⲈⲦⲬⲠⲞ

15. ⲘⲠⲈⲞⲞⲨ ⲀⲨⲰ ⲠⲈⲦⲞⲨⲰⲚϨ
ⲈⲂⲞⲖ ⲘⲠⲈⲞⲞⲨ ⲈⲂⲞⲖ ⲬⲈ ⲞⲨⲀ
ⲠⲈ ⲈⲂⲞⲖ ϨⲚ ⲚⲈⲒⲈⲞⲞⲨ ⲚⲀⲒ ⲈⲦ
ⲀϨⲈⲢⲀⲦⲞⲨ ⲘⲠⲔⲰⲦⲈ ⲘⲠⲒⲚⲞϬ
ⲚⲆⲨⲚⲀⲘⲒⲤ ⲠⲀⲒ ⲈⲦⲞⲨⲘⲞⲨ

20. ⲦⲈ ⲈⲢⲞⲨ ⲬⲈ ⲆⲞⲌⲞⲔⲢⲀⲦⲰⲢ Ⲉ
ⲦⲈ ϨⲘ ⲠⲈⲨⲞⲨⲰⲚϨ ⲈⲂⲞⲖ ⲀⲨ
ⲀⲘⲀϨⲦⲈ ⲈⲬⲚ ϨⲈⲚⲚⲞϬ ⲚⲈⲞⲞⲨ
ⲚⲀⲒ ⲚⲈ ⲚⲆⲨⲚⲀⲘⲒⲤ ⲈⲚⲦⲀⲨ
ⲦⲀⲀⲨ ⲘⲠⲈⲠⲢⲞⲠⲀⲦⲰⲢ ⲈⲚⲦⲀⲨ

25. ⲔⲀⲀⲨ ϨⲘ ⲠⲀⲒⲰⲚ ⲚⲦⲘⲀⲀⲨ
ⲀⲨⲰ ϨⲈⲚⲦⲂⲀ ⲚⲦⲂⲀ ⲚⲈⲞⲞⲨ
ⲀⲨⲦⲀⲀⲨ ⲚⲀⲨ ⲀⲨⲰ ϨⲈⲚⲀⲄ
ⲄⲈⲖⲞⲤ ⲀⲨⲰ ϨⲈⲚⲀⲢⲬⲀⲄⲄⲈ
ⲖⲞⲤ ⲀⲨⲰ ϨⲈⲚⲖⲒⲦⲞⲨⲢⲄⲞⲤ

30. ⲬⲈ ⲈⲨⲈⲆⲒⲀⲔⲞⲚⲒ ⲚⲀⲨ ⲚⲚⲀⲐⲨ
ⲖⲎ ⲀⲨⲰ ⲀⲨϮ ⲦⲈⲌⲞⲨⲤⲒⲀ ⲚⲀⲨ
ⲚϨⲰⲂ ⲚⲒⲘ ⲀⲨⲰ ⲀⲨⲦⲀⲘⲒⲞ
ⲚⲀⲨ ⲚⲞⲨⲚⲞϬ ⲚⲚⲀⲒⲰⲚ ⲀⲨⲰ
ⲀⲨⲔⲰ ⲚϨⲎⲦⲨ ⲚⲞⲨⲚⲞϬ ⲘⲠⲖⲎ

35. ⲢⲰⲘⲀ ⲀⲨⲰ ⲞⲨⲚⲞϬ ⲚϨⲒⲈⲢⲞⲚ
ⲀⲨⲰ ⲚⲆⲨⲚⲀⲘⲒⲤ ⲦⲎⲢⲞⲨ ⲈⲚⲦⲀⲨ

1. ϪΙΤΟΥ ΕΝΤΑΥΚΑΑΥ ΝϨΗΤϤ ΑΥⲰ
ΑϤΤΕΛΗΛ ⲙⲙΟΥ ΝⲙⲙΑΥ ΕΥ
ϪΠΟ ΝΝΕΥϹⲰΝΤ ΝΚΕϹΟΠ ΚΑ
ΤΑ ΠΟΥΕϨϹΑϨΝΕ ⲙΠΙⲰΤ Ε
5. ΘΗΠ Ϩⲙ ΠΚΑΡⲰϤ ΠΑΙ ΕΝΤΑΥ
ΤΝΝΟΟΥ ΝΑϤ ΝΝΕΙⲙΝΤΡⲙⲙΑ
Ο ΑΥⲰ ΠΕΚΛΟⲙ ΝΤⲙΝΤΕΙⲰΤ
ΑΥΤΑΑΥ ΝΑϤ ϪΕ ΑϤΚΑΑΥ ΝΕΙ
ⲰΤ ΝΝΕΝΤΑΥϣⲰΠΕ ⲙΝΝ
10. ϹⲰϤ ΑΥⲰ ΤΟΤΕ ΑϤⲰϣ ΕΒΟΛ
ΕΥϪⲰ ⲙⲙΟϹ ϪΕ ΝΑϣΗΡΕ ΝΑΙ
ΕϮϮ ΝΑΑΚΕ ⲙⲙΟΟΥ ϣΑΝΤΕ
ΠΕϪϹ ϪΙ ⲙΟΡⲪΗ ΝϨΗΤΤΗΥ
ΤΝ ΑΥⲰ ΟΝ Ϥϣϣ ΕΒΟΛ ϪΕ
15. ϮϹΒΤⲰΤ ΓΑΡ ΕΠΑΡϨΙϹΤΑ ⲙ
Ν ΟΥΠΑΡΘΕΝΟϹ ΕϹΟΥΑΑΒ
ΝΟΥϨΑΙ ΝΟΥⲰΤ ΠΕϪϹ ΑΛΛΑ
ΕΠΙΔΗ ΑΥΝΑΥ ΕΤΕΧΑΡΙϹ ΕΝ
ΤΑ ΠΙⲰΤ ΕΤϨΗΠ ΤΑΑϹ ΝΑΥ
20. ΝΤΟϤ ϨⲰⲰϤ ΠΕΠΡΟΠΑΤⲰΡ
ΑϤΟΥⲰϣ ΕΚΤΕ ΠΤΗΡϤ ΕϨΟΥΝ
ΕΠΙⲰΤ ΕΘΗΠ ϪΕ ΠΕϤΟΥⲰϣ
ΠΕ ΠΑΙ ΕΤΡΕ ΠΤΗΡϤ ΚΟΤϤ Ε
ΡΟϤ ΑΥⲰ ΝΤΕΡΕϹΝΑΥ ΕΝΕΙ
25. ⲙΝΤΝΟϬ ΝϬΙ ΤⲙΑΑΥ ΝΑΙ ΕΝ
ΤΑΥΤΑΑΥ ⲙΠΕϹΠΡΟΠΑΤⲰΡ
ΑϹΡΑϣΕ ΕⲙΑΤΕ ΑΥⲰ ΑϹΤΕ
ΛΗΛ ⲙⲙΟϹ ΕΤΒΕ ΠΑΙ ϹϪⲰ ⲙ
ⲙΟϹ ϪΕ ΑΠΑϨΗΤ ΕΥⲮΡΑΝΕ ΑΥ
30. Ⲱ ΑΠΑΛΑϹ ΤΕΛΗΛ ⲙΝΝϹⲰϹ
ΑϹⲰϣ ΕΒΟΛ ΟΥΒΕ ΤϬΟⲙ ΝΑΠΕΡ
ΑΝΤΟϹ ΤΑΙ ΕΤΑϨΕΡΑΤϹ ϨΑΤⲙ
ΠΑΙⲰΝ ΕΘΗΠ ⲙΠΙⲰΤ ΤΑΝΙ
ΝΟϬ ΝΔΥΝΑⲙΙϹ ΝΕΟΟΥ ΤΑΙ
35. ΕΤΟΥⲙΟΥΤΕ ΕΡΟϹ ϨΑΤΝ ΝΕΟΟΥ
ϪΕ ΤΡΙΓΕΝΙΘΛΟϹ ΕΤΕ ΤΑΙ ΤΕ

L

MS. f. 126R

C.S. p. 40

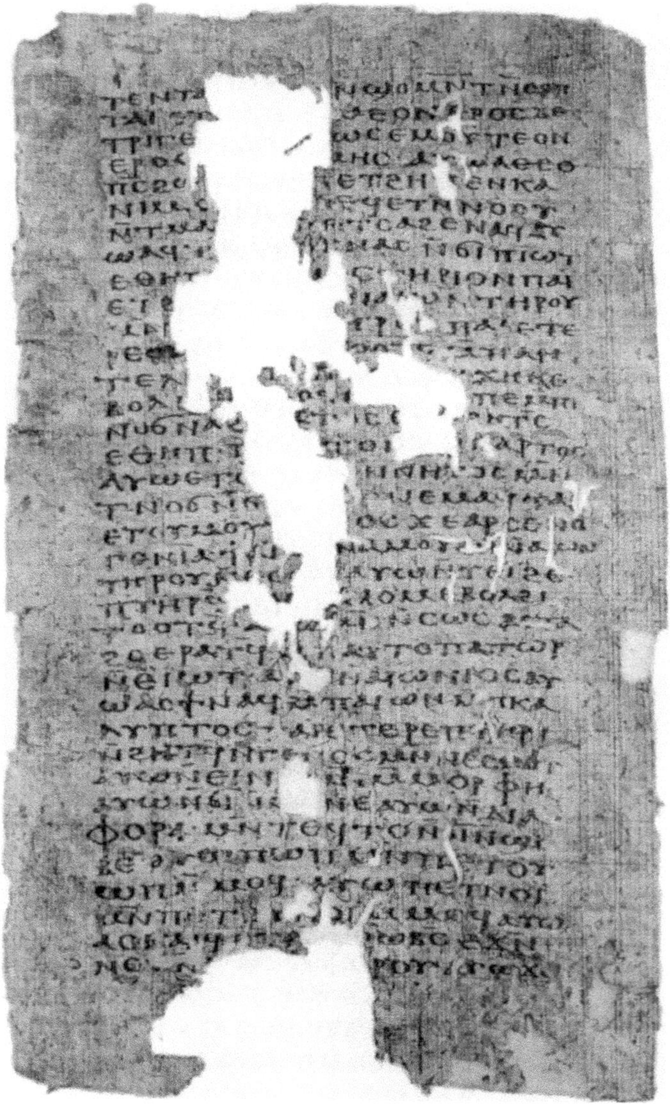

1. ⲦⲉⲚⲦⲀⲨⲬⲠⲞⳓ ⲚⲰϢⲞⲙⲚⲦ ⲚⳓⲞⲠ
ⲦⲀⲒ ⲈⲦⲞⲨⲙⲞⲨⲦⲈ ⲞⲚ ⲈⲢⲞⳓ ⲬⲈ
ⲦⲢⲒⲄⲈⲚⲎⳓ ⲀⲨⲰ ⳓⲈⲙⲞⲨⲦⲈ ⲞⲚ
ⲈⲢⲞⳓ ⲬⲈ ⳨ⲀⲢⲙⲎⳓ ⲀⲨⲰ ⲀⳓⳓⲞ

5. Ⲡⳓ ⳨ⲰⲰⳓ ⲙⲠⲈⲦ⳨ⲎⲠ ⲈⲚⲔⲀ
ⲚⲒⲙ ⲬⲉⲔⲀⲀⳓ ⲈⲨⲈⲦⲚⲚⲞⲞⲨ
ⲚⲦⲙⲀⲀⲨ ⲙⲠⲈⲦⳓⲀϩⲈ ⲚⲀⲨ ⲀⲨ
ⲱ ⲀⲨⲦⲚⲚⲞⲞⲨ ⲚⲀⳓ ⲚϬⲒ ⲠⲒⲰⲦ
ⲈⲐⲎⲠ ⲙⲠⲙⲨⳓⲦⲎⲢⲒⲞⲚ ⲠⲀⲒ

10. ⲈⲦϩⲰⲂⳓ Ⲉ⳨Ⲛ ⲚⲀⲒⲰⲚ ⲦⲎⲢⲞⲨ
ⲙⲚ ⲚⲈⲞⲞⲨ ⲦⲎⲢⲞⲨ ⲠⲀⲒ ⲈⲦⲈ
ⲢⲈ ⲞⲨⲔⲖⲞⲙ ⲚⲦⲞⲞⲦⳓ ⲙⲠⲀⲚ
ⲦⲈⲖⲎⳓ ⲈⲦⲈ ⲠⲀⲒ ⲠⲈ ⲈⲨⲬⲎⲔ Ⲉ
ⲂⲞⲗ ⲚⲨⲦⲀⲗⲞⲨ Ⲉ⳨Ⲛ ⲦⲀⲠⲈ ⲙⲠⲒ

15. ⲚⲞϬ ⲚⲀϩⲞⲢⲀⲦⲞⳓ ⲈⲦⲚϩⲎⲦⳓ
ⲈⲐⲎⲠ ⲠⲀⲒ ⲈⲦⲞ ⲚⲀⲮⲐⲀⲢⲦⲞⳓ
ⲀⲨⲰ ⲈⲦⲞ ⲚⲀⲄⲈⲚⲚⲎⲦⲞⳓ ⲙⲚ
ⲦⲚⲞϬ ⲚϬⲞⲙ ⲈⲦⲚⲈⲙⲀⲨ ⲦⲀⲒ
ⲈⲦⲞⲨⲙⲞⲨⲦⲈ ⲈⲢⲞⳓ ⲬⲈ ⲀⲢⳓⲈⲚⲞ

20. ⲄⲈⲚⲒⲀ ⲦⲀⲒ ⲈⲦⲚⲀⲙⲞⲨϩ ⲚⲚⲀⲒⲰⲚ
ⲦⲎⲢⲞⲨ ⲚⲈⲞⲞⲨ ⲀⲨⲰ ⲚⲦⲈⲒϩⲈ
ⲠⲦⲎⲢⳓ ⲚⲀ⳨Ⲓ ⲔⲖⲞⲙ ⲈⲂⲞⲗ ϩⲒ
ⲦⲞⲞⲦⳓ ⲀⲨⲰ ⲙⲚⲚⳓⲰⳓ ⲀⳓⲦⲀ
ϩⲞ ⲈⲢⲀⲦⳓ ⲙⲠⲀⲨⲦⲞⲠⲀⲦⲰⲢ

25. ⲚⲈⲒⲰⲦ ⲀⲨⲰ ⲚⲀⲒⲰⲚⲒⲞⳓ ⲀⲨ
ⲱ ⲀⳓⲦⲚⲀⲨⲙⲠⲀⲒⲰⲚ ⲙⲠⲔⲀ
ⲗⲨⲠⲦⲞⳓ ⲠⲀⲒ ⲈⲦⲈⲢⲈ ⲠⲦⲎⲢⳓ
ⲚϩⲎⲦⳓ ⲚⲄⲈⲚⲞⳓ ⲙⲚ ⲚⲈⳓⲙⲞⲦ
ⲀⲨⲰ ⲚⲈⲒⲚⲈ ⲙⲚ ⲙⲙⲞⲢⲪⲎ

30. ⲀⲨⲰ ⲚϬⲒⲚⲙⲒⲚⲈ ⲀⲨⲰ ⲚⲀⲒⲀ
ⲪⲞⲢⲀ ⲙⲚ ⲦⲈⲨⲦⲞ ⲚϬⲒⲚⲱϢⲒ
ⲂⲈ ⲀⲨⲰ ⲠⲰⲠ ⲙⲚ ⲠⲈⲦⲞⲨ
ⲱⲠ ⲙⲙⲞⳓ ⲀⲨⲰ ⲠⲈⲦⲚⲞⲒ
ⲙⲚ ⲠⲈⲦⲞⲨⲚⲞⲒ ⲙⲙⲞⳓ ⲀⲨⲰ

35. ⲀⳓⲔⲀⲀⳓ ⲈⲦⲢⲈⲨϩⲰⲂⳓ Ⲉ⳨Ⲛ
ⲚⲈⲦⲚϩⲎⲦⲞⲨ ⲦⲎⲢⲞⲨ ⲀⲨⲰ ⲬⲈ

30 α. Owing to the bad condition of the original, Woide was unable to read this word, and wrote ϣⲓⲛⲉ=*questions*. Dr Schmidt proposes to substitute ϣⲓⳓⲉ. This seems unlikely, as the word occurs in the next line. I suggest ⲙⲓⲛⲉ, the left half of the ⲙ being visible.

1. ⲕⲁⲁⲥ ⲉⲩⲛⲁϯ ⲙⲡⲉⲧⲥⲟⲡⲥⲡ ⲙ
ⲙⲟⲩ ⲁⲩⲱ ⲁⲥϯ ⲛⲁⲩ ⲙⲙⲏⲧⲉ
ⲛⲇⲩⲛⲁⲙⲓⲥ ⲁⲩⲱ ⲯⲓⲧⲉ ⲛϩⲉⲛ
ⲛⲁⲥ ⲁⲩⲱ ⲟⲩⲡⲉⲛⲧⲁⲥ ⲛⲛⲁⲓ
5. ⲱⲛ ⲁⲩⲱ ⲁⲩϯ ⲛⲁⲩ ⲛϩⲉⲛⲯⲱⲥ
ⲧⲏⲣ ⲁⲩⲱ ⲁⲩϯ ⲧⲉⲍⲟⲩⲥⲓⲁ ⲛⲁⲩ
ⲉϫⲛ ⲛⲉⲑⲏⲡ ⲧⲏⲣⲟⲩ ϫⲉⲕⲁⲁⲥ
ⲉⲩⲛⲁⲭⲁⲣⲓⲍⲉ ⲛⲛⲉⲛⲧⲁⲩⲁ
ⲅⲱⲛⲓⲍⲉ ⲁⲩⲱ ⲁⲩⲡⲱⲧ ⲛ
10. ⲧⲛ ⲑⲩⲗⲏ ⲙⲡⲁⲓⲱⲛ ⲉⲁⲩ
ⲕⲁⲁⲥ ⲛⲥⲱⲟⲩ ⲁⲩⲱ ⲁⲩⲡⲱⲧ
ⲉϩⲣⲁⲓ ⲉⲡⲁⲓⲱⲛ ⲙⲡⲁⲩⲧⲟ
ⲡⲁⲧⲱⲣ ⲁⲩϫⲓ ⲛⲁⲩ ⲙⲡⲉⲣⲏⲧ
ⲉⲛⲧⲁⲩⲉⲣⲏⲧ ⲙⲙⲟⲩ ⲛⲁⲩ ϩⲓ
15. ⲧⲙ ⲡⲉⲧϫⲱ ⲙⲙⲟⲥ ϫⲉ ⲡⲉ
ⲧⲛⲁⲕⲁ ⲉⲓⲱⲧ ϩⲓ ⲙⲁⲁⲩ ϩⲓ ⲥⲟⲛ
ϩⲓ ⲥⲱⲛⲉ ϩⲓ ⲥϩⲓⲙⲉ ϩⲓ ϣⲏⲣⲉ
ϩⲓ ϩⲩⲡⲁⲣⲝⲓⲥ ⲁⲩⲱ ⲛϥϥⲓ ⲙ
ⲡⲉⲩⲥⳁⲟⲥ ⲛϥⲟⲩⲁϩϥ ⲛⲥⲱⲓ
20. ϥⲛⲁϫⲓ ⲛⲛⲉⲣⲏⲧ ⲉⲛⲧⲁⲓ ⲉⲣⲏⲧ
ⲙⲙⲟⲟⲩ ⲛⲁⲩ ⲁⲩ ⲡⲙⲩⲥⲧⲏⲣⲓ
ⲟⲛ ⲙⲡⲁⲓⲱⲧ ⲉⲑⲏⲡ ϯⲛⲁⲧⲁⲁⲩ
ⲛⲁⲩ ϫⲉ ⲁⲩⲙⲉⲣⲉ ⲡⲉⲧⲉ ⲡⲱ
ⲟⲩ ⲡⲉ ⲁⲩⲱ ⲁⲩⲡⲱⲧ ⲉⲃⲟⲗ ⲙ
25. ⲡⲉⲧⲡⲏⲧ ⲛⲥⲱⲟⲩ ϩⲛ ⲟⲩϫⲓ
ⲛϭⲟⲛⲥ ⲁⲩⲱ ⲁⲩϯ ⲛⲁⲩ ⲙⲡⲱⲟⲩ
ϣⲟⲩ ⲁⲩⲱ ⲡⲣⲁϣⲉ ⲁⲩⲱ ⲡⲧⲉ
ⲗⲏⲗ ⲁⲩⲱ ⲡⲟⲩⲛⲟⲩ ⲁⲩⲱ ϯⲣⲏ
ⲛⲏ ⲁⲩⲱ ⲑⲉⲗⲡⲓⲥ ⲁⲩⲱ ⲧⲡⲓⲥ
30. ⲧⲓⲥ ⲁⲩⲱ ⲧⲁⲅⲁⲡⲏ ⲁⲩⲱ ⲧⲁⲗⲏ
ⲑⲓⲁ ⲉⲧⲉ ⲙⲉⲥⲡⲱⲛⲉ ⲁⲩⲱ
ⲧⲁⲓ ⲧⲉ ⲑⲉⲛⲛⲁⲥ ⲉⲛⲧⲁⲩⲭⲁⲣⲓ

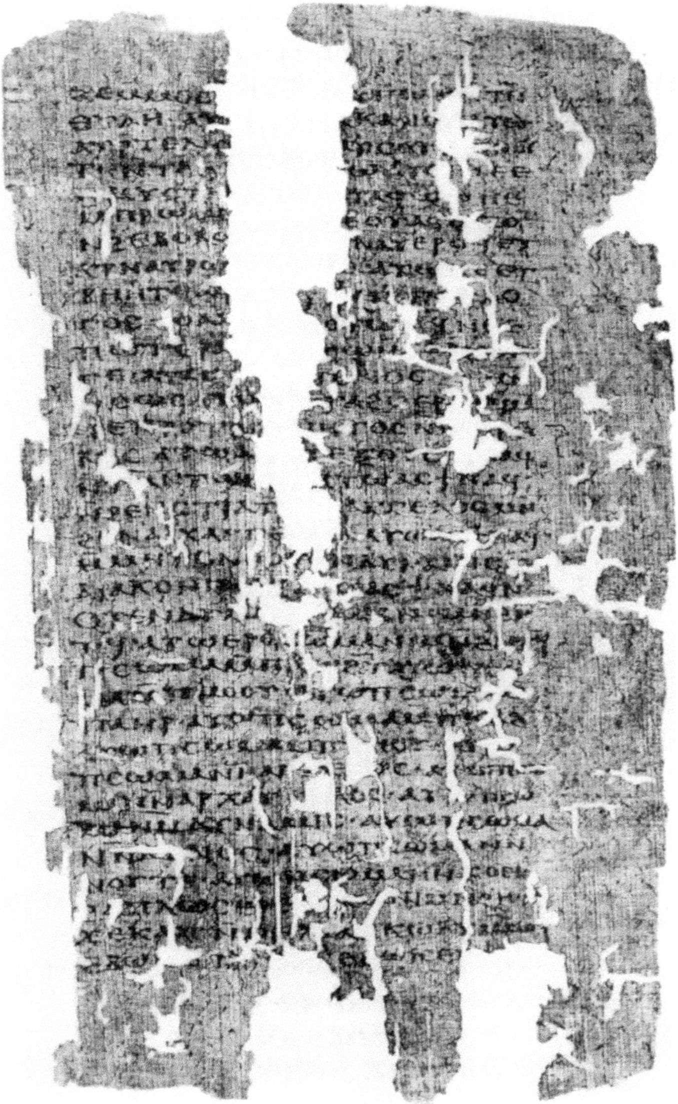

1. ϫε ⲙⲙⲟⲥ ⲛⲛⲉⲛⲧⲁⲩⲡⲱⲧ ⲛⲧⲛ
ⲑⲩⲗⲏ ⲁⲩⲱ ⲁⲩⲣⲙⲁⲕⲁⲣⲓⲟⲥ ⲁⲩⲱ
ⲁⲩⲣⲧⲉⲗⲓⲟⲥ ⲁⲩⲱ ⲁⲩⲥⲟⲩⲛ ⲡⲛⲟⲩ
ⲧⲉ ⲛⲧⲁⲗⲏⲑⲓⲁ ⲁⲩⲱ ⲁⲩⲉⲓⲙⲉ ⲉ
5. ⲡⲙⲩⲥⲧⲏⲣⲓⲟⲛ ⲉⲛⲧⲁⲩϣⲱⲡⲉ
ⲙⲡⲣⲱⲙⲉ ϫⲉ ⲉⲧⲃⲉ ⲟⲩ ⲁⲩⲟⲩⲱ
ⲛϩ ⲉⲃⲟⲗ ϣⲁⲛⲧⲟⲩⲛⲁⲩ ⲉⲣⲟⲩ ⲉⲩ
ⲁⲧⲛⲁⲩ ⲣⲱ ⲉⲣⲟⲩ ⲡⲉ ⲁⲩⲱ ϫⲉ ⲉⲧ
ⲃⲏⲏⲧⲩ ⲁⲩⲗⲟⲅⲣⲫⲏ ⲉⲡⲉⲩⲗⲟ
10. ⲅⲟⲥ ϣⲁⲛⲧⲟⲩⲥⲟⲩⲱⲛⲩ ⲛⲥⲉ
ⲡⲱⲧ ⲉⲣⲁⲧⲩ ⲁⲩⲱ ⲛⲥⲉⲣⲛⲟⲩ
ⲧⲉ ⲁⲩⲱ ⲛⲥⲉⲣⲧⲉⲗⲓⲟⲥ ⲙⲛ
ⲛⲥⲱⲥ ⲁⲧⲙⲁⲁⲩ ⲧⲁϩⲟ ⲉⲣⲁⲧⲩ ⲙ
ⲡⲉⲡⲣⲟⲧⲟⲅⲉⲛⲏⲧⲟⲥ ⲛϣⲏⲣⲉ
15. ⲛⲁⲥ ⲁⲩⲱ ⲁⲥϯ ⲧⲉⲍⲟⲩⲥⲓⲁ ⲛⲁⲩ
ⲛⲧⲙⲛⲧϣⲏⲣⲉ ⲁⲩⲱ ⲁⲥϯ ⲛⲁⲩ
ⲛϩⲉⲛⲥⲧⲣⲁⲧⲓⲁ ⲛⲁⲅⲅⲉⲗⲟⲥ ⲙⲛ
ϩⲉⲛⲁⲣⲭⲁⲅⲅⲉⲗⲟⲥ ⲁⲩⲱ ⲁⲥϯ ⲛⲁⲩ
ⲙⲙⲛⲧⲥⲛⲟⲟⲩⲥ ⲛⲇⲩⲛⲁⲙⲓⲥ ⲉⲩ
20. ⲇⲓⲁⲕⲟⲛⲓ ⲛⲁⲩ ⲁⲩⲱ ⲁⲥϯ ⲛⲁⲩ ⲛ
ⲟⲩⲉⲛⲇⲩⲙⲁ ⲉⲣϩⲱⲃ ⲛⲓⲙ ⲛϩⲏ
ⲧⲩ ⲁⲩⲱ ⲉⲣⲉ ⲥⲱⲙⲁ ⲛⲓⲙ ⲛϩⲏⲧⲩ
ⲡⲥⲱⲙⲁ ⲙⲡⲕⲱϩⲧ ⲁⲩⲱ ⲡⲥⲱ
ⲙⲁ ⲙⲡⲙⲟⲟⲩ ⲁⲩⲱ ⲡⲥⲱⲙⲁ ⲙ
25. ⲡⲁⲏⲣ ⲁⲩⲱ ⲡⲥⲱⲙⲁ ⲙⲡⲕⲁϩ
ⲁⲩⲱ ⲡⲥⲱⲙⲁ ⲙⲡⲧⲛⲟⲩ ⲁⲩⲱ
ⲡⲥⲱⲙⲁ ⲛⲛⲁⲅⲅⲉⲗⲟⲥ ⲁⲩⲱ ⲡⲥⲱ
ⲙⲁ ⲛⲛⲁⲣⲭⲁⲅⲅⲉⲗⲟⲥ ⲁⲩⲱ ⲡⲥⲱ
ⲙⲁ ⲛⲛⲇⲩⲛⲁⲙⲓⲥ ⲁⲩⲱ ⲡⲥⲱⲙⲁ
30. ⲛⲛⲇⲩⲛⲟⲥ ⲁⲩⲱ ⲡⲥⲱⲙⲁ ⲛⲛ
ⲛⲟⲩⲧⲉ ⲁⲩⲱ ⲡⲥⲱⲙⲁ ⲛⲛⲁⲇⲟⲉⲓⲥ
ϩⲁⲡⲗⲱⲥ ⲉⲣⲉ ⲥⲱⲙⲁ ⲛⲓⲙ ⲛϩⲏⲧⲩ
ϫⲉⲕⲁⲁⲥ ⲛⲛⲉ ⲗⲁⲁⲩ ⲕⲱⲗⲩ ⲙⲙⲟⲩ
ⲉⲃⲱⲕ ⲉⲡϫⲓⲥⲉ ⲏ ⲉⲃⲱⲕ ⲉⲡⲉⲥⲏⲧ

1. ЄПNOYN ΑΥШ ПΑΙ ПЄΙПРΟΤΟΓЄ
ΝΗΤШР ЄΝΤΑ ΝΑПϨΟΥΝ ΜΝ ΝΑ
ПΒΟλ ЄРΗΤ ΝΑΥ ΜПЄΤΥΝΑΟΥΑШϤ
ΤΗΡϤ ΑΥШ ПΑΙ ПЄ ЄΝΤΑΥΔΙΑ

5. ΚΡΙΝЄ ΝΘΥλΗ ΤΗΡС ΑΥШ ΝΘЄ
ЄΝΤΑΥ ПΑϨΤϤ ЄΒΟλ ЄΧШС Ν
ΘЄ ΝΟΥϨΑλΗΤ ЄШΑΥПШРШ ЄΒΟλ
ΝΝЄΥΤΝϨ ЄΧΝ ΝЄΥСΟΟΥϨЄ
ΤΑΙ ΤЄ ΘЄ ЄΝΤΑΥΑΑС ΝΘΥλΗ

10. ΝϬΙ ПЄПРΟΤΟΓЄΝΗΤШР ΑΥ
Ш ΑΥΤΟΥΝΟС ΝϨЄΝΤΒΑ Ν
ΤΒΑ ΝЄΙΔΟС Η ΝΓЄΝΟС
ΝΤЄРЄ ΘΥλΗ ϨΜΟΜ ΑСΒШλ
ЄΒΟλ ΜПΑШΑΙ ΝΝΔΥΝΑΜΙС

15. ЄΤΝΜΜΑΥ ΑΥШ ΑΥ˙ΤΟШ Є
ϨΡΑΙ ΝΘЄ ΜПРШΤ ΑΥШ ΑСПΟΡΧΟΥ
ЄΒΟλ ΚΑΤΑ ΓЄΝΟС ΑΥШ ΚΑ
ΤΑ ЄΙΔΟС ΑΥШ ΑΥ†ΝΟΜΟС
ΝΑΥ ЄΜЄРЄ ΝЄΥЄРΗΥ ΑΥШ

20. ЄΤΑΙЄ ПΝΟΥΤЄ ΑΥШ ЄСΜΟΥ
ЄРΟΥ ΑΥШ ЄШΙΝЄ ΝСШϤ ΧЄ
ΝΙΜ ПЄ ΑΥШ ΧЄ ΟΫ ΟΥ ПЄ
ΑΥШ ΝСЄРШПΗРЄ ΜПΜΑ ЄΝ
ΤΑΥЄΙ ЄΒΟλ ΝϨΗΤϤ ΧЄ ΥϬΗΟΥ

25. ΑΥШ ϤΜΟΚϨ ΑΥШ ΝСЄΤΜ
ΚΟΤΟΥ ЄРΟΥ ΝΚЄСΟП ΑλλΑ Є
ПШΤ ΝСΑ ПЄΝΤΑΥ† ΝΟΜΟС
ΝΑΥ ΑΥШ ΑΥΝΤΟΥ ЄΒΟλ ϨΜ
ПΚΑΚЄ ΝΘΥλΗ ЄΤΟ ΜΜΑΑΥ

30. ΝΑΥ ΑΥШ ΑΥΧΟΟС ΝΑΥ ΧЄ ΟΥ
ΝΟΥΟЄΙΝ ШΟΟП ЄΒΟλ ΧЄ Μ
ПΑΤΟΥЄΙΜЄ ЄПΟΥΟЄΙΝ ΧЄ
ΝЄΥШΟΟП ПЄ ΧΝ ΜΜΟΝ

23. ·· deleted word.

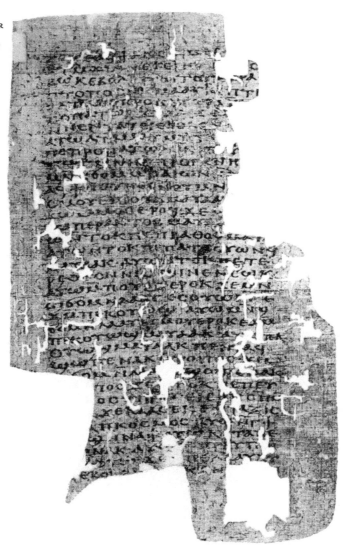

ⲓ ⲧⲟⲧⲉ ⲁⲩⲧⲁⲛⲥⲙⲙⲉ ⲉⲧⲟⲟⲧⲟⲩ
ⲉⲧⲙⲭⲓ ⲛⲛⲉⲩⲉⲣⲏⲩ ⲛⲃⲟⲛⲥ ⲁⲩ
ⲃⲱⲕ ⲉⲃⲟⲗ ϩⲓⲧⲟⲟⲧⲟⲩ ⲉϩⲣⲁⲓ ⲉ
ⲡⲧⲟⲡⲟⲥ ⲛⲧⲙⲁⲁⲩ ⲙⲡⲧⲏⲣϥ
5. ϩⲁⲧⲙ ⲡⲉⲡⲣⲟⲡⲁⲧⲱⲣ ⲙⲛ ⲡⲁⲩ
ⲧⲟⲡⲁⲧⲱⲣ ⲭⲉⲕⲁⲁⲥ ⲉⲩⲉϯ ⲧⲱⲱ
ⲛⲛⲉⲛⲧⲁⲩⲉⲓ ⲉⲃⲟⲗ ϩⲛ ⲑⲩⲗⲏ
ⲁⲩⲱ ⲁⲧⲙⲁⲁⲩ ⲙⲡⲧⲏⲣϥ ⲙⲛ
ⲡⲉⲡⲣⲟⲡⲁⲧⲱⲣ ⲙⲛ ⲡⲁⲩⲧⲟⲡⲁ
10. ⲧⲱⲣ ⲙⲛ ⲡⲉⲡⲣⲟⲅⲉⲛⲏⲧⲱⲣ
ⲙⲛ ⲛϭⲟⲙ ⲙⲡⲁⲓⲱⲛ ⲛⲧⲙⲁⲁⲩ
ⲁⲩϯ ⲛⲟⲩⲛⲟϭ ⲛϩⲩⲙⲛⲟⲥ ⲉⲩ
ⲥⲙⲟⲩ ⲉⲡⲓⲟⲩⲁ ⲙⲁⲩⲁⲁⲩ ⲉⲩ
ⲭⲱ ⲙⲙⲟⲥ ⲉⲣⲟϥ ⲭⲉ ⲛⲧⲟⲕ ⲡⲉ
15. ⲡⲁⲡⲉⲣⲁⲛⲧⲟⲥ ⲙⲁⲩⲁⲁⲕ ⲁⲩ
ⲱ ⲛⲧⲟⲕ ⲡⲉ ⲡⲃⲁⲑⲟⲥ ⲙⲁⲩⲁⲕ
ⲁⲩⲱ ⲛⲧⲟⲕ ⲡⲉ ⲡⲁⲧⲥⲟⲩⲱⲛϥ
ⲙⲁⲩⲁⲁⲕ ⲁⲩⲱ ⲛⲧⲟⲕ ⲡⲉⲧⲉ
ⲣⲉ ⲟⲩⲟⲛ ⲛⲓⲙ ϣⲓⲛⲉ ⲛⲥⲱⲕ
20. ⲁⲩⲱ ⲙⲡⲟⲩϩⲉ ⲉⲣⲟⲕ ⲭⲉ ⲙⲛ
ϣϭⲟⲙ ⲛⲗⲁⲁⲩ ⲉⲥⲟⲩⲱⲛⲅ ⲉ
ⲭⲙ ⲡⲉⲕⲟⲩⲱϣ ⲁⲩⲱ ⲙⲛϣ
ϭⲟⲙ ⲛⲗⲁⲁⲩ ⲉⲥⲙⲟⲩ ⲉⲣⲟⲕ ⲉⲭⲙ
ⲡⲉⲕⲟⲩⲱϣ ⲙⲁⲩⲁⲁⲕ ⲁⲩⲱ ⲡⲉⲕ
25. ⲟⲩⲱϣ ⲙⲁⲩⲁⲁⲕ ⲡⲉⲛⲧⲁⲩ
ϣⲱⲡⲉ ⲛⲁⲕ ⲛⲧⲟⲡⲟⲥ ⲭⲉ ⲙⲛ
ϣϭⲟⲙ ⲛⲗⲁⲁⲩ ⲉϣⲱⲡⲉ ⲛⲁⲕ
ⲛⲧⲟⲡⲟⲥ ⲭⲉ ⲛⲧⲟⲕ ⲡⲉ ⲡⲉⲩ
ⲧⲟⲡⲟⲥ ⲧⲏⲣⲟⲩ ⲉⲓⲥⲟⲡⲥ ⲙ
30. ⲙⲟⲕ ⲭⲉⲕⲁⲁⲥ ⲉⲕⲉϯ ⲧⲁⲍⲓⲥ
ⲛⲛⲁⲡⲕⲟⲥⲙⲟⲥ ⲁⲩⲱ ⲛⲅϯ
ⲧⲱϣ ⲛⲛⲁⲧⲟⲣϣ ⲕⲁⲧⲁ ⲡⲉ
ⲧⲉϩⲛⲁⲕ ⲁⲩⲱ ⲙⲡⲣⲗⲩⲡⲓ ⲛ
ⲛⲁⲧⲟⲣϣ ⲭⲉ ⲙⲡⲉⲗⲁⲁⲩ ⲗⲩ
35. ⲡⲓ ⲉⲃⲟⲗ ϩⲓⲧⲟⲟⲧⲕ ⲉⲛⲉϩ ⲁⲩⲱ

---

12 α. 3rd pers. sing. pron. in error for 3rd pers. plur.

LV
MS. f. 130v
C.S. p. 45

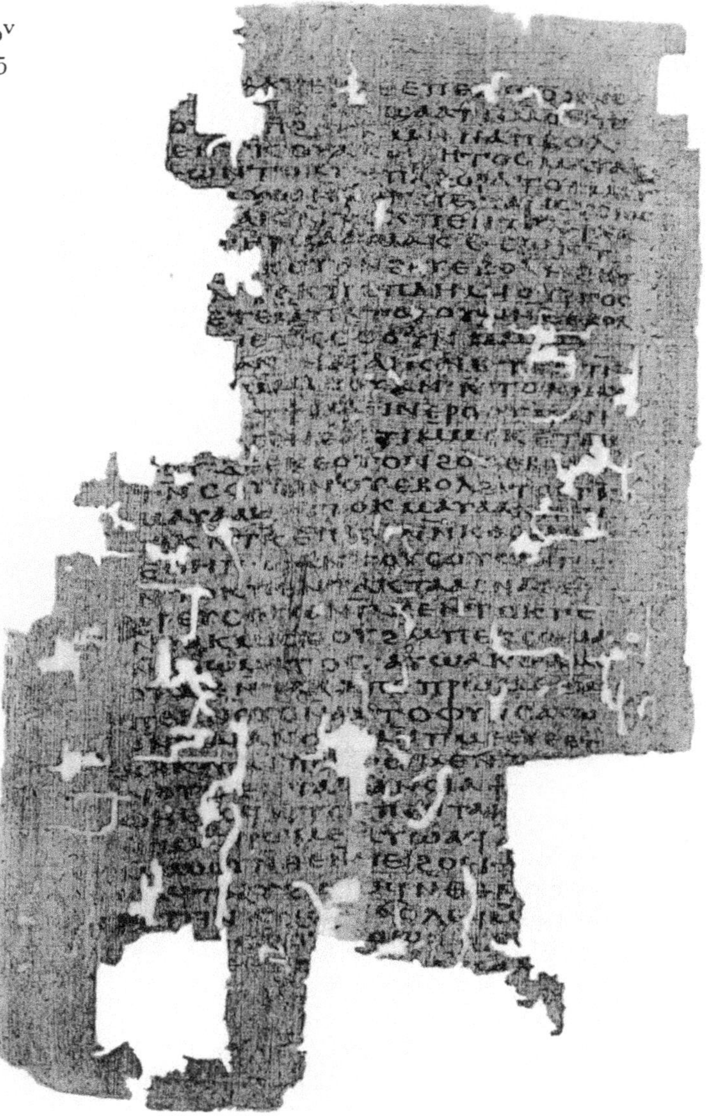

1. ⲙ̄ⲡⲉ ⲗⲁⲁⲩ ⲉⲓⲙⲉ ⲉⲡⲉⲕϣⲟⲭⲛⲉ
ⲛⲧⲟⲕ ⲡⲉⲧⲟⲩϣⲁⲁⲧ ⲙⲙⲟⲕ ⲧⲏ
ⲣⲟⲩ ⲛⲁⲡϩⲟⲩⲛ ⲙⲛ ⲛⲁⲡⲃⲟⲗ
ϫⲉ ⲛ̄ⲧⲕ ⲟⲩⲁⲭⲱⲣⲏⲧⲟⲥ ⲙⲁⲩⲁⲕ

5. ⲁⲩⲱ ⲛⲧⲟⲕ ⲡⲉ ⲡⲁϩⲟⲣⲁⲧⲟⲥ ⲙⲁⲩ
ⲁⲁⲕ ⲁⲩⲱ ⲛⲧⲟⲕ ⲡⲉ ⲡⲁⲛⲟⲩⲥⲓⲟⲥ
ⲙⲁⲩⲁⲁⲕ ⲛⲧⲟⲕ ⲡⲉⲛⲧⲁⲕϯ ⲭⲁ
ⲣⲁⲕⲧⲏⲣ ⲙⲁⲩⲁⲁⲕ ⲉⲥⲱⲛⲧ
ⲛⲓⲙ ⲁⲕⲟⲩⲟⲛϩⲟⲩ ⲉⲃⲟⲗ ⲛϩⲏⲧ

10. ⲕ ⲛⲧⲟⲕ ⲡⲉ ⲡⲇⲏⲙⲓⲟⲩⲣⲅⲟⲥ
ⲛⲛⲉⲧⲉ ⲙⲡⲁⲧⲟⲩⲟⲩⲱⲛϩ ⲉⲃⲟⲗ
ϫⲉ ⲛⲁⲓ ⲉⲧⲉ ⲕⲥⲟⲟⲩⲛ ⲙⲙⲟⲟⲩ
ⲙⲁⲩⲁⲁⲕ ⲛⲁⲓ ⲁⲛⲟⲛ ⲉⲧⲉ ⲛⲧⲛ
ⲥⲟⲟⲩⲛ ⲙⲙⲟⲟⲩ ⲁⲛ ⲛⲧⲟⲕ ⲙⲁⲩ

15. ⲁⲁⲕ ⲡⲉⲧϯ ⲙⲁⲉⲓⲛ ⲉⲣⲟⲟⲩ ⲛⲁⲛ
ϫⲉⲕⲁⲁⲥ ⲉⲛⲉⲁⲓⲧⲓ ⲙⲙⲟⲕ ⲉⲧⲃⲏ
ⲧⲟⲩ ϫⲉ ⲉⲕⲉⲟⲩⲟⲛϩⲟⲩ ⲉⲃⲟⲗ ⲛ
ⲧⲛⲥⲟⲩⲱⲛⲟⲩ ⲉⲃⲟⲗ ϩⲓⲧⲟⲟⲧⲕ
ⲙⲁⲩⲁⲁⲕ ⲛⲧⲟⲕ ⲙⲁⲩⲁⲁⲕ ⲡⲉⲛ

20. ⲧⲁⲕⲛⲧⲕ ⲉⲡϣⲓ ⲛⲛⲕⲟⲥⲙⲟⲥ
ⲉⲑⲏⲡ ϣⲁⲛⲧⲟⲩ ⲥⲟⲩⲱⲛⲅ
ⲛⲧⲟⲕ ⲡⲉⲛⲧⲁⲕ ⲧⲁⲁⲥ ⲛⲁⲩ ⲉ
ⲧⲣⲉⲩ ⲥⲟⲩⲱⲛⲅ ϫⲉ ⲛⲧⲟⲕ ⲡⲉ
ⲛⲧⲁⲕ ⲙⲉⲥⲓⲟⲟⲩ ϩⲙ ⲡⲉⲕⲥⲱⲙⲁ

25. ⲛⲁⲥⲱⲙⲁⲧⲟⲥ ⲁⲩⲱ ⲁⲕⲧⲁⲙⲓⲟ
ⲟⲩ ϫⲉ ⲛⲧⲁⲕ ⲭⲡⲉ ⲡⲣⲱⲙⲉ ϩⲙ
ⲡⲉⲕⲛⲟⲩⲥ ⲛⲁⲩⲧⲟⲯⲩⲏⲥ ⲁⲩⲱ
ϩⲛ ⲧⲇⲓⲁⲛⲟⲓⲁ ⲙⲛ ⲡⲙⲉⲉⲩⲉ ⲉⲧ
ϫⲏⲕ ⲡⲁⲓ ⲡⲉ ⲡⲣⲱⲙⲉ ⲛϫⲡⲟ ⲛ

30. ⲛⲟⲩⲥ ⲉⲛⲧⲁ ⲇⲓⲁⲛⲟⲓⲁ ϯ ⲙⲟⲣ
ⲯⲏ ⲉⲣⲟⲩ ⲛⲧⲟⲕ ⲡⲉⲛⲧⲁⲕϯ ⲛⲕⲁ
ⲛⲓⲙ ⲙⲡⲣⲱⲙⲉ ⲁⲩⲱ ⲁⲩⲫⲟⲣⲓ
ⲙⲙⲟⲟⲩ ⲛⲑⲉ ⲛⲛⲉⲓϩⲟⲉⲓⲧⲉ ⲁⲩ
ⲱ ⲁⲩⲧⲁⲁⲩ ϩⲓⲱⲟⲩ ⲛⲑⲉ ⲛⲛⲉⲓ

35. ϣⲧⲏⲛ ⲁⲩⲱ ⲁⲩϭⲟⲗⲉϥ ⲙⲡⲥ
ⲱⲛⲧ ⲛⲑⲉ ⲟⲩⲣϣⲱⲛ ⲡⲁⲓ ⲡⲉ
ⲡⲣⲱⲙⲉ ⲉⲧⲉⲣⲉ ⲡⲧⲏⲣϥ ϣⲗⲏⲗ ⲉ

1. ⲥⲟⲩⲱⲛⲩ ⲛⲧⲟⲕ ⲙⲁⲁⲩⲁⲁⲕ
ⲡⲉⲛⲧⲁⲕⲟⲩⲉϩⲥⲁϩⲛⲉ ⲙⲡⲣⲱⲙⲉ
ϫⲉⲕⲁⲁⲥ ⲉⲩⲉⲟⲩⲱⲛϩ ⲉⲃⲟⲗ ⲛⲥⲉ
ⲥⲟⲩⲱⲛⲅ ⲉⲃⲟⲗ ϩⲓⲧⲟⲟⲧⲩ ϫⲉ ⲛ

5. ⲧⲟⲕ ⲡⲉⲛⲧⲁⲕ ϫⲡⲟⲩ ⲁⲩⲱ ⲁⲕⲟⲩ
ⲱⲛϩ ⲉⲃⲟⲗ ⲕⲁⲧⲁ ⲡⲉⲕ ⲟⲩⲱϣ
ⲛⲧⲟⲕ ⲡⲉⲧϯ ϣⲗⲏⲗ ⲉϩⲣⲁⲓ ⲉⲣⲟⲕ
ⲡⲓⲱⲧ ⲙⲙⲛⲧⲉⲓⲱⲧ ⲛⲓⲙ ⲁⲩⲱ
ⲡⲛⲟⲩⲧⲉ ⲛⲛⲟⲩⲧⲉ ⲛⲓⲙ ⲁⲩⲱ

10. ⲡϫⲟⲉⲓⲥ ⲛϫⲟⲉⲓⲥ ⲛⲓⲙ ⲡⲁⲓ ⲁⲛⲟⲕ
ⲉⲧⲥⲟⲡⲥⲡ ⲙⲙⲟⲩ ϫⲉⲕⲁⲁⲥ ⲉⲩⲉ
ϯ ⲧⲁϩⲓⲥ ⲛⲛⲁⲉⲓⲇⲟⲥ ⲙⲛ ⲛⲁϯ
ⲟⲩⲱ ⲛⲁⲓ ⲛⲧⲁϯⲟⲩⲣⲟⲧ ⲛⲁⲩ
ϩⲙ ⲡⲉⲕⲣⲁⲛ ⲁⲩⲱ ϩⲛ ⲧⲉⲕ ϭⲟⲙ

15. ⲡⲙⲟⲛⲁⲣⲭⲏⲥ ⲙⲁⲩⲁⲁⲩ ⲁⲩⲱ ⲡⲁⲧ
ϣⲓⲃⲉ ⲙⲁⲩⲁⲁⲩ ⲙⲁ ⲛⲁⲓ ⲛⲟⲩϭⲟⲙ
ⲁⲩⲱ ϯⲛⲁⲧⲣⲉ ⲛⲁⲧⲟⲩⲱ ⲥⲟⲩ
ⲱⲛⲅ ϫⲉ ⲛⲧⲟⲕ ⲡⲉ ⲡⲉⲩⲥⲱⲧⲏⲣ
ⲁⲩⲱ ⲛⲧⲉⲣⲉ ⲧⲙⲁⲁⲩ ϭⲱ ⲉⲥⲥⲟⲡ

20. ⲥⲡ ⲙⲡⲁⲡⲉⲣⲁⲛⲧⲟⲥ ⲁⲩⲱ ⲡⲉ̄ⲁ
ⲅⲛⲱⲥⲧⲟⲥ ⲁⲩⲱ ⲡⲉⲧⲙⲟⲩϩ ⲙ
ⲡⲧⲏⲣⲩ ⲁⲩⲱ ⲉⲩⲧⲁⲛϩⲟ ⲙⲙⲟ
ⲟⲩ ⲧⲏⲣⲟⲩ ⲁⲩⲱ ⲁⲩⲥⲱⲧⲙ ⲉ
ⲣⲟⲥ ⲙⲛ ⲛⲉⲧⲛⲙⲙⲁⲥ ⲉⲧⲏⲡ ⲉ

25. ⲣⲟⲥ ⲧⲏⲣⲟⲩ ⲁⲩⲱ ⲁⲩⲧⲛⲛⲟⲟⲩ
ⲛⲁⲥ ⲛⲟⲩⲇⲩⲛⲁⲙⲓⲥ ⲉⲃⲟⲗ ϩⲙ ⲡⲣⲱ
ⲙⲉ ⲡⲁⲓ ⲉⲧⲟⲩⲉⲡⲓⲑⲩⲙⲓ ⲉⲛⲁⲩ ⲉ
ⲣⲟⲩ ⲁⲩⲱ ⲁⲩⲉⲓ ⲉⲃⲟⲗ ϩⲙ ⲡⲁⲡⲉⲣ
ⲁⲛⲧⲟⲥ ⲛϭⲓ ⲡⲓⲥⲡⲓⲛⲑⲏⲣ ⲛⲁⲡⲉⲣ

30. ⲁⲛⲧⲟⲥ ⲡⲁⲓ ⲉⲛⲧⲁ ⲛⲁⲓⲱⲛ ⲣ
ϣⲡⲏⲣⲉ ⲙⲙⲟⲩ ϫⲉ ⲉⲛⲉⲩϩⲏⲡ
ⲧⲱⲛ ⲡⲉ ⲉⲙⲡⲁⲧⲩⲟⲩⲱⲛϩ ⲉ
ⲃⲟⲗ ϩⲙ ⲡⲁⲡⲉⲣⲁⲛⲧⲟⲥ ⲛⲉⲓⲱⲧ
ⲡⲁⲓ ⲉⲛⲧⲁⲩⲟⲩⲱⲛϩ ⲡⲧⲏⲣⲩ ⲉ

35. ⲃⲟⲗ ⲛϩⲏⲧⲩ ⲁⲩⲱ ⲉⲣⲉ ⲡⲁⲓ ϩⲏⲡ

---

13. The 1st pers. sing. pron. has probably been
omitted in error, the word should be ⲛⲧⲁⲓϯⲟⲩⲣⲟⲧ.

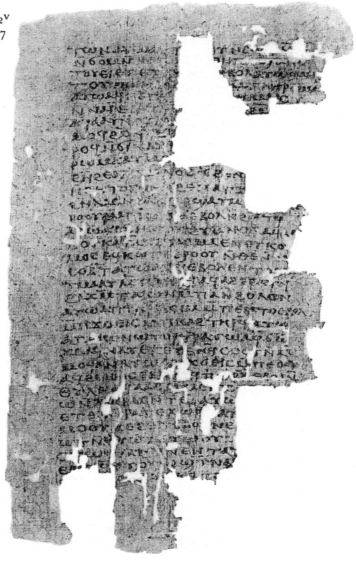

1. ⲧⲱⲛ ⲁⲩⲱ ⲁⲩⲟⲩⲁϩⲟⲩ ⲛⲥⲱⲩ ⲛϭⲓ
ⲛϭⲟⲙ ⲛⲛⲁⲓⲱⲛ ⲛⲉⲑⲏⲡ ϣⲁⲛ
ⲧⲟⲩⲉⲓ ⲉⲡⲉⲧⲟⲩⲟⲛϩ ⲉⲃⲟⲗ ⲁⲩⲱ ϣⲁⲛ
ⲧⲟⲩⲡⲱϩ ⲉ ϫ ⲓⲉⲣⲟⲛ ⲙⲡⲗⲏⲣⲱⲙⲁ

5. ⲁⲩⲱ ⲁⲩϩⲟⲡⲩ ϩⲛ ⲛⲁⲩⲛⲁⲙⲓⲥ
ⲛⲛⲁⲓ ⲉⲛⲧⲁⲩⲉⲓ ⲉⲃⲟⲗ ϩⲙ ⲡⲉⲑⲏⲡ
ⲁⲩⲁⲁⲩ ⲛⲟⲩⲕⲟⲥⲙⲟⲥ ⲁⲩϥⲟⲣⲓ ⲙ
ⲙⲟⲩ ϩⲙ ϫ ⲓⲉⲣⲟⲛ ⲁⲩⲱ ⲁⲩⲛⲁⲩ ⲉ
ⲣⲟⲩ ⲛϭⲓ ⲛⲁⲩⲛⲁⲙⲓⲥ ⲙⲡⲉⲡⲗⲏ

10. ⲣⲱⲙⲁ ⲁⲩⲙⲉⲣⲓⲧⲩ ⲁⲩⲥⲙⲟⲩ ⲉⲣⲟⲩ
ϩⲛ ϩⲉⲛϩⲩⲙⲛⲟⲥ ⲉϩⲉⲛⲁⲧϣⲁϫⲉ
ⲛϩⲏⲧⲟⲩ ⲛⲉ ⲉϩⲉⲛⲁⲧⲭⲟⲟⲩ ⲛⲉ
ϩⲛ ⲗⲁⲥ ⲛⲥⲁⲣⲝ̄ ⲉϣⲁⲩⲙⲟⲕⲙⲉⲕ ⲉ
ⲣⲟⲟⲩ ϩⲙ ⲡⲣⲱⲙⲉ ⲉⲃⲟⲗ ⲛϩⲏⲧⲩ

15. ⲁⲩⲱ ⲁⲩϫⲓ ⲙⲡⲉⲩϩⲩⲙⲛⲟⲥ ⲁⲩⲁⲁⲩ
ⲛⲟⲩⲕⲁⲧⲁⲡⲉⲧⲁⲥⲙⲁ ⲉⲛⲉⲩⲕⲟⲥ
ⲙⲟⲥ ⲉⲩⲕⲱⲧⲉ ⲉⲣⲟⲟⲩ ⲛⲑⲉ ⲛⲟⲩ
ⲥⲟⲃⲧ ⲁⲩⲱ ⲁⲩⲉⲓ ⲉⲃⲟⲗ ⲉⲛⲧⲟϣ ⲛ
ⲧⲙⲁⲁⲩ ⲙⲡⲧⲏⲣⲩ ⲁⲩⲁϩⲉⲣⲁⲧⲩ

20. ϩⲓϫⲙ ⲡⲁⲓⲱⲛ ⲙⲡⲁⲛϩⲟⲗⲱⲛ
ⲁⲩⲱ ⲁⲡⲧⲏⲣⲩ ⲕⲓⲙ ⲙⲡⲉⲙⲧⲟ ⲉⲃⲟⲗ
ⲙⲡⲭⲟⲉⲓⲥ ⲙⲡⲕⲁϩ ⲧⲏⲣⲩ ⲁⲩⲱ
ⲁⲡⲁⲓⲱⲛ ϣⲧⲟⲣⲧⲣ ⲁⲩⲱ ⲁⲩϭⲱ
ϫⲉ ⲁⲩⲛⲁⲩ ⲉⲡⲉⲧⲉ ⲛ̄ⲥⲟⲟⲩⲛ ⲙ

25. ⲙⲟⲩ ⲁⲛ ⲁⲩⲱ ⲁⲡⲭⲟⲉⲓⲥ ⲙⲡⲉⲟⲟⲩ
ⲁⲩϩⲙⲟⲟⲥ ⲉϩⲣⲁⲓ ⲁⲩⲡⲱⲣϫ ⲉⲃⲟⲗ ⲛ
ⲑⲩⲗⲏ ⲁⲩⲁⲁⲥ ⲙⲙⲉⲣⲟⲥ ⲥⲛⲁⲩ ⲁⲩ
ⲱ ⲛⲭⲱⲣⲁ ⲥⲛⲧⲉ ⲁⲩⲱ ⲁⲩϯ ⲧⲟϣ
ⲉⲧⲉⲭⲱⲣⲁ ⲧⲉⲭⲱⲣⲁ ⲁⲩⲱ ⲁⲩⲧⲁ

30. ⲙⲟⲟⲩ ϫⲉ ϩⲉⲛⲉⲃⲟⲗ ⲛⲉ ϩⲛ ⲟⲩⲉⲓ
ⲱⲧ ⲛⲟⲩⲱⲧ ⲁⲩⲱ ⲟⲩⲙⲁⲁⲩ ⲛ
ⲟⲩⲱⲧ ⲁⲩⲱ ⲛⲉⲛⲧⲁⲩⲡⲱⲧ
ⲉⲣⲁⲧⲩ ⲁⲩⲟⲩⲱϣⲧ ⲛⲁⲩ ⲁⲩϯ
ⲛⲁⲩ ⲛⲧⲉⲭⲱⲣⲁ ⲉⲧⲥⲁⲟⲩⲛⲁⲙ

1. ⲙⲙⲟⲩ ⲁⲩⲱ ⲁⲩⲭⲁⲣⲓⲍⲉ ⲛⲁⲩ ⲙⲡⲱ
ⲛⲍ ϣⲁ ⲉⲛⲉⲍ ⲁⲩⲱ ⲧⲙⲛⲧⲁⲧⲙⲟⲩ
ⲁⲩⲱ ⲁⲩⲙⲟⲩⲧⲉ ⲉⲧⲉⲧⲥⲁⲟⲩⲛⲁⲙ
ϫⲉ ⲧⲉⲭⲱⲣⲁ ⲙⲡⲱⲛⲍ ⲁⲩⲱ ⲧⲉⲧⲥⲁ
5. ⲍⲃⲟⲩⲣ ϫⲉ ⲧⲉⲭⲱⲣⲁ ⲙⲡⲙⲟⲩ ⲁⲩⲱ
ⲁⲩⲙⲟⲩⲧⲉ ⲉⲧⲉⲭⲱⲣⲁ ⲉⲧⲥⲁⲟⲩ
ⲛⲁⲙ ϫⲉ ⲧⲉⲭⲱⲣⲁ ⲙⲡⲟⲩⲟⲉⲓⲛ ⲁⲩ
ⲱ ⲧⲉⲧⲥⲁⲍⲃⲟⲩⲣ ϫⲉ ⲧⲉⲭⲱⲣⲁ ⲙ
ⲡⲕⲁⲕⲉ ⲁⲩⲱ ⲁⲩⲙⲟⲩⲧⲉ ⲉⲧⲉⲭⲱ
10. ⲣⲁ ⲉⲧⲥⲁⲟⲩⲛⲁⲙ ϫⲉ ⲧⲉⲭⲱⲣⲁ ⲛ
ⲧⲁⲛⲁⲡⲁⲩⲥⲓⲥ ⲁⲩⲱ ⲧⲉⲭⲱⲣⲁ ⲉⲧⲥⲁ
ⲍⲃⲟⲩⲣ ϫⲉ ⲧⲉⲭⲱⲣⲁ ⲙⲡⲍⲓⲥⲉ ⲁⲩⲱ
ⲁⲩⲛ ⲍⲉⲛⲧⲟϣ ⲟⲩⲧⲱⲟⲩ ⲁⲩⲱ ⲍⲉⲛ
ⲕⲁⲧⲁⲡⲉⲧⲁⲥⲙⲁ ⲟⲩⲧⲱⲟⲩ ϫⲉ ⲉ
15. ⲛⲉⲩⲛⲁⲩ ⲉⲛⲉⲩⲉⲣⲏⲩ ⲁⲩⲱ ⲁⲩⲕⲱ
ⲛⲍⲉⲛⲯⲩⲗⲁⲍ ϩⲓϫⲛ ⲛⲉⲩⲕⲁⲧⲁⲡⲉ
ⲧⲁⲥⲙⲁ ⲁⲩⲱ ⲁⲩϯ ⲛⲍⲉⲛⲧⲁⲓⲟ
ⲉⲛⲁϣⲱⲟⲩ ⲛⲛⲉⲛⲧⲁⲩⲟⲩⲱϣⲧ
ⲛⲁⲩ ⲁⲩⲱ ⲁⲩⲁⲁⲩ ⲛⲛⲟϭ ⲉϫⲛ ⲛⲉⲛ
20. ⲧⲁⲩⲁⲛⲧⲓⲗⲉⲅⲉ ⲁⲩⲱ ⲁⲩⲟⲩⲱⲍⲙ
ⲛⲁⲩ ⲁⲩⲱ ⲁⲩⲥⲱⲣ ⲉⲃⲟⲗ ⲛⲧⲉⲭⲱ
ⲣⲁ ⲉⲧⲥⲁⲟⲩⲛⲁⲙ ⲉⲍⲉⲛⲭⲱⲣⲁ
ⲉⲛⲁϣⲱⲟⲩ ⲁⲩⲱ ⲁⲩⲁⲁⲩ ⲛⲧⲁ
ⲝⲓⲥ ⲧⲁⲝⲓⲥ ⲁⲩⲱ ⲁⲓⲱⲛ ⲁⲓⲱⲛ
25. ⲁⲩⲱ ⲕⲟⲥⲙⲟⲥ ⲕⲟⲥⲙⲟⲥ ⲁⲩⲱ
ⲙⲡⲉ ⲡⲉ ⲁⲩⲱ ⲥⲧⲉⲣⲉⲱⲙⲁ
ⲥⲧⲉⲣⲉⲱⲙⲁ ⲁⲩⲱ ⲙⲡⲏⲩⲉ ⲙ
ⲡⲏⲩⲉ ⲁⲩⲱ ⲛⲧⲟⲡⲟⲥ ⲧⲟⲡⲟⲥ
ⲁⲩⲱ ⲙⲙⲁ ⲙⲁ ⲁⲩⲱ ⲛⲭⲱⲣⲏⲙⲁ
30. ⲭⲣⲱⲣⲏⲙⲁ ⲁⲩⲱ ⲁⲩⲧⲱϣ ⲛⲁⲩ
ⲛⲍⲉⲛⲛⲟⲙⲟⲥ ⲁⲩϯ ⲛⲁⲩ ⲛⲍⲉⲛ
ⲁⲛⲥⲙⲙⲉ ϫⲉ ϭⲱ ϩⲙ ⲡⲁϣⲁϫⲉ
ⲁⲩⲱ ϯⲛⲁϯ ⲛⲏⲧⲛ ⲙⲡⲱⲛⲍ ϣⲁ
ⲉⲛⲉⲍ ⲁⲩⲱ ϯⲛⲁⲧⲛⲛⲟⲟⲩ ⲛⲏ
35. ⲧⲛ ⲛⲍⲉⲛⲇⲩⲛⲁⲙⲓⲥ ⲁⲩⲱ ϯⲛⲁ
ⲧⲁϫⲣⲱⲧⲛ ϩⲛ ϩⲉⲛⲡⲛⲁ ⲛϭⲟⲙ

LIX
MS. f. 134^{v}
C.S. p. 49

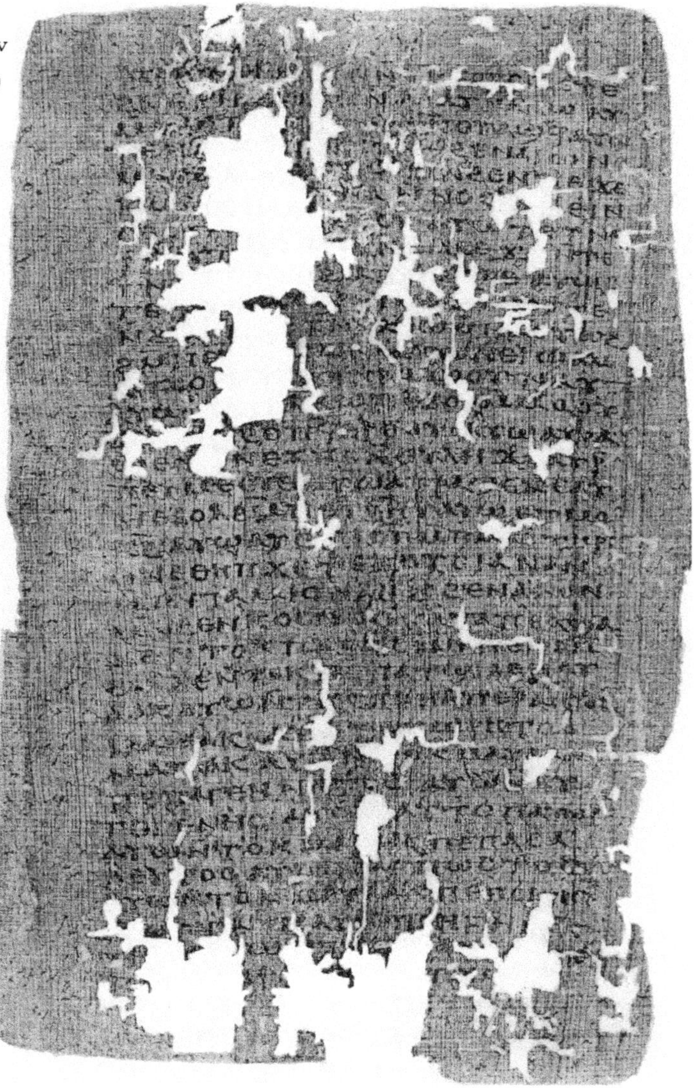

1. ⲁⲩⲱ ϯⲛⲁϯ ⲛⲏⲧⲛ ⲛⲟⲩⲉⲍⲟⲩⲥⲓⲁ ⲉⲧⲉ
ⲅⲛⲏⲧⲛ ⲁⲩⲱ ⲙⲛ ⲗⲁⲁⲩ ⲛⲁⲕⲱⲗⲩ
ⲙⲙⲱⲧⲛ ⲉⲡⲉⲧⲉⲧⲛⲟⲩⲁϣϥ ⲁⲩⲱ
ⲧⲉⲧⲛⲁⲭⲡⲟ ⲛⲏⲧⲛ ⲛⲅⲉⲛⲁⲓⲱⲛ
5. ⲙⲛ ⲅⲉⲛⲕⲟⲥⲙⲟⲥ ⲙⲛ ⲅⲉⲛⲡⲉ ⲭⲉ
ⲕⲁⲁⲥ ⲉⲣⲉ ⲛⲉⲡⲛⲁ ⲛⲛⲟⲉⲣⲟⲛ ⲉⲓ ⲛ
ⲥⲉⲟⲩⲱⲅ ⲛⲅⲏⲧⲟⲩ ⲁⲩⲱ ⲧⲉⲧⲛⲉ
ⲣⲛⲟⲩⲧⲉ ⲛⲧⲉⲧⲛⲉⲓⲙⲉ ⲭⲉ ⲛⲧⲉ
ⲧⲛⲅⲉⲛⲉⲃⲟⲗ ⲅⲙ ⲡⲛⲟⲩⲧⲉ ⲁⲩⲱ
10. ⲧⲉⲧⲛⲉⲛⲁⲩ ⲉⲣⲟⲩ ⲉⲩⲟ ⲛⲛⲟⲩⲧⲉ
ⲛⲅⲏⲧⲧⲏⲩⲧⲛ ⲁⲩⲱ ϥⲛⲁⲟⲩⲱⲅ
ⲅⲙ ⲡⲉⲧⲛⲁⲓⲱⲛ ⲁⲩⲱ ⲛⲉⲓϣⲁⲭⲉ
ⲁⲡⲭⲟⲉⲓⲥ ⲙⲡⲧⲏⲣϥ ⲭⲟⲟⲩ ⲛⲁⲩ
ⲁⲩⲱ ⲁⲩⲁⲛⲁⲭⲱⲣⲓ ⲉⲃⲟⲗ ⲙⲙⲟⲟⲩ
15. ⲁⲩⲱ ⲁⲩⲅⲟⲡϥ ⲉⲣⲟⲟⲩ ⲁⲩⲱ ⲁⲩⲣⲁ
ϣⲉ ⲛϭⲓ ⲛⲉⲭⲡⲟ ⲛⲑⲩⲗⲏ ⲭⲉ ⲁⲩⲣ
ⲡⲉⲩⲙⲉⲉⲩⲉ ⲁⲩⲱ ⲁⲩⲣⲁϣⲉ ⲭⲉ ⲁⲩ
ⲉⲓ ⲉⲃⲟⲗ ⲅⲙ ⲡⲉⲧϭⲏⲩ ⲁⲩⲱ ⲉⲧⲙⲟ
ⲕⲅ ⲁⲩⲱ ⲁⲩⲥⲟⲡⲥⲡ ⲙⲡⲙⲩⲥⲧⲏⲣⲓ
20. ⲟⲛ ⲉⲑⲏⲡ ⲭⲉ ϯⲉⲍⲟⲩⲥⲓⲁ ⲛⲁⲛ
ⲛⲧⲛ ⲧⲁⲙⲓⲟ ⲛⲁⲛ ⲛⲅⲉⲛⲁⲓⲱⲛ
ⲙⲛ ⲅⲉⲛⲕⲟⲥⲙⲟⲥ ⲕⲁⲧⲁ ⲡⲉⲕϣⲁ
ⲭⲉ ⲛⲧⲟⲕ ⲡⲭⲟⲉⲓⲥ ᵃⲙⲛ ⲡⲉⲕⲅⲙ
ⲅⲁⲗ ⲭⲉ ⲛⲧⲟⲕ ⲡⲉ ⲡⲁⲧϣⲓⲃⲉ ⲙⲁⲩ
25. ⲁⲁⲕ ⲁⲩⲱ ⲛⲧⲟⲕ ⲡⲉ ⲡⲁⲡⲉⲣⲁⲛⲧⲟⲥ
ⲙⲁⲩⲁⲁⲕ ⲁⲩⲱ ⲡⲁⲭⲱⲣⲏⲧⲟⲥ
ⲙⲁⲩⲁⲁⲕ ⲁⲩⲱ ⲛⲧⲟⲕ ⲙⲁⲩⲁⲁⲕ
ⲡⲉ ⲡⲁⲅⲉⲛⲛⲏⲧⲟⲥ ⲁⲩⲱ ⲛⲁⲩ
ⲧⲟⲅⲉⲛⲏⲥ ⲁⲩⲱ ⲛⲁⲩⲧⲟⲡⲁⲧⲱⲣ
30. ⲁⲩⲱ ⲛⲧⲟⲕ ⲙⲁⲩⲁⲁⲕ ⲡⲉ ⲡⲁⲥⲁ
ⲗⲉⲩⲧⲟⲥ ⲁⲩⲱ ⲛⲁⲅⲛⲱⲥⲧⲟⲥ
ⲁⲩⲱ ⲛⲧⲟⲕ ⲙⲁⲩⲁⲁⲕ ⲡⲉ ⲡⲥⲓⲅⲏ
ⲁⲩⲱ ⲧⲁⲅⲁⲡⲏ ⲁⲩⲱ ⲧⲡⲏⲅⲏ ⲙⲡ
ⲧⲏⲣϥ ⲁⲩⲱ ⲛⲧⲟⲕ ⲙⲁⲩⲁⲁⲕ ⲡⲉ
35. ⲡⲁⲧⲅⲩⲗⲏ ⲁⲩⲱ ⲡⲁⲧⲭⲱⲅⲙ

23 α. Dr Schmidt states that the sign :/: follows this word in the original, and that Woide referred it to a phrase which he said was written in the margin. This was no longer to be seen when M. G. Schwartze inspected the text. The disappearance was probably due to the fact that since Woide's day the margins had been trimmed. For the significance of the phrase, vide note 5, LIX (comm.).

LX
MS. f. 136R
C.S. p. 50

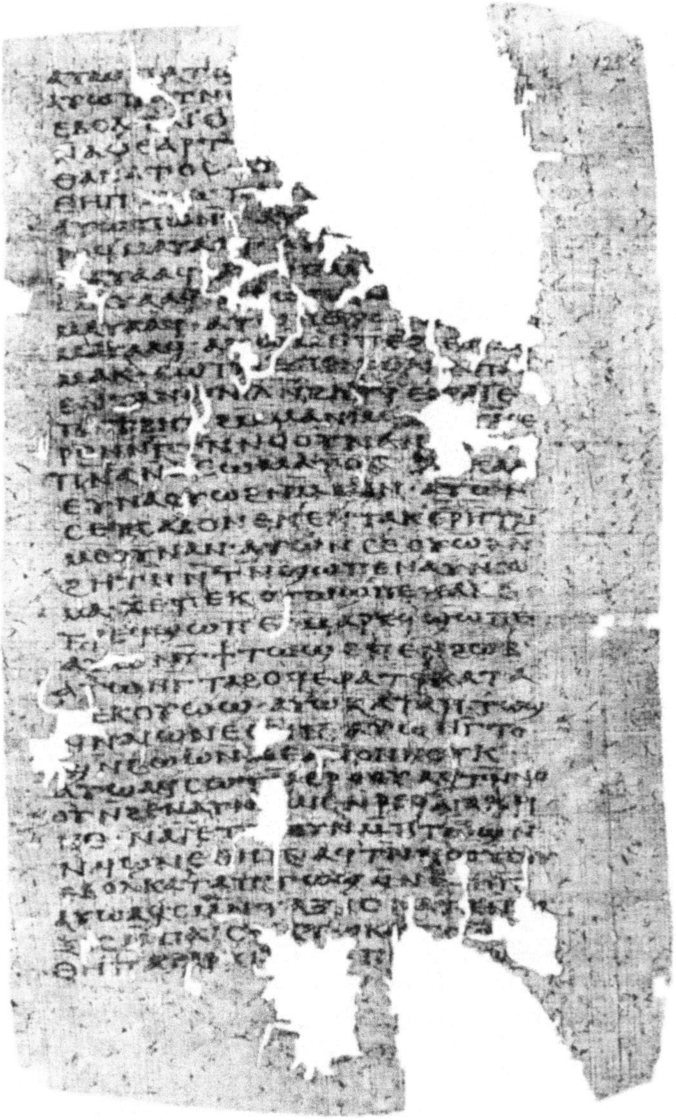

1. ⲁⲩⲱ ⲡⲁⲧϣⲁϫⲉ ⲉⲧⲉⲩⲅⲉⲛⲉⲁ
ⲁⲩⲱ ⲡⲁⲧⲛⲟⲓ ⲛⲧⲉⲩϭⲓⲛⲟⲩⲱⲛϩ
ⲉⲃⲟⲗ ϩⲁⲓⲟ ⲥⲱⲧⲙ ⲉⲣⲟⲓ ⲡⲓⲱⲧ
ⲛⲁⲫⲑⲁⲣⲧⲟⲥ ⲁⲩⲱ ⲡⲓⲱⲧ ⲛⲁ
5. ⲑⲁⲛⲁⲧⲟⲥ ⲁⲩⲱ ⲡⲛⲟⲩⲧⲉ ⲛⲛⲉ
ⲑⲏⲡ ⲁⲩⲱ ⲡⲟⲩⲟⲉⲓⲛ ⲙⲁⲩⲁⲁⲩ
ⲁⲩⲱ ⲡⲱⲛϩ ⲁⲩⲱ ⲡⲁⲧⲛⲁⲩ ⲉ
ⲣⲟϥ ⲙⲁⲩⲁⲁⲩ ⲁⲩⲱ ⲡⲁϩⲣⲏⲧⲟⲥ
ⲙⲁⲩⲁⲁⲩ ⲁⲩⲱ ⲡⲁⲙⲓⲁⲛⲧⲟⲥ
10. ⲙⲁⲩⲁⲁⲩ ⲁⲩⲱ ⲡⲁⲇⲁⲙⲁⲛⲧⲟⲥ
ⲙⲁⲩⲁⲁⲩ ⲁⲩⲱ ⲡⲉⲧϣⲟⲟⲡ ⲛϣⲟⲣⲡ
ⲙⲁⲩⲁⲁⲩ ⲁⲩⲱ ⲙⲛ ⲡⲉⲧϩⲓⲑⲏ ⲙ
ⲙⲁⲕ ⲥⲱⲧⲙ ⲉⲡⲉⲛϣⲗⲏⲗ ⲡⲁⲓ
ⲉⲛⲧⲁⲛϣⲗⲏⲗ ⲛϩⲏⲧϥ ⲉϩⲣⲁⲓ ⲉ
15. ⲡⲉⲧϩⲏⲡ ϩⲙ ⲙⲁ ⲛⲓⲙ ⲥⲱⲧⲙ ⲉ
ⲣⲟⲛ ⲛⲅⲧⲛⲛⲟⲟⲩ ⲛⲁⲛ ⲛϩⲉⲛ
ⲡⲛⲁ ⲛⲁⲥⲱⲙⲁⲧⲟⲥ ϫⲉⲕⲁⲁⲥ
ⲉⲩⲛⲁⲟⲩⲱϩ ⲛⲙⲙⲁⲛ ⲁⲩⲱ ⲛ
ⲥⲉⲧⲥⲁⲃⲟⲛ ⲉⲛⲉⲛⲧⲁⲕⲉⲣⲏⲧ ⲙ
20. ⲙⲟⲟⲩ ⲛⲁⲛ ⲁⲩⲱ ⲛⲥⲉⲟⲩⲱϩ ⲛ
ϩⲏⲧⲛ ⲛⲧⲛϣⲱⲡⲉ ⲛⲁⲩ ⲛⲥⲱ
ⲙⲁ ϫⲉ ⲡⲉⲕⲟⲩⲱϣ ⲡⲉ ⲡⲁⲓ ⲉ
ⲧⲣⲉⲩ ϣⲱⲡⲉ ⲙⲁⲣⲉϥϣⲱⲡⲉ
ⲁⲩⲱ ⲛⲅϯ ⲧⲱϣ ⲉⲡⲉⲛϩⲱⲃ
25. ⲁⲩⲱ ⲛⲅⲧⲁϩⲟⲩ ⲉⲣⲁⲧϥ ⲕⲁⲧⲁ
ⲡⲉⲕⲟⲩⲱϣ ⲁⲩⲱ ⲕⲁⲧⲁ ⲡⲧⲱϣ
ⲛⲛⲁⲓⲱⲛ ⲉⲑⲏⲡ ⲁⲩⲱ ⲛⲅⲧⲟ
ϣⲛ ϩⲱⲱⲛ ϫⲉ ⲁⲛⲟⲛ ⲛⲟⲩⲕ
ⲁⲩⲱ ⲁⲩⲥⲱⲧⲙ ⲉⲣⲟⲟⲩ ⲁⲩⲧⲛⲛⲟ
30. ⲟⲩ ⲛϩⲉⲛⲇⲩⲛⲁⲙⲓⲥ ⲛⲣⲉϥⲇⲓⲁⲕⲣⲓ
ⲛⲉ ⲛⲁⲓ ⲉⲧⲥⲟⲟⲩⲛ ⲙⲡⲧⲱϣ ⲛ
ⲛⲁⲓⲱⲛ ⲉⲑⲏⲡ ⲁⲩⲧⲛⲛⲟⲟⲩⲥⲟⲩ
ⲉⲃⲟⲗ ⲕⲁⲧⲁ ⲡⲧⲱϣ ⲛⲛⲉⲑⲏⲡ
ⲁⲩⲱ ⲁⲩⲥⲙⲛⲧⲁⲝⲓⲥ ⲕⲁⲧⲁ ⲛⲧⲁ
35. ⲝⲓⲥ ⲙⲡⲇⲓⲥⲉ ⲁⲩⲱ ⲕⲁ ⲡⲧⲱϣ ⲉ
ⲑⲏⲡ ⲁⲩⲁⲣⲭⲓ ϫⲓⲛ ⲙⲡⲉⲥⲏⲧ ϣⲁ

12 α. τ written above the line.

LXI
MS. f. 136v
C.S. p. 51

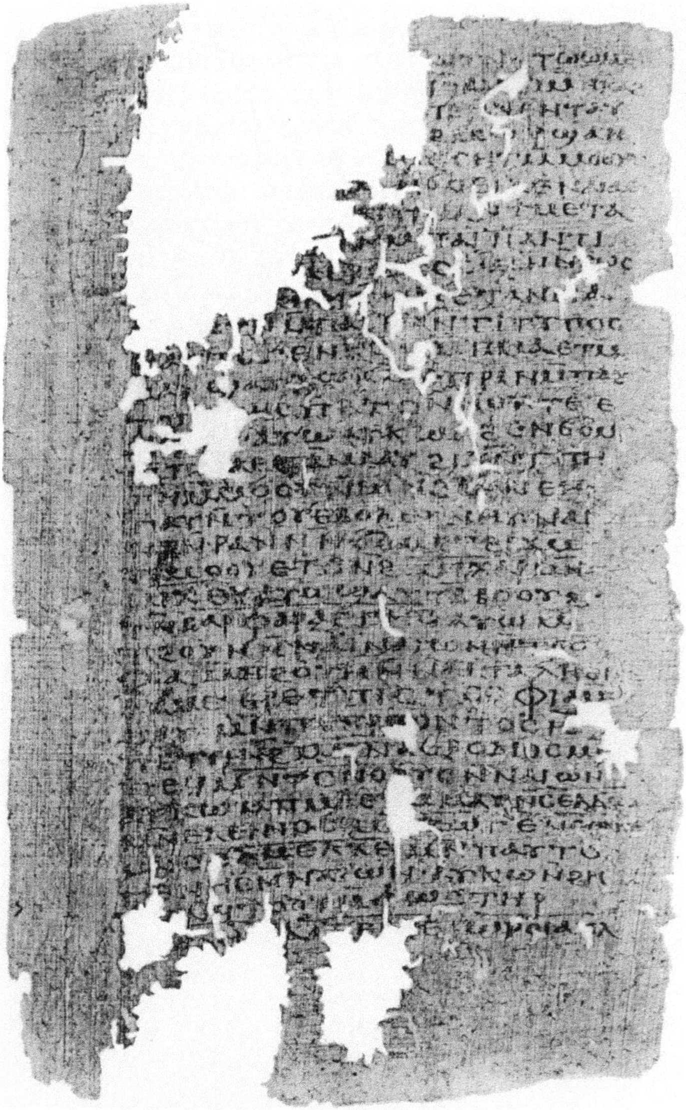

1. ⳍⲣⲁⲓ ⲭⲉⲕⲁⲁⲥ ⲉⲣⲉ ⲡⲕⲱⲧ ⲛⲁⲧⲱⲱⲙⲉ
ⲉⲛⲉⲩⲉⲣⲏⲩ ⲁⲩⲱ ⲁⲩⲧⲁⲙⲓⲟ ⲙⲡⲕⲁⳍ
ⲛⲁⲏⲣ ⲙⲙⲁ ⲛϣⲱⲡⲉ ⲛⲛⲉⲛⲧⲁⲩ
ⲉⲓ ⲉⲃⲟⲗ ⲭⲉ ⲉⲧⲉⲃⲱ ⳍⲓⲭⲱⲩ ϣⲁⲛ
5. ⲧⲁⲭⲣⲟ ⲛⲛⲉⲧⲙⲡⲉⲥⲏⲧ ⲙⲙⲟⲟⲩ
ⲙⲛⲛⲥⲱⲥ ⲡⲙⲁ ⲛϭⲟⲉⲓⲗⲉ ⲛⲁⲙⲉ
ⲙⲡⳍⲟⲩⲛ ⲙⲡⲁⲓ ⲡⲙⲁ ⲛⲧⲙⲉⲧⲁ
ⲛⲟⲓⲁ ⲙⲡⳍⲟⲩⲛ ⲙⲡⲁⲓ ⲛⲁⲛⲧⲓ
ⲧⲩⲡⲟⲥ ⲛⲁⲉⲣⲟⲇⲓⲟⲥ ⲙⲛⲛⲥⲱⲥ
10. ⲧⲡⲁⲣⲟⲓⲕⲏⲥⲓⲥ ⲧⲙⲉⲧⲁⲛⲟⲓⲁ
ⲙⲡⳍⲟⲩⲛ ⲙⲡⲁⲓ ⲛⲁⲛⲧⲓⲧⲩⲡⲟⲥ
ⲛⲁⲩⲧⲟⲅⲉⲛⲏⲥ ⳍⲙ ⲡⲙⲁ ⲉⲧⲙ
ⲙⲁⲩ ϣⲁⲩⲭⲱⲕⲙ ⲉⲡⲣⲁⲛ ⲙⲡⲁⲩ
ⲧⲟⲅⲉⲛⲏⲥ ⲡⲉⲧⲟ ⲛⲛⲟⲩⲧⲉ ⲉ
15. ⲭⲱⲟⲩ ⲁⲩⲱ ⲁⲩⲕⲱ ⲛⳍⲉⲛϭⲟⲙ
ⲙⲡⲙⲁ ⲉⲧⲙⲙⲁⲩ ⳍⲓⲭⲛ ⲧⲡⲏ
ⲅⲏ ⲙⲙⲟⲟⲩ ⲛⲱⲛⳍ ⲛⲁⲓ ⲉⲛ
ⲧⲁⲩⲛⲧⲟⲩ ⲉⲃⲟⲗ ⲉⲩⲛⲏⲩ ⲛⲁⲓ
ⲛⲉ ⲛⲣⲁⲛ ⲛⲛϭⲟⲙ ⲉⲧⳍⲓⲭⲙ
20. ⲡⲙⲟⲟⲩ ⲉⲧⲟⲛⳍ ⲙⲓⲭⲁⲣ ⲙⲛ
ⲙⲓⲭⲉⲩ ⲁⲩⲱ ϣⲁⲩⲧⲃⲃⲟⲟⲩ ⳍⲓ
ⲧⲛ ⲃⲁⲣⲯⲁⲣⲁⲅⲅⲏⲥ ⲁⲩⲱ ⲙ
ⲡⳍⲟⲩⲛ ⲛⲛⲁⲓ ⲛⲁⲓⲱⲛ ⲛⲧⲥⲟ
ⲫⲓⲁ ⲙⲡⳍⲟⲩⲛ ⲛⲛⲁⲓ ⲧⲁⲗⲏⲑⲓⲁ
25. ⲛⲁⲙⲉ ⲉⲣⲉ ⲧⲡⲓⲥⲧ ⲥⲟⲫⲓⲁ ⲙ
ⲙⲁⲩ ⲙⲛ ⲡⲉⲡⲣⲟⲱⲛⲧⲟⲥ ⲓⲥ
ⲡⲉⲧⲟⲛⳍ ⲙⲛ ⲛⲁⲉⲣⲟⲇⲓⲟⲥ ⲙⲛ
ⲡⲉⲩⲙⲛⲧⲥⲛⲟⲟⲩⲥ ⲛⲛⲁⲓⲱⲛ
ⲁⲩⲕⲱ ⲙⲡⲙⲁ ⲉⲧⲙⲙⲁⲩ ⲛⲥⲉⲗⲗⲁⲱ
30. ⲙⲛ ⲉⲗⲉⲓⲛⲟⲥ ⲙⲛ ⳍⲱⲅⲉⲛⲉⲑⲗⲏⲥ
ⲙⲛ ⲥⲉⲗⲙⲉⲗⲭⲉ ⲙⲛ ⲡⲁⲩⲧⲟ
ⲅⲉⲛⲏⲥ ⲛⲛⲁⲓⲱⲛ ⲁⲩⲕⲱ ⲛⳍⲏ
ⲧⲩ ⲛⲩⲧⲟⲟⲩ ⲙⲫⲱⲥⲧⲏⲣ
ⲏⲗⲏⲗⲑ ⲇⲁⲩⲉⲓⲇⲉ ⲱⲣⲟⲓⲁⲏⲗ

TRANSLATION
AND
COMMENTARY

TRANSLATION
AND
COMMENTARY

N.B.

Marginal References. E.g.

I	Top numeral (I) denotes translator's sequence and arrangement of leaves of the Coptic text;
MS. f. 138ᴿ	MS. f. 138ᴿ = folio number in Codex Brucianus;
C.S. p. 52	C.S. p. 52 = page number in Dr Schmidt's transcript and German translation.

Reference Numbers in the Notes. E.g. (vide II) = top numeral of the Marginal Reference, *i.e.* II = II, MS. f. 138ᵛ, C.S. p. 53.

Greek Words in the Text. The Coptic form, spelling, and terminations are retained, but to obviate the use of Coptic type, ordinary Greek letters are employed, e.g. ανουσιος = ⲁⲛⲟⲩⲥⲓⲟⲥ, ʻικων = ϩⲓⲕⲱⲛ.

[ ] Denote emendations and restorations of the Coptic text made by Dr Schmidt supplementary to those of Woide-Schwartze.

⟨ ⟩ Denote emendations and restorations made by present translator.

" They understood the Mystery that became Man, because for this he was manifested, till they saw HIM who is indeed invisible".

The Treatise, LI

" Philip saith unto Jesus: Lord, show us the Father and it is enough for us. Jesus saith unto him: So long a while have I been with you, and you have not known me: Philip, he that hath seen me hath seen the Father".

Sahidic N.T. John, XIV, 8–9

COPTIC GNOSTIC TREATISE
from the
CODEX BRUCIANUS

[The title and beginning are wanting]

[in]comprehensible: him they comprehended not: the Father of the Universes[1], and ⟨the Bounds⟩ of the Universes, ⟨and the Space⟩ of these Universes. Without substance (ανουσιος)[2], invisible (α˙ορατος), unknown, infinite (απεραντος), [and] unknowable (αγνωστος) ⟨is he⟩. In[comprehensible] is he in his un[attainable], unapproachable Image (˙ικων)[3]: by this the Universes are enclosed[4]: thus within it ⟨they move to and fro⟩[5]. [Itself] without bodily form (ατσωμα), it setteth bounds to them all. Itself incorporeal (ασωματος) and without substance (ανουσιος), it [setteth bounds] to them all.

This is the Father ineffable (απο˙ρητος), unutterable (α˙ρητος), inconceivable (ακαταγνωστος)[6], invisible (α˙ορατος), immeasurable (αμετρητος) and infinite (απεραντος)[7]. Within his own Self did he present himself to the mass of those (things) that were in him. And to the mass without substance (ανουσιος) he presented the Thought (επινοια) of his greatness, until he made them in non-substance (ανουσιος). But (δε), as to him, through his own Members (μελος)[8] incomprehensible is he. He made himself to be Space (τοπος)[9] for his Members (μελος), to cause them to dwell in him and know him, because he is their Father, who did emanate (προβαλε)[10] them from his First Conception (εννοια)[11], which became Space (τοπος) for them, making them in non-substance (ανουσιος), so that they shall know him: for (γαρ) through none of all the things that are can he be known[12].

I
MS. f. 138^R
C.S. p. 52

1. *Universes*. The construction of the Coptic term should be noted, the sing. noun, *universe, whole*, being prefixed by both plur. and sing. def. arts., and—where rendered *these universes*—by plur. dem. pro. and sing. def. art. Thus constructed, the word must bear the sense of *unity* and *completeness, uniqueness* being precluded by the plur. art. Whilst *wholes* is the rendering least liable to misunderstanding, *universes* is adopted in the translation as being the more euphonious term. The word occurs frequently in the present treatise, but the only other instance in Coptic literature known to me is in the unpublished *Apocryphon of John* (Codex Berolinensis), from which extracts were translated into German and published by Dr Carl Schmidt (*Iren. u. seine Quelle in adv. haer.* 1, 29, reprinted from *Philotesia*, Berlin, 1907). In the *Apocryphon*—a Gnostic writing bearing a close doctrinal relationship to the present treatise—the term is used in a like sense and connection (p. 6, German trans.). The Greek equivalent, τὰ ὅλα, occurs many times in the writings of Irenaeus (*Adv. Haer.* Bk I), Hippolytus (*Ref. Haer.* Bks v and vi) and Epiphanius (*Haer.* xxi), in passages where the Fathers are recording the Ophite, Valentinian and Marcosian systems. The use of the term is the same as in our treatise. A close contextual parallel is found in the baptismal formula of the Marcosian School: "*Into the Name of the unknowable Father of the Wholes, etc.*" (ἀγνώστου Πατρὸς τῶν ὅλων) (Iren. 1, xiv, 2). τὰ ὅλα can, of course, be rendered *universals*, but this word has a specific meaning which does not seem applicable in the present case. Study of the context in the above-mentioned instances, in both Coptic and Greek texts, makes it clear—in my view—that by *wholes* or *universes* are denoted the Aeons of the Pleroma of the Valentinian and related systems of the Gnosis, the symbolism of the term signifying the fact that a complete and perfect Aeon—such as those of the Pleroma—was a unified, consubstantial being of dual sex. This notion of the constitution of an Aeon would follow on the view—seemingly taught by the Gnostic Schools to which our treatise is doctrinally related—regarding the nature of the First Cause. While these particular speculations most usually presented him as a Monad, the fact that he was the originating source of all that is and contained the potentiality of every mode of being, admitted the element of femininity. This was represented by his ἔννοια, i.e. his conceptive Mind. These notions may have been derived from the pre-Christian Gnosis of Simon Magus. That teacher gave to the Unbegotten Infinite Power—his First Principle—the dual name of *Power-Silence* (δύναμις σιγή), which Power—so he held—"*existed in oneness*". From this "*one Root*" there proceeded Simon's Second Principle—*Mind of the Wholes* (νοῦς τῶν ὅλων) and *Thought* (ἐπίνοια), "*a masculo-feminine Power after the likeness of the Pre-existing Infinite*

Power", and "*having the female within it*" (Hippol. *Ref. Haer.* VI, 18). Following on this, the other Aeons were produced after the same manner and likeness. In this view of the constitution of an Aeon, we get the first adumbration of a separation of the sexes, the all-comprising unity of the Unbegotten First Principle being reflected, in the begotten being, as a masculo-feminine power, substantially one, but sexually dual. Regarding the names, numbering and grouping of the Aeons in the Valentinian and allied systems, some discrepancies are to be observed in the records of the Church Fathers. The nearest parallel to our treatise is found in Iren. I, xxvii, where the writer describes a system, now known also in a Coptic translation of the original, in the above-mentioned *Apoc. of John* (Codex Berolinensis). This particular section of the treatise of Irenaeus is extant, in full, in Latin only, but portions are also known through an abstract—possibly from the Greek original—made by Theodoret (*Haer. Fab.* I, 13). This is valuable for a comparison of terms. In the system thus recorded, as also in our treatise, the Triad—Father, Mother, and Son—is the ground of the cosmogonical process. In both cases we meet with the Pentad, i.e. the Five Members of the Father, which—it is learned from the *Apoc. of John*—by duplication of itself, becomes the masculo-feminine Decad (*vide infra*, and II; also pp. 9 and 14, *Apoc. of John*, German trans.). While the records of the Church Fathers show some variation in naming and grouping the Aeons, they agree in making the full complement of the Pleroma to be thirty. According to the cosmology of the Valentinian and related systems, there was a triple series of Aeons, consisting of an Ogdoad, a Decad and a Dodecad, each series being produced through the medium of the preceding one, the three series together constituting the Triacontad. In most of the records the Aeons are distinguished by these group numbers, but in our treatise we find group names, *Members* and *Universes* or *Wholes*, while the designations, *Powers*, *Worlds* and *Glories*, are terms applicable to all. In our treatise there is no mention of the Ogdoad as such. Nor is it referred to by name in the correlative system in Iren. I, xxvii, but four conjunctions amongst the highest Aeons are there clearly indicated, a list of eight names being given. The eight names of the Ogdoad are also found in the *Apoc. of John*. In both these texts, the male members are Monogenes, Nous, Thelema and Logos, but there is disagreement in regard to the names of their syzygies. The Ogdoad of the Valentinians was differently constituted, and does not agree, in nomenclature, with the *Apoc. of John* or Iren. I, xxvii. On the present page of our treatise, we learn of the production of a Pentad —i.e. the Members of the Father—through the medium of his ἔννοια. The Pentad is also mentioned in the *Apoc. of John*, with the addi-

[5]

tional information that by duplication of itself—that is by means of feminine syzygies—the Pentad becomes the Decad (*vide infra*, note 8). According to these theories, the Pleroma—viewed as a *whole*—represented *unity*. In pursuance of this idea, every Aeon had his pleromal form and was a unified being, i.e. a masculo-feminine consubstantiality. This appears to be the import of the term *universe* or *whole* used as an alternative designation for the members of the Pentad, who, by union with their feminine counterparts, constituted the Decad. In II, xiii, 1, Irenaeus comments on the Valentinian doctrine of the Aeons, and thus concludes his remarks: "*For there is a necessity, in their opinion, that a female Aeon should exist together with a male one, inasmuch as she is, so to speak, [the forth putting of] his affection*". Neither the Dodecad nor the Triacontad is mentioned in our treatise as being a definite group of Aeons. The Twelve Deeps (*vide* XIII and XIX), and the Twelve Fathers surrounding the Sētheus (*vide* XX), probably stand for the former group. In the *Apoc. of John*, the list of names of the Ogdoad is followed by an account of the production of four great Luminaries and the emission of four more groups of Aeons—three Aeons in each group. These latter constitute the Dodecad in that system. On XI of our treatise, we learn that from the *Members* of the Father each *Power* came forth. This is no doubt a reference to the fact that one series of Aeons came from another. But although each succeeding efflux was farther removed from the Supreme Being, he was, nevertheless, regarded as the originating Source of the entire Pleroma of Aeons. As stated in the *Apoc. of John*, previously cited: "*all of them came into being in the Silence of an* ἔννοια" (p. 10, German trans.). As will be seen, *infra*, the ἔννοια is manifested as the Divine Image (εἰκών), and forms the initial Boundary between the Deity and his creation, the Universes being enclosed in it (cf. also XI). The word translated *universes* also occurs frequently in the treatise in the sing. num. Thus written, it denotes sometimes the Pleroma of the Aeons, and sometimes the totality of the cosmos, and can be rendered *all, whole*, or *universe*. But when followed, as it frequently is, by the plur. pro. *they*, it usually signifies the individual Aeons, and may be translated *All things*. The word is so employed in the Sahidic text of the fourth Gospel, i.e. in John i, 3: "*All things* were made by him". There is another group of Aeons mentioned in the treatise. These are entitled *outside Aeons* and *outside Worlds*. They do not come under the heading of *universes*, being exterior to the unity of the Pleroma. Also, there is for them necessity for "salvation", consisting in a process of making *whole*, in respect both of substance and gnosis. More will be heard of this in the course of the treatise.

[6]

2. ανουσιος. While it is to be inferred from the statements of the Patristic writers that the word οὐσία was allowed a somewhat fluid interpretation in Gnostic circles of the day, *substance* appears to be the usage adopted by the writer of the present treatise. When used of the Supreme Being, the adjectival form of the word, prefixed, as here, with the αν priv., may perhaps have been regarded as synonymous with *super-substantial*, thus denoting, not a deprived, but a transcendental condition. οὐσία, however, in Gnostic thought, seems sometimes to have stood for *substance* in the simple sense of the *stuff* of which things are made, and thus interpreted, ἀνούσιος could appropriately, and without derogative effect, be applied to the Divine Being who is without substance in the sense of not being made of anything. Cf. Hippol. VI, 29, recording Valentinian beliefs: "...*the Father was alone, unoriginated, having no place, no time, no counsellor, nor any other thing that by any means could be deemed to be* οὐσία". There are many instances in the Patristic records of the Valentinian and allied systems where οὐσία can be interpreted to mean the *stuff* of created things, e.g. Hippol. VI, 33 —with adjectives defining its particular quality—we get, ψυχικὴ οὐσία = *soul substance*, and δαιμονία οὐσία = *demon substance*. In Iren. I, i, 10, ὑλικὴ οὐσία = *material substance*, and, *ibid*. 8, ἐνύδρη οὐσία = *watery substance*, all of which *stuffs* were differentiations of the fundamental substances (ὑποστατικὰς οὐσίας) of the phenomenal creation (*vide* Hippol. VI, 32, and Iren. I, i, 7 and 8). In Iren. I, i, 3 and 8, the word οὐσία is found standing alone and unqualified for *material substance*. In the system of the Gnostic Marcus, we find the term ἀνούσιος applied—as in our treatise— to the Supreme Being (*vide* Iren. I, viii, 1, Hippol. VI, 42, and Epiph. *Haer.* XXXIV, 4), in connection with which use of the word, Wigan Harvey remarks that οὐσία bore a twofold interpretation in the days when theological language was still vague and loose. It conveyed the same meaning as our word *being*, while it also meant *material substance*; in which sense only, he adds, can the Deity be said to be ἀνούσιος (note 3, p. 129, Iren. *Adv. Haer.* edit. Harvey). On p. xcii of his "Preliminary Observations" Harvey notes "the assertion of Aristotle, that οὐσία imports *material* and *bodily* substance". And again, in note 3, p. 17, he remarks that Philo spoke of "*unformed matter* as οὐσία ἄτακτος, using the word οὐσία for the complex idea of *material substance*". Cf. also Grabe's note on the use of ἀνούσιος in relation to the Deity (Iren. *Adv. Haer.* I, p. 66, note 3, edit. E. J. Grabe, Oxford, 1702): "*If the heretics have called God* ἀνούσιος, *that is, having no substance, and have denied substance to the Deity in the ultimate sense of material substance as* οὐσία *is defined by the philosophers, that is, subject to accidents and bound by certain limitations, they cannot be proved to be in error....But since the word substance can*

I
MS. f. 138ᴿ
C.S. p. 52

[7]

I
MS. f. 138ᴿ
C.S. p. 52

*be freed from all that corruption (*faece*), so certain Fathers have not feared to attribute it in sincerity and in the proper sense to God*".

3. By the production of the εἰκών, i.e. the Divine Image, the Supreme Being is self-revealed to himself. Cf. the previously cited *Apoc. of John* (p. 8, German trans.), where, following an attempted description of the Deity in abstract terms, the text proceeds: "*His eternity (*αἰών*) is imperishable, in stillness abiding, in silence reposing . . . who, by himself alone, contemplates himself in his own Light surrounding him, which Light is the source of the Water of Life. . . . And he adorned all the Aeons and all the Worlds . . . the while he contemplates his own Image, the while he sees it in the pure Water of Light surrounding him. And his Thought (*ἔννοια*) performed a work, it manifested itself and stood before him, springing from the Ray of Light . . . the complete Forethought (*πρόνοια*) of the Whole . . . the Image of the Invisible One, namely, the perfect Power, the Barbēlo, the perfect Aeon of Glory. . . . This is the First Thought (*ἔννοια*), his Image, it became a First Man, namely, the Virginal Spirit (*παρθενικὸν πνεῦμα*), the Triple-male, the Triple-power, the Triple-named, the Thrice-begotten, the Unageing Aeon, the Male-female, that from his Forethought (*πρόνοια*) came forth*". It is important to notice the designation, *a First Man*, applied here to the Divine Image. (For a proposed interpretation of the name Barbēlo (ⲃⲁⲣⲃⲏⲗⲱ), *vide* note 11, XII.) The corresponding passage in Irenaeus (I, xxvii, 1) contains much less detail. XIV of our treatise may also be compared: "*This is the Image of the Father: this is the Mirror of the Whole: 'this is the Mother of all the Aeons, this same which encompasses all Deeps. This is the Monad that is inconceivable*". In this passage the εἰκών is equated with the Monad. For parallel thought in the N.T., cf. Col. i, 15: "*the Image (*εἰκών*) of the Invisible God, the First-born of every creature: in him were All things created, in heaven and on earth, visible and invisible, whether Thrones, or Dominations, or Princedoms, or Powers*". These four terms are designations of four of the Angelic hierarchies, the counterparts—in Jewish and Christian doctrine—of the Aeons of the Pleroma of Gnosticism.

4. Literally: "*their enclosure* (or *circumscription*) *is by means of it*", that is to say, the all-containing εἰκών forms the boundary between the Deity and his creation. The Coptic term signifies à circumscribed place. The word is employed in Ezek. v, 2 to denote a state of siege.

5. A parallel statement occurs on XI, where see note 5.

6. ἀκαταγνωστος. From γιγνώσκω = *to perceive, have knowledge of*. In classical Greek use this word has the derived meaning of *uncondemned, blameless*. By the Copt writer of our treatise Greek terms are almost always employed with their radical meanings; many instances of this will be noted throughout the text. ἀκατά-

[8]

γνωστός here signifies *not perceivable by the mind*. This interpretation
is confirmed by another occurrence on XIV, where the word is
employed in a sentence with an explanatory clause: "*this is the
Monad which is* ακαταγνωστος, *or* (η) *of which all are ignorant*".

7. By the use of negative terms, the Gnostics attempted to
define a state of being which, standing in relation to nothing what-
soever, could truly be called *ineffable*. This non-related definition
was applied to the Deity even in the phase of the activity of his
ἔννοια, for his ἔννοια was his self-thinking, and what he thought was
himself. The Gnostics of our treatise, however, in common with
the Valentinians, conceived of a still more severely abstract state
when they applied the designation *Silence* (σιγή) to the Divine
Being. This served to denote a condition prior to the activity of
the ἔννοια. On VI, the idea is embodied in a hymn: "*I bless thee,
the Light—even by himself unthought!*"

8. As previously observed (note 1), according to the doctrine of
this treatise and the *Apoc. of John*, the duplicated Pentad of Members of the Father is the counterpart of the Decad of Valentinian
cosmology. As in the case of the εἰκών, the *Apocryphon* throws additional light on these speculations. In that text the word *Members*
does not occur in such excerpts as Dr Schmidt has made accessible
in German translation, but we read of the *Pentad*, obviously the
equivalent of the Five Members. The passage from the *Apoc. of
John*, cited *supra* in note 3, continues thus: "*And the Barbēlo* (= the
εἰκών) *asked of him* (i.e. the Invisible Spirit), *to give Foreknowledge
(*πρόγνωσις). *He consented, and when he had consented, Foreknowledge
was manifested and ranged itself with Thought* (ἔννοια), *that is to say:
Forethought* (πρόνοια). *And they praised the Invisible One, and the
perfect Power, the Barbēlo, because through it they had come into being.
And again, this Power* (i.e. Foreknowledge) *asked for the gift of In-
corruptibility* (ἀφθαρσία). *He consented, and when he had consented, In-
corruptibility was manifested and ranged itself with Thought and Foreknowledge, while it praised the Invisible One and the Barbēlo, because
through* [*the Barbēlo*] *it had come into being. And it asked for the gift of
Everlasting Life* (αἰωνία ӡωή). *He consented, and when he had consented,
Everlasting Life was manifested. And they ranged themselves and praised
him* (the Invisible Spirit) *and the Barbēlo, because through it they had
come into being in the manifestation of the Invisible Spirit. This is the
Pentad of the Aeons of the Father, the First Man, the Image of the Invisible One, namely: the Barbēlo, and the* ἔννοια, *and the* πρόγνωσις, *and
the* ἀφθαρσία, *and the* αἰωνία ӡωή. *This is the male-female Pentad, that
is to say, it is the Decad of the Aeons*" (p. 9, German trans.). It will
be observed that in the above passage, the designation *First Man*
is, for the second time, applied to the Divine Image (*vide* previous
citation from the *Apocryphon* in note 3). As remarked in note 1, the

I

MS. f. 138ᴿ

C.S. p. 52

[9]

Aeons were emanated as consubstantial dualities; thus in the *Apoc. of John* we learn that the male-female Pentad equals the Decad.

9. Through the activation of the Divine Will, Thought (ἔννοια) became Space. The conception of the Deity as τόπος was also a Jewish one. Cf. the Septuagint reading of Exod. xxiv, 10: καὶ εἶδον τὸν τόπον = *"and they saw the Place"*, rendered, in the Vulgate and the Authorized Versions: *"and they saw the God of Israel"*. In later Kabbalistic developments, the En Soph = τὸ ἀπέραντον (the Infinite) received the name Makom = ὁ τόπος. The belief was that God is in his nature boundless and endless, that beyond him and without him there is naught. Yet while he contains all things in himself and is the Space of all, the All is not his space. This conception of the nature of the Divine Being can be paralleled in several passages in our treatise. On LIV, in a prayer to the Deity the following occurs: *"thy Will alone became Space* (τοπος) *for thee, because it is not possible for any to be space for thee, in that of all, thou art the Space"*. This again recalls the speculations of the Kabbalists, to the effect that when the En Soph willed to reveal himself, he withdrew within himself and formed around him a void. The notion of the Deity creating Space by means of his ἔννοια is found in another Coptic Gnostic work in the same collection as our treatise, i.e. the *Books of Ieou* (Codex Brucianus). Whilst being instructed concerning the origin of the universe, the Disciples make the following enquiry of the Master: *"O our Lord, how then did all these Spaces come into being? Or again, how did these Fatherhoods within them come into being? And their Orders also, through what cause came they into being? Or again, we ourselves, through what cause have we arisen? Jesus spake unto them, saying: 'They came into being on account of this little Thought, [the] one the Father left behind and withdrew not to himself. He withdrew himself altogether to himself except this little Thought which he left behind and withdrew not to himself. I shone forth in this little Thought proceeding from my Father. I was projected and streamed forth in it. I shone forth in him, he emanated me, I being the first of his Emanations and his whole Likeness and Image* (ἱκων). *He having emanated me, I stood before him. Again shone forth this little Thought and gave out another Voice. This is the Second Voice. Thereafter all these Spaces were in being. This is the Second Emanation'"*. The passage continues with an account of the sounding of the Third Voice and the subsequent coming into being of other spaces one from another (Coptic text in *T. u. U. Altchristl. Lit.* Bd vɪɪɪ, p. 88, edit. C. Schmidt, Leipzig, 1892).

10. This word—of frequent occurrence in other Coptic Gnostic texts (e.g. *Pistis Sophia* (Cod. Ask.) and the two *Books of Ieou* (Cod. Bruc.))—is found this once only in our treatise. The meaning is well conveyed in the passage from the *First Book of Ieou*, cited *supra*, in

note 9. Emanation implies a flowing or streaming forth from some
source, connection with which remains unbroken, that which is
poured forth having no separate existence of its own. Thus emanation differs entirely from creation.

I
MS. f. 138ᴿ
C.S. p. 52

11. It is not clear what shade of difference in meaning the
writer assigned to ἔννοια and ἐπίνοια (*vide supra*). Some distinction
must be intended, as the words are placed in contiguity on the
present page, and again on **XXXII**. In both places ἐπίνοια comes
first. The thinking out or devising of a scheme or purpose is perhaps intended, while ἔννοια may denote the complete thought held
in the mind. In the Patristic records (*vide* Irenaeus and Hippolytus) the terms are used interchangeably in Simonian, Ophite,
Valentinian and Marcosian doctrine.

12. Literally: "*for he is an unknown one through all things*".

¹He it is who made his ⟨Image of⟩ Light after the manner ⟨of a Thought⟩, and after the manner of a ⟨Conception, and⟩ after the manner of a ⟨Spark of Light. He⟩ gave being to his Members ² in the Thought (επινοια) of his greatness. From his Thought (επινοια) he brought them forth, and they were made in non-substance (ανουσιος)³, namely, his Members (μελος). But (δε) [as to these], of the Place (τοπος) [incomprehensible?] are they. Each one of his Members (μελος) [is accounted as] a myriad. And each one saw him ⟨in the⟩ Son, for the Father's perfections are his. And the Father sealed (σφραγιζε) ⟨the Name⟩ of his Son ⁴ within [them, so that] they shall know him within themselves. And the Name within them moved them, causing them to see the Unseen and Unknown One ⁵. And they gave glory to the One Alone and the Conception (εν-νοια) that was in him, and the Intelligible Word (λογος νοερον), giving glory to the Three which be but One ⁶: because through him they were made in non-substance (ανουσιος). And the Father took their whole likeness, and he made it as a City (πολις) or (η) a Man ⁷. In him he portrayed (ζωγραφι) ⁸ the Universes, namely, all these Powers (δυναμις). Each one in the City (πολις) knew him, each one gave myriads of praises to the Man or (η) the City (πολις) of the Father, who is in all things. And the Father took the praise, and he made it as the outer vesture (ενδυμα) of the Man.

1. As is shown by the photographic reproduction, the papyrus of this folio is much perished, about half the text of the first ten lines having disappeared. Three words only of the first line now remain, but C. G. Woide—who in the eighteenth century was the first to copy the text—was able to read as far as a second pronoun which he transcribed as the poss. pro., third pers., sing. num., fem. gen. The subject-matter of this page is the same as that of the preceding one, where only three nouns of fem. gen. occur. The three

are interrelated. The first mentioned is the εἰκών, this is followed   II
by ἐπίνοια, and thirdly by ἔννοια. My choice of these three nouns for MS. f. 138ᵛ
the proposed restoration is further substantiated by comparison   C.S. p. 53
with a statement in the *Apoc. of John*, quoted in note 3, I, in which
the εἰκών is described as formed of Light, and equatable with the
ἐπίνοια and the ἔννοια. Also, on VI of our treatise, in a Song of
Praise, we read: "*I bless thee, the Light Thought* (επινοια)". And
again, on XII, where it is said that the Monad—equalling the
εἰκών (*vide* note 3, I)—came from the Father as a Spark of Light.

2. The text has: "⟨He⟩ gave being to *them*".

3. That is to say, in God all things *are* as pure ideas. Cf.
note 2, I.

4. = the Monogenes. As will be seen by reference to XXVI,
our Gnostics taught that the Monogenes was first begotten in the
Monad (= the ἔννοια and the εἰκών), and that in and through him
all subsequently created entities had their being. For details relating to the production of the Monogenes, reference may again
be made to the *Apoc. of John*. Following an account of the origination of the Decad (*vide* passage quoted in note 8, I), the text proceeds: "*Gazing deeply into him* (i.e. the Invisible Spirit), *the pure
Light within, the Barbēlo* (= the ἔννοια and the εἰκών) *turned itself to
him and gave birth to a blessed Light Spark* (σπινθήρ): *this, however, in
greatness, was not its equal. This is the Monogenes, who manifested himself to the Father, the* αὐτογένητος *God. [This is] the First-born Son of
the Whole, from the Spirit of pure Light. And the Invisible Spirit rejoiced
on account of the Light that had come into being, which was manifested in
the beginning, in the First Power, namely, his* πρόνοια, *the Barbēlo. And
he anointed him with his Grace, so that he was made complete, and no deficiency was in Christ, he being anointed with his Grace, while the Invisible
Spirit poured*(?) *himself over him*" (p. 10, German trans.). The conclusion of this passage recalls the statement in our treatise: "*the
Father's perfections are his*".

5. The Valentinians taught that the Monogenes alone had full
and perfect knowledge of the Father and his perfections, having
been produced in that Gnosis whereby the Divine Being knew
himself. Thus through the Monogenes alone could knowledge of
the Father be obtained. Cf. the Valentinian source in the *Excerpt.
ex Theodot.*: "*Now since the Father was unknown, he willed to be
known by the Aeons, and through his own* ἐνθύμησις (heart's-desire), *he
knew himself and brought forth the Spirit of Gnosis which is in Gnosis,
namely, the Only-begotten* (μονογενής). *He, then, who came forth from
Gnosis, is also Gnosis, that is, the Son, for the Father is known through the
Son.... Now the Only-begotten Son, remaining in the bosom of the Father,
interpreted the* ἐνθύμησις—*as put forth from the bosom of the Father—*

[13]

through Gnosis, to the Aeons" (§ 7, *Excerpt. ex Theodot. Clem. Alex.*
Bd III, edit. Stählin, Leipzig, 1909).

6. In the Triad we have a Gnostic conception of the Trinity in
Unity, which, in their view, contained a feminine principle, i.e.
the ἔννοια of the Father. Signifying the power of conception, this
feminine principle was hidden in the Father as a Thought. In
previously quoted passages (note 3, I), it was observed that the
ἔννοια is to be equated with the εἰκών, and the latter with the Monad,
which is further designated: "*the Mother of all the Aeons*". A similar
reference to the Triad is found in the *Apoc. of John* (p. 14, German
trans.): "*...the Three, the Father, the Mother, and the Son, the perfect
Power*". Reflecting the conception of the Triad as originating
source of all, the cosmos was represented as a tripartite unit, and
this idea of triplicity in unity is repeated again and again in each
succeeding state, space and subdivision of the cosmos. Together
with reflection or re-enaction of antecedent events, it is the basic
cosmological idea in the system of our Gnostics. The group of
schools—called variously Naassenes, Ophites, Peratae and Sethians
—whose doctrines were possibly derived from the pre-Christian
Gnosis of Simon Magus, all held this view of the triple constitution
of the universe, and made the originating Principle to be a Triad.
This relationship of basic ideas is a strong argument in favour of
Dr Carl Schmidt's theory that both our treatise and the *Apoc. of
John* emanated from some circle in the aforesaid group (*vide* latter
part of note 6, III). The fact that correspondences with what are
generally regarded as specific Valentinian doctrines become increasingly apparent as the treatise develops is no argument against
Dr Schmidt's theory. For Valentinus undoubtedly based much
of his doctrinal system on that of his predecessors. Also many of
the early doctrines may have come down to us only in their
Valentinian dress, for the reason that in this latter form they were
more accessible for purposes of criticism by the Church Fathers
of the second and third centuries. As the influence of the developed
Gnosis of Valentinus became widespread, the more primitive
forms of doctrine would be superseded.

7. A reference to the Aeon Anthropos. According to the
Valentinian and some related schools (e.g. of Ptolemy (Iren. I, vi)
and Marcus (*ibid.* vii)), this Aeon and his syzygy Ecclesia were
reckoned the fourth pair in the primary Ogdoad. In the system
of our treatise, and its correlative in the *Apoc. of John* and Iren. I,
xxvii, he bears a more important significance. As observed in
note I, I, the primary Ogdoad is not mentioned by name either in
our treatise or the *Apocryphon*, but in the latter text and its correspondence in Iren. I, xxvii, the names are given of the four pairs
of Aeons of which it was constituted according to the tenets of that

[14]

particular school: and in that category, the name of the Anthropos **II**
does not appear. A second important variant concerns the name MS. f. 138ᵛ
of the syzygy of the Anthropos, which is not *Ecclesia*—as with the C.S. p. 53
Valentinians—but *Gnosis* (Iren. I, xxvii, 1). Finally, more emphasis seems to be laid on the Anthropos as the revelation of a
particular aspect of the Deity. Excerpts from the *Apoc. of John*
given in notes 3 and 8, I, show that the term *Man* was first predicated of the Divine Image, viewed both as a Monad (note 3)
and as the male-female Pentad of Members = the Decad (note 8).
Secondly, as stated in our treatise, the Father took the whole like-
ness of his Members and made thereof a City or a *Man*, who was
thus created after the likeness of the Pentad of Members = the
First Man. This defines the Anthropos as the image of the Image.
It is to be inferred from our treatise (*vide* note 4, III), that the
Decad—which came into being by duplication of the Pentad of
Members = the First Man—is the *hidden* Decad. In the *Apoc. of
John* (p. 14, German trans.), the Anthropos is designated the *First
Manifestation*. That he is the Decad *manifested* is perhaps the idea.
Following an account of the origination of the Monogenes =
Christ, and a list of the pairs of Aeons constituting the primary
Ogdoad, the *Apoc. of John* thus describes the production of the
Anthropos: "*From Foreknowledge* (πρόγνωσις), *and the perfect Mind*
(τέλειος νοῦς) . . . [*through*] *the good pleasure of the great Invisible Spirit,
and the good pleasure of the Autogenes* (= Christ), [*was produced*] *the
perfect and true Man, the first Manifestation. He was called Adam, and
was placed over the First Aeon*. . . .*And the Invisible Spirit gave him an
unconquerable intelligible* (νοερός) *power. He* (i.e. the Man) *spake and
said: 'I glorify and praise the Invisible Spirit, because through him all
things have come into existence'*". Cf. the corresponding passage in
Irenaeus, which is prefaced by similar statements concerning the
Monogenes and the Aeons: "*All things, then, being established, the
Autogenes further produces a Man, perfect and true, who is called Adamas*
(= unconquerable), *because neither has he himself been overcome, nor
those from whom he sprang*. . . .*Further, perfect Gnosis* (Γνῶσιν τελείαν)
*was sent forth by the Autogenes together with Man, and conjoined to him,
hence he attained to the gnosis of him who is above all. Unconquerable
power was also conferred on him by the ⟨Invisible⟩ Spirit, and All things
reposing sang praises to the great Aeon*". This excerpt is from the
Latin text of Irenaeus (I, xxvii, 1), the incorporated Greek terms
being from the version of Theodoret (*Haer. Fab.* I, 13). With these
passages, cf. the following in our treatise: XIV, "*from these incorporeal
Members the Man came into being*"; LV, "*this is the Man of Mind* (νους)
begotten, to whom Thought (διανοια) *gave form* (μορφη)"; XVIII
(following a reference to the Monogenes), "*through him, the Man
was revealed*"; XVI, "*Adam, who is of the Light*"; XLV–XLVI,

[15]

II
MS. f. 138ᵛ
C.S. p. 53

"*Adamas, the Man of Light*"; IV, "*He made him to be unconquerable, after the pattern of the Unconquerable One . . .*". Cf. also the Man's Song of Praise commencing on V. In the system attributed by Hippolytus to the Naassene School, we find an Anthropos doctrine very similar to that of our treatise, in that it postulates a prototypal *First* and *Second Man*, vide *Ref. Haer.* v, 6: "*These [Naasseni], by their own statement, honour before all things else, a Man, and a Son of Man. Now this Man* (i.e. the second) *is male-female* (ἀρσενόθηλυς), *and is called by them Adamas. Hymns also, many and various, are made to him . . . in some such form as this: 'From thee, Father, and through thee, Mother, the two deathless Names: O Progenitor of Aeons! O Citizen of Heaven! O Man of Great Name!' And they hold that the gnosis of him is the beginning of the capacity for the gnosis of God*". Cf. the treatise (*infra*): "*Each one in the City knew him, each one gave myriads of praises to the Man or the City of the Father, who is in all things*". This last phrase—"*the Man . . . who is in all things*"—presents the Anthropos both as a cosmogonic principle and a special revelation of God. The same notion is found in the Gnostic speculations recorded in the Pseudo-Clementine *Recognitions* and emanating probably from the Elkesaite or Ebionite School. There, the Primal Adam is described as "*the true prophet running through the ages and speeding to rest*". He is said to manifest in a series of prophetic figures beginning with the historic Adam and ending with Jesus Christ (*Recog.* i, 52). The Adamas κατ' εἰκόνα was also the ideal prototype of the manifested cosmos. This is implied in his second designation, the *City*. Cf. Philo of Alexandria (*De op. Mund.* § 24): "*For the intelligible City is nothing else but the Reason of the Architect determining in his Mind to found a City perceptible by the senses*". Philo also draws a clear distinction between humanity as personified in the Primal Adam who was created after God's Image and belonged to the noumenal world, and the humanity of the phenomenal creation as represented by Adam and Eve: "*the one is created, pertains to the material world, and is in possession of a definite quality, consists of soul and body, is either man or woman, and of a mortal nature; the other, after the Image of God, is Idea, Genus, Counterpart, belonging to the intelligible world, without body, neither male nor female . . . immortal, incorruptible*" (*De op. Mund.* § 134).

8. From ϫⲱⲅⲣⲁⲫⲉⲱ = *to draw from life*, i.e. to copy or reproduce the living model. Cf. the statement on V: "*this is the Man made corresponding to each Aeon*". Also on XIV: "*from these incorporeal Members the Man came into being*".

his belly after the pattern (τυπος) of the Holy Pleroma
('ιερον πληρωμα)². He made his sinews coming one
from another after the pattern (τυπος) of ⟨the⟩³ hundred myriad Powers (δυναμις) less four myriads. He
made the twenty digits after the likeness of the two
Decads (δεκας)—the Decad (δεκας) that is hidden and
the manifested Decad (δεκας)⁴. He made ⟨the⟩ navel of
his belly after the likeness of the Monad (μονας)⁵ which
is hidden in the Sētheus (σηθευς)⁶. He made the great
intestine after the likeness of the Sētheus (σηθευς) who
is Lord over the Pleroma (πληρωμα), and the small intestine he made after the likeness of the Ennead ('εννας)
⟨hidden in⟩ the Sētheus (σηθευς). He made his womb
(μητρα)⁷ after the pattern (τυπος) of the innermost
part of the Holy ('ιερον) [Pleroma] . . . .

. . . .
. . . . he made
his knees after the pattern (τυπος) of the still (ερημος=
ηρεμος)⁸ and unknown ones (αυγνωστος) who minister
(διακονι) to the Whole and rejoice with those who shall
be saved⁹. He made his members (μελος) after the
pattern (τυπος) of the Deep (βαθος)¹⁰ in which are
three hundred and sixty-five Fatherhoods¹¹, in accordance with (κατα) the pattern (τυπος) of the Fatherhoods.

1. A folio is missing here. Judging from the final statement on
II, a description of the Man's exterior form was to be expected.
Also some reference to the head and upper part of his body.
2. πληρωμα. As employed by the Gnostics, this term denotes two
principal ideas. Collectively, it represents the fullness of the Divine
perfections and attributes, thus standing in sharp contrast, as a
positive conception, to the negative ineffable aspect of the Deity
of which the human mind can form no definite notion. Secondly,

it stands for the Ideal World, the perfect archetype and pattern, hidden in Heaven, of which all subsequent phenomenal manifestation is an imperfect copy. In our treatise, the Twelve Deeps of the Pleroma denote the Divine perfections (XIII–XIV), while the Ideal World is represented by a concept called the *Indivisible*, of which the innermost part is the Pleroma, the latter being further defined as the Holy Place, wherein the Sētheus dwells (*vide* XVI and XXVI)—*Sētheus* being a designation for the Deity as Creator (*vide infra*, note 6).

3. The article is omitted in the text, but as with the other correspondences, a particular antitype is intended. The symbolical relationship between the Powers and the sinews *coming one from another*, arises from the fact that in the cosmological scheme each group of Aeons (= the *Powers*) was produced from the preceding one.

4. "*the Decad that is hidden and the manifested Decad.*" For the *hidden* Decad, *vide* latter part of note 8, I. In the system of our treatise and the *Apoc. of John*, the Decad results from the duplication of the Pentad of Members of the Father. Of this Pentad, the ἔννοια of the Father (= the εἰκών and the μονάς) is a member (*vide* citation from *Apoc. of John* (p. 9) in note 8, I). At the same time, so it is said, it contains the other Members in itself: "*all of them came into being in the Silence of an* ἔννοια" (*ibid.* p. 10). The Valentinian and allied systems, such as that of our treatise and the *Apoc. of John*, are based on the imitative principle, events in each succeeding stage of creation duplicating those of the preceding order. Thus one may expect to find the manifested Decad exhibiting the same features as the hidden one. On XVIII, mention is made of the Universal Womb of Creation. From this issues forth an Ennead of Powers connected with the coming phenomenal manifestation. After giving the names of these Powers, the Universal Womb is thus defined: "*this is the inconceivable Beginning, the Mother of the Ennead, which is completed to a Decad in the Monad of the Unknowable*". As pointed out in note 7, II, the Pentad of Members—which, duplicated, equals the hidden Decad—is entitled the *First Man*, while the Anthropos—made in the likeness of the First Man and called the *First Manifestation*—probably represents the manifested Decad.

5. The Monad is the Divine Forethought of the whole creation, issuing from the ἔννοια of the Father (*vide* note 3, I). All that was preordained to be was foreshadowed therein. As we learn *infra*, and on XXVI, the Monad was hidden in the *Sētheus*—a term used, seemingly, to denote the creative phase of the Deity, and having, most probably, the significance of *movement* (*vide* next note). The symbolism employed in the present passage to describe the configuration of the prototypal Man, also some of the actual terms

[18]

used with reference to his abdominal parts (*vide infra*), strongly recall the notions of the Sethian School on the subject of creative processes. Hippolytus, in the *Ref. Haer.* (v, 19 and x, 11), gives two accounts of the doctrines of these Gnostics, but the obscurity of his language suggests that he did not altogether understand the meaning of what he wrote. Some correspondence of ideas, however, seems clear. He likens Heaven and Earth to a great Womb with a navel in the midst. And he makes it evident that *movement*—in our text symbolized by the intestines of the Man and by the term *Sētheus*—was regarded by the Sethian Gnostics as the originating creative force.

6. *Sētheus.* A proper noun, used in this treatise to designate the Deity in his rôle as Creator. On XXVI, it is definitely stated that the Sētheus is God, and that the Monad and the Monogenes are in his ἔννοια: "*This is the Monogenes who is in the Monad...which is in Sētheus as it were a Thought. And this is Sētheus who dwelleth in the Holy Place...he being God*". The term Sētheus presents the Divine Being under his second aspect, as God the Father and Creator, dwelling within the Pleroma which is the emanation of his Thought. The Deity under his first and inconceivable aspect—called, in our treatise, the *Silence*—is prior to the Pleroma. The meaning of the appellation Sētheus may be sought in its derivation. Like the Aryan *Seth*, Hamitic *Set*, and the Semitic *Sheth*, it may be derived from the same root as the Greek verbs σείω = *to move to and fro*, and σήθω = *to shake*. An example of a noun thus derived occurs in Num. xxiv, 17, where—in the Septuagint Version—the sons of *Seth* are mentioned. In the Revised Version the word σήθ is taken to be a common noun, and the passage is translated "sons of *tumult*," a rendering which, according to the authority in Hastings' *Dictionary of the Bible*, is undoubtedly correct. Throughout our treatise, the designation Sētheus denotes the creative and dynamic phase of the Divine Being. Etymologically considered, the term probably means the *Mover*. Also in the statement *infra*, where the intestines of the Anthropos are likened to the Sētheus, the idea of *movement* seems implied. With further reference to the meaning inherent in terms derived from σείω and σήθω, it may be remarked that the word *sistrum* (σεῖστρον) is by some etymologists assigned to the same root. The sistrum, an instrument constantly named and pictured in Egyptian records, is always associated with creative processes, and is more particularly the symbol of Isis, the Nature Goddess. It represented the movement, which, it was supposed, was the origin of manifested life (cf. Plu. *de Is. et Osir.* edit. Squire, vol. LXIII, pp. 1–3). That the work of creation was believed by the Egyptians to be the result, initially, of movement on the part of the Deity is recorded by Plutarch. After relating a story about

III
MS. f. 141ᴿ
C.S. p. 54

[19]

2-2

III
MS. f. 141ᴿ
C.S. p. 54

the Creator, which states that his legs formed originally one limb, in consequence of which, not being able to walk, he lived in solitude, till Isis by separating the two limbs enabled him to go forth, Plutarch adds, that this story *"enigmatically hints that the Mind and Reason* (νοῦς καὶ λόγος) *of God, after progression within itself in the invisible and unmanifested, came forth into genesis by means of motion"* (*ibid.*). Students of Gnosticism will call to mind the sect bearing the name of *Sethiani*, a title which—in view of the appellation *Sētheus* given to the Creator in the present treatise—suggests a link with the school whence our text emanated. Hippolytus, in the *Ref. Haer.*, gives two accounts of the teaching of the Sethians, from which it is to be inferred that there was a fundamental doctrine in their system which regarded *movement* as the activating cause of creation (*vide* also preceding note). We further learn from Hippolytus (*Ref. Haer.* v, 6) that the sect whom he calls Sethians claimed for themselves the title of *Gnostics*, while the orthodox Christians called them *Ophites* and *Naassenes*. Theodoret, who copies the account of Irenaeus, calls them *Ophites* and *Sethians* (Theodor. *Haer. Fab.* I, 14). The probability is—with regard to these different titles—that what the Church Fathers represent as separate sects are merely subdivisions of, or offsets from, a main group, which possibly traced its doctrines back to the pre-Christianized Gnosis of Simon Magus. To this same source are probably to be referred the basic doctrines of the Basilidian and Valentinian systems. The apparent differences observable in the teachings of a given group of sects are due, in the main, to special emphasis being laid on certain features, or to developments and variants in points of detail. The source whence Irenaeus derived his information regarding the School of Gnostics described by him in I, xxvii, has come to light, in Coptic translation, in the treatise, previously cited, entitled *Apocryphon of John* (Cod. Berol.). Dr Schmidt, as the result of an exhaustive enquiry into the subject, concludes that the originals of the present treatise and the *Apoc. of John* must have issued from those Gnostic circles that went by the name of *Sethiani*. In the course of this enquiry, Dr Schmidt gives the reasons for his belief that the Gnostic sect with which Plotinus deals in the second Ennead (*Against the Gnostics*) is the Sethian group, and he points to well-substantiated correspondences between their teachings and the doctrines in the *Apoc. of John* and our treatise (*Plotin. Stellung z. Gnost. u. Kirch. Christentum. T. u. U. n. f.* Bd v, C. Schmidt). Epiphanius also treats of the Sethian sect (Epiph. *Haer.* 40), and he further mentions the name of *Seth*, son of Adam, *"father of the spiritual seed"*, to whom Irenaeus also refers. In the *Apoc. of John* also, we hear of *Seth*, son of the archetypal Adam. It has been suggested, by Dr Schmidt and other authorities, that it was from this personage that the *Sethians* took their name. Having regard, however, to the probable meaning of the title *Sētheus* and its application in the present treatise—which in the view of Dr Schmidt came from Sethian circles—the opinion may be ventured that the designation of the sect originated from the fundamental doctrine of their school, whereby they contended that *movement* was the primal cause of all manifestation. And that further, and for the same reason, these Gnostics bestowed upon the Creator the name of Sētheus = the *Mover*. This view seems borne out by a statement of Theodoret: " *They say that* Σήθ *is a Divine Power* (θείαν τινα δύναμιν), *and that therefrom the* Σηθιανοί *derived their name*" (Theodor. *Haer. Fab.* 1, xiv).

III

MS. f. 141ᴿ

C.S. p. 54

7. The Anthropos, being the prototype of *humanity*, is at once male and female. The Naassene Gnostics taught a similar doctrine, and conceived of the cosmos under the similitude of a Man who was ἀρσενόθηλυς (Hippol. v, 6, *vide* also note 7, II).

8. The spelling ερημος appears twice in the text, ηρεμος occurs twelve times. As *still* (ηρεμος) always suits the context, the vowel transposition is presumably due to carelessness, or to that indifference in the use of Greek vowels noticeable among Coptic scribes.

9. Can be rendered: " *those who shall be made whole*". The statement has reference, most probably, to the salvation of the *outside* Aeons. Cf. latter part of note 1, I.

10. Referring to the *Immeasurable Deep* which surrounds the Pleroma. Details will be found on XXXIV *et seq*.

11. The relationship between the 365 and Adamas, i.e. the Anthropos, is again emphasized on XVI.

. . . .

. . . .

. . . .

he made ⟨the⟩ hair of his body after the pattern (τυπος) of the worlds (κοσμος) of the Pleroma (πληρωμα). He filled him with knowledge like unto the All-wise (πανσοφος). He completed him inwardly with mystery (μυστηριον) like unto the Sētheus (σηθευς), and he completed him outwardly like unto the Indivisible¹. He made him to be unconquerable, after the pattern (τυπος) of the Unconquerable One who is in every place—the One and Only One in the Whole—whom none doth comprehend. He made him encompassing his fellow², after the pattern (τυπος) of the Covering (καλυπτος)³ which veils the hidden Mysteries (μυστηριον)⁴. He made his ⟨feet of Light⟩⁵ after the pattern (τυπος) of the Indivisible—⟨they were named⟩, saying: Feet of ⟨Light⟩. [He made the] four extremities⁶ after the pattern (τυπος) of the Four Gates (πυλη), and he made the two thighs (μερος = μηρος)⁷ after the pattern (τυπος) of the countless Beginnings (μυριαρχος)⁸, those of the Right-hand and those of the Left-hand. He made his necessities of nature (αναγκαιον)⁹ after the pattern (τυπος) of those that go out and those that come in, and the two loins after (V) [the pattern of the Silence].

V

1. The philosophic background of the Valentinian and related systems was largely coloured by Platonism. In our treatise the Indivisible (Deep) seems to be the counterpart of the Platonic Ideal World viewed as an indivisible unit. Later in the treatise some account of its potentialities is given, the cosmos being ideally actualized in it. On XXIX we learn that its Crown contains the subjective qualities of every kind of created life.

2. The Coptic word rendered *fellow* is a noun of sing. num., almost invariably preceded—as here—by a plur. pronoun. It can be translated *companion, partner, mate, neighbour,* terms denoting reciprocity, this being the import of the plur. pronoun. The word

[22]

also equals the Greek ἀλλήλων, compound reciprocal pronoun, meaning *one another*. Thus the passage might be rendered: "*he made him, encompassing one another*". As previously remarked (note 1, I), the Aeons of the Pleroma were emanated in pairs, each with a syzygy, the two together forming a single consubstantial being. Although the actual name nowhere appears in our treatise, we have, in the present passage, a reference to the syzygy of the Aeon Anthropos. As stated in note 7, II, while the Valentinians named the syzygy *Ecclesia* ('Ἐκκλησία), the Gnostics dealt with by Irenaeus in I, xxvii, taught a variant in this respect and called the partner of the Anthropos *Gnosis* (Γνῶσις). As the doctrines of this school are closely related to those of our treatise in all that concerns the Pleroma and the Aeons, it is probable that they were in agreement as to this name. In *Adv. Haer.* I, xxvii, after giving a list of the first pairs among the Aeons, and relating the production—by the Autogenes (= Monogenes and Christ)—of "*a Man, perfect and true* ("Ἄνθρωπον τέλειον καὶ ἀληθῆ), *whom they call Adamas*", Irenaeus continues: "*Further, perfect Gnosis* (Γνῶσιν τελείαν) *was sent forth by the Autogenes, together with Man and conjoined* (ὁμόζυγα) *to him, whereby he attained to the knowledge of him who is above all.... Also from Anthropos and Gnosis there sprang forth* (βεβλαστηκέναι) *the Tree* (Ξύλον) *which is itself also called Gnosis*" (I, xxvii, 1). (The Greek terms are from the version of Theodoret (*Haer. Fab.* I, 13).) The latter part of this passage will recall the teaching of the Naassenes in relation to the Anthropos: "*they hold that gnosis of him is the beginning of the capacity for the gnosis of God*" (*vide* note 7, II). Duality of nature in unity of substance was the mode of being of the Aeons of the Pleroma. They represented the various modes of the Divine subsistence, and, as personifications, were constituted in likeness of nature to the Divine Being, with whom, according to the doctrine of some of the schools, was his ἔννοια, and according to others his co-eternal *Silence* (Σιγή). A noteworthy example of this conception of the nature of even the highest beings is seen in the Valentinian reading and interpretation of the prologue to the fourth Gospel: "*In the Beginning was the Word* (Λόγος) . . . *and that which came to be in Him is Life* (Ζωή)". By the *Beginning*, these Gnostics understood the Monogenes, in whom—according to their reading—the Logos was. While in the words "*that which came to be in Him*", *Him* refers to the Logos, in whom was his syzygy Zoe (*vide* § 6, *Excerpt. ex Theodot.*). The same notion can, of course, be read into the Biblical story of the creation of Adam and Eve, the latter being "*bone of bone and flesh of flesh*" of the body of Adam. And again, in the corresponding Christian doctrine of the mystical union between Christ and the Church.

3. καλυπτος. Verbal adj. from καλύπτω = *to cover over, to veil*.

[23]

Obviously the word is not used adjectivally in this sentence. One must regard it as an instance of the Coptic scribe's haphazard use of Greek words. καλύπτρα must be the intention.

4. *Hidden Mysteries* probably denotes the Aeons of the Pleroma. They were enclosed by the εἰκών, which thus constituted their *covering* (*vide* note 4, I).

5. About a third of this folio—following the words *feet of*—has perished. The final ten lines are taken from Woide's transcript. The extant portion of the text is all but illegible, and judging by the tentative and inaccurate spelling of some of the words in Woide's copy, its condition was probably but little better in his day. The change from the sing. noun meaning *foot*, transcribed by Woide, to *feet*, which I propose, depends on the substitution of an ⲛ for a ⲧ in the Coptic word (initial letters of the pronouns agreeing respectively with the plur. and sing. numbers). Examination of the photographic reproduction will show that one letter is as likely as the other. The first two letters of the Coptic word for *light* (ⲟⲩⲟⲉⲓⲛ)—my proposed restoration—are the same as the first two letters of the Coptic word for *right* (ⲟⲩⲛⲁⲙ), Dr Schmidt's suggestion. My reasons for substituting *feet of light* for *right foot* (*vide* Dr Schmidt) are that *the right foot and the left* are mentioned on the succeeding folio. Also that the Indivisible—to which the *feet* are likened—was a creation of Light (*vide* XVII).

6. The Coptic word here equals ἄκρον, *tip* or *extremity*, the extremities of the body, i.e. *hands* and *feet*, being intended. The symbolical correspondence with the Four Gates of the Pleroma (*vide* XV–XVI) is perhaps to be explained in the sense that hands and feet are man's means of contact with the exterior world, as are a city's gates with that which lies outside it.

7. ε standing for η.

8. μυρίαρχος. From μυρίος = *countless, numberless*, and ἄρχω = *to begin*. This composite word affords a good example of the Coptic use of Greek root meanings. It is constructed and employed in the same way as is the term μοναρχία by the Gnostics of the *Apoc. of John* (p. 6, German trans.) and Hippolytus (ɪx, 10). *Vide* also μοναρχης, on LVI of our treatise, sole *source* or *origin*, not sole *ruler*, being the meaning in these passages. The interpretation given to μυρίαρχος in later classical Greek—i.e. *ruler of myriads*—would be without significance in the present passage where we have a series of symbolical relationships. The word occurs nowhere else, nor would *ruler of myriads* relate to anything in the treatise. On XIII, αρχος occurs again, prefixed, in this instance, by the αν priv., thus meaning *without origin*. There the context includes an explanatory clause, confirming the use of ἀρχός in the sense of *origin* or *beginning*. Throughout the present section, the treatise

deals with initial creative processes. The simile of the *Right-hand* and the *Left-hand*—here mentioned for the first time—is used, primarily, in the treatise—as in Gnosticism generally—to denote the spiritual and material principles. Thus by the *countless Beginnings, those of the Right-hand and those of the Left-hand,* the initial processes of both creations are intended. Cf. Clem. *Hom.* II, 16: "*In the Beginning, God, who is One, like a Right-hand and a Left, made the Heaven first, and then the Earth*".

MS. f. 141ᵛ
C.S. p. 55

IV

9. From ἀνάγκη, L. and S. 2 = *necessity, natural want,* such as *hunger,* etc. The context likens the αναγκαιον to "*those that go out and those that come in*". This suggests that the term here stands for the nutritive and excretive processes.

V
MS. f. 143ᵛ
C.S. p. 56

. . . .

. . . . . He made ⟨the genitals⟩¹ of his body, [the one after the] pattern (τυπος) of Aphredōn (αφρηδων) ⟨and⟩ the other after the pattern (τυπος) of Mousanios (μουσανιος)². And he made ⟨the soles⟩ of his feet, the right foot after the pattern (τυπος) [of the] All-manifest (πανδηλος), and the left foot after the pattern (τυπος) of the Mother underlying all 3. This is the Man made corresponding to (κατα) each Aeon (αιων): this same the Whole desired (επιθυμει) [to know] 4. This is the All-perfect One (παντελιος): this is the Man of God: he being also himself a god. And invisible (αʿορατος) is he, and unknowable (αγνωστος) is he, and all-still (πανηρεμος) is he, and uncontainable (αχωρητος) 5 is he, and unmoved (ασαλευτος) is he. To scorn him it behoveth not: to bless him it behoveth —the while he saith:—

"I bless thee, the Father of all fathers of Light.

I bless thee, the infinite (απεραντος) Light, every infinitude (απεραντος) excelling.

I bless thee, the Light uncontainable (αχωρητος), every uncontainable (αχωρητος) surpassing.

I bless thee, the Light unutterable (αʿρητος), every unutterable (αʿρητος) preceding.

I bless thee, the Light incorruptible (αφθαρτος), every incorruptible (αφθαρτος) excelling.

V
MS. f. 143ᵛ
C.S. p. 56

1. The Anthropos is masculo-feminine. The missing word probably stood for the male generative organs, the female organ of procreation, i.e. the womb, having been mentioned on III. If an infiltration of ideas from the Basilidian Gnosis be admitted (*vide* next note), the symbolical relationship between Aphredōn and Mousanios and the male generative organs of the bi-sexual Anthropos, is presumably due to the fact that Aphredōn and Mousanios were subordinate creative and ruling Powers in the space outside the Pleroma, called, in our treatise, the place of the *Midst* (*vide* next note).

2. *Aphredōn* and *Mousanios*. The great beings who bore these
names belong to a somewhat later stage in the cosmogonic process, but their significance may best be considered here, at the
point where they first come into the symbolism. It was the
practice of the Gnostics to people all the spheres in their cosmos,
and assign to these embodiments names expressive of their attributes. To analyse the names of Aphredōn and Mousanios may
therefore furnish some clue to their significance, barely ad-
umbrated by the brief allusions to them in the text. It is tenable
that the Copts may have derived the proper noun ⲁϥⲣⲏⲇⲱⲛ from
the Greek root ΦΡΑΔ, whence comes φράζω = *to speak, to declare*,
etc. and ἄφραστος = *unuttered, undeclared*. Granted this derivation,
and prefixed, as is this word, by the α priv., Aphredōn would
bear the meaning of *unuttered*. As regards the change of vowel from
ⲁ to ⲏ, comment is required, although this substitution will not
cause surprise to anyone familiar with the fluid use of Greek
vowels by the Copts. Also it will be noted that similar vowel inter-
changes occur in other Greek words found in this treatise. The
Coptic language retains many of the characteristics of its parent
tongue, Egyptian. Old Egyptian writings employ no vowels,
groups of consonants are by us made pronounceable by the in-
sertion of a short ε between them. Consequently, the translitera-
tion and pronunciation of the hieroglyphs is only approximately
equivalent. Later, when the Copts adopted the Greek alphabet,
the Greek vowels came into general use in writing Coptic, but the
habit—among the earlier people—of omitting any indication of
vowel sounds in writing, seems to have resulted—in their successors
—in an indifference, or perhaps an uncertainty, as to which particular vowel should be used. This uncertainty, it must be remarked, is as frequently to be observed in their writing of Greek
words as Coptic. In early texts, ε and ⲏ are both found standing
for ⲁ; ⲁ for ε and ο; ⲟⲩ for ω, and so on. W. E. Crum, in his *Intro.
to Coptic Ostraca*, 1902, gives a detailed list of these vowel inter-
changes, and adds: "*there is conspicuous inaccuracy in the use of vowels
throughout certain texts*", and he proceeds to note, in particular, the
frequency with which these inaccuracies occur in the Codex
Brucianus, a collection of which the present treatise forms part.
Mousanios, the second proper name, occurs twice in the treatise,
coupled with that of *Aphredōn*, the two being related in significance.
A Greek word, affording—in the not too rigid linguistic sense of
the Copts—a possible etymological source and an appropriate
meaning, is μοῦσα, *vide* L. and S. μοῦσα II = *song, eloquence*, etc.
(e.g. τίς ἥδε μοῦσα = *what strain is this?*), the general sense of
utterance being perhaps allowed the word. If these conjectured
derivations—ΦΡΑΔ and μοῦσα—are accepted, the names Aphre-

V

MS. f. 143ᵛ

C.S. p. 56

[27]

V
MS. f. 143^v
C.S. p. 56

dōn and Mousanios bear the contrasted meanings of *unuttered* and *uttered*. In the endeavour to discover possible analogies to Aphredōn and Mousanios, by reference to Gnostic systems showing relationship of doctrine with our treatise, we find the idea of two cosmical rulers developed with much detail in a system recorded by Hippolytus in the *Ref. Haer.* and attributed by him to Basilides. Although, in detail, this system does not greatly resemble that of our treatise, more than one of the main cosmological speculations may be correlated with it; e.g. (1) the σπέρμα τοῦ κόσμου, single all-containing Seed of the cosmos; (2) the one Sonship of triple division; (3) the μεθόριον πνεῦμα, the Boundary Spirit; (4) the two great Rulers of the cosmos, Ἄρρητος and Ῥητός. The analogies in our treatise are: (1) the all-containing Monad; (2) the Monogenes of Triple-power; (3) a Boundary delimiting the Pleroma; and (4) Aphredōn and Mousanios (presumably). An outline of the Basilidian cosmogony—in so far as concerns these analogies—may be briefly presented. The not-existing-God (οὐκ ὤν θεός), having pre-ordained a cosmos, cast down a single Seed—produced from not-existing-things—containing in itself the whole seed mass of the cosmos. In this Seed was the Sonship, a unity, triply divided, of the same essence as the not-existing-God. This Sonship effects the salvation of the whole cosmos, as, in our treatise, does the Monogenes of Triple-power. The first part of the Sonship ascended at once to the highest realms. The second part also rises, borne aloft by the Holy Spirit—also contained in the cosmical Seed—as a wing. The Holy Spirit remained below the Sonship—but not altogether severed therefrom—to form the Firmament or Boundary between the highest Heaven and the rest of the cosmos where the third part of the Sonship remained. This lower portion of the cosmos consisted of the Ogdoad and the Hebdomad; the lowest region—called by Basilides, the Formlessness—being included in the Hebdomad. Following the rising of the first and second parts of the Sonship, and the formation of the Boundary, two great Rulers arose from the cosmical Seed. The first was head of the whole cosmos below the Boundary, the second, ruler of all that was below himself. The first was designated "*Unuttered*" (ἄρρητος), the second "*Uttered*" (ῥητός). Excerpts from Hippolytus, relating to the two Rulers, may be given: "*When therefore the firmament which is above the heaven was in being, there escaped and was engendered from the cosmical germ and universal seed mass, the great Ruler, head of the cosmos . . . he, [Basilides says,] is more unuttered* (ἄρρητος) *than unuttered* [*things*]. *. . .He, [when] engendered, raised and lifted himself up and was borne wholly up as far as the firmament . . . this is what they denominate Ogdoad, where the great Ruler has his throne. . . . Then the entire heavenly creation, that is, the aetherial* [*world*], *he himself, the great wise demiurge fashioned.*

[28]

...When all aetherial things, then, were in order, again from the uni-   V
versal seed mass another Ruler ascended...and this one is named by   MS. f. 143ᵛ
them: uttered (ῥητός). *And this space is called: Hebdomad. And this*   C.S. p. 56
Ruler is the governor and demiurge of all things below himself" (*Ref. Haer.*
VII, 23 and 24). "*The great Ruler, the Ogdoad, was king and lord, as*
it seemed, of all things, but [*in reality*] *of this space between, the Heb-*
domad was king and lord. And the Ogdoad is unuttered (ἄρρητος),
[*whereas*] *the Hebdomad is uttered* (ῥητός)" (*ibid.* 25). If the conjectured interpretations for the names Aphredōn and Mousanios
be allowed—i.e. Aphredōn = *unuttered* and Mousanios = *uttered*
(*vide supra*)—we have a striking etymological coincidence with the
designations of the two Rulers of Basilides. It is not, however,
suggested that the two pairs are absolute equations, although as far
as can be seen from the scanty references to Aphredōn and
Mousanios in the treatise, their positions in the cosmos are similar.
In the Basilidian scheme of cosmogonical partitioning, there was
a primary division of the cosmos into two parts, the world *above*,
and the world *below* the Firmament (*Ref. Haer.* VII, 23). The two
great Rulers had their place in the world below, in which were included the Ogdoad, the Hebdomad, and the Formlessness. In the
system of our treatise and that of Valentinus, emphasis is laid more
particularly on the triple partitioning of the cosmos, the three
divisions being called the *Within* (i.e. the Pleroma), the place of
the *Midst*, and the *Without*, the two last being located in the world
below the Firmament of Basilides. In the scheme of our Gnostics,
Aphredōn and Mousanios have their positions in the place of the
Midst. The meagre treatment accorded to the two in our treatise
is in striking contrast to the wealth of detail given and the importance assigned to the analogous pair in the system of Basilides.
Since in the presentation of the cosmic drama, our treatise would
lose little by their exclusion, the inference is that their introduction
serves some not quite obvious end. Certain indications suggest
what that end may be. As pointed out in note 6, II, the cosmology
of our treatise is grounded on two main ideas: (1) triplicity in
unity as regards the constitution of the universe, and (2) re-
enactment, in each successive sphere, of all antecedent events, together with the duplication of the dramatis personae. About two-
thirds of the treatise is concerned with creative processes in the
upper world and the place of the Midst, and with the beings related to these spaces. The remaining portion deals with the creation of the lower world, the abode of entities of lesser degree, and
the sphere of human existence. More particularly as regards the
latter part, the scheme of things—though not identical in every
detail—resembles that of Valentinus. Our treatise presents the
Mother—corresponding to the lower Sophia of Valentinus—

[29]

V
MS. f. 143^v
C.S. p. 56

operating as general creator, and through her first-begotten Son, forming and fashioning the diverse kinds and species of the lower creation, thus acting in imitation of God the Father and Creator, who, through his Only-begotten Son, created all things. With the Mother are associated two great Beings, called the Propator and the Autopator. The former takes a share in the creative processes, while the two exercise ruling functions, and correspond in position to the Demiurge and the Cosmokrator of the Valentinian tradition. The Propator and the Autopator occupy prominent positions in the cosmogony of the lower world; thus the idea suggests itself that Aphredōn and Mousanios were introduced into the drama of the *middle* region, by the exponents of the system, to provide the prototypes required by the principle of repetition. In no other extant system are two pairs of Rulers found with this particular significance, and possibly the appearance of the two, in a spatially suitable position, in the system of Basilides, may have suggested their adoption as the necessary prototypes of the Propator and the Autopator, while the borrowing of the significant Basilidian names might reasonably follow. The absolute prototypes of the two Rulers in the triple series are, of course, to be recognized in the two aspects of the Deity in the world *Within* (*vide* XI, XII, and XV). In regard to the significance of the terms *unuttered* and *uttered*, some explanation is required. The racial inheritance of Egyptian tradition influenced the schools of Gnosticism that flourished in Egypt, and in early and late Egyptian texts, as also in all Gnostic writings, enormous importance was attached to the power exercised in giving utterance to a name. By speaking the name, the Gnostics understood the calling into existence of the distinguishing character and essential qualities of a being; *form*, in the metaphysical sense, was thus given to him, by enclosing him, so to speak, within the limits of his own nature, which nature had been defined by the speaking of his name. To say, therefore, of a being, that he was *uttered*, was equivalent to saying that he was *manifested*, *made*, while to be defined as *unuttered*, was to be *unmanifested*, *unmade*. The account given by Hippolytus of the two great Rulers in the Basilidian system, discloses that the first one, the *unuttered*, was ruler of the Ogdoad, i.e. the noumenal world, whereas the second, the *uttered*, was lord of the Hebdomad, the world of phenomena. The name of the first was said to be *unuttered*, because in the regions—and to the entities—of the phenomenal world his mode of being was incomprehensible. As far as their powers of perception went, he was non-existent, unmade. They had not heard his name, which, in their terms, was indefinable and inexpressible. The second Ruler, on the other hand, belonging as he did to the phenomenal world, had a definable,

[30]

comprehensible nature. He was *uttered*, made. The term Aphredōn
—conjectured to mean *unuttered*—besides occurring several times
in the treatise as a proper name, is twice used adjectivally (XVII
and XX).

3. The substratum of phenomenal manifestation. The reference
is not to the feminine principle of the Triad, mentioned on II, but
to the reflection of that principle in the manifested cosmos, where
the *Mother* stands for the basic substance of all created things.

4. Cf. the beliefs of the Naassene Gnostics, quoted in note 7, II:
"*And they hold that the gnosis of him is the beginning of the capacity for
the gnosis of God*" (Hippol. v, 6).

5. As employed in the treatise, this word bears the meaning:
not to be contained in a place.

VI
MS. f. 143ᴿ
C.S. p. 57

[I bless] (VI) thee, the ⟨Light Source of⟩ [every Light].

I bless ⟨thee⟩, the Light [unspeakable].

[I bless] thee, the Light—even by himself unthought.

I [bless] thee, the unbegotten (αγεννητος) Light.

I bless thee, the self-alone-[caused] (αυτο—)¹ Light.

I bless [thee], the Forefather (προπατωρ) of Light, every forefather (προπατωρ) excelling.

I [bless] thee, the invisible (α‘ορατος) Light, [every] invisible (α‘ορατος) preceding.

[I] bless thee, the Light Thought (επινοια), every thought (επινοια) excelling.

I bless thee, the God of Light, who art before all gods.

I bless thee, the Gnosis (γνωσις), which to all gnosis (γνωσις) is the Light.

I bless thee, the Light unknowable (αγνωστος), every unknowable (αγνωστος) preceding.

I bless thee, the still (ηρεμος) Light, every stillness (ηρεμος) preceding.

I bless thee, the all-powered (παντοδυναμος) Light, every all-power (παντοδυναμος) excelling.

I bless thee, the triple-powered (τριδυναμος) Light, every triple-power (τριδυναμος) excelling.

I bless thee, the undivided (ατδιακρινε) Light—and (δε) thou art he who separates (διακρινε) all Light.

I bless thee, the uncommingled (‘ιλικρινες) Light, all uncommingled (things) (‘ιλικρινες) excelling.

VI
MS. f. 143ᴿ
C.S. p. 57

1. *Vide* note 1, VII.

.   .   .   .
.   .   .   .
.   .   .   .

I bless thee, [the One who] all things knoweth (νοι),
whereas himself, [no one doth know].

I bless [thee, the One] who in himself the Whole
possesseth, whereas himself, [none doth] possess.

[I bless] thee, who begettest all in unbegottenness
(—αγεννητος), [inasmuch as] him, none hath begotten.

I [bless] thee, the Source (πηγη) of the Whole, [and]
of all things.

I bless [thee], truly the self-alone-begotten (αυτογενης) ¹ [Light], preceding all the self-alone-begotten (αυτογενης).

[I] bless thee, truly the unmoved (ασαλευτος) Light:
thou art the [Light] of those who in thy [Light]
were moved.

I bless thee, the Silence of all silences of Light.

I bless thee, the Saviour (σωτηρ) of all saviours
(σωτηρ) of Light.

I bless [thee], the unconquerable [Light] alone.

I bless thee, who to all spaces (τοπος) of the Whole
alone art Space (τοπος).

I bless [thee], who alone art Wise (σοφος), and who
alone art Wisdom (σοφια).

I bless [thee] ,the All-mystery (πανμυστηριον) alone.

[I] bless thee, the All-perfect (παντελιος) Light alone.

I bless thee, the only Unattainable One.

---

1. αυτογενης, with which may be associated—for a consideration
of the import of the prefix—the correlative terms αυτογενητος and
αυτοπατωρ (IX and LIX). There are several instances in the
treatise where meanings peculiar to Gnostic thought are attached

to Greek words (e.g. on I, IV and V). In some cases the context makes this clear, in others, an explanatory clause follows the word and defines the meaning. In the case of αὐτογενής, the manner in which the term is on occasions employed, is ample indication that the simple rendering of αὐτο as *self*, does not—in these particular instances—represent the full intention of the Gnostic writer, the more significant self-*alone* being implied (*vide* L. and S. 1926, I, 3, αὐτός = μόνος, *by oneself, alone*). αὐτο occurs several times prefixed both to γένης and γεννητός. As employed in our treatise, there is a difference in meaning between the two combinations, and with the exception of their use as designations of the Supreme Deity, the terms are not interchangeable. Thus their significance must be sought by reference to the context, and in the special sense of the verbal forms whence they are derived. In the first term— αὐτογενής—γενής may be derived from γείνομαι = *to be begotten, to be born.* By adopting self-*alone* as the meaning of the prefix αὐτο, we have a definition—not of one who begets himself—but of an entity *begotten by a single agent.* Thus an αὐτογενής is the product of an αὐτοπάτωρ, a *self-alone-father* or *sole parent*, one who has the power to produce offspring without a partner. On LIX both these terms occur in a prayer addressed to the Hidden Mystery = the First Cause: "*Thou alone art Unbegotten and Self-alone-begotten* (αυτο-γενης) *and the Self-alone-Father* (αυτοπατωρ)". The ascription of *self-alone parenthood* to the First Cause is not peculiar to the thought of our treatise. It occurs also in the doctrine of the Gnostic Marcus as recorded by Hippolytus, and by Epiphanius who copied the now-lost Greek treatise of Irenaeus. Marcus relates that the manner of coming into being of all things was revealed to him in vision: "*When the Primal [Being], the Self-alone Father* (τὸ πρῶτον ὁ πατὴρ αὐτοῦ), *who is unimaginable and without substance* (ἀνούσιος), *who is neither male nor female, willed his ineffability to be uttered, and the invisible to take form, he opened his mouth, and a Logos like to himself went forth*" (Hippol. *Ref. Haer.* VI, 42). The corresponding passage in Epiphanius (*Haer.* XXXIV, 4), which agrees in all other respects, substitutes ὁ πατὴρ ὤδινεν = *the Father was in travail*, for ὁ πατὴρ αὐτοῦ. The use, as an alternative, of this term with a feminine implication appears to emphasize the completeness and unity of the generative power of the *sole parent.* The Latin translator of Irenaeus, entirely missing the meaning of Marcus, proposes to read "*cuius pater nemo est*" for the Greek sentence! In the passage in our treatise to which the present note relates, αὐτο-γενής is predicated of the Supreme Being: "*in very deed the* αυτογενης *Light*". Here, the Light—a name continually applied to the Deity in the treatise—is not only the sole begetter, but is also that which is begotten by the sole parent, i.e. himself. It is of course obvious

that were αὐτογενής used only in relation to the First Cause, VII
question as to the significance of the prefix would not arise—*self* MS. f. 145ᴿ
or *self-alone begotten* being equally applicable to him. But the C.S. p. 58
matter is otherwise when we find the word applied, in our
treatise, to the Mother, to certain Aeons of the middle space of the
cosmos, to the Forefather of the lower creation, and, once, to the
Christ. As a designation for the Monogenes, αὐτογενής is used re-
peatedly in the correlative texts of Iren. I, xxvii and the *Apoc. of
John* (Cod. Berol.), while a significant instance occurs in the pro-
nouncements of Marcus (*vide* Epiph. *Haer.* xxxiv, 5): "...*the self-
alone begotten and father-donated Word*" (τὸν αὐτὸν γεννήτορα καὶ
πατροδότορα λόγον). This application of the term affords positive
proof that the simple rendering *self* cannot be the meaning of αὐτο
as used by these teachers, for never in the beliefs of any school of
Gnostic thought, nor, indeed, in the tenets of any theology, has
the Monogenes been held to be *self*-begotten. Indeed, to speak
thus of the Son would utterly confound the conception of sonship.
Giving, however, to αὐτός the significance of the synonymous term
μόνος, self-*alone*, the application of αὐτογενής to the Monogenes is
justified, the qualifying term having reference, not to his own, but
to the Father's generative act, he being begotten by the Father in
unpartnered generation. Elucidation of the term as applied to
beings of a lower status, as also of its use as a designation for the
second category of being, and the middle space of the universe,
is deferred until such instances occur. The second combination,
αὐτογένητος, may be derived from γεννάω (of a male parent) = *to
beget, to generate*. This word has a rigorously restricted application
in our treatise, where, in contradistinction to the dually applicable
and dually significant αὐτογενής, it is reserved for the Supreme Deity
alone. It signifies *one who by himself alone begets himself.* On IX we
have an instance, where the meaning is defined by a preceding
sentence: "...*the Fruit of himself alone...who alone gave birth to
himself...an* αυτογενητος *is he*". Of the First Cause only can it be
said that he, acting alone, begets himself. Whereas, in the case of
the Monogenes, the Father—again acting alone—begets the Son,
who is thus αὐτογενής, i.e. *self-alone begotten* by the Father.

VIII
MS. f. 145ᵛ
C.S. p. 59

. . . .

[I bless] thee, [thyself] the Good (αγαθος), and [thou dost every] good (αγαθος) reveal.

I bless thee, [thyself] the Light, and thou dost every [Light] reveal.

I bless [thee], who [all Mind] awakest, who givest Life to every soul (ψυχη).

[I bless thee], Repose (αναπαυσις) of those who are ⟨in Silence⟩¹.

I bless thee, [in] all Fatherhoods abiding—from [the Beginning] until now all seek for [thee]—in that thou art their [quest].

[Yea], hearken to the supplication of the [Man] in every place²—this same who [prays] with his whole heart."

³This is the [Father] of every father, [the God] of every god, and [the Lord] of every lord. The [Son] among all sons is he, [and] the Saviour [σωτηρ) among [all] saviours (σωτηρ). The Invisibility (α'ορατος) of all invisibles (α'ορατος) is he, and [the Silence] of all silences (σιγη). The Infinitude (απερ-αντος) of all infinitudes (απεραντος) is he, the Un-containability (αχωρητος) of all the uncontainables (αχωρητος). Abysmal depth is he to all of the Abyss, a Space (τοπος) is he to every space (τοπος). The One and Only Intelligible One (νοερον) is he, who is before [all] Mind (νους).

VIII
MS. f. 145ᵛ
C.S. p. 59

1. The Coptic word proposed in restoration of the text is of suitable length, and is suggested by comparison with other passages of similar import, e.g. X, "*all Life is in him. All Repose is in him*"; XV, "*from the Father every Name arose, whether unutterable...or all Names that are in the Silence*"; XXXVI, "*the Mystery of the Silence, this which uttereth all things*". Cf. also LV: "*Thou art the Maker of the things not yet revealed, these which thou alone dost know*".

2. *Vide* II: "*the Man or the City of the Father, who is in all things*". VIII
Cf. also the statement of the Naassene Gnostics: "...*the masculo-* MS. f. 145ᵛ
feminine Man who is in all things" (Hippol. *Ref. Haer.* v, 8). C.S. p. 59

3. The Man's Song of Praise being ended, the treatise resumes
the original theme with a description of the nature and attributes
of the Deity. The substance of what follows is closely paralleled in
the *Apoc. of John,* where a description of the Supreme Being is
found in which similar terminology is used (pp. 6–7, German
trans.).

Again, a Mind (νους) [is he, who is] before all mind (νους). [And] incomprehensible is he, whilst ⟨all⟩ he ⟨comprehends⟩. Without like [is he, who is before] all likeness. ⟨Exalted⟩ is he ⟨beyond⟩ all ⟨height⟩, widespread is he ⟨beyond⟩ all ⟨breadth⟩. And ⟨before⟩ all ⟨breadth⟩ is he, and [before] every height. And [he is] wise (σοφος), beyond (παρα) ⟨all⟩ wisdom (σοφια), holy is he, beyond (παρα) all ⟨holiness⟩. Good (αγαθος) is he, exceedingly, beyond (παρα) all goodness (αγα-θος): himself he is the Seed of all good things (αγαθον), and he, again, is pregnant with them all—the Self-alone-caused (αυτοφυης), or (η) Fruit of himself alone. Before the Universes were, is he who alone to himself gave birth—and from all time is he. A self-alone-generated (αυτογενητος)¹ and an Everlasting One is he. No name hath he to whom all names belong. He hath foreknown these Universes: he contemplates (θεωρι) the Universes, he looketh on the Universes, he hearkeneth to the Universes. Mighty is he, exceedingly, beyond (παρα) all might. Upon his Face that none can comprehend, it is not possible to look. One and selfsame in fashion is his being²: without substance (ανουσιος), still (ηρεμος), unknowable (αγνωστος), and the All-mystery (πανμυστηριον) is he.

1. Reference may be made to note 1, VII.

2. Text: "*he exists in a form* (or *fashion*) *of oneness*". Cf. the comments of Irenaeus on the mode of being of the Father: "*He is a simple uncompounded Being, without diverse parts, and altogether similar and equal to himself*" (Iren. II, xv, 3).

And the All-wise (πανσοφος) [is he, and] ⟨the⟩ All-
source (παναρχος) [1], [and] ⟨the All-space⟩, to whom
belongeth every ⟨space⟩, they being all in him. [And]
all Light [is] in him, [and] all Life is in him. [All] Repose (αναπαυσις) is in him, and ⟨all Silence⟩ is in him.
And ⟨the Father is in him⟩, and the Mother and the Son
[are in him]. This is the Blessed One (μακαριος) alone,
for (γαρ) of him ⟨the⟩ Universes are in need (χρια),
since (γαρ) [all] through him have Life. He in [him-
self] these Universes knows, the Universes in himself he
contemplates (θεωρι). Uncontainable (αχωρητος) is he
himself, whilst (δε) the Universes he contains (χωρι),
possessing them in him. Beyond him doth not anything
exist, but (αλλα) in him the Universes are. To them all
he setteth bounds, he encloses them, and all exist in
him. The Father, he, of all the Aeons (αιων), he being
before them all. Beyond him is not any space (τοπος),
nothing intelligible (νοερον) is, nor (ουτε) aught that
cometh forth [2], except the One Alone. His incompre-
hensibility they behold: it is within them all, because
he is the bounds of all—but (δε) him they comprehended not. At him they are amazed, because he setteth
bounds unto them all, (and) they strive (αγωνιζε)—[3]

X
MS. f. 147ᵛ
C.S. p. 61

1. For the significance of ἀρχός in the treatise, *vide* note 8, IV.
2. Dr Schmidt considers the spelling of this word to be incorrect, and proposes to transpose two letters, which alters it to the
Coptic for *omnino = altogether*. In this case the sentence could
perhaps be read: "nor any thing *at all*". The word in question
may, however, be the pronominal form of the Egyptian verb
_pr_ = *to go forth through birth or begetting*.
3. One or more leaves are missing at this point. The page
placed in succession—according to my arrangement of the MS—
deals with the same subjects as the preceding ten, i.e. the First
Cause, the Members and Universes, and the Archetypal Man or
City, the detailed consideration of these topics being there brought
to a conclusion.

X
MS. f. 147ᵛ
C.S. p. 61

He set him up¹ to cause a striving (αγωνιзε)² in the City (πολις) wherein their Likeness ('ικων) is. And in this they move, and in this they live. And this same is the House of the Father, the Vesture (ενδυμα) of the Son, the Power of the Mother, and the Likeness ('ικων) of the Pleroma (πληρωμα)³.

This is he, the Primal Father of the Universes. This is he, the Primal Ever-living One (αει)⁴. This is he, the King of the Unattainables. This is he in whom the Universes move to and fro⁵: he giveth form (μορφη) to them within himself. This is he, the self-alone-caused (αυτοφυης), self-alone-generated (αυτογεννητος)⁶ Space (τοπος). This is he, the Deep (βαθος)⁷ of the Universes. This verily is he, the Greatness beneath the Abyss. This is he from whom All things⁸ came forth: before him was silence, none spoke of him, for unspeakable, unimaginable (ατνοι) is he. This is he, the Primal Source (πηγη)⁹, whose Voice did penetrate in every place. This is he, the Primal Sound, till All things heard (αισθανε) and apprehended (νοι). This is he whose Members (μελος) are accounted a myriad myriad Powers (δυναμις)¹⁰, from them each (Power) came forth¹¹.

1. A reference to the *Man*, a title synonymous with *City*, *vide* II: "*And the Father took their whole likeness, and he made it as a City or a Man*".

2. Or, *to cause them to strive*. The final sentence on the preceding page tells of a striving on the part of the Aeons to comprehend the incomprehensible Father. Here the subject is resumed, while a statement as to the manner in which such knowledge was to be obtained is found on II, following the account of the creation of the Man or City: "*each one in the City knew him, etc.*"

3. The subject of the City is here concluded. In the succeeding paragraph a description of the First Cause is resumed.

4. αει = *for ever*. On p. cxviii of the Preface of his edition of the text of Irenaeus, Wigan Harvey says that Aristotle derived the word *aeon* (αιων) from this term: ἀεὶ ὤν = *ever-living* (*De Cael.* 1, 9; *Met.* vii, 107, 2 b). The Valentinians applied the term to the

Supreme Deity, speaking of him as the Pre-living Aeon (Αἰῶνα προόντα) (Iren. 1, i, 1).

5. The Coptic word means to *wander*, to *roam* or *float about*. It was used previously, on I, in relation to the εἰκών and the *Universes*: "*thus within it* (the εἰκών) *they move to and fro*". The word is derived from the hieroglyphs, and occurs in the inscriptions with reference to the flowing to and fro of the Waters of the Inundation. In our passage, the meaning is God as primaeval Space in which the Universes floated about.

6. *Vide* note 1, VII.

7. βάθος, signifying *depth* or *height*. A term used both by the Sethian and Valentinian Gnostics to denote the unfathomable nature of the First Cause (Iren. 1, i, 1, and 1, xxviii, 1). The term serves to show the utter impossibility for the human mind to conceive the mode of the Divine subsistence before he revealed himself as Creator and Father. Being, however, a positive rather than a negative definition, it exhibits him as potentially containing all things in himself.

8. A reference to the Aeons, also *infra* (*vide* latter part of note 1, I).

9. The foregoing appellations—*Primal Father*, *Primal Everliving One*, *Deep*, and *Primal Source*—are the equivalents of four Valentinian designations for the First Cause. Cf. Iren. 1, i, 1: "*They maintain, then, that in the invisible and unutterable height above, there exists a certain perfect* αἰῶνα προόντα (*Pre-living Aeon*). *And this they call* προαρχή (*Pre-Source*), προπάτωρ (*Fore-Father*) *and* βυθός (*Deep*)".

10. Cf. II: "*Each one of his Members is accounted as a myriad*". The context has reference to the later emanations which came into being through the medium of the Members of the Father, *vide* note 1, I.

11. There is a full stop and a pause of some length at this point in the script, where the account of the first phase in the cosmogonical process is brought to a conclusion.

[41]

(XI) The Second Space (τοπος) ¹ came into being: He shall be called Creator (δημιουργος), Father², Reason (λογος), Source (πηγη), and Mind (νους), and Man³, Eternal (αιδος), and Infinite (απεραντος). (XII) This is the Support (στυλος), this is the Guardian (επισκοπος), this is the Father of the Whole. He it is upon whose Head the Aeons (αιων) are a Crown, darting forth rays (ακτιν). The Fullness of his Face is the Ignorance⁴ in the outside Worlds (κοσμος), these which at all times seek after his Face. They desire to know him because his Word reaches them, and they long to see him. To the Spaces (τοπος) outside the Pleroma (πληρωμα) pierces the Light of his Eyes, and the Word (λογος) that proceeds from his Mouth penetrates the heights and the depths. The Hair of his Head is the number of the hidden Worlds (κοσμος)⁵, the circumference⁶ of his Face is the pattern (?) (κατ‘ικων) of the Aeons (αιων), the Hairs of his Face are the number of the outside Worlds (κοσμος)⁷. The outstretching of his Hands is the manifestation of the Stauros (στρος)⁸, the outstretching of the Stauros (στρος) is the Ennead (‘εννας) on the Right-hand and on the Left⁹, the stock whence sprang the Stauros (στρος) is the unconquerable Man. This is the Father, this is the Source (πηγη) welling forth from the Silence¹⁰, this same for whom they seek in every place. This is the Father: as it were a Spark of Light from him came forth the Monad (μονας)¹¹, ⟨beside⟩ which all the Worlds (κοσμος) that are shall be accounted naught.

1. By the definitive conclusion, on the preceding page, of the first subject of the discourse, and the present use of the term *Second* Space in relation to the Deity, the second stage in the cosmogonical process is inaugurated. For a previous use of the term τόπος in this connection, *vide* note 9, I. The *Space* there mentioned is the first, and relates to the Members of the Father. While the

Deity's initial act was one of self-revelation by the production of   XII
his own Image, the emanation of his Members marked the first   MS. f. 94^v
stage of the process whereby he revealed himself to his creation.   C.S. p. 2
This was a revelation of Fatherhood. *Vide* I: "*He made himself to
be Space for his Members, to cause them to dwell in him and know him,
because he is their Father, who did emanate them from his First Conception which became Space for them*". The notion of the Deity determining to reveal himself in Fatherhood is finely expressed in
Valentinian thought: "*But [the Father] was alone and solitary, as they
say, and reposing alone within himself. When, however, he became productive, it seemed good to him, at one time, to beget and lead forth that
which was most beautiful and most perfect in himself, for [the Father]
loved not solitude. For he, [Valentinus] says, was all love, but in truth,
love is not love, unless there be something to be loved*" (Hippol. VI, 29).
The titles which follow in our treatise on this and the succeeding
page, are all of Valentinian usage. They serve to define the comprehensible attributes and qualities whereby the incomprehensible Deity enters into relationship with his creatures.

2. The title *Primal Father* relates to the Deity in his remoter
aspect as the ultimate Space and Source of all (*vide* I). The names
Father and *Second Space* convey the notion of a more intimate
relationship with the creation. Cf. Iren. I, vi, 2: "*When the Fore-
Father* (προπάτωρ) *conceived the Thought of bringing forth, he received
the name of Father* (πατήρ)".

3. Cf. Irenaeus, recording the beliefs of the Ptolemaic School
of Valentinians: "*There are yet others among them who declare that the
Fore-Father of the Wholes* (προπάτορα τῶν ὅλων), *the Fore-Source* (προ-
άρχην), *and the Primal-unimaginable One* (προανεννόητον) *is called Man*
("Ανθρωπον), *and that this is the great and abstruse mystery, namely, that
the Power which is above all others and contains the Wholes* (τὰ ὅλα) *in his
embrace, is termed Man; hence does the Saviour also style himself: Son of
Man*" (Iren. I, vi, 3). Also in the Valentinian source in Epiphanius
(*Panar.* 31, 5) it is said that the *Father of Truth*—a title of the
Monogenes—bore the mystical name *Man:* "*The perfected ones
named him in a familiar way 'Man', because he was the antitype of the
pre-existing Unbegotten One*". This same mystery is referred to on
LI–LII of our treatise: "*And they understood the Mystery that became
Man—because for this he was manifested, till they saw HIM who is indeed
invisible*". This uncompromising assertion, by the Gnostics, of the
Manhood of God, was no doubt understood in the sense that the
Divine Nature contains in itself, in an eminent manner, all the
perfections of humanity.

4. Meaning: the Deficiency of Knowledge *without* equals the
Fullness of Knowledge *within*. The Coptic word for ignorance is a
composite one, *the state of not-knowing*, i.e. *deficient in knowledge*. On

[43]

the present page we meet the first allusion to the history of the Aeon Sophia and the circumstances that arose in the cosmos in consequence of her actions. Although in the first half of the treatise, the Mother (= the Sophia) is not mentioned by name— nor indeed in any part is her fall from the Pleroma related—from the present point onwards the cosmology becomes increasingly involved in her story. That the writer of our treatise makes allusion to details without relating the story itself, is due, doubtless, to his assuming on the part of his readers complete familiarity with this fundamental doctrine of the Gnosis. Whilst the story is commonly understood in all the systems doctrinally related to our treatise, the tragedy of the Sophia's fall, and its consequences, is found in its fullest known form in the system of Valentinus. The Valentinian School had two main developments, the Eastern or Anatolic, and the Western or Italic, the latter being the more evolved form. While the fundamental doctrines are the same in both cases, there are differences in form and in development of detail between the two. Although the system of our treatise has its own distinctive character, there is clear doctrinal relationship with the Valentinian Gnosis, more particularly in the second half. But most of the doctrines are simply alluded to, and such particulars as are given are barely enough to suggest that the tendencies are Eastern in character. More particularly as regards the doctrine of the Sophia and her fall are the allusions slight, and the manner of presenting the incidents differs considerably from what we find in the accounts of the Church Fathers. In order to relate the references in our treatise, it is necessary to summarize the story as it is found in its fullest known form in the treatises of Irenaeus (*Adv. Haer.*) and Hippolytus (*Ref. Haer.*). These two accounts, in certain points of detail, are supplementary to one another. It must be remarked that in the treatise of Irenaeus, the Church Father frequently confuses the Eastern and Western forms of Valentinianism, but for the purposes of a summary to which the doctrines of our treatise may be related, this may be disregarded. The production of the Dodecad of Aeons of the Pleroma is represented as taking place in pairs, as the result of the conjunction of a primary pair: Νοῦς (Mind) & Ἀλήθεια (Truth) (Hippol. vi, 29; Iren. I, i, 1). Of these Aeons, the only one who had immediate knowledge of the Father was Νοῦς (= the Monogenes), who sprang directly from him. To the other Aeons he was unknown. All, however, had a desire to know the Author of their being, which desire was in accordance with the Father's Will (Iren. I, i, 2. Cf. also note 5, II). But the youngest Aeon of the Dodecad, Sophia, suffered this desire independently from her partner Thelētos (θελητός = personification of the Divine will and intention in Sophia's regard). And

reaching forward by herself, she strove to enter into immediate
communion with the Father. Perceiving also, that whilst the
Aeons—as being themselves begotten beings—begat progeny by
conjugal intercourse, the Unbegotten Father generated and
brought forth by himself alone, Sophia desired to search into and
comprehend his nature, that she might emulate his generative act
and achieve a work in no wise inferior to his (Hippol. vi, 30).
Finding, however, that she could not attain her desire—she having
aimed at an impossibility—Sophia became involved in ignorance
and suffering, and was in danger of being altogether dissolved in
her desire (Iren. i, i, 2). Further, in making her attempt to imitate
the Father's creative act, she transgressed the Divine will and intention for a created being, by forsaking her syzygy Theletos. Her
transgression, however, was due to a deficiency of knowledge, for
she, a begotten being, incomplete in nature apart from her syzygy,
was unable to comprehend the fullness of nature of the uncreated
Being, who, as the originating principle of all things, alone possessed the full power of unpartnered generation. Unable, then,
to acquire the power of the Unbegotten One, Sophia projected
that only, which she—by herself—could project, a deficient and
formless substance, "*a female fruit*" (καρπὸς θῆλυς), which possessed
nothing from the male (Iren. i, i, 3). The Sophia's substance was
also called the *Abortion* (ἔκτρωμα) (Hippol. vi, 31), the idea being
that in giving birth to this substance which was of *herself alone*,
she brought forth an abortive image of a perfect Aeon, i.e. herself.
As her power and her knowledge were deficient, so also was that
which she brought forth, and on the two contrasted ideas, *Fullness* and *Deficiency*, hangs the whole story of the Sophia and the
created universe. As a result of what had come to pass, Sophia
herself was thrown into great agony of mind, whilst the other
Aeons, fearing that what was subsequently born from them would
be equally formless and imperfect, were involved in ignorance,
confusion and fear. This disturbed condition was rectified by
command of the Father—through the projection of two additional
Aeons. The one was called *Christ & Holy Spirit* by the Valentinians
and *Guardian of the Pleroma* by our Gnostics (Iren. i, i, 3; Hippol.
vi, 31; and XVI of our treatise). The other was entitled Horos
("Ορος), Stauros (Σταυρός), and various other names (Hippol. vi,
31). By the former, stability and repose were restored to the
Aeons, and Sophia, separated from the formless substance to
which she had given birth, was reunited to her partner and returned to her former state within the Pleroma. The Stauros then
formed a *palisade* around the complete Aeons, enclosing them, and
screening off the deficient substance which was then excluded
from the Pleroma. From this unformed and deficient substance,

XII
MS. f. 94ᵛ
C.S. p. 2

called by the Valentinians the *Sophia outside* (ἡ ἔξω Σοφία, Hippol. VI, 31), the whole exterior creation arose. The Gnostic speculation which divided the cosmos into three regions was noted on II (*vide* note 6). In our treatise, these are called the *Within*, the *Midst* and the *Without*. They correspond, in the nomenclature of another system (the Peratic), to the ἀγέννητος, the αὐτογέννητος and the γεννητός spaces (*vide* note 6, XXVI and note 1, XXVIII). The *Within* is the hidden world of the Pleroma, the *Midst* and the *Without*—with their related entities—came into being from the substance of the Sophia *outside*. The place of the *Midst*—μεσότητος τόπος of the Valentinians—was immediately exterior to the Pleroma and was also denominated the *second Ogdoad* (Iren. II, xviii, 1). This space, according to Hippolytus (VI, 36), *is* the Sophia *outside*. (Cf. the *outside Worlds* of our treatise, *supra*.) The condition of ignorance, in which the Sophia *inside* the Pleroma became involved owing to her presumptuous act, was, of course, inherent in the nature of her formless offspring, the Sophia *outside*, who had been cast out of the Pleroma wherein no imperfection can abide. In II, iii, 3, Irenaeus says that the Valentinians "speak of what is *without* and what is *within* in reference to *knowledge* and *ignorance*, and not in respect of local distance". Cf. the *Fullness* and *Ignorance* referred to in our passage. Other incidents relating to the Sophia's career will be noted as the references occur in the treatise. The foregoing is a summary of the more important version of the story as it is given in Valentinian form. While in all the systems the main features of this important doctrine would be the same, it is unlikely that the similarity extended to all the details. As is clear in the case of the Anthropos (note 7, II), and as will become evident in regard to many of the personifications figuring in our treatise, while the occurrence of identical names points to a correspondence with Valentinian and kindred speculations, some variation in respect of the significance and functions of the beings in question will usually be observed.

5. Meaning: the Worlds *within* the Pleroma.

6. The same word as on I, i.e. *enclosure*. In both cases *delimitation* is implied.

7. That is: in the place of the *Midst*, outside the Pleroma.

8. στρος = σταυρός, rendered *Cross* in the N.T., primarily means an upright *pale* or *stake*. With the Valentinians the idea was that of a palisade or fence, forming a boundary that could not be overpassed either as regards the laws of being or capacity for knowledge. In their system, as a definite personification, the Aeon Stauros received various names descriptive of his functions. According to Hippolytus his principal purpose was the security of the Pleroma, and the exclusion therefrom of the deficient sub-

[46]

stance of the Aeon Sophia (*vide supra*, note 4). Hippolytus says
that in order "*that the shapelessness of the Abortion might in no way be
visible to the complete Aeons, the Father again projected one Aeon, namely
the Stauros. Who, having been born great from the great and perfect Father,
and projected as a guard and palisade to the Aeons, became the Boundary
of the Pleroma, holding together in himself all the thirty Aeons.... And
he is called Horos* ('ορος), *because he marks off from the Fullness* (πλήρωμα) *the Deficiency* (ὑστέρημα) *outside*" (Hippol. VI, 31). Cf. our
treatise: "*The outstretching of his* [*the Father's*] *Hands is the manifestation
of the Stauros*". Also XIV: "*These are the Worlds in which up-sprang
the Stauros*". The foregoing passages all treat the Stauros as a delimitation. As with all the main concepts in the cosmology of our
Gnostics, the Boundary is threefold. Referring to I, we find that
the Father brings the first Boundary into being by the creation of
his own Image (*vide* note 3, I). By the Image, the Universes are
circumscribed and enclosed. The Boundary in this case is *inwards*,
and divides the Incomprehensible Deity from his creation. The
second Boundary is the Stauros. This relates to the Second Space,
and, enclosing the Thirty Aeons, separates the Pleroma from the
world outside. Cf. Iren. I, v, 1: "*He* (Valentinus) *also supposes two
boundaries* (ὅρους), *one of which was between* βυθός *and the rest of the
Pleroma, dividing the begotten Aeons from the Unbegotten Father, while
the other marks off the Mother from the Pleroma*". According to our
treatise, the stretching forth of the Father's Hands brings the
second Boundary, i.e. the Stauros, into being. In I, i, 3, Irenaeus
gives a few more details: "*The Father then projected, by means of the
Monogenes, the afore-mentioned Horos, after his own Image...they term
this Horos also Stauros*". The third Boundary is the Stauros or Cross
of the earthly redemptive scheme, *vide Excerpt. ex Theodot.* § 42:
"*The Stauros* (σταυρός) *is the Sign of the Boundary* (ὅρος) *of the
Pleroma. As Horos divides the lower world from the Pleroma, so the
Stauros separates the faithful from the unfaithful*". It is clear from the
manner in which the word Stauros is written in the MS, that the
form of the Cross pictured by the Gnostics was not the con-
ventional + of modern art, but ⊤. Under this form the symbol
represented both Horos and Stauros—the delimiting *boundary* of
the spiritual world, above which all is unity, and the *pale* or *stake* set
up in the material universe, by which all things are divided into the
Right hand and the Left hand. In our treatise, the Cross, as such, is
not mentioned, but on LVII, following a reference to the descent of
the Saviour to earth, we read that he divided Matter into two parts
and two places, and called the one, the *Right-hand* and *Place of
Life*, and the other, the *Left-hand* and *Place of Death*. A point of
correspondence between our treatise and the system recorded in
Iren. I, xxvii, i, is seen in the statement *supra*: "*The stock whence*

[47]

sprang the Stauros is the unconquerable Man". This is a reference to the Anthropos. On IV—where the manner of creation of the Anthropos is described—we read: "*He* (the Father) *made him to be unconquerable after the pattern of the Unconquerable One"*. Here, the *Unconquerable One* equals the Divine Image or First Man, in whose likeness the Second Man—created *unconquerable*—was made (*vide* note 7, II). In I, xxvii, I, Irenaeus gives the import of *unconquerable* in this connection. After describing the production of the first conjunctions amongst the highest Aeons, he continues: "*The Autogenes* (= the Monogenes) *further produces a Man, perfect and true, who is called Adamas* (= unconquerable) *because neither has he himself been overcome, nor those from whom he sprang"*. Irenaeus goes on to give the name of the syzygy of the Anthropos, i.e. *Gnosis* (*vide* note 2, IV), and concludes: "*from Anthropos and Gnosis sprang forth that Tree* (ξύλον), *which is itself also called Gnosis"*. Here ξύλον equates with σταυρός, and both denote the Cross.

9. In this passage, the simile of the Right and Left hands denotes the spiritual and material creations. The number *nine* is not characteristic of Gnostic systems in general, though categories of nine gods and goddesses occur in Egyptian mythology. Enneads are, however, mentioned several times in our treatise, where they have a bearing on both creative and redemptive processes. The separation of the dextral and sinistral principles which was effected by the manifestation of the Stauros is again brought about by the descent of the Saviour (LVII–LVIII). The outstretching of the Stauros, which effects the first separation, is the pre-figurement of the stretching forth of the Saviour upon the Cross, with the good and the bad thieves standing for the principles of the Right and the Left.

10. *Source* and *Silence*. Terms denoting the positive and negative aspects of the First Cause. The imagery suggests an ultimate fountain head of all that is conceivable, expressible, and approachable, arising from that which is inconceivable, inexpressible, and unapproachable. In Valentinian doctrine also we find the concept *Silence* used to define the state or mode of the Divine self-subsistence prior to any form of revelation. But it would also seem possible—if we accept the statements of Irenaeus in I, i, I and I, v, I—that a section of the Valentinian School regarded Silence (σιγή) as a definite personification and the actual syzygy of the Deity. In the first passage Irenaeus says that the Eternal and Unbegotten Father "*remained throughout endless ages in deep stillness and repose, together with his* ἔννοια, *who is also called* χάρις *and* σιγή". This language is not, however, altogether conclusive, and Hippolytus, in the *Ref. Haer.*, states quite definitely that Valentinus taught that the Unbegotten Father was "*without female, solitary, and abiding*

alone within himself" (VI, 29). As it is impossible to reconcile the notion of a syzygy for the Father with the Valentinian belief that the Sophia's transgression was due to her ignorance that he alone had the power to generate without a partner, one may conclude that the view which presents the First Principle as a Monad, represents the original doctrine of Valentinus, from which, perhaps, some of his followers may have later departed. But in any case, the state of duality, implied by a partner, could only be a secondary condition where the First Cause is concerned. For until he gave expression to his ἔννοια, neither that ἔννοια itself, nor σιγή, nor any other companion, can have had independent existence. Also the belief in the singleness of being of the Unbegotten Father which precluded the possibility of an independent partner, did not prohibit the inclusion of a feminine potency in the monadic source which is the comprising unity of all powers and all modes of being. It seems probable that the Valentinian and allied forms of the Gnosis were developed from the earlier Simonian system, and it appears that Simon Magus was the first to postulate *Silence* as the originating source of all. Eusebius (*de Eccl. Th.* II, 9) quotes a statement of that teacher: "*God was also Silence* (ἦν θεὸς καὶ Σιγή)*"* (Harvey's trans. *vide* note 1, p. 98, *Sancti Irenaei.* W. Harvey, 1857). Hippolytus (VI, 18) says that Simon wrote in his *Great Announcement* that all the Aeons came from "*one Root, which is Power-Silence* (Δύναμις Σιγή), *unseen, incomprehensible"*.

XII
MS. f. 94ᵛ
C.S. p. 2

11.   According to statements in our treatise (XIV) and the *Apoc. of John* (p. 8, German trans.), the Monad is to be equated with the εἰκών and ἔννοια of the Father. In the *Apocryphon*, the ἔννοια is also called πρόνοια, that is to say, it is the complete Divine Forethought of the whole cosmos (*vide* note 3, I). In the present passage we learn that the Monad came forth from the Father as a Spark of Light. (Cf. the passage cited from the *Apoc. of John* in note 3, I, where it is said that the ἔννοια was manifested as a Ray of Light.) On the next page (XIII), we read that by the shining of the Monad all things were *moved*, that is, *aroused, raised up to life*. On XXIV, we find the Monad likened to a laden ship, a planted field, and an inhabited city. This imagery presents the Monad as the all-containing germ of the cosmos. While this concept of the cosmical Seed is not a prominent one in the Valentinian system, we find it, as a basic idea, in the cosmology attributed to Basilides by Hippolytus (*Ref. Haer.* VII, 1–27). One probable point of contact between the doctrine of our treatise and that system has already been noted in the case of the two superior Rulers of the cosmos—Aphredōn and Mousanios (*vide* note 2, V). Others will be observed in the course of the treatise. Comparison of the Basilidian beliefs regarding the origin and nature of the σπέρμα

τοῦ κόσμου (cosmical Seed) with what our treatise has to say concerning the Monad shows a close relationship of ideas. *Vide* Hippolytus: "*[The] not-existing God* (οὐκ ὢν θεός), *made [the] not-existing cosmos out of not-existing [things], casting down and planting a single Seed, having in itself the whole seed mass of the cosmos*" (vii, 21). "*[God] spake and it came to pass. And this—as these men say—is what was declared by Moses: 'Let there be Light'. Whence, says [Basilides], came the Light? From nothing. For it is not written whence, but only that it came forth from the Voice of the Speaker.... This is the Seed that contains in itself the whole seed mass*" (*ibid.* 22). Hippolytus illustrates his meaning by the example of an egg, a whole that cannot be divided, but that contains the manifold substances, parts, colours, etc., of the bird that is to be. In this manner, the Seed of the cosmos—a whole and indivisible thing—contained, potentially, all the things of the cosmos in itself (*ibid.* 21). The proposed equation of the all-containing Monad with the cosmical Seed of Basilides may perhaps be substantiated from another quarter. In the *Apoc. of John* (*vide* citation in note 3, I), the title Barbēlo (ⲃⲁⲣⲃⲏⲗⲱ) is given as the proper name of the εἰκών and ἔννοια of the Father, which εἰκών is further to be equated with the Monad (XIV, and note 3, I). The derivation and meaning of this term Barbēlo has long been debated by commentators. In his latest published work, *Church and Gnosis*, Cambridge, 1932, (pp. 54–55, 58–60), Prof. F. C. Burkitt proposes an interesting solution of the puzzle. He first points out that the title is utilized in the same connection as in the *Apoc. of John*, by certain "so-called Gnostics" who are described by Epiphanius in *Haer.* xxvi, 92. These particular Gnostics resided in Egypt, not far from Alexandria. The *Apoc. of John*, whilst written, most probably, originally in Greek, exists in a Coptic version, and Prof. Burkitt considers it reasonable to suppose that geographically, it had an Egyptian origin. He therefore proposes to derive Barbēlo from the Coptic ⲃⲗ̄ⲃⲓⲗⲉ, a feminine word—as is also ⲃⲁⲣⲃⲏⲗⲱ—meaning "a seed", "a single grain". The transcription of the liquids in old Egyptian dialects is often uncertain and presents no difficulty here. In the passage from Hippolytus (quoted *supra*) recording the Basilidian beliefs, we find the following: "*The not-existing God made the not-existing cosmos out of not-existing things, casting down and planting a single Seed* (σπέρμα) ..." (vii, 21). "*And the Seed of the cosmos* (σπέρμα τοῦ κόσμου) *contained all things in itself, as the grain* (κόκκος) *of mustard comprises, in the smallest compass, all things simultaneously— roots, stem, branches, leaves, innumerable seeds, etc.*" (*ibid.*). The word κόκκος (*grain*), used in this passage as descriptive or explanatory of the σπέρμα τοῦ κόσμου, is the exact Greek equivalent of the Coptic ⲃⲗ̄ⲃⲓⲗⲉ (*vide* Sahidic version of John xii, 24).

The same by its shining moved all things, and they received Gnosis (γνωσις), Life, and Hope ('ελπις), Repose (αναπαυσις), Love (αγαπη), and Upraising (αναστασις) [1], Faith (πιστις), Rebirth [2], and the Seal (σφραγις) [3]. This is the Ennead ('εννας) that came from the unoriginated (αναρχος) [4] Father, who alone to himself is Father and Mother, whose Fullness (πληρωμα) encompasses the Twelve Deeps (βαθος) [5]:

α. The first Deep (βαθος) is the All-source (παν-πηγη), from out of it all sources (πηγη) came.

β. The second Deep (βαθος) is the All-wise (παν-σοφος), from out of it came all the wise (σοφος).

γ. The third Deep (βαθος) is the All-mystery (παν-μυστηριον), from it, or (η) out of it, came every mystery (μυστηριον).

δ. And (δε) the fourth Deep (βαθος) is the All-gnosis (πανγνωσις), from out of it all gnosis (γνωσις) came.

ε. The fifth Deep (βαθος) is the All-holy (παν-'αγνον), from out of it came all holiness (?) ('αγνον) [6].

ϛ. The sixth Deep (βαθος) is the Silence (σιγη), in this is every silence.

ζ. The seventh Deep (βαθος) is the Door of non-substance (ανουσιος) [7], from out of it came forth all substance (ουσια).

η. And (δε) the eighth Deep (βαθος) is the Fore-father (προπατωρ) (Deep), from it, or (η) out of it, all forefathers (προπατωρ) arose.

θ. And (δε) the ninth Deep (βαθος) (is) an All-father (παντοπατωρ), that is, a self-alone-father (αυτοπατωρ) [8] (Deep), (XIV) in this is every fatherhood, it being father alone to them.

XIV

[51]   4-2

1. Or *awakening*. This seems to be the meaning of ἀνάστασις in the present passage which is descriptive of happenings at the dawn of creation. The Septuagint affords many instances of the use of the word in this sense.

2. At this early cosmological stage—relating to the creation of the Aeons—there cannot be any reference to regeneration in the N.T. sense. Probably initiation into gnosis of the Father is intended. This was imparted to the first created Aeons by the Monogenes, *vide* note 5, II.

3. Referring perhaps to the sealing of the Name of the Son, whereby the Aeons were *moved* and gained knowledge of the Father, *vide* note 5, II.

4. Literally, *"the Father without origins"*, meaning, *no father* and *no mother*, other, that is, than himself. *Vide* sequence: *"who alone to himself is Father and Mother"*.

5. The designations of the Twelve Deeps indicate that they represent the Divine attributes and qualities called into being. Their detailed description is the revelation, in terms of multiplicity, of the unity of the Divine perfections which is the Pleroma, while their presentation as Deeps implies their reaching back into the depths of the Eternal Being of God. As Deeps, the Twelve embody abstract conceptions, but when referred to later (XX and XXI)—where they are said to be in the Deep of Sētheus—they assume a more concrete quality and are called the *Twelve Fatherhoods*. As such, each possesses a triplicity of aspects denoting his relationship to the cosmos as a triply divided unit. The description of the Twelve Deeps, given on the present page, is by way of parenthesis. When ended, the subject of the Father is resumed.

6. Judging by the particulars given of the fourth and sixth Deeps, a noun rather than an adjective seems required here. *All holy ones* might, however, be the intention.

7. For the significance of ἀνούσιος in Gnostic thought, *vide* note 2, I. The *Silence* and the *Door of non-substance* are mentioned again on XXXVI, following a reference to Five Powers contained in the Immeasurable Deep which immediately surrounds the Pleroma. Four of these Powers bear the same names as four of the components of the above-mentioned Ennead, i.e. Love—Hope—Faith—Gnosis. In relation to the fourth, i.e. Gnosis, the statement follows: *"through this they knew the Primal Father, through whose Will they came to be. And they knew the Mystery of the Silence, which uttereth all things and is hidden, the Primordial Monad, through whom the Whole was made in non-substance (ἀνούσιος). This is the Mystery . . . this is the Door of God"*.

8. For the significance of the prefix αὐτο as employed in our treatise, *vide* note 1, VII. As there remarked, αὐτός appears to be

[52]

synonymous with μόνος, and thus has the force of self-*alone*, an αὐτοπάτωρ being one who can act independently and produce offspring without the aid of a partner. This is implied by the context of the present passage: "*it* (the Deep) *being father alone to them*", i.e. *sole parent*. The designations of the Twelve Deeps show that they stand for the perfections and attributes of the One who is the All-father, and who, pre-existing in silence and solitude within himself, willed and brought forth, by himself alone, the Beauty and Perfection that was in him. Cf. also Eph. iii, 14–15: "*I bow my knees to the Father . . . of whom every Fatherhood in Heaven and Earth is named*".

XIII
MS. f. 96ᴿ
C.S. p. 3

XIV
MS. f. 96ᵛ
C.S. p. 4

1. The tenth Deep (βαθος) is the All-power (παντο-δυναμις) (Deep), from out of it all powers came.

1α. And (δε) in the eleventh Deep (βαθος) is the first Invisible (α‘ορατος)¹, from this came all invisibles (α‘ορατος).

1β. And (δε) the twelfth Deep (βαθος) is the Truth (αληθια), from this came forth all truth.

This is the Truth (αληθια) which encloses them all. This is the Image (‘ικων) of the Father²: this is the Mirror of the Whole: this is the Mother of all the Aeons (αιων), this same which encompasses all Deeps (βαθος). This is the Monad (μονας) that is inconceivable (ακαταγνωστος)³, or (η) of which all are ignorant: this uncharactered One (ατχαρακτηρ)—which in itself every character (χαρακτηρ)⁴ contains—and which to everlasting ages shall be blessed.

This is the Father Everlasting: this is the Father unspeakable, unimaginable (ατνοι), unperceivable, untranscendable. In him All things were made substantial (ευνουσιος =ενουσιος?)⁵. And they rejoiced, and they exulted: they brought forth myriads upon myriads of Aeons (αιων) in their joy: they were called, saying: "The Births of Joy", because they rejoiced with the Father. These are the Worlds (κοσμος) in which up-sprang the Stauros (στρος)⁶, and from these incorporeal (ασωμα-τος) Members (μελος) the Man came into being⁷.

XIV
MS. f. 96ᵛ
C.S. p. 4

1. Or perhaps *invisibility*. Obviously an adjective doing duty for a noun.

2. The Twelfth Deep, i.e. the *Truth*, is here equated with the εἰκών and the μονάς. The designation, *Mother of all the Aeons*, recalls a teaching of Valentinus, to the effect that the Father—who was alone—engendered and projected Νοῦς & 'Αλήθεια (*Mind & Truth*), which pair became the Origin and Mother of all the Aeons within the Pleroma (Hippol. vi, 29). The Mother of the phenomenal creation, called by the Valentinians, the Sophia, is the reflection of this great Mother principle.

3. *Vide* note 6, I.

[54]

4. χαρακτηρ = a *distinctive mark* or *characteristic*.

5. There is some uncertainty about this word, which, as it stands, is unknown. In his 1905 translation of the text, Dr Schmidt proposes to read ἀνούσιος, a term which occurs in other passages (e.g. on I and XXXVI). An alternative would be to delete the υ, and read ἐνούσιος. This was previously suggested by Dr Schmidt in his 1892 edition. The phrase can then be rendered, "*All things were made substantial in him*". In this way we get a sense that accords with the meaning of the context, which deals with the consolidation of the Pleroma and re-establishment of the Aeons following the disturbance created by the transgression of the youngest of their number, Sophia (*vide* note 4, XII). As the result of her ignorant and presumptuous attempt at generation—apart from her syzygy, Thelētos—there had appeared among the complete and perfect Aeons a deficient and unformed substance, at the sight of which those beings were filled with fear and agitation. *Vide* Hippol. VI, 31: "*Ignorance, then, having arisen in the Pleroma through Sophia, and formlessness owing to the offspring of Sophia, tumult came about within. For the Aeons [feared] that what would be born from them would also be begotten shapeless and imperfect, and that decay would finally seize upon them all. Whereupon, all the Aeons took refuge in prayers to the Father...*". Hippolytus goes on to say that the Father hearkened to the prayers of the Aeons, and with a view to their tranquillization, ordered the projection of the Aeon *Christ & Holy Spirit* (cf. note 4, XII), and himself projected the Aeon *Stauros* (*vide* XII, and *infra*). The latter formed a palisade around the Aeons and hid the deficient substance from their sight. Irenaeus, relating the same incident, tells us that the Aeon *Christ & Holy Spirit* was projected "*in accordance with the Forethought of the Father*", "*for the purpose of consolidating and establishing the Pleroma*" (Iren. I, i, 4). By his agency the ignorance of the Aeons was removed, they obtained a certain gnosis of the Father, and were instructed concerning the laws and limitations of their own mode of being. Finally, their equilibrium and confidence having been restored, they were taught to render thanks to the Father. *Vide* Iren. I, i, 4: "*The Wholes* (τὰ ὅλα), *then, being established and brought to a state of perfect repose, they* (the Valentinians) *next tell us that these beings sang praises with great joy to the Forefather, who himself shared in the abounding exultation*". The subsequent action of the Aeons, which was expressive of their joy and thankfulness, is then described by Irenaeus. This sequel is mentioned in our treatise on XX (*vide* note 9, XIX, and note 3, XXVII).

6. *Vide* note 8, XII.

7. Cf. II: "*The Father took their whole likeness* (i.e. of his Members) *and he made it as a City or a Man*".

XIV
MS. f. 96ᵛ
C.S. p. 4

[55]

This is the Father and the Source (πηγη) of all—complete are all his Members (μελος). From the Father every Name arose, whether (ειτε) unutterable (α῾ρητον), or (ειτε) incorruptible (αφθαρτον), or (ειτε) inconceivable (ακαταγνωστος), or (ειτε) invisible (α῾ορατος), or (ειτε) simple (῾απλουν), or (ειτε) still (ερημος = ηρεμος), or (ειτε) mighty (δυναμις)¹, or (ειτε) almighty (πανδυναμις), or (ειτε) all Names that are in the Silence. All these arose from the Father, whom, as the stars of the firmament (στερεωμα) in the night the outside Worlds (κοσμος)² behold. Even as men desire (επιθυμει) to see the sun, in this way also the outside Worlds (κοσμος) desire (επιθυμει) to see him, because of his Invisibility which is round about him. To the Aeons (αιων) at all times it is he who giveth Life: through his Word the Indivisible knew the Monad (μονας), to comprehend it³, and through his Word the Holy Pleroma (῾ιερον πληρωμα) came into being.

This is the Father, the Second Creator (δημιουργος)⁴. Through the breath of his Mouth Forethought (προνοια) created those that were not. Through his Will (θελημα) they came into being, for he it is who commanded the Whole, and caused it to be.

1. A noun doing duty for the corresponding adjective. Similarly the next word, πανδυναμις.

2. The *outside Worlds* came into being from the substance of the Sophia *outside*. *Vide* latter part of note 4, XII.

3. This sentence is rather a puzzle. The word translated *comprehend* is very indistinct in the text and is possibly incorrect. The Monad of our treatise and the cosmical Seed of the Basilidian Gnosis appear to be kindred conceptions (*vide* note 11, XII), while the Indivisible suggests the counterpart of the Ideal World in the Platonic sense, i.e. the world of archetypal ideas wherein the manifold varieties of created substances have a real subjective existence. In the thought of our treatise, the Indivisible stands midway between the Monad and the phenomenal universe, and

seems to be the actualization of the former in the subjective world
wherein are the true counterparts of all natural substances and
existences. The Monad issues from the ἔννοια of the Father as the
complete Divine Forethought (πρόνοια) of the *Whole*. By utterance
of the Creative Word it is brought into actualization in the Indivisible. Such may be the meaning of the present passage.

XV

MS. f. 98ᴿ

C.S. p. 5

4. Cf. XI–XII, where the Father receives the designation,
Second Space.

(XV) In this wise made he the Holy Pleroma (ʿιερον πληρωμα) ¹: Four Gates (πυλη) ², (XVI) four Monads (μονας) being in it, one Monad (μονας) to each Gate (πυλη), and six Supporters (παραστατης) to each Gate (πυλη), making twenty-four Supporters (παραστατης). And four and twenty myriad Powers (δυναμις) to each Gate (πυλη), nine Enneads (ʿεννας) to each Gate (πυλη), ten Decads (δεκας) to each Gate (πυλη), twelve Dodecads (δωδεκας) to each Gate (πυλη), and five Pentads (πεντας) of power to each Gate (πυλη), and a Guardian (επισκοπος) ³ who has Three Aspects, an unbegotten (αγεννητος) aspect, a true (αληθια) aspect, and an unutterable (αʿρητος) aspect, to each Gate (πυλη). One of his aspects looketh from the Gate (πυλη) to the outside Aeons (αιων), another looketh within to the Sētheus (σηθευς), and another looketh to the height⁴. And in each Monad (μονας) (is)⁵ the Sonship. Aphredōn (αφρηδων) is there⁶, with his Twelve Righteous ones (χς) ⁷, he being there, namely, the Forefather (προπατωρ) ⁸. Adam (αδαμ), who is of the Light, is in that place⁹, and his three hundred and sixty-five Aeons (αιων) ¹⁰. There also is the perfect Mind (τελιος νους) ¹¹, while they surround a Rule (κανουν = κανων) ¹², which is in everlastingness (αθανασια) ¹³. The unutterable (αʿρητος) aspect of the Guardian (επισκοπος) looketh within to the Holy of Holies, which is boundless (απεραντος) (XVII) and the sum (κεφαλη) ¹⁴ of the Holy Place (ʿιερον). To this there are two aspects, one looking to the space (τοπος) of the Deep (βαθος), and the other looking to the space (τοπος) of the Guardian (επισκοπος), who is wont to be called:—The Servant ¹⁵.

1. The Pleroma is here presented as the Holy City. It is the abode of the Aeons, while in the innermost part—called the Holy of Holies—dwells the Sētheus (*vide infra* and XXVI).

2. In the account of the creation of the Archetypal Man or City   XVI
it was said that the four extremities of the Man's body, i.e. the   MS. f. 98ᵛ
hands and feet, correspond to the Four Gates (*vide* note 6, IV).   C.S. p. 6
The Gates of the Holy City are in contact with the inner world of
the Pleroma, and with the exterior world, where are the outside
Aeons.

3. The Guardian appears to correspond, in position and functions, with the Valentinian Aeon *Christ & Holy Spirit*. According
to that cosmology, he was projected, by command of the Father,
for the restoration and security of the Aeons of the Pleroma (*vide*
latter part of note 4, XII, and note 5, XIV). *Infra*, he receives the
further title of *Servant* or *Minister*. In the *Apoc. of John*, besides
being called the *Servant*, he is described as the Christ through
whom All things were consolidated (p. 13, German trans.). This
identification is not directly made in our treatise, but is probably
implicit in a reference to the activities of *Christ the Prover*, on XIX.
The sentence there quoted from the Prologue to the Fourth
Gospel: "*through him it is All things were made*", is seemingly parallel
to the definition: "*through whom All things were consolidated*". There is
perhaps an echo of Basilidian thought in the use of *Servant* or *Minister*
as second name for the Aeon *Christ & Holy Spirit*. According to
Clement of Alexandria (*Strom.* II, 8), the Holy Spirit was called *the
Ministering Spirit* (τὸ διακονούμενον πνεῦμα) by Basilides. Again, in
§ 16, *Excerpt. ex Theodot.*, it is stated that *the Minister* (ὁ διάκονος)
was a Basilidian name for the Holy Spirit. The Valentinian notion
of the dual nature of all the heavenly Beings (*vide* note 1, I), which
made of *Christ & Holy Spirit* a single consubstantial Aeon, is not
discernible in Basilidian thought, but the Holy Spirit is definitely
associated with that manifestation of the Christ which Basilides
called the Sonship of Triple Power (*vide* Hippol. VII, 22). Following
immediately on the depositing of the cosmical Seed by the
not-existing God, a Sonship, of triple division, was revealed
therein. Of this, the first part straightway ascended to the presence
of the not-existing God. The second part was also borne aloft,
equipped, as with a wing, by the Holy Spirit, and drawing nigh
to the first part of the Sonship, left the Holy Spirit near that
"*blessed place*", i.e. the Pleroma, but not altogether severed from
itself. Thus the Holy Spirit—now called the Boundary Spirit (τὸ
μεθόριον Πνεῦμα)—remained in the place of the *Midst*, forming the
Boundary between the Pleroma and the space outside (*ibid.* 23).
In our treatise, the Guardian—called the Servant, and equating,
presumably, with the Valentinian Aeon *Christ & Holy Spirit*—has
his place in the Gates, that is to say, he looks inwards and outwards from the Boundary of the Pleroma.

4. The Coptic word rendered *aspect* in this passage means a *face*,

a *shewing*, an *appearance*. Of the three aspects of the Guardian, the unutterable aspect looks inwards to the innermost part of the Pleroma, where dwells the Sētheus, and another faces outwards to the worlds outside. It is not clear what is intended by the direction of the third aspect, but probably some reference to the middle space is intended.

5. A word is certainly missing here; the restoration conveys a suitable idea.

6. Aphredōn is conjectured to be a Ruler in the middle space of the cosmos (*vide* note 2, V). He has his place outside the Boundary of the Pleroma.

7. χͷ. Contraction of χρηστός = *good, right, serviceable. Righteous* is here taken to signify the quality of *rightness*, i.e. being right and fitted for a particular calling or function. The Twelve belong to Aphredōn, one of the Rulers in the place of the *Midst*. They probably have some connection with the divisions of upper cosmical space, figured, according to the Gnostics, by the Twelve Zodiacal Signs (*vide* Iren. 1, x).

8. Aphredōn is the prototype of the Forefather of the phenomenal creation (*vide* latter part of note 2, V, and XLI).

9. By *Adam* is here intended the Archetypal Man, created after the Image of God (for particulars, *vide* note 7, II). The statement that Adam is *of the Light* is repeated on XLV–XLVI, where he is called "*Adamas, the Man of Light*". The notion that the primal Man was a creation of Light is a prominent one in Kabbalistic speculations, the Adam Kadmon of that tradition being an emanation from the Infinite Light. The source of the idea may perhaps be the Zoroastrian notion that man's ideal nature was formed first. An interesting parallel occurs in the fragments of Zosimus, a Greek writer of the fourth century. In the book entitled *Authentic Memorandum concerning the Letter Omega* there is a reference to the name of Adam: "... *the Primal Man is called by us* (Greeks and Egyptians) *Thoth, and by them* (Chaldaeans, Parthians, Medes and Hebrews) *Adam...in relation to his body. Thus the embodied Adam is called Thoth in relation to his outward seeming, but his inner man, the spiritual, possesses an authentic [name] and a [name] appellative. While we are ignorant up till now of the authentic [name]...his appellative name, on the other hand, is called* φῶς (*Light*), *from whence it follows that men are spoken of as* φῶτας (*mortals*)". There is here a play of words, i.e. φῶς, contraction of φάος = *Light*, and φώς = a *man, a mortal*. (Text of Zosimus in *Les Alchimistes grecs*, M. Berthelot, vol. 1, pp. 230–1.)

10. The 365 Aeons are related to Adam, the Archetypal Man. On XXXVI there is mention of 365 Fatherhoods in the Immeasurable Deep which is localized in the place of the *Midst*, outside the Pleroma. By means of the 365—so it is said—the Year is divided.

On III we learned that the members of the Archetypal Man were XVI
created to correspond to the 365 Fatherhoods in the Immeasurable MS. f. 98ᵛ
Deep. Another probable link with Basilidian thought is suggested C.S. p. 6
by these statements (*vide* Hippol. VII, 26, and Iren. I, xix, 4). In
the system of Basilides we meet the 365. They are designated
Heavens, and the Year is said to contain 365 days in conformity
with the number of the Heavens. According to both Hippolytus
and Irenaeus, the chief of the 365 bore the title Abrasax ('Αβρασάξ),
for the reason that the letters of this word represent numbers
amounting to 365 (i.e. α = 1, β = 2, ρ = 100, α = 1, σ = 200,
α = 1, ξ = 60). This is also noted by Augustine (*de Haer.* 4).
Epiphanius, partly following Irenaeus and partly a lost treatise of
Hippolytus, says that the Basilidians regarded Abrasax as the
archetype of all things, and spoke of 365 as being the number of
parts of man's body as well as the days of the year (Epiph. *Haer.*
69, 73 f.). This latter statement corresponds closely with the remarks on III of our treatise, regarding the members of the body
of the Archetypal Adam. In view of these correspondences in sym-
bolology, the suggestion may perhaps be hazarded that Abrasax
was the name given by the Basilidian Gnostics to the Archetypal
Man, who, it may be remarked, is not otherwise mentioned at all in
their cosmology, an omission which would be somewhat unaccount-
able. The word is found on numerous so-called Gnostic gems,
where it may stand simply for the number 365, meaning the solar
year. At the same time, the figure which appears on many of these
gems—usually portrayed with the body and legs of a man and the
head of a cock—probably symbolical of the dawn—with the solar
disc or light rays surrounding him—may well be representative of
the Man of Light. Returning to our treatise, it appears that both
the 12, belonging to Aphredōn (*vide supra*), and the 365, belonging to Adam, not only represented divisions of time and space,
but were also embodiments and living ideas. The probable connection of the 12 with the Zodiacal Signs has been noted (*supra*,
note 7). On XXIII both the 12 and the 365 are spoken of in
relation to the divisions of the year. On XXIX the two numbers
are again mentioned. There, the 365 seem to stand for the archetypal
qualities of substance. The notion which made personifications of
the 365 was a familiar one in Egypt, where there are 365 gods and
goddesses—unnamed—to whom the days of the year were assigned, while a further notion emphasizing the Gnostic idea of the
intimate relationship between the number 365 and the bodily
constitution of man is found in the *Pistis Sophia*, where it is related
that the mysteries of embryology are consummated by a hierarchy
of 365 Powers (Coptic text, p. 344 *et seq.* edit. Petermann).

11. It is difficult to interpret or even to comment on some of

these passages. While many of the terms are met with in other Gnostic writings, some of the incidents are without parallel either in the Patristic records or extant Gnostic texts. With regard to the τέλειος νοῦς, we meet the phrase in the *Apoc. of John*. On p. 9 (German trans.), we learn that a Power called πρόγνωσις is included in the Pentad of Members of the Father (*vide* citation in note 8, I); on p. 10, *ibid.*, that the νοῦς is brought forth by the Invisible Spirit (i.e. the Father), at the request of the Monogenes; while on p. 11, *ibid.*, we are informed that the πρόγνωσις and the νοῦς form a conjunction. These particulars are corroborated in the corresponding accounts in Irenaeus (I, xxvii) and Theodoret (*Haer. Fab.* xiii). After relating the production of the Monogenes, Irenaeus states: "*Moreover, they maintain, that this was Christ, who again—according to them—requested that νοῦς should be given him as an assistant, and νοῦς came forth accordingly*". Irenaeus then gives the names of the other Powers associated with the Monogenes, and concludes: "*conjunctions will thus be formed...the νοῦς and the πρόγνωσις*". Returning to the correlative text in the *Apoc. of John* (p. 14, German trans.), we find the following: "*From πρόγνωσις and the τέλειος νοῦς...* [*through*] *the good pleasure of the great Invisible Spirit and the good pleasure of the Autogenes* (= Monogenes) [*was produced*] *the perfect and true Man, the first Manifestation. He was called Adam, and was placed over the first Aeon*". The Power called πρόγνωσις is not mentioned in our text, but the origination of Adam through the νοῦς is referred to on LV: "*This is the Man of Mind* (νους) *begotten*". Also, in the passage *supra*, Adam is associated with the νοῦς.

12. The significance of this term is not obvious. If the orthography is to stand, i.e. ⲕⲁⲛⲟⲩⲛ (= κανοῦν, Attic form of κάνεον) = a *basket*, it must be regarded as a container for sacrificial offerings. The word was so employed to designate a receptacle for sacrificial fruits or grain used in processions at certain religious feasts in Athens (*vide* L. and S., under κάνεον). But the spelling κανοῦν was of local use only, and the interpretation is unsatisfactory for the reason that while the word occurs many times in the treatise, in one instance only could the context support the idea of an offering, and then not a sacrificial one. A more likely explanation seems to be that the word—written κανουν by the Coptic scribe—is intended for κανών, i.e. a *rule*, a *norm*, or *standard* of excellence. As regards the change of vowels in the Greek word, in Coptic use the diphthong ⲟⲩ frequently takes the place of ω, and substitutions of one vowel for another are often found in early Coptic scripts (*vide* W. E. Crum, *Intro. to Coptic Ostraca*, 1902, quoted in note 2, V). Throughout the treatise, the ⲕⲁⲛⲟⲩⲛ is associated with creative or perfective processes, and it comes on the scene whenever such processes are described. The idea is thus suggested that it

represents the *rule* or *standard* of excellence to which—in their degree—all created things must conform. Another point must be noted. In every context where the word appears, the κανουν is associated with a Triad. On four occasions this fact seems emphasized, the number being given in addition to a description of the members of the Triad (XXXIII and XLV). In two cases, simply the names appear, as above—Aphredōn, Adam and the τελιος νους—and on XXXVII. In one instance, we are told that three great Beings—each of triple aspect—are standing by the κανουν (XXXI). In the treatise, triads and powers of triple aspect relate to the cosmos as a triply divided unit, and, in later instances, have special reference to the pneumatic, psychic and hylic principles of the creation.

13. Meaning, presumably, an unalterable standard.

14. Signifying *head*, as the culminating or principal part. On III we learn that the Sētheus is Lord of the Pleroma, and on XXVI that he dwells in the Holy Place as King and as God. There are two aspects to the Holy Place, the one facing inwards to the Deep of Sētheus, and the other facing outwards to the Boundary of the Pleroma, where is the Guardian.

15. The Guardian who was mentioned *supra*. He is probably to be equated with the Christ who consolidated the Pleroma (*vide supra*, note 3). He is mentioned again *infra* (XVII), under his second title of *Servant* or *Minister*. The Coptic word there translated *servant* can also be rendered *boy*, the terms being probably synonymous in the dialect. This synonymity, indeed, is observed to-day in many countries of the East, where *boy* is the general appellation for the house servant. As employed in the present connection, however, the intention is definitely *servant*, for on XXVII–XXVIII, where the appellation is again used, the Greek διακονος takes the place of the Coptic word. In the *Apoc. of John* (pp. 12–13, German trans.), we meet with a reference to the *Servant*, who is there further described as the Christ with Twelve Aeons. The first mention of the Christ by name, in our treatise, occurs on XIX, where he is said to wear Twelve Aspects, and is called *Christ the Prover* (χς δογιμαστης). He is doubtless to be identified with the *Servant*, i.e. the Christ with Twelve Aeons, in the *Apoc. of John*. On XXVII–XXVIII, we read of another *Servant*, designated by our Gnostics, "*Fruit of the Whole*" (XIX–XX), and by the Valentinians, "*Joint Fruit of the Whole Pleroma*". Irenaeus speaks of him as the second Christ, and of the Aeon *Christ & Holy Spirit* as the first (Iren. I, i, 5). The Saviour who was manifested on earth was the third. The Patristic writings relative to the several manifestations of the Christ are confusing, probably for the reason that the Fathers failed to grasp the meaning of the Gnostics, and accused

them of postulating three distinct and separate Beings, whereas their intention was a threefold manifestation of the One, i.e. the Monogenes. Viewing the cosmos as a tripartite unit, and believing, as they did, that some form of salvation or restoration was required for the whole, they taught that the Saviour was manifested in the three divisions in a form and manner suited to the mode of being and needs of each. Thus, according to Valentinian theories, the first Christ, who was the stabilizer of the Pleroma and the Aeons, was a dual-natured, consubstantial Being, called *Christ & Holy Spirit*, in conformity with the dual mode of being of the entities of the Pleroma. This dual title does not occur in our treatise, but it is of interest to remark that, as late as the second century A.D., in orthodox circles of the day, a distinction between the second and third Persons of the Trinity was not always clearly defined. In the second-century book of *Allegories*, entitled *The Shepherd of Hermas*, used for public reading in the Churches, the Son of God and the Holy Spirit are, in two passages, identified with one another (*Sim.* IX, I, and v, 6, 5). The Gnostic notion of the several manifestations of the One Divine Being would not have seemed an extravagant or even a novel theory to the thinkers of those days, familiar with Jewish religious history. Many of the appearances on earth of angels, recorded in the O.T., were regarded as manifestations of Jehovah. In our treatise, the first of the three manifestations of the Christ is called the *Servant* and *Guardian* of the Pleroma. According to Valentinus, the principal work of the first Christ was the restoration of the Aeons and the security of the Pleroma. The present passage in our treatise, that cited *supra* from the *Apoc. of John*, the references above to the *Guardian*, and on XIX to *Christ the Prover*, all relate to him. The second Christ, also called the *Servant*—who was manifested after the re-establishment of the Pleroma, of which he was the perfect Fruit (*vide* Iren. I, i, 4)—is mentioned on XIX–XX and XXVII–XXVIII of our treatise. He was concerned with the salvation of the worlds outside the Pleroma, and the sphere of his operations was the place of the *Midst*. The third manifestation was the Saviour of the earthly dispensation. Some reference to his activities will be found on LI and LVII–LIX of our treatise. Passages identifying the Monogenes with the triple manifestation of the Christ will be met with on XVII: "*A Monogenes...who manifests Three Powers*", and "*a Monogenes...who is himself the Triple-Power*". And again, on XLIX, where he is described as the one who was "*Thrice-born*" and "*Thrice-begotten*". While we do not find the appellation *Servant* predicated, in our treatise, of the third and earthly manifestation of the Christ, in the Valentinian source, *Excerpt. ex Theodot.*, it is so applied in a statement referring to the manifestation of the Logos on earth: "*he is said to have put on the form of a Servant*" (§ 19). Again, in *The Shepherd of Hermas*, cited *supra*, with reference to his work in the *Vineyard of the Lord*, the Son of God is called "*The Servant*" (ὁ δοῦλος) (*Sim.* v, 2). Cf. also the Pauline epistle: "*He emptied himself, and took on him the form of a Servant*" (Philip. ii, 7).

XVI

MS. f. 98ᵛ

C.S. p. 6

XVII
MS. f. 100ᴿ
C.S. p. 7

And there is a Deep (βαθος) there, which is wont to be called: "The Light", or (η) "The Light-maker"¹. An Only-begotten (μονογενης)² is in it, he being hidden. He it is who manifests Three Powers, and who in every power is mighty. This is the Indivisible (Deep), never was this divided, the Whole was disclosed in it, for thereto belong the powers³. To this (Deep) there are three aspects, an invisible (αʿορατος) aspect, an all-power (παντοδυναμις) aspect, and an unuttered (αφρηδων) aspect, and it is wont to be called: "Aphredōn Pēksos" (αφρηδων πηξος)⁴. In it is hidden an Only-begotten (μονογενης), who is himself the Triple-Power (τριδυναμις).

When the Idea cometh out from the Deep (βαθος), Aphredōn (αφρηδων)⁵ taketh the Thought (επινοια), and to the Only-begotten (μονογενης) presents it. To the Servant the Only-begotten (μονογενης) presents it, and as far as the Space (τοπος) of the Triple-Power (τριδυναμις) they bring it out to all the Aeons (αιων), and they complete them⁶, and they take them to the unbegotten (αγεννητος) Five⁷.

XVII
MS. f. 100ᴿ
C.S. p. 7

1. This Deep is the *Indivisible, vide infra.* On XX it is designated the first of the Twelve Fatherhoods in the Deep of Sētheus, which is the ultimate Deep of creation. *Infra,* we learn that from this Deep the *Idea* comes forth. The intention may be the forthcoming of the plan or design of the macrocosm, as it existed, consummated and complete, in the Mind of the Creator. Cf. note 3, XV.

2. *An Only-begotten . . . who manifests Three Powers.* The statement is repeated almost word for word a few lines below: *an Only-begotten . . . who is himself the Triple-Power.* This is the first mention of the Monogenes, by name, in the treatise. The reiterated description of his nature and powers may serve to draw attention to what is a basic idea in the cosmology: the principle of triplicity in unity (*vide* note 6, II). The starting-point of these speculations was the belief held by these Gnostics in regard to the Godhead whom they defined as "*the Three which be but One*" (II). Following on this they taught that what the Deity conceived in his εννοια was after his own likeness. Thus the Divine Forethought of the creation

was a Monad containing the triply divided cosmos. The term μονογενής has received more than one interpretation in religious philosophy: e.g. begotten as the *only one* of his kind, *unique*: begotten by the Father *alone*, i.e. of a *sole* parent: and begotten as the *sole* Son of his Father. None of these interpretations accords with the particular notion of our cosmology, which requires that the Power operating in the cosmos should be of like nature with that cosmos and with the Deity in whose ἔννοια both were begotten. As previously noted in regard to other Greek words used in the treatise, the original meaning of the prefix represents the intention of the writer, i.e. μονάς = a *unit*. Thus while μονογενής is rendered *only-begotten* in the translation, *only* is to be understood as signifying *one*-ly, i.e. *in oneness begotten*, or *begotten as a unit*, the title denoting both the manner of origin and the nature of the Monogenes, he being the *begotten unity* proceeding from the *unbegotten unity* of the Father. This conception of the essential unity of the Son of God is set forth by Clement of Alexandria: "*God then, not being a subject for demonstration, cannot be the object of science. But the Son is wisdom and knowledge and truth, and all else that has affinity thereto. He is also susceptible of demonstration and of description. And all the powers of the Spirit, becoming collectively one thing, terminate in the same point, that is, in the Son. . . . And the Son is neither simply one thing as one thing, nor many things as parts, but one thing as all things; whence also he is all things. For he is the circle of all powers enfolded and united into one unity. Wherefore the Word is called the Alpha, of whom alone the end becomes the beginning and ends again at the original beginning without any break*" (*Strom.* IV, Cap. xxv, Clem. Alex. *Die Griech. Christl. Schrift.* Bd II, p. 317, 1806, Leipzig). On the next page (XVIII), the word μονογενής occurs as an adjective qualifying λόγος. The significance is the same: a Word that is *One*. The employment of the word as an adjective in philosophy, to mean *oneness of nature*, is not peculiar to our treatise. An instance may be cited from the fragments of the Greek philosopher Parmenides which is conclusive, and admits of no alternative in translation, since the word is applied to the First Cause, and can therefore have no reference to generation. The writer, in the course of his teaching as to the "Way of Truth", attempts a description of the nature of the Supreme Being: "*There remaineth yet one theme of the Way: that there is a Being of whom there are full many tokens that he is uncreate* (ἀγένητον) *and imperishable* (ἀνώλεθρον), *whole* (οὖλον), *of one kind* (μουνογενές), *unmoved* (ἀτρεμές), *and without end* (ἀτέλεστον)" (Parm. *Carm. Relig.* 11, 57–60, in *Frag. Philos. Graec.* edit. F. C. Mullach, Paris, 1860, tome I, p. 120). In his article on Parmenides (*Dict. of Greek and Roman Biog.* edit. Wm Smith, vol. III, p. 124), Christian A. Brandis, in treating of this passage, regards οὖλον μουνογενές as one phrase and translates *"entirely of one sort"*. The second designation of the Monogenes in our treatise, i.e. *Triple-Power*, denotes his relationship to the triply divided cosmos. Thus, as Monogenes Logos he is the One Word in whom the Father created all things, and as Triple-Power he denotes the three-times-manifested Christ, who appears and operates in the three regions of the cosmos, under a form and in a manner in conformity with the requirements of each. In these respects the doctrine of our treatise coincides with that of Valentinus. In the Basilidian cosmogony, the Nous (= the Monogenes) is again the Power through whom all things were created, the Triple-Sonship being his mode of manifestation in the triply divided cosmos (Iren. I, xix, 1, and Hippol. VII, 22).

3. We learn, on XXIX, that the Indivisible possesses a Crown which contains the ideal qualities of every form of created life. Further, that all *gnosis* and all *mind* are in it, and that all Powers receive *light* from it—meaning, perhaps, intellectual illumination. Indivisible and simple in itself, as representing the one *Idea*, it contains simultaneously all qualities and characteristics as elements of the Idea. As the *arena* of the universe (*vide* XXX), it is the subjective field of the evolutionary process.

4. πηξος, a noun formed from πήγνυμι, *to fix, to consolidate*. The term should perhaps be rendered *fixity*, or *stability*. The word αφρηδων is here used adjectivally, meaning *unuttered*, i.e. *undeclared, undisclosed* (*vide* note 2, V). It is perhaps allowable to paraphrase, and translate the name *hidden stability*. The intention seems to be an insistence on the undiscerned immutability underlying mutable appearances.

5. Here, Aphredōn is a proper noun, denoting one of the great Rulers in the place of the *Midst*.

6. Interpretation of this passage is tentative. The Space of the Triple-Power is the Immeasurable Deep, which immediately surrounds the Pleroma and is therefore in the place of the *Midst*, where also are Aphredōn and Mousanios, the two Rulers of that space. *Vide* XXXVI: *" This is the Immeasurable Deep . . . which encircles the Holy Pleroma. The Triple-powered One is over it. . . . And over it is Mousanios . . . There also is Aphredōn"*. The place of the *Midst* is the region to which was banished the deficient substance of the Sophia—called the *outside Sophia* by the Valentinians, the *outside Worlds* and *outside Aeons* by our Gnostics (*vide* XII). The process of completing these Aeons may perhaps be the counterpart of an operation spoken of by the Valentinians as the *enformation in respect of substance* (μόρφωσις κατ' οὐσίαν). *Vide* XIX (note 5), where the incident is again mentioned.

7. These must be the Five Members of the Father. They were emanated, not begotten (*vide* note 10, I). Emanation means re-

taining unbroken connection with the originating source. This is
implicit in the term *Member*. On XV it is stated that the Members
of the Father are *complete*, i.e. perfect beings. They doubtless represent the standard of excellence for aeonic beings, to which—in
their degree—the later creations must conform. The κανουν mentioned on XVI may perhaps be connected with the process of
completing the outside Aeons.

XVII

MS. f. 100ᴿ

C.S. p. 7

[69]

(XVII) There is again another Space (τοπος) which is called: "Deep" (βαθος). Three Fatherhoods are in it. The first (Fatherhood) there is the covered (καλυπτος) one, (XVIII) that is to say, the Hidden God. In the second Father(hood) the Five Trees¹ are standing, and in their midst is a Trapeza (τραπεζα)². Standing on the Trapeza (τραπεζα) is an Only-begotten Word (λογος μονογενης)³. Twelve aspects of the Universal Mind (νους) is he, and to him is rendered the adulation of all. At his appearing All things rejoiced, him the Indivisible strove (αγωνιζε)⁴ to know, and through him the Man was revealed⁵. In the third (Fatherhood) is the Silence (σιγη) and the Source (πηγη). On this Twelve Righteous ones (χς)⁶ are gazing, seeing themselves therein. And in it is the Love (αγαπη) and the Universal Mind (νους), and Five Seals (σφραγις).

And after this is the Universal Womb (παμμητωρ)⁷ from which the Ennead (ʻεννας) was manifested—whose names are these: "The Foremost" (πρωτια), "That-which-*IS*-in-all" (πανδια), "The All-begetting" (παν-γενια), "Revealing-glory" (δοξοφανια), "Begetting-glory" (δοξογενια), "Ruling-glory" (δοξοκρατια), "Be-getting-males" (αρσενογενια), "God-with-us" (λωια), "God-unto-everlasting" (ιουηλ)⁸. This is the inconceivable (ακαταγνωστος) Beginning, the Mother of the Ennead (ʻεννας), which is completed to a Decad (δεκας) in the Monad (μονας) of the Unknowable (αγνωστος).

1. There is no clue to the significance of the Five Trees in our treatise. They are several times mentioned in the *Pistis Sophia* (Cod. Ask.) and in the *Books of Ieou* (Cod. Bruc.). In these texts they represent a company or order (ταξις) in one of the spaces outside the Pleroma. An interesting reference occurs in the *Second Book of Ieou*, p. 70 (Text in *Gnost. Schrift. in Kopt. Sprache,* C. Schmidt, Leipzig, 1892). The Saviour is instructing his disciples respecting the spaces (τοποι) through which they must pass to attain

to the Treasury of Light. Having received from him the Mystery   XVIII
of the Forgiveness of Sins, they will go upwards and inwards, MS. f. 100ᵛ
through space after space, each with its companies of Guardians,   C.S. p. 8
who will deliver up to them the Mystery, the Seal, and the great
Name of the Space. Coming to the Space and Company of the
great god Iao, they will go inwards, and reach the Company of
the Seven Amens. And again, going within, they will come to
"*the Company of the Five Trees, which are the unmoved* (ἀσάλευτος)
Trees". The adjective may perhaps be expressive of immutability.
In the *Pistis Sophia*, the *Five Trees* are described as Kings in the in-
heritances of the Light (*Pistis Sophia*, edit. J. H. Petermann,
Berol. 1851, p. 192).

2. Probably a shortened form of τετράπεζα = *a four-footed object*
or *standing*. The word is used in the *Pistis Sophia* and in the N.T.
with the significance of a *table* for food and drink, either spiritual
or material; but that meaning seems inapplicable here. In our
passage, the τραπεζα is connected with a Monogenes Logos, and,
on XIX, with the first manifestation of the Sonship, i.e. *Christ the
Prover*. The term occurs nowhere else in the treatise. The association of the *One Word* with a quadruplicity of some sort may relate
to a notion current at that time in Christian circles, with regard
to a *fourfold covenant*, and the presentation of the one Word of
revelation through the fourfold Gospel. A passage from the
treatise of Irenaeus suggests this relationship of ideas. After com-
plaining that the Gnostics utilize the Gospels in an illegitimate
manner, appealing sometimes to one only and ignoring the others,
with a view to substantiating their individual doctrines, the Church
Father says: "*It is not possible that the Gospels can be either more or
fewer in number than they are. For since there are four zones of the cosmos
in which we are, and four universal winds—the Church being dispersed
throughout the earth, and the pillar and support and the breath of life of the
Church being the Gospel—it is fitting that she should have four pillars,
breathing forth immortality on all sides, and renewing the life of men. For
which reason it is evident that the Logos, the Artificer of all things—who is
seated upon the Cherubim, who holds all things together, and who was
manifested to men—gave us the Gospels, in form fourfold, but in spirit,
one....For the Cherubim, too, have four appearances, and their appearances figure the modes of operating of the Son of God*" (Iren. III, xi, 11).
Irenaeus then describes the four *appearances*, i.e. *lion, calf, man* and
eagle, which signify, according to him, the kingship, priesthood,
humanity and protective functions of the Logos. After which, he
concludes the matter by stating: "*For the living creatures are fourfold,
and the Gospel is fourfold, as is also the mode of operating of the Lord. And
on this account were ·four universal covenants given to mankind*" (i.e.
under Adam, Noah, Moses, and through the Gospel (*ibid.*)). In

[71]

XVIII
MS. f. 100ᵛ
C.S. p. 8

Strom. v, Clement of Alexandria mentions the same fourfold covenant. Speaking of the veiled entrance to the Holy of Holies, he says: "*Four pillars are there, denoting the sacred quaternion* (τετράς) *of ancient covenants*" (Cap. vi, p. 348).

3. μονογενης. Here used adjectivally, and signifying *oneness*. *Vide* note 2, XVII.

4. Cf. the passage on XV: "*through* [*the Father's*] *Word, the Indivisible knew the Monad, to comprehend it*".

5. Not a reference to Archetypal Man, but to the revelation of the Deity through the εικών, described on LI–LII as "*the Mystery that became Man*". Cf. also XI–XII, where the designation *Man* is used for the Father.

6. χϲ. Contraction for χρηστόϲ.

7. The most usual rendering of this word, i.e. *Mother of All*, is represented in the treatise by a Coptic term. That *Universal Womb* is the meaning here is corroborated by a statement on XLV, to the effect that a πανμητωρ is placed *in* the Mother of the Universe (*vide* also note 5, XXXI).

8. These names, of Greek derivation, appear again on XLVII, where their interpretation is given in Coptic. The last two are perhaps Semitic, the λ and ηλ standing for the word *God*, while the remaining letters may be permutations of the so-called mystery vowels.

(XVIII). After these things there is another Space (τοπος), which is wide-spread. A great wealth is hidden in it, (XIX) which supplies (χωρηγι) the Universe. This is the Immeasurable Deep (βαθος αμετρητος)¹. There is a Trapeza (τραπεζα)² there, round which are gathered three great Powers³: these are still (ηρεμιος), inconceivable (ακαταγνωστος), and infinite (απεραντος). There is a Sonship⁴ in their midst, called: "Christ the Prover" (χς δογιμαστης)⁵. He it is who proves (δογιμαζε) and seals (σφραγιζε) each one with the Seal (σφραγιζ) of the Father, while he sends them to the Primal Father who exists in himself alone. Through him it is All things were made, and without him was nothing made⁶. And this Christ (χς) wears (φορι) Twelve Aspects, a boundless (απεραντος) aspect, an uncontainable (αχωρητος) aspect, and an unutterable (α῾ρητος) aspect, a simple (῾απλουν) aspect, an incorruptible (αφθαρτον) aspect, and a still (ηρεμιος) aspect, an inconceivable (ακαταγνωστος) aspect, an invisible (α῾ορατος) aspect, and a triple-power (τριδυναμις) aspect, an unmoved (ασαλευτος) aspect, an unbegotten (αγεννητος) aspect, and an uncommingled (῾ιλικρινες) aspect.

And as to that Place⁷, Twelve Sources (πηγη) are there. These are called: "The Rational Sources" (πηγη λογικον)⁸, while they are full of Life Eternal. And again they are called: "Deeps" (βαθος), and yet again: (XX) "Twelve Containing-places" (χωρημα), for in them they possess all Fatherhood Spaces (τοπος), and the Fruit (καρπος) of the Whole, which they produce, this is the Christ (χς) who in himself possesses the Whole⁹.

XX

1. We learn on XXXVI that this Deep surrounds the Pleroma, and on XXXIV that the *things of the Within*—meaning the spiritual creations within the Pleroma—and *the things of the Without*—i.e.

XIX
MS. f. 102ᴿ
C.S. p. 9 the things of the phenomenal creation—are looking upon it. It appears to be the treasury and supply source of the universe, in regard both to spiritual and material wealth. It is localized in the place of the *Midst*, and is in touch with the noumenal and phenomenal worlds.

2. *Vide* note 2, XVIII.

3. *Greatnesses* in the Coptic.

4. This is the first mention of the Sonship in our treatise. Reference may be made to note 11, XII, where the Monad—= the complete Divine Forethought of the whole cosmos—is tentatively related to the Basilidian concept of the cosmical Seed. The speculations of our Gnostics in regard to the Sonship tend to confirm this relationship. Basilides taught that the Seed of the cosmos deposited by the not-existing God, contained a Sonship (υἰότης)—a unity of triple division—through the instrumentality of which the development and also the salvation of the triply divided cosmos was brought about (Hippol. VII, 22–27). The use of this term *Sonship*—so far as I am aware—is peculiar to Basilides and our Gnostic writer. In our treatise, the Monogenes—whose title as such denotes the unity of the Sonship in the Monad—is manifested as the Triple-Power in the tripartite cosmos (*vide* XVII and XXXVIII). The Triple Sonship of Basilides and our treatise corresponds to the threefold manifestation of the Christ in the Valentinian system. The first of these manifestations—i.e. the Christ who consolidated the Pleroma—is probably referred to on XVI–XVII as the *Guardian* and *Servant*, and *infra* as *Christ the Prover*.

5. χ̅ς̅ δογιμαστης. From δοκιμάζω, *to prove, to test, to hold good after trial*. This is the first mention of the Christ, by name, in the treatise. As in none of the extant sources is there anything resembling this passage, it can only be tentatively related. The region in which the operations of *Christ the Prover* are enacted is the Immeasurable Deep, which is outside the Pleroma, in the place of the *Midst* (*vide* note 1, *supra*). It is therefore probable that we are dealing with the counterpart of an incident in the Valentinian history of the Sophia *outside*, and that *Christ the Prover* is to be equated with the first Christ—the Aeon *Christ & Holy Spirit* of the Valentinians—who, after effecting the stabilization of the Aeons within the Pleroma, extended himself through the Boundary, and gave shape to the deficient and formless substance of the Sophia *outside*. It may be as well, at this point, to reaffirm the fact, in regard to correlations with Valentinian doctrines, that while the main features of that cosmology have their analogies in the system of our treatise, in most cases the actual details vary considerably, as do also the nomenclature and the terminology (cf. note 4, XII).

The incidents, to which it is conjectured the present passage in our treatise may relate, are given more fully by Irenaeus than any other writer. The substance to which the Sophia *within* had given birth—together with the afflictions (πάθη) she endured—having been separated from her and banished from the "*light and fullness*", was abandoned in places of "*darkness and vacuity*", "*without form or figure, like an abortion, because she possessed nothing from a male parent. But the Christ, dwelling on high, took pity on her, and having extended himself beyond the Stauros, he gave form to her in respect of substance only* (μόρφωσις κατ' οὐσίαν), *but not in respect of gnosis*" (Iren. I, i, 7). Hippolytus gives an additional detail, to the effect that when the *outside* Sophia had been given form by *Christ & Holy Spirit*, the latter Aeon returned to the Pleroma. Reverting to our treatise, it seems probable that the work of *Christ the Prover* in the space outside the Pleroma—which consisted in some process of perfecting for the entities of that space—has its counterpart in the work of the first Christ on behalf of the Sophia *outside*. On XVII there is an earlier reference to a process of completing the outside Aeons, which possibly relates to the same incident. The fact that the sentence from the *Prologue* to the fourth Gospel—quoted *infra*— is used in relation to *Christ the Prover* tends to confirm his identification with the first Christ—the Aeon *Christ & Holy Spirit* of the Valentinians—"*through whom*", according to the *Apoc. of John*, "*All things were consolidated*" (p. 13, German trans.). As read by the Valentinians, the *Prologue* related, not to the creation of the world, but to the production, through the Monogenes, of the Aeons of the Pleroma, to which Aeons "*the Logos* (= Christ) *afterwards imparted form*" (Iren. I, i, 18).

6. John i, 3. The second clause of this sentence from the *Prologue* is repeated on XXVI, where we find a longer citation from the Fourth Gospel. In his *Commentary* on the Gospel of St John, Origen deals at length with the sentence in point, giving his views on the meaning of the terms *all things* and *nothing*. *Nothing* he regards as the equivalent of *not-being*, and *not-being* as synonymous with *evil*. On XLIV–XLV of our treatise—in relation to creative processes in the lower cosmos—we read: "*Then that-which-is was separated from that-which-is-not, and that-which-is-not is the Evil* (κακια) *which appeared in Matter* ('υλη)". This follows the lines of Origen's argument, which he works out thus: "*As for the meaning of the words Nothing and Not-being, they would appear to be synonymous. For Nothing can be spoken of as Not-being, and the Not-being can be described as Nothing. The Apostle appears to count the things which are not, not among the things which have no existence whatever, but rather among the things which are evil. To him the Not-being is evil. . . . We may also notice how evil men, on account of their wickedness, are said not to be, from the*

XIX
MS. f. 102ᴿ
C.S. p. 9

Name of God in Exodus: 'For the Lord said to Moses: I AM, that is My Name'. . . . The Saviour praises him, saying: 'None is good but One, God the Father'. The good then, is the same as Him-who-is. Over against good, is evil or wickedness, and over against Him-who-is, is that-which-is-not. Whence it follows that evil and wickedness are that-which-is-not" (*Com. in Joh.* tome II, 13).

7. The word used here is not the Greek τόπος, but a Coptic term for locus = *place*. We are now taken back, for the space of a paragraph, to the Pleroma, and a consideration of the action of the Aeons which followed on their restoration by the first Christ (*vide infra*, note 9). By *that Place* is intended the *Holy Place*, i.e. the Pleroma (cf. ἱερον on XVI). The Twelve Sources are the Twelve Deeps of the Pleroma presented under a more concrete aspect (*vide* note 5, XIII).

8. Considered concurrently with what we are told on XVII (*vide* notes 1 and 3) and XXX about the Indivisible, this concept of the πηγη λογικον gives some indication of the form of evolutionary doctrine taught by our Gnostics, and further recalls the fact that the theory of absolute evolution, first advanced by the early Greek philosophers, reappeared, in a scarcely modified form, in the philosophic thought of the deeper Christian minds, such as St Basil, St Augustine and Origen. These doctors asserted that the mass of unformed matter was endowed with formative and creative qualities—the πηγη λογικον of our treatise, the *seminales rationes* of the later Scholastic philosophy. With these views, the Gnostics would, of course, be completely familiar.

9. In this passage we meet a close correspondence with a specific Valentinian doctrine. The *Fruit of the Whole* of our treatise is the counterpart of the *Joint Fruit of the Whole Pleroma* (κοινὸς τοῦ πληρώματος καρπός) (Hippol. VI, 32) of the latter system. In both cosmologies this Being represents the second manifestation of the Christ. There are some discrepancies in the Patristic accounts regarding his origination, but in view of statements on XXVII, it appears that the beliefs of our Gnostics coincided with what Irenaeus tells us in I, i, 4. The Church Father states that after the Pleroma had been consolidated and repose restored to the Aeons by the first Christ, these beings, as an expression of their thankfulness and joy, blended together the gifts and perfections of them all and produced a Being whom they called the *Constellation* of the Pleroma and the *Fruit* of them all. The outburst of joy which preceded this action of the Aeons was first mentioned in our treatise on XIV (*vide* note 5). The account from Irenaeus, quoted in that note, continues thus: " *Then out of gratitude for the beneficences conferred on them, the whole Pleroma of Aeons, with one design and desire, and with the concurrence of Christ & Holy Spirit—their Father also setting*

[76]

the Seal of his approval on their conduct—brought together what each one XIX
had in himself of greatest beauty and preciousness, and uniting and com- MS. f. 102ᴿ
bining all these contributions so as skilfully to blend the whole, they pro- C.S. p. 9
duced, to the honour and glory of βυθός (i.e. the Father), *a Being of most*
perfect beauty, both the Constellation (ἄστρον) *of the Pleroma, and the*
perfect Fruit (καρπός) *[of it], Jesus. Him they also call Saviour, and*
Christ, and—from his paternal origin, Logos—and All things (πάντα),
because he was sprung from them all" (Iren. I, i, 4). A key to the
Christology of our Gnostics—which closely agrees with that of
Valentinus—will be found on XVII of the treatise, in two statements which both define the nature of the Monogenes and indicate the mode of his manifestation in the cosmos: *"A Monogenes...who manifests Three Powers"*, and, *"A Monogenes, who is
himself the Triple-Power"*. In his capacity as μονογενής (= *one in
nature*, vide note 2, XVII), he is related to the cosmos as a *whole*,
while the designation *Triple-Power* signifies his association with
the universe as triply divided, the Three Powers denoting his three
manifestations in the terms and mode of being corresponding to
the three divisions. As previously stated (note 15, XVI), the first
of these manifestations was the Aeon *Christ & Holy Spirit* in
Valentinian terminology, = in our treatise, the *Guardian*, the first
Servant, and probably, *Christ the Prover*. In I, i, 4, Irenaeus says that
this first manifestation was a direct emanation from the Monogenes
in accordance with the Forethought of the Father (τοῦ Μονογενῆ
...προβαλέσθαι συζυγίαν κατὰ προμήθειαν τοῦ Πατρὸς...χριστὸν
καὶ Πνεῦμα ἅγιον), while from the *Apoc. of John* we get the additional information that he was anointed by the Father (*vide* p. 10,
German trans.): *"...he (the Father) anointed him with his Grace,
and thus he was made perfect, and no deficiency was in Christ, because he
had anointed him with his Grace"*. The sphere of operation of the first
Christ was the Pleroma, where his mission was the restoration of
the Aeons. As regards the production of the second Christ—called
Joint Fruit of the Whole Pleroma by the Valentinians (Hippol. VI,
32, and Iren. I, i, 4), and *Fruit of the Whole* by our Gnostics—the
idea seems to be that by blending together their most precious
gifts the Aeons produced the vehicle for the second manifestation.
Vide above citation from Iren. I, i, 4, and XXVII of our treatise—
where the manner of his production is described with more detail
—also XXXIII, where it is stated that *he was made a Body of Light*.
That the meaning of the Gnostics was the formation of a body or
vehicle of manifestation is also deducible from a further statement
on XXXIII, to the effect that the Grace of the Monogenes descended on this Being and that he was anointed Christ. We have
thus a re-enactment of what took place at the manifestation of the
first Christ. (*Vide* above citation from Iren. I, i, 4, and *ibid.* II, xiv, 2:

[77]

XIX
MS. f. 102ᴿ
C.S. p. 9

"they affirm that a projection was made by Monogenes—Christ & Holy Spirit". And again, *ibid*.: *". . .Christ, whom they describe as having, according to the Father's Will, been produced by Monogenes"*.) While his place of origin was the Pleroma, the second Christ—*Fruit of the Whole*—was destined to bring about the salvation of the place of the *Midst*, for which purpose he was sent forth later from the Pleroma. Of this happening more will be heard in the course of the treatise. It must be noted, in passing, that according to the beliefs of the Valentinians, the manner of production of the third Christ—the Saviour of the world—was once more a re-enactment —but in the place of the *Midst*—of the earlier occurrences in the spiritual realms. His vehicle or body was formed of the elements of the middle space. With this belief our treatise is in agreement. According to one of the schools—that of the Ophites or Sethians— a material body, formed in the womb of the Virgin Mary, was added for the purposes of his earthly mission. But whether of animal nature, or purely apparitional—as held by the Valentinians—upon this body of the Saviour, the *Name of the Son* (τὸ ὄνομα ὅπερ ἐστιν ὁ υἱὸς ὁ μονογενής)—that is, the power of the Monogenes—descended at the time of his baptism, when the Voice from Heaven proclaimed: *"This is my Only Beloved Son"* (Matt. iii, 17, and Mark i, 11, Gk text, Oxford, 1905). Thus it will be seen that the triple manifestation of the Christ is a threefold dispensation—from the Father—of the saving power of the Monogenes. If one may judge from the tone of the Patristic writers commenting on these doctrines, the elaborate Christology of the Gnostics was misunderstood and misinterpreted by its critics, with the exception, perhaps, of Clement of Alexandria. Equally with the orthodox Christian, the Gnostic asserted of the Monogenes that *"of Him and by Him and in Him are all things"* (Rom. xi, 36). And this conception of his all-containing unity was logically held by them to comprise and relate to every phase, condition and state of being included in their elaborate cosmogony. But concurrently with this view of his fundamental unity, they taught that he presented different aspects in accordance with the mode of being in the particular sphere of his operations, that is to say, his personal revelation was made in the terms of the different states and places where he appeared. To these several aspects of revelation, the Valentinian and related schools gave separate names, thus leading the Church Fathers to suppose that they taught the existence of distinct and separate Christs. *Vide* Iren. ɪᴠ, Praef. 2: *"They utter blasphemy against our Lord, by cutting off and dividing Jesus from Christ, and Christ from the Saviour, and again, the Saviour from the Word, and the Word from the Only Begotten"*. Again, in ɪɪɪ, xvii, 8, Irenaeus remarks that it was against these doctrines that the Apostle wrote

[78]

in I John, iv, 2: "*Every spirit which separates Jesus Christ is not of God,*   XIX
but of Anti-christ" (agreeing with Vulgate rendering). That the real   MS. f. 102^R
intention was several manifestations of the undivided unity of the   C.S. p. 9
Monogenes can be learned from the fragments of Valentinian
doctrine in the *Excerpt. ex Theodot.*, e.g. in § 4, following a reference
to the Saviour's coming to earth: "*He was also the Light of the upper
regions, and he who was manifest in the flesh lost not his former dignity, nor
did he abandon his former abode in coming here.... But he was with the
Father even while he was here and everywhere*". Again, in § 7: "*But he
who was manifest here was not now the Monogenes, but, the Apostle says,* '*the
Glory as of the Monogenes*'. *Because the First-born in the creation is Jesus,
in the Pleroma, the Monogenes. But he is always the same, showing himself
in each place in a form that can be comprehended there. And never is he who
descended severed from him who remains. For the Apostle says:* '*He who
ascended is he who descended*'". With their belief in a unified, but
triply divided cosmos, were bound up the Gnostics' speculations
regarding salvation, which, in the view of the Valentinian and
related schools, consisted in a restorative process for the invisible
as well as the visible world. The Power operating this redemption
was always the Monogenes, the hidden unity of the *Whole*, manifesting, in the tripartite cosmos, as the threefold Christ—the
Triple-Power of our treatise. The Gnostic redemptive scheme was
an elaborate one, designed to bring purification, enlightenment
and rectification to the entities of the whole cosmos. For the
Aeons of the Pleroma, purification consisted in the removal from
among them of the deficient substance to which the youngest
Aeon, Sophia—through her passion and ambitious error—had
given birth. Their enlightenment and rectification were brought
about through information concerning the laws and limitations
of their mode of being, and through gnosis of the fact that only as
revealed in the Monogenes can the Father be known. The redemptive process in the second and third regions is dealt with later
in the treatise. In connection with these speculations, it is of
interest to remember that the belief in salvation being required
for the whole cosmos was held by Origen, who taught the Gnostic
doctrine regarding the inter-relation of all things. In *Com. in Joh.*,
tome I, 15, he says that the Gospel in its widest sense is "*for the
whole world*", not for our earth only, but for the universal system
of the heavens and the earth. In *Cel.* iii, 17, he advances the view
that the death of Christ was salutary for the whole cosmos, and of
avail for heavenly beings, if not for expiation of sin, yet for ad-
vancement in blessedness (*vide* also *Hom. in Lev.* i, 3; ii, 3; *Rom.* v,
s.f. i, 4; *Hom. in Luc.* x). Again, in *De Princ.* iv, pr. Graec. 2, he
allows that the Passion of Christ may be made available—perhaps
in some other shape—in the spiritual world. At times Origen

[79]

XIX
MS. f. 102ᴿ
C.S. p. 9

appears to teach that the Divine Word was actually manifested to other orders of beings in a manner corresponding to their nature, even as he was revealed as soul to the souls in Hades (*Sel. in Ps.* iii, 5). In this sense, also, he thought that "*He became all things to all*", an angel to angels, etc. (*Com. in Joh.* tome I, 34). (*Vide* Art. on Orig. vii, 2, A.W.W.D. in *Dict. of Christ. Biog.* 1877.)

After all these things is the Deep (βαθος) of Sētheus (σηθευς), which is the innermost of all. This the Twelve Fatherhoods surround, and this, moreover (δε), is in their midst[1]. To each there are three aspects[2].

XX
MS. f. 102ᵛ
C.S. p. 10

> The first among them is the Indivisible. To this there are three aspects: a boundless (απεραντος) aspect, an invisible (α‘ορατος) aspect, and an unutterable (α‘ρητος) aspect.

> The second Father is (of) uncontainable (αχωρητος) aspect, unmoved (ασαλευτος) aspect, and undefiled (αμιαντος) aspect.

> The third Father has an inconceivable (ακαταγνωστος)[3] aspect, an incorruptible (αφθαρτος) aspect, and an unuttered (αφρηδων)[4] aspect.

> The fourth Father has a silence (σιγη) aspect, a source (πηγη) aspect, and an unattainable aspect.

> The fifth Father has a still (ηρεμιος) aspect, an all-power (παντοδυναμις) aspect, and an unbegotten (αγεννητος) aspect.

> The sixth Father has an all-father (παντοπατωρ) aspect, a (XXI) self-alone-father (αυτοπατωρ)[5] aspect, and a progenitor (προγενητωρ) aspect.

XXI

1. The Dodecad was previously mentioned on XIII (*vide* note 5) and XIX.

XX
MS. f. 102ᵛ
C.S. p. 10

2. The three aspects possessed by each Fatherhood have relation to the cosmos as a triply divided unit. The exact import of these qualities is not stated. While some of the terms used previously to describe the Twelve Deeps (*vide* XIII–XIV) are here repeated, only in the case of the Twelfth Father does one of his qualities correspond with that of the Deep of the same number, *vide* XIV: "*And the Twelfth Deep is the Truth*". For the rest, it is evident that exact correspondences are not intended. The Deep of Sētheus—which the Twelve surround—is the ultimate Deep of

XX

MS. f. 102^v

C.S. p. 10

creation. (For the significance of the term *Sētheus*, *vide* note 6, III.) The qualities may perhaps signify specific creative powers, but as *aspects*, they seem to denote definite personifications, *vide* **XXI**: "*These are the Twelve Fathers . . . in their number making Thirty-six*".

3. *Vide* note 6, I.

4. *Vide* latter part of note 2, V.

5. *Vide* note 1, VII, and note 8, XIII.

The seventh Father has an all-mystery (πανμυσ-τηριον) aspect, an all-wise (πανσοφος) aspect, and an all-source (παντπηγη) aspect.

The eighth Father has a light aspect, a repose (αναπαυσις) aspect, and an upraising (αναστασις) aspect.

The ninth Father has a covered (καλυπτος) aspect, a first-manifested (προδοφανης) aspect, and a self-alone-begotten (αυτογενης) aspect.

And (δε) the tenth Father has a thrice-strong (τρισαρσης) aspect, an unconquerable (αδαμας) aspect, and an uncommingled (ʻιλικρινες) aspect.

And (δε) the eleventh Father has a triple-power (τριδυναμις) aspect, a complete (τελιος) aspect, and a sparkling (σφινθηρ), or (η) raying aspect.

The twelfth Father has a truth (αληθια) aspect, a forethought (προνοια) aspect, and an after-thought (επινοια) aspect.

These are the Twelve Fathers that surround the Sētheus (σηθευς), in their number making thirty-six[1]. And those that are exterior to them received character (χαρακτηρ)[2] from them, and therefore, to them at all times, is glory given.

There is again another Twelve[3] surrounding the head (of the Deep)[4]. Upon them is a diadem: rays (ακτιν) they cast forth to the Worlds (κοσμος) around them from the Light of the Only-begotten (μονογενης) who (XXII) is hidden in (the Deep): this same for whom all seek.

---

1. *Vide* note 1, XX.
2. χαρακτηρ = *characteristic*, or *distinctive mark impressed on anything.*
3. The Twelve Fatherhoods in the Right-hand of the Monogenes (*vide* XXIII).
4. The text reads: "surrounding *its* head", meaning the topmost part of the Deep. Also *infra*, "the Only-begotten, who is hidden in *it*".

¹The spoken word, indeed (μεν = μην), (exists) to cause us to comprehend (χωρι)² him through those who excel in uttering these things. And (ηδη = ηδε) as far as we are concerned, it is not possible in any other way to apprehend (voι) them, that is to say, (of) ourselves. To speak of him indeed (μεν = μην), with a tongue of flesh (σαρξ), even as he is, this is impossible. For (γαρ) they are great ones who excel in powers (δυναμις), to cause them to learn through an inborn thought, (εvvoια) ³ after which they follow. Even though (ειμητι) there be not found in anything a kinship (συγγενης) ⁴ to these things, it is possible, regarding him, to learn about the places whence he came. For (γαρ) each thing is wont to follow its race. Since ('oτι) then, in truth (μεν = μην), man is a kinsman (συγγενης) of mysteries (μυστηριον), by this means he learned of the Mystery (μυστηριον). They did homage, namely, the Powers (δυναμις) of the mighty Aeons (αιων), to the power (δυναμις) of Marsanes (μαρσανης) ⁵, saying: Who is this who beheld these things with his own eyes⁶, that is, concerning him who in this manner was revealed? Nicotheos (vικοθεος) ⁷ spake concerning him, he had seen him, for he is one who was in that place⁸. He spake and said: He *IS*, even the Father, who excels all perfection (τελιος): he revealed the invisible (α'ορατος),

XXIII   (XXIII) perfect (τελιος) Triple-Power (τριδυναμις). They saw him, each one of the perfect (τελιος) men⁹, they spake concerning him, whilst they gave him glory, each after (κατα) his own manner.

1. A short space in the script follows the final words on XXI, and the writer interpolates comments of his own, suggested, apparently, by the preceding statements to the effect that the worlds on which the Light has shined seek after the Monogenes. Teachers and teaching, he would have us understand, exist for the

purpose of throwing light on the mystery and explaining it—so far as is possible in human speech—to those who, lacking the intuitive faculty by which alone such matters are personally apprehended, can learn in no other way. My rendering of the passage is rather free, it being difficult to translate. In the preface to his 1892 edition of the Coptic text, Dr Schmidt suggests a reason for the difficulty, and states his opinion that the whole treatise betrays the tone of a Coptic translation from the Greek. In support of this view he draws attention to verbal translations of Greek phrases, and to passages, where—contrary to the usual custom of the Coptic language, which requires that Greek substantives should be in the nom. case—the translator has left the original Greek unchanged. As containing a whole paragraph, translated word for word, either on account of the corruption of the Greek text, or perhaps owing to want of comprehension on the part of the writer, Dr Schmidt cites the present page. The meaning of the passage, however, seems clear enough, and on XXIII, where the writer ends his comments, the subject proper of this section of the treatise, i.e. the Monogenes and his operations in the cosmos, is resumed.

2. From χωρέω. L. and S. III, transit. = *to hold, to contain, to make room for.*

3. εννοια = an *intuition*.

4. συγγενης = *akin, cognate, of like kind.* In things that are solely of this world, there is nothing of like nature to this mystery, nor can it be comprehended by the faculties of sense. Man, however, owing to his spiritual nature, is akin thereto.

5. Marsanes is apparently one of the *great ones* just mentioned. By his innate powers of spiritual perception he could comprehend the mystery, for which reason the Powers of the great Aeons did him reverential homage. Epiphanius, in his treatise against the Gnostics, mentions two prophets of the Sethian School called Martiades and Marsianos. In view of the probable Sethian origin of the present treatise, Marsanes is perhaps identifiable with Marsianos. Epiphanius states that the two prophets asserted that they had at one time been carried up into heaven, returning to earth after three days (Epiph. *Adv. Haer.* 40). If the Marsanes of our treatise and Marsianos are one and the same person, it will be to this temporary translation to heaven that reference is made in the comment: "*who beheld these things with his own eyes*". Mention of Marsianos—said to be a *heretic*—occurs also in an extract from a letter of Serapion of Antioch, quoted by Eusebius (*Eccles. Hist.* VI, 12).

6. Text, "*in front of his face*".

7. Presumably another of the *great ones* gifted with the power of intuiting what cannot be put into speech. The name of Nicotheos occurs in the fragments of the Greek writer Zosimus (fourth

century). He is twice spoken of as the possessor of secret know-ledge. In the book entitled: *Authentic Memorandum concerning the Letter Omega*, Zosimus writes: "*The Letter ⲱ is formed of two rounded parts, it belongs to the Seventh Zone, [that of] Saturn, according to the declaration of embodied beings. For, according to the unembodied, it is something other, which cannot be uttered. Nicotheos, the hidden one* (κεκρυμμένος), *alone knoweth [it]*". Later, in the same book, after stating that the Primal Man is called Thoth and Adam in relation to his outward appearance, while his inner man, the spiritual, has an authentic name, Zosimus adds: "*. . .we are ignorant, up to the present, of the authentic [name]—for Nicotheos, who cannot be found* (ὁ ἀνεύρετος), *alone knoweth these things*". (Text in *Les Alchimistes grecs*, M. Berthelot, vol. I, pp. 228, 231.) Another reference to Nicotheos is found in Porphyry's *Life* of Plotinus. He states that when the latter came to Rome in A.D. 244, he found the Gnostic sects in possession of a considerable body of literature which they had preserved from an earlier date. Amongst these works was included an *Apocalypse* of Nicotheos.

8. Or: "*who was there*", meaning in the place of heavenly vision.

9. That is, the *great ones*, mentioned above, among whom are to be reckoned Marsanes, Nicotheos, and probably Phōsilampes (*vide* XXV).

¹This is the Only-begotten (μονογενης) who is hidden   XXIII
in the Sētheus (σηθευς): "The Dark Light" have they   MS. f. 106^R
called him, because through the excess of his Light they   C.S. p. 13
themselves were darkened: this is he through whom the
Sētheus (σηθευς) is King². This is the Only-begotten
(μονογενης): in his Right-hand are Twelve Fatherhoods after the pattern (τυπος) of the Twelve Apostles
(αποστολος), and in his Left are Thirty Powers (δυναμις), each being accounted Twelve³. To each there
are two aspects after the pattern (τυπος) of the Sētheus
(σηθευς), one aspect looking into the innermost Deep
(βαθος), and (δε) the other looking out upon the Triple-
Power (τριδυναμις). And each Fatherhood in his Right-
hand makes three hundred and sixty-five Powers (δυναμις), according (κατα) to the word which David
(δαυειδ) spake, in that he said: "I shall bless the Crown
of the Year in thy Goodness (-χς)⁴".

Now all these Powers (δυναμις) surround the Only-
begotten (μονογενης) after the fashion of a Crown,
while they give Light to the Aeons (αιων) in the Light
of the Only-begotten (μονογενης), as has been written,
(XXIV) saying: "In thy Light shall we see Light"⁵.   XXIV

---

1. The main discourse is now resumed.   XXIII
2. In our treatise, *Sētheus* is a name predicated of the Deity as   MS. f. 106^R
Creator (*vide* note 6, III). But even as a king is not a king if with-   C.S. p. 13
out subjects over whom to exercise his rule, so God himself was
without a kingdom until he sent forth the Only-begotten Word, in
whom, and through whom, all things were made.
3. The Twelve Fatherhoods and Thirty Powers in the Right
and Left hands of the Monogenes are, in the first place, reflections
of the Dodecad and Triacontad of Aeons of the Pleroma, and together with them are mirrored in the divisions of time and space.
Hippolytus, in the *Ref. Haer.* (VI, 53), gives the theories of the
Marcosian Gnostics in this connection: "...*the Moon, traversing the
heavens completely in 30 days, typifies, they say, by these days, the number
of the Aeons...the Sun, completing his journey and terminating his
cyclical return to his former place in 12 months, shows forth the Dodecad*...

[87]

XXIII
MS. f. 106ᴿ
C.S. p. 13

the perimeter of the Zodiacal circle has 360 degrees, and each Zodiacal sign has 30. Thus by means of the circle, they say, the connection of the 12 with the 30 is observed". As regards the Dodecad, the sequence of reflection is carried on to the Twelve Apostles. *Vide § 25, Excerpt. ex Theodot.:* " *The Apostles, he says, took the place of the Dodecad of the Zodiac. For as [the world of] generation is under the government of those Signs, so is [the world of] regeneration under the government of the Apostles".* Cf. note 15, LXI.

4. -χϲ, contraction of χρηϲτόϲ = *good, serviceable,* with Coptic prefix forming an abstract noun. Cf. Ps. lxiv, 12 (Vulg.): " *Thou shalt bless the crown of the year with thy goodness".*

5. Cf. Ps. xxxv, 10 (Vulg.): " *In thy Light we shall see Light".*

And the Only-begotten (μονογενης) is borne upon them, as it is written again: "The Chariot ('αρμα) of God is ten thousandfold". And again, saying: "Thousands are rejoicing, because the Lord is among them"[1]. This same is he who dwelleth in the Monad (μονας) which is in the Sētheus (σηθευς), and which came from the Place of which none can say where it is, which came from the One who is before the Universes—who is the One Alone. From him it is the Monad (μονας)[2] came, in the manner of a ship, laden with all good things (αγαθον), and in the manner of a field, filled, or (η) planted with every kind (γενος) of tree, and in the manner of a city (πολις), filled with all races (γενος) of mankind, and semblances ('ικων) of kings. This is the fashion of the Monad (μονας)—all these being in it: there are twelve monads (μονας) as a crown upon its head—each being accounted twelve: there are ten decads (δεκας) surrounding its shoulders, nine enneads ('εννας) surrounding its body, and seven hebdomads ('εβδομας) under its feet—each being accounted seven. And to its veil (καταπετασμα) which surroundeth it in the manner of a defence (πυργος) there are twelve Gates (πυλη), and twelve myriad (XXV) Powers (δυναμις) upon each Gate (πυλη), and they are called: "Archangels" (αρχαγγελος), and again, saying: "Angels" (αγγελος). This same is the Mother-city (μητροπολις)[3] of the Only-begotten (μονογενης).

1. Ps. lxvii, 18 (Vulg.): "*The Chariot of God is attended by ten thousands; thousands of them that rejoice; the Lord is among them in Sina, in the Holy Place*".

2. *Vide* note 11, XII.

3. Referring to the Monad, μητρόπολις is used in the sense of *place of origin, home*.

This same is the Only-begotten (μονογενης) of whom Phōsilampes (φωσιλαμπης) [1] spake and said: He *IS*, before the Whole: Who came from the infinite (απεραντον), uncharactered (ατχαρακτηρ), unfashioned (ατσχημα), and self-alone-begotten One (αυτογενης), who to himself gave birth: Who came from the unspeakable and immeasurable One (αμετρητος), who truly (οντως) and veritably *IS*, the One who *IS* in himself, that is to say, the One who veritably *IS*, even the incomprehensible Father, who *IS* in his Only-begotten (μονογενης) Son [2]. And the Whole abideth in the unspeakable, unutterable (α῾ρητος), unruled and untroubled One (ατενωχλι), of whose Godhood no one can speak: for the same is no godhood [3]. And when Phōsilampes (φωσιλαμπης) apprehended (νοι), he spake and said: "Through him are those who verily (οντως) and truly *ARE*, and those who verily are not. This is he through whom they are—even the hidden who truly *ARE*, and the manifest, who verily are not".

1. Probably another of the *great ones*, possessing spiritual insight, spoken of on XXII.

2. The same idea is expressed in John xiv, 9: "*He that hath seen me, hath seen the Father*". Also John i, 18: "*No man hath seen God at any time; the Only-begotten Son, who is in the bosom of the Father, he hath declared him*". Cf. also § 10, *Excerpt. ex Theodot.*: "*. . .the Face of the Father is the Son, through whom the Father is known*".

3. Nothing—not even divinity—can be predicated of the First Cause.

This verily is he: the Only-begotten (μονογενης) God.
When All things knew him, they were deified [1]: and
through this Name—even God—they were made
surpassing great. This same is he of whom John
(ιω‘αννης) spake and said: "In the Beginning [2] he
was, even the Word (λογος). And the Word (λογος)
was with God, and the Word (λογος) was God. Without
him was nothing made, and that which was made in
him is Life" [3].

This is the Only-begotten (μονογενης) who is in the
Monad (μονας), dwelling in it as it were a City (πολις) [4]:
and this is the Monad (μονας) which is in Sētheus
(σηθευς) as it were a Thought (εννοια): and this is
Sētheus (σηθευς) who dwelleth in the Holy Place
('ιερον) as it were a King—he being God.

This is he: the fashioning Word (λογος δημιουργος) [5],
who commanded all things and caused them to work.
This is he: the fashioning Mind (νους δημιουργος),
in accordance (κατα) with the command of God the
Father. This same the Creation doth supplicate as
('ως) God, and as ('ως) Lord, and as ('ως) Saviour
(σωτηρ), and as ('ως) one to whom all are subject ('υπο-
τασσε). At his comeliness and beauty all are amazed:
All things of the Within are as a Crown upon his
Head, and those of the Without are underneath his
Feet, while around him and about are those belonging
to the Midst [6]—and they bless him, saying:—

1. In this sentence, *All things* and *they* denote the Aeons of the
Pleroma. The word for *All things* is the same as is used in the
Sahidic text of John i, 3: "*All things* were made by him". The
Valentinians interpreted the Prologue to the Fourth Gospel as
relating to the creation of the Aeons. *Vide* Iren. I, i, 18: "*they teach
that John, the disciple of the Lord...wishing to speak of the origin of the
Wholes* (τῶν ὅλων), *in accordance with the manner in which the Father
brought forth the All* (τὰ πάντα), *lays down* [*as*] *Beginning* (ἀρχή) *that*

XXVI
MS. f. 108ᵛ
C.S. p. 16

which was first begotten by God, who is called both Only-begotten Son and God, in whom, after a seminal manner, the Father brought forth the All (τὰ πάντα). *Through* (ὑπό) *the same, the Word* (λόγος) *was produced, and in* (ἐν) *him, the whole substance of the Aeons, to which the Word afterwards gave form"*. The members of the Ogdoad of Aeons are then shown to be all indicated in the Prologue (John i, 1–4 and 14).

2. John i, 3–4. According to both Irenaeus (1, i, 18–19), and the narrator in the *Excerpt. ex Theodot.* (§ 6), the Valentinians made a distinction between the Monogenes and the Logos, and identified the Monogenes with the *Beginning*, in which, according to their reading of the Prologue, the Logos was. By our Gnostics, the Monogenes and the Logos are not distinguished from one another, the Monogenes Logos is said to be in the Monad (*vide infra*), and the Monad is equated with the Beginning, *vide* XXXVI: "*they knew the Mystery of the Silence, this which uttereth all things and is hidden—the Primordial Monad, through whom the Whole was made in non-substance*". In this passage, the Coptic term translated *primordial*, and used adjectivally, equals the Greek ἀρχή = *beginning, origin*. It is also employed *supra*, for *Beginning*, in the citation from the Prologue, and similarly in the Sahidic text of the Fourth Gospel. The Gnostics of the *Apoc. of John* made the same distinctions and identifications as are found in our treatise. Passages from the two texts, cited and compared in note 3, I, reveal that the πρόνοια of the Father, the εἰκών, the Barbēlo and the Monad are equations, that is, different aspects of the One Divine Thought (ἔννοια). A further passage from the *Apocryphon* equates the *Beginning* with the πρόνοια and the Barbēlo, and indicates the manner of origin of the Monogenes therefrom: "*Gazing deeply into him* (i.e. the Invisible Spirit = the Father), *the pure Light within, the Barbēlo turned itself to him and gave birth to a blessed Light Spark.... This is the Monogenes, who manifested himself to the Father....And the Invisible Spirit rejoiced because of the Light which had come into being, which was manifested in the Beginning, in the First Power, that is to say, in his* πρόνοια, *the Barbēlo*" (*Apoc. of John*, p. 10, German trans.).

3. "*Without him was nothing made, and that which was made in him is Life.*" This rendering, which in Greek texts is dependent on punctuation, differs from that adopted in translation in the A.V. and R.V., and in the revised and authorized version of the Vulgate (London, 1914). Before the fourth century, however, it appears to have been of almost universal acceptance, and is found in nearly all Ante-Nicene texts, being adopted by Irenaeus, Tertullian, Augustine, etc. Amongst moderns, it is accepted by Westcott, Loisy, and von Soden, and it appears in Nestle's text of the Vulgate, 1906. Most recent commentators, however, prefer the other reading: "*Without him was not anything made that was made.*

In him was Life, etc.", for the reason that the older reading suggests that something was created in the Word, and that, as some of the Fathers noted, e.g. St John Chrysostom, would contradict the statement that the Word was God. In our Coptic text, however, the occurrence of the word *and*, joining the two clauses, makes any alternative reading impossible. Alternatives are also ruled out in the case of the Coptic (Sahidic) text of the Fourth Gospel (*Fragments Sahidic du Nouveau Testament*, preserved in the Bibliothèque nationale de Paris, edit. Paul Geuthner, 68 Rue Mazarine, Paris, 1908). In this latter version, the word *and* does not occur between the clauses, but the third verse ends with a full stop at the words: "*without him was not anything made.*", while the fourth verse reads thus: "*That which was made in him is Life, and the Life is the Light of men*". It will be observed that the fifth clause of the Prologue: "*All things were made through him*", is omitted in our passage. It was, however, given previously, on XIX, together with the sixth clause. The final words of the citation: "*that which was made in him* (meaning, in the Logos) *was Life*", were interpreted by the Valentinians to substantiate their doctrine of the dual nature of the Aeons of the Pleroma, λόγος & Ζωή (*Word & Life*), forming, in their belief, a single consubstantial Being (Iren. 1, i, 1 and 18). Cf. also note 2, IV.

XXVI
MS. f. 108ᵛ
C.S. p. 16

4. *Vide* note 3, XXIV.

5. δημιουργος. The word is here employed with the sense of *fashioner*. The Valentinians taught that, in the Monogenes, God the Father brought forth the All (τὰ πάντα): that through him the Logos was produced, and in him, the whole substance of the Aeons, "*to which the Logos himself afterwards imparted form*" (*vide supra*, note 1). Later, in the same passage, Irenaeus says: "*For the Logos was the author of form and beginning to all the Aeons that came into being after him*" (Iren. 1, i, 18).

6. The three divisions of the universe are mentioned here: the *Within*, the *Without*, and the *Midst*. These designations are also found in Valentinian terminology. Most Gnostic schools recognized a tripartite division of the cosmos, and a related threefold category of being. By the Peratae, a group doctrinally related to the Ophites or Sethians, the three regions were denominated ἀγέννητος = *unbegotten*, αὐτογέννητος = *self-alone-begotten*, and γεννητός = *begotten*, designations which appear to have been recognized also by the Gnostics of our treatise, *vide* note 1, XXVIII.

XXVII
MS. f. 110ᴿ
C.S. p. 17

"Holy: Holy: Holy: the ααα, ηηη, εεε, οοο, υυυ, ωωω"¹, that is to say: "Among the living thou art the Living One: among the holies thou art the Holy One: among those who are, thou art the One who *IS*. And thou art Father among fathers, thou art God among gods, thou art Lord among lords, and among spaces (τοπος) thou art Space (τοπος)". And they bless him, saying: "Thou art the House, and thou the Dweller in the House". And again they bless him, saying to the Son within him hidden²: "Thou art, thou art, O Only-begotten (μονογενης): Light, and Life, and Grace (χαρις)!"

Then (τοτε) Sētheus (σηθευς) sent the Spark (σπινθηρ) into the Indivisible. And it shone and made Light for all the Space (τοπος) of the Holy Pleroma ('ιερον πληρωμα)³. And they saw the Light of the Spark (σπινθηρ), and rejoiced, and offered myriads upon myriads of glories unto the Sētheus (σηθευς) and unto the Spark (σπινθηρ) of Light that had shone forth: in that in this they saw their whole likeness. And they portrayed (ʒωγραφι) the Spark (σπινθηρ) among them as a Man of Light and Truth⁴. And they named

XXVIII

(XXVIII) him, saying: "All-formed" (παντομορφος), and "Uncommingled" ('ιλικρινες). And they called him: "Unmoved" (ασαλευτος), and all the Aeons (αιων) named him: "All-powered" (παντοδυναμος)⁵. This is the Servant (διακονος)⁶ of the Aeons (αιων), and he ministers to (διακονι) the Pleroma (πληρωμα).

XXVII
MS. f. 110ᴿ
C.S. p. 17

1. It is clear that the vowel triplicities should correspond numerically with the statements following. One may therefore conclude that the threefold ιῶτα was omitted in error from the vowel series.

2. By the *Son* is meant the Sonship of Triple-Power, the manifestation of the Monogenes in the triply divided cosmos. *Vide* XVII and XXXVIII.

3. In our treatise, and the *Apoc. of John, Spark of Light* is a name

[94]

for the Monogenes and Christ. *Vide* the passage from the *Apocryphon* quoted in note 2, XXVI: "...*a blessed Light Spark....This is the Monogenes, who manifested himself to the Father*". And, in continuation of the same passage: "*And the Invisible Spirit rejoiced because of the Light which had come into being...and he anointed him with his Grace, and thus he was made perfect, and no deficiency was in Christ*" (p. 10, German trans.). The sending forth of the Spark of Light is three times recorded in our treatise. On the present page the shining is in the Pleroma, the world of the *Within*. On XXVIII it descends to the place of the *Midst*, and on LVI to the lower cosmos, the world of the *Without*. By the threefold appearance of the Spark of Light is intended the triple manifestation of the Christ in the three divisions of the cosmos. The shining of the Spark in the Pleroma clearly means spiritual illumination, removal of ignorance through *gnosis* being one of the principal factors in the Gnostic redemptive scheme. The paragraph which follows refers to this restorative work as wrought in the Pleroma by the first Christ, an event previously recorded on XIV (*vide* note 5). From this point onwards, creative and redemptive processes in the tripartite cosmos are the theme of the discourse, and for reasons of completeness, perhaps, it was deemed necessary to refer back to what took place in the first of the three divisions. As observed in note 9, XIX, the Gnostic belief in the unity and inter-relation of all things involved a restorative process for the entire cosmos, this being wrought throughout by the hidden Monogenes, manifesting and operating as the Triple-Power or Threefold Christ. For the Aeons of the Pleroma this was the work of the first Christ, i.e. the Aeon *Christ & Holy Spirit*. In I, i, 4, Irenaeus says that he enlightened the ignorance of the Aeons by announcing among them what related to the Father—namely, that he can be comprehended only through the Monogenes—and by informing them concerning the laws and limitations of their own nature, and, further, that the Holy Spirit taught them to give thanks. Stability and repose having been restored, the Aeons with great joy sang praises to the Father, and as a mark of their gratitude for beneficences conferred on them, brought together the gifts of greatest beauty that each possessed, and produced—to the honour and glory of the Father—a Being of perfect beauty, called the Constellation of the Pleroma and the perfect Fruit of it. The presentment of this incident and the terminology used are different in our treatise. Here the Sētheus equals God the Father (*vide* note 6, III), the Spark of Light is the Christ, while the myriads of glories offered to the Father must correspond to the precious gifts brought together by the Aeons. The rejoicing of the Aeons, subsequent to their restoration, was first mentioned on XIV, *vide* note 5.

XXVII
MS. f. 110ᴿ
C.S. p. 17

[95]

XXVII
MS. f. 110ᴿ
C.S. p. 17

4. The action of the Aeons in producing the perfect Fruit—which followed on their restoration by the first Christ—was previously mentioned on XX (*vide* note 9, XIX). The Being thus formed represented the body or vehicle for the second manifestation of the Christ. That the Aeons depicted him as a Man of Light and Truth in the likeness of the Spark of Light, is an additional detail not found in the Valentinian sources. Ζωγραφέω means to draw from nature, to copy the living model. It will be observed that this action of the Aeons was in imitation of that of the Father, as recorded on II, where it is said that he took the whole likeness of his Members—that is to say, the likeness of the First Man—and made it as a City or a (second) Man, who was thus the image of the Image (*vide* notes 7 and 8, II).

5. παντομορφος, παντοδυναμος—meaning that he possessed the perfections and powers of all the Aeons. Cf. Iren. II, xxxii, 4: "*the Saviour, compounded of them all, who derived his being from the collected gifts of all, and whom they term also, 'All things' (omnia), as being formed of them all*". Also *ibid*. III, xvi, 2: "*who was also termed 'All' (πᾶν), because he possessed the names of all those who had produced him*". His title, ʼιλικρινες, denotes the singleness and unity of his nature, for although all the Aeons contributed to his formation, Irenaeus tells us that their contributions were skilfully blended into a *whole*. *Vide* citation from Iren. I, i, 4 in note 9, XIX.

6. For the use of the designation *Servant* in relation to the first and second manifestations of the Christ, *vide* note 15, XVI.

And the Indivisible sent the Spark (σπινθηρ) from
the Pleroma (πληρωμα), and the Triple-powered One
(τριδυναμος) cometh down to the Self-alone-begotten
(αυτογενης) Spaces (τοπος) 1. And they 2 saw the
Grace (χαρις) of the Aeons (αιων) of the Light which
was freely bestowed (χαριζε) on them: and they rejoiced, because the One who *IS* was come forth among
them. Then (τοτε) were the Veils (καταπετασμα)
opened, and the Light reached down to the Matter
('υλη) below, and to those that were without form and
without likeness 3, and thus they acquired the likeness
of the Light. Some, on the one hand (μεν), rejoiced, because the Light came to them and thus they were made
rich. Others lamented, because they were made poor,
and that which they had was taken away 4. And thus
came Grace (χαρις) into being when it came forth, and
thus was captivity (χμαλωσια) taken captive (αιχμαλωτιζε) 5. To the Aeons (αιων) who to themselves
received the Spark (σπινθηρ) honour was given, and
Guardians (φυλαξ) 6 were sent to them, which are:
Gamaliēl (γαμαλιηλ) and Strempsoukos (στρεμ-
ψουχος), (XXIX) and Agramas (αγραμας) and his
company. And they gave aid (βοηθος) to those who
believed (πιστευε) in the Spark (σπινθηρ) of Light.

1. At this point the treatise enters definitely on the history of
the cosmos exterior to the Pleroma. This outside region was
previously referred to on XII (*vide* spaces *outside*). The enlightenment of the Aeons within the Pleroma—an operation which resolved their ignorance and was the main factor in the redemptive
process for the spiritual world (*vide* note 3, XXVII)—is followed
by the illumination of the space outside, where, as required by the
principle of reflection, there will be a re-enactment of antecedent
events. The *ignorance in the outside Worlds* was mentioned on XII,
vide note 1 (cf. also note 5, XIX). By the Gnostics of our treatise—
as also by the Valentinians—the region immediately outside the
Pleroma was called the place of the *Midst*. On the present page it

XXVIII
MS. f. 110ᵛ
C.S. p. 18

is further designated *Self-alone-begotten Spaces*, a term employed also by the Peratic School for the second region of the cosmos (Hippol. v, 12). The latter school spoke of the three divisions as ἀγέννητος, αὐτογενής and γεννητός, categorical terms embodying the notion of a series of generative modes in declining order, i.e. ἀγέννητος = *unbegotten*, having *no* parents: αὐτογενής = *self-alone-begotten*, i.e. begotten by *one* parent acting alone: and γεννητός = *begotten* in the normal manner by *two* parents. (For the significance attached to αὐτογενής, *vide* note 1, VII.) In the usual nomenclature of our treatise and that of the Valentinians, the three regions are termed the *Within*, the *Midst* and the *Without* (*vide* XXVI). The place of the *Midst* was the abode of the *outside* Sophia, after her exclusion from the Pleroma (Hippol. vi, 31). The fall of the Sophia's substance into the space *outside* followed on the attempt of the Sophia *within* to search into the nature of the incomprehensible Father, and—forsaking her natural conjunction within the Pleroma—to emulate him in his capacity of αὐτοπάτωρ, i.e. a *self-alone parent*, one able to beget and bring forth without the aid of a partner, Sophia being ignorant of the fact that the Father alone possessed the power thus to act completely and perfectly (Hippol. vi, 30 and 31). But while the fruit of the Sophia's attempt was an imperfect and unformed substance—since it lacked the formative principle of a male parent—it was, nevertheless, αὐτογενής, that is, *begotten by herself alone*, and it was from this chaotic substance, after it had been given form through the operation of the first Christ (Iren. i, i, 7, and Hippol. vi, 31), that were produced the entities that peopled the place of the *Midst*, for which reason this region immediately outside the Pleroma was called: *"Self-alone-begotten Spaces"*. The Aeons of the Light (*infra*), whose Grace, it is stated, was exhibited to the imperfect entities of the middle space, must be the complete and perfect Beings of the Pleroma.

2. Meaning the entities of the Self-alone-begotten Spaces.

3. This is not a reference to the material world as ordinarily understood. The Self-alone-begotten Spaces—to which the Light of the Spark reached down when the veils of the Pleroma were opened—equal the place of the *Midst*. This region—second of the three divisions of the cosmos—was intermediate between the world of spirit and that of gross matter. In other terms, it is the psychical realm. The use of the word ὕλη in relation to this space requires explanation. ὕλη is employed in this treatise and in Valentinian terminology with the general sense of *material, stuff*. Thus there were, in the first place, two substances only—spirit and matter, the Right-hand and the Left-hand—and all that was not pure spirit was of a material nature. Continuing this categorical

division, both spirit and matter were subjected to a qualitative distinction, the spiritual substance being of masculine *or* feminine quality—the complete spiritual being, of course, possessing both— while matter was divided into the light and the heavy, i.e. the psychic and the hylic, the former being regarded as a refined sort of matter, entirely different from the gross matter of the world. This psychic substance, as indeed all the *materia* of the universe, owed its origin to the Sophia's substance, and, like all her *self-alone-begotten* productions, it was incomplete, inchoate and undefined, until impressed upon with the likeness of the things of the world of Light.

4. As here employed, *matter* denotes the material entities of the cosmos, things of the psychic order in particular. The passage seems to indicate that there was a power of choice for the inhabitants of the *Midst*, which equals the psychical world. On XII, the entities who belong to this region are styled *outside Worlds*, and on XVI, *outside Aeons*, while on LXI they are spoken of as the *Self-alone-begotten Aeons* who belong to the space of the Sophia. In this intermediate region, the *outside* Sophia dwelt in ignorance and darkness, banished from the world of Light. And to this region, for her salvation, the Christ from on high came down, extending himself through the Boundary, and imparting enformation to her substance, but without conveying gnosis (*vide* note 5, XIX). In I, i, 7 and 8, Irenaeus tells us that having effected this work, the Christ "*withdrew his influence and returned to the Pleroma leaving Sophia to herself, in order that she, becoming sensible of her sufferings, as being severed from the Pleroma, might be influenced by the desire for better things*". Finding herself alone, in the midst of darkness and vacuity, she passed through every kind of affliction (πάθος), including ignorance, and turned herself to supplicate the Light that had forsaken her. Thus the place of the Midst was the place of the Sophia's repentance, the turning point in her career, from whence she looked upwards seeking the Light. From one view point, the Sophia is to be regarded as the spiritual soul (ψυχή) of the universe. The psychic substance, which was held to be intermediate between spirit and gross matter, was held by the Valentinians to have a power of choice. Irenaeus says that being the mean between the spiritual and the material, it "*passes to the side to which inclination draws it*" (i, i, 11). This seems to be the explanation of the present passage in our treatise. The offer made to the entities of the place of the *Midst* is the Grace of God—already possessed by the perfect Aeons of the Light—which now comes down to the middle region. The acceptance or rejection of the offer appears to be a matter of choice. The passage seems to reflect the teaching embodied in Matt. xiii, 12: "*For he that hath to him shall be given, and he shall*

[99]

XXVIII
MS. f. 110ᵛ
C.S. p. 18

abound. But he that hath not, from him shall be taken away that also which he hath".

5. Seemingly a paraphrase of Eph. iv, 7–9: *"But to everyone is given Grace according to the measure of Christ. Wherefore he saith: Ascending on high, he led captivity captive".*

6. Or *protectors*. There is no clue to the identity of the three, but their purpose is clearly to assist the entities of the psychic order who belong to this space, and who are described as *"those who had faith in the Spark of Light".* While these entities are quite definitely not the psychic race of mankind—for the human kingdom has not yet come into being—it is clear that the conditions which make for "salvation" are the same for all who belong to the psychic order, whether aeons or men. As we learn from Irenaeus (I, i, 11), recording the Valentinian teaching in this relation, the first condition was *faith* (cf. also note 3, LIII).

¹And in the Space (τοπος) of the Indivisible there
are Twelve Sources (πηγη), and over them are Twelve
Fatherhoods, surrounding the Indivisible as it were
Deeps (βαθος), or (η) as it were Veils (καταπετασμα).
And upon the Indivisible there is a Crown, in which is
every kind (γενος) of life: every triple-powered (τριδυναμος) kind (γε), every uncontainable (αχωρητος)
kind (γενος), and every infinite (απεραντος) kind
(γενος), every unutterable (α῾ρητος) kind (γενος), every
silent (σιγη) kind (γενος), and every unknowable
(αγνωστος) kind (γενος), every still (ηρεμιος) kind
(γενος), every unmoved (ασαλευτος) kind (γενος), and
every first-manifested (προδοφανης) kind (γενος), every
self-alone-begotten (αυτογενης) kind (γενος), and every
true (αληθια) kind (γενος)—all these being in (the
Crown). And in it are all kinds (γενος), and all Gnosis
(γνωσις), and from out of it all Powers receive Light,
and all Mind (νους) was manifested in it. This is the
Crown which the Father of the Universes gave to the
Indivisible: in it are three hundred and sixty-five kinds
(γενος) ²: and they shine, and they fill the Whole (XXX)
with incorruptible and unfading Light.

XXIX
MS. f. 112ᴿ
C.S. p. 19

XXX

1. The Indivisible was first mentioned on XVII. On XXX we
learn that it is the arena, or assembling place of the universe. The
365 γένη contained in the Crown seem to represent the ἰδέαι or
patterns—in the subjective world—of the various modes of existence in the objective universe.

2. The 365 in this Deep were spoken of on III, in connection
with the creation of the Archetypal Adam. They are there called
Fatherhoods. On XVI, they again appear, and are assigned to
Adam as his aeons. Cf. note 10, XVI.

XXIX
MS. f. 112ᴿ
C.S. p. 19

XXX
MS. f. 112ᵛ
C.S. p. 20

This is the Crown that giveth power to every Power (δυναμις). And this is the Crown for which all the Immortals (αθανατος) pray, and from this (Crown) shall invisibility (ἀ‘ορατος)¹ be restored ⟨them⟩² on the Day of Joy—namely, to those that through the Will (θελημα) of the Unknowable were manifested first—which are these: "The Foremost" (προτια), "That-which-*IS*-in-all" (πανδια), "The All-begetting" (πανγενια), and those of their company³. Then all the invisible (ἀ‘ορατος) Aeons (αιων) shall receive their Crown therefrom, and with invisibility (ἀ‘ορατος) shall flee above, all these Crowns being received from the Crown of the Indivisible: and in the Incorruptible One all shall be made complete. And on this account they pray, who have received bodies (σωμα), desiring to leave the body (σωμα) behind, that they may receive the Crown laid up for them in the Incorruptible Aeon (αιων)⁴.

And this is the Indivisible, which was made the assembling-place (αγων)⁵ for the universe. And to it were all things freely given (χαριζε) through him who is exalted above all things. And there was given to it freely (χαριζε) of the Immeasurable Deep (βαθος αμετρητον)⁶. In it the Fatherhoods cannot be numbered, and in its uncharactered (ατχαρακτηρ) Ennead (‘εννας) are contained the characters (χαρακτηρ) of all created things.

XXX
MS. f. 112ᵛ
C.S. p. 20

1. Probably an instance of a Greek word used alternately as a noun and adjective (*vide infra*). In early Coptic texts, Greek adjectives frequently do duty for the corresponding nouns, no change being made in the terminations, e.g. in our treatise: IV, καλυπτος; IX, αγαθος; XV, δυναμις; and *supra*, αθανατος. This use of one part of speech for another is also seen in Greek texts, e.g. I Cor. xv, 53–54, where φθαρτός stands for *corruptibility* and θνητός for *mortality*.

2. The text has the 3rd pers. sing., but the pronoun relates to *those* that were manifested.

3. Referring to the Ennead of Powers, which at the first came forth from the Universal Womb of creation (*vide* XVIII).

4. The translation of the foregoing is uncertain. The passage appears to relate to an ultimate process of restoration whereby certain manifested entities will be enabled to re-enter the invisible world. The *body* they desire to abandon is not—in the case of these particular beings—a physical body, but a vehicle of manifestation. The Valentinians held that all created beings have bodies in this sense. Cf. § 10, *Excerpt. ex Theodot.*: "*But neither spiritual nor intelligible* [*beings*], *nor archangels, nor first-created ones are without form, shape, body. But each has its own form and body corresponding to its own rank among spiritual things . . . for nothing that is created for the universe is without form*". Also § 11: "*There is one glory of celestials, another of terrestrials, in form and body, one of angels, another of archangels. If you compare intelligible bodies with earthy bodies or with starry bodies they certainly seem to be without form, but if you compare them with the Son, they seem to have size and solidity*".

5. αγων = *place of assembly, for games*, etc. The Indivisible is the arena where the evolutionary drama unfolds subjectively.

6. This Deep contains the wealth and resources of the universe (*vide* note 1, XIX); also the means and gifts of Grace by help of which the Divine scheme of salvation for the beings of the outer cosmos may be accomplished. This is to be inferred from the context (XXXI), and from statements on XXXV–XXXVI, where we learn that the Immeasurable Deep contains Five Powers: Love, Hope, Faith, Gnosis, Peace, which are directed to this end.

XXX
MS. f. 112ᵛ
C.S. p. 20

(XXX) And its Ennead ('εννας) maketh (XXXI) twelve enneads ('εννας), and in the midst of it there is a Space (τοπος) called: "The god-bearing," or (η), "The god-begetting Land"¹. This is the Land of which it has been said: "He that tills his land shall be satisfied with bread and shall enlarge his threshing-floor". And again it has been said: "The king of the field that hath been tilled is above all"². And all these Powers in this god-begetting land receive Crowns upon their heads, and by this the Receivers (παραλημπτωρ)³ are wont to be known—by means of the Crown upon their heads—whether or not they are from the Indivisible⁴.

And again within (the Indivisible) is the Universal Womb (πανμητωρ). In this there are seven Wisdoms (σοφια)⁵, nine Enneads ('εννας) and ten Decads (δεκας). And a great Rule (κανουν = κανων)⁶ is in their midst, and a great Invisible (Power) (α'ορατος) is set up over it, and a great Unbegotten (Power) (αγεννητος), and a great Uncontainable (Power) (αχωρητος), there being to each three aspects. And they offer the supplication and the praise and the hymn ('υμνος) of the Creation upon the Rule (κανουν = κανων) which is there —which is in the midst of the Universal Womb (παμ-μητωρ), and in the midst of the seven Wisdoms (σοφια), and in the midst of the nine Enneads ('εννας), and in the

XXXII midst of the Decads (δεκας)—these being set (XXXII) upon the Rule (κανουν = κανων) for a perfecting by the Fruit (καρπος) of the Aeons (αιων), this which he commanded them, namely the Only-begotten (μονο-γενης), who is hidden in the Indivisible.

1. Frequently, in Gnostic thought, personifications, such as Aeons and other great Powers, stood also for the spaces to which they were related, and of which, in consequence, they possessed the denominations. The present passage is concerned with the

Immeasurable Deep, which, according to the cosmology of our Gnostics, surrounded the Pleroma, and was localized in the space of the *Midst*. As already stated (notes 3 and 4, XXVIII), this space contained the psychic substance of the creation, and was the dwelling of the Sophia *outside*. Besides her local relationship to this region, the substance of the *outside* Sophia formed the substratum of the lower cosmos that was to be (*infra*, note 6). The Valentinians gave her the additional names of: "*The Good Land*", and "*Jerusalem*" (Hippol. VI, 30 and 34). Cf. also Iren. IV, i, 1: "*For they maintain that their aeons and gods and fathers and lords are also still further termed 'heavens', together with their Mother, whom they also call, 'The Land', and 'Jerusalem', while they also style her many other names*".

XXXI
MS. f. 114ᴿ
C.S. p. 21

2. Paraphrasing Prov. xii, 11, and Eccles. v, 8. These quotations, and the designations "*god-bearing*" and "*god-begetting Land*", have reference to the opportunities for salvation afforded to all who are of the region.

3. Or perhaps *inheritors*. The term παράλημπτωρ occurs frequently in the *Pistis Sophia* (Cod. Ask.), and three times in the *Books of Ieou* (Cod. Bruc.), as the name of certain Powers concerned with the embodiment and release of the souls of mankind. The rendering *Receivers* is in keeping with what is stated in those texts regarding their functions, but relationship between them and the παραλήμπτορες of our treatise is not obvious.

4. The Coptic can be read: *derived from* or *out of the Indivisible*. The import of the passage is obscure.

5. The πανμητωρ containing Seven Wisdoms is, of course, to be related to the Sophia. Cf. § 46, *Excerpt. ex Theodot.*: "*First then the Saviour was the universal Creator. But Sophia in the next place built a house for herself and strengthened it with Seven Pillars*". The πανμητωρ with the Seven Wisdoms is in the Indivisible, which is the counterpart, seemingly, of the Ideal World. The original notion is perhaps that in the Divine Wisdom are the ἰδέαι or exemplar forms of all created things. In Valentinian belief, the πανμήτωρ and Seven Wisdoms represented the second, or lower, Ogdoad (7 + 1), which—spatially regarded—was the abode of the *outside* Sophia (Hippol. VI, 34). This is also the import of the present reference to the region. Another correlation of the Seven Pillars may be made with the Seven Planets or planetary spheres. The simile of the Nature goddess surrounded by the Seven Stars is found in the Naassene cosmology, the notion being derived from Egypt. The Egyptians spoke of Isis as "*seven-mantled Nature, covered and enwrapped by seven aetherial mantles—for so they call the wandering stars*" (Hippol. V, 7). In the accounts given by Celsus, Origen and Irenaeus, of the doctrinal system of the Ophites or Sethians, the idea

appears under the guise of an Ogdoad composed of the Mother and Seven Sons. The latter bear Hebrew names, and Irenaeus says that they represent *heavens, virtues, powers, angels* and *creators*. According to Origen, they are equatable with the Seven Planets (Orig. *c. Cels.* VI, 31–32; and Iren. I, xxviii, 3). The source is perhaps Babylonian.

6. The κανουν is conjectured to be a *rule* or *standard* of excellence appointed for the creation. It was first mentioned on XVI (*vide* note 12). Reference in the present passage to the Universal Womb suggests that early creative processes are in question, while mention of the Seven Wisdoms makes conclusive the relationship of this space to the Sophia (*vide supra*, note 5). By *the Creation*—of which the *supplication, praise* and *hymn* are offered on the κανουν (*infra*)—is to be understood the Sophia's *substance*, to which the first Christ imparted form and figure, when, extending himself beyond the Boundary, he gave her *enformation in respect of substance. Vide* note 5, XIX, and note 4, XXVIII. Continuing, from this point, the Sophia's story, Irenaeus relates that after the Christ had returned to the Pleroma, Sophia strained herself, seeking after the Light that had forsaken her. But being stopped by the Boundary (i.e. Horos), she resigned herself to every sort of affliction to which she was subject—grief, because she could not attain her object, fear, lest life should fail her, and further, a newborn desire of turning to him who had given her life. At one time she wept and lamented, on account of being left alone in darkness and vacuity. At another, reflecting on the Light that had been present with her, she would be filled with joy. Then again she would be struck with fear, and sink into consternation and bewilderment. " *This concourse [of afflictions] and [her] substance, so they say, became the material* (ὕλης) *out of which the world was produced*" (Iren. I, i, 7). " *When therefore the Mother had endured all her afflictions* (πάθη) . . . *she turned herself to supplicate the Light that had forsaken her*" (*ibid.* 8). Hippolytus tells the same story, and gives the sequel as follows: " *Then Christ who was in the Pleroma had compassion on her beseeching, as had all the Aeons, and they sent forth outside the Pleroma, the Joint Fruit of the Pleroma, to be a spouse to Sophia outside, and to set right the afflictions she endured while seeking after Christ. The Fruit, then, arriving outside the Pleroma, and finding her amidst the four primary afflictions, namely, in fear and grief and perplexity and supplication, he set right her afflictions, but did not think it fitting, when correcting them, that they should be destroyed.* . . . *He, therefore, as an Aeon so great, and the offspring of the whole Pleroma, caused the afflictions to stand apart from her, and he made them into fundamental substances* (ὑποστάτους οὐσίας) " (Hippol. VI, 32). The foregoing gives the Valentinian account of the incident. As with earlier references to the Sophia's story, it is merely touched on in our treatise, and

such details as are given show some variation from the Valentinian XXXI
version. This particular incident is, however, again mentioned on MS. f. 114ᴿ
XXXVII, and is there more fully described. The Mother's *prayers* C.S. p. 21
are added to the *supplications, praises* and *hymns*. This brings the
notion numerically into line with the Valentinian category of the
four πάθη from which the substances of the phenomenal universe
were formed. Thus, in our treatise, the *praises, hymns, supplications*
and *prayers*, take the place of the four afflictions, and are perfected
by the Fruit of the Aeons in accordance with the standard of excellence (κανουν) appointed for the creation that is to be (*vide infra,*
and XXXVII). It may be remarked that the narration of this
incident on the present page is anticipatory, for not until we
reach XXXIII do we hear of the anointing of the Fruit of the
Aeons, an event which preceded his going forth from the Pleroma.
The second account—on XXXVII—is, of course, in place. One
of the difficulties of interpreting this text arises from the fact that
while in broad outline there is historical sequence, this is often
disregarded where incidents and details are concerned, and the
narrative sometimes dodges about, giving particulars of one space
and another, or one personage and another, regardless of the
temporal relationship of such particulars to the whole.

XXXII
MS. f. 114ᵛ
C.S. p. 22

And before (the Only-begotten) there is a Source (πηγη), which Twelve Righteous ones (χρς)[1] surround. On the head of each one is a Crown with twelve Powers (δυναμις) encircling it. And they bless the King, the Only-begotten (μονογενης), saying: "For thy sake we have been clothed (φορι) with glory, and through thee we saw the Father of the Whole—ααα and ωωω—and the Mother of All things[2] who in every place is hidden: she who is the Thought (επινοια) of every aeon (αιων), she who is the Conception (εννοια) of every god and every lord, she who is the Gnosis (γνωσις) of all invisibles (α'ορατος). And thy Likeness ('ικων) is the Mother of all (things) uncontainable (αχωρητος), and the power of all infinitudes (απεραντος)". And they bless the Only-begotten (μονογενης), saying: "Through thy Likeness ('ικων) we saw thee and we fled to thy Feet[3]. In thee were we established, and we received the unfading Crown of which all learned through thee: Glory be to thee, O Only-begotten (μονογενης), for ever!" And with one accord all said: "Amen ('αμην)"[4].

XXXII
MS. f. 114ᵛ
C.S. p. 22

1. Contraction of χρηστός. (For significance of term, vide note 7, XVI.) On XXIII we read of Twelve Fatherhoods associated with the Monogenes and connected with the divisions of the Year. There does not appear to be any relationship between them and the Twelve χρηστοί beyond the reflective one. The number Twelve is always associated with the Monogenes, and in accordance with the principle of repetition, each dodecad reflects the preceding one, the series terminating with the Twelve Apostles connected with the earthly manifestation of the Monogenes.

2. Judging by the context, by *Mother of All things* must be intended the Monad (cf. XIV, note 2, and V).

3. This is a puzzling passage on account of the second reference to the 'ικων. The first to be mentioned is presumably the Monad = the 'ικων of the Father (*vide* note 3, I), while the origin of the Monogenes in the Monad is made clear on XXIV–XXV (cf. also note 4, II). But the remarks that follow the second reference are

inapplicable where the Divine Image is concerned. If one may XXXII
regard the references as independent statements, the second MS. f. 114ᵛ
'ικων may be the Fruit of the Aeons, who was portrayed by those C.S. p. 22
beings in the likeness of the *Spark of Light*—a title of the Monogenes
(*vide* XXVII–XXVIII). In the treatise, the Monogenes is several
times described as *hidden*, his mode of manifesting being through
the Triple-Power or threefold Christ. Of these manifestations the
Fruit of the Aeons was the second. The sentence, *through thy Likeness we saw thee*, could thus be explained.

4. With this termination, direct reference to the Monogenes and
the Indivisible Deep is at an end, and the discourse proceeds with
a more or less detailed account of creative and redemptive operations in the space of the *Midst*.

XXXIII
MS. f. 116ᴿ
C.S. p. 23

¹And he was made a Body (σωμα) of Light, and he penetrated the Aeons (αιων) of the Indivisible till he reached to the Only-begotten (μονογενης) who is in the Monad (μονας)—this same that in quietude (υσυχια = ησυχια) or (η) stillness (ηρεμος) abides². And ⟨he⟩ received the Grace (χαρις) of the Only-begotten (μονογενης)—that is, his Christhood (-χς)³—and he received the Everlasting Crown. This is the Father of all the Sparks (σπινθηρ), this is the Head of all immortal (αθανατος) bodies (σωμα)⁴, and through him was caused the raising up (αναστασις) of bodies (σωμα)⁵.

⁶Now (δε) outside the Indivisible, and outside its uncharactered (ατχαρακτηρ) Ennead ('εννας)—this same in which all characters (χαρακτηρ) are found—there is another three Enneads ('εννας), each being accounted nine. And in each one is a Rule (κανουν = κανων), to which three Father(hoods) are gathered—these are boundless (απεραντος), unutterable (α'ρητος), and uncontainable (αχωρητος). And in the second, in the midst, there is a Rule (κανουν = κανων), and three Fatherhoods are in it—these are invisible (α'ορατος), unbegotten (αγεννητος), and unmoved (ασαλευτος). Again, in the third, there is a Rule (κανουν = κανων), and three Fatherhoods are in it—these are still (ηρεμος), unknowable (αγνωστος), and triple-powered (τριδυναμος). And through these All things⁷ learned of God

XXXIV

(XXXIV), and they fled to him, and they brought forth an innumerable multitude of aeons (αιων).

XXXIII
MS. f. 116ᴿ
C.S. p. 23

1. The discourse resumes the subject of the Christ, who was the Fruit of the Whole Pleroma. As related on XXVII–XXVIII, he was formed by the Aeons as a Man, in the likeness of the Spark of Light. The notion is evidently the preparation of a vehicle for the second manifestation of the Christ, for we read, *infra*, that he presented himself to the Monogenes—the unitary aspect of the Triple Sonship—whose Grace he received, and by whom he was anointed

as Christ (cf. note 9, XIX, and note 4, XXVII). This event is the   XXXIII
pre-figurement, in the super-terrestrial career of the Christ, of   MS. f. 116ᴿ
the phenomenon which followed the baptism in Jordan, when,   C.S. p. 23
according to the belief of the Valentinians, the Name (ὄνομα) of
the Son, i.e. the Power of the Monogenes, descended on the Man,
Christ Jesus (§ 26, *Excerpt. ex Theodot.*).

2. The statement on XVII is recalled, to the effect that the
Monogenes is hidden in the Indivisible, his mode of manifesting
in the cosmos being through the Triple-Power of Sonship.

3. Contraction of χριστός, with the Coptic prefix of *condition*, and
meaning, *the state of being Christ.*

4. That is to say, he is himself the Spark of Light, and the
Father of the future spiritual Seed, i.e. the *immortal bodies* which
will be brought forth by the Mother of the lower cosmos as the
result of his ministrations. The Valentinians spoke of "*the elect
Seed* (τὸ ἐκλεκτὸν σπέρμα)" as "*a Spark, kindled by the Logos*" (§ 1,
Excerpt. ex Theodot.). Cf. note 3, L.

5. Following on an operation by the Saviour, described by the
Valentinians as the transmutation of her afflictions, the Mother was
provided with the primary substances of creation (*vide* XXXI and
XXXVII). To these she later gave form and fashion when she
had obtained the necessary knowledge, as the result of her "*enformation in respect of gnosis*" (*vide* note 5, XXXVIII, and note
3, XL).

6. We now get some description of the space immediately outside the Pleroma, called the place of the *Midst*. Here is the Immeasurable Deep which contains all provision for the setting up
of the world *without* (*vide* next page). The κανουν again comes into
prominence, with the Triads that are always associated with
creative processes and have numerical relation to the three principles of creation.

7. Meaning, the *outside* Aeons.

[111]

XXXIV
MS. f. 116ᵛ
C.S. p. 24

Furthermore, concerning (κατα) these Enneads (ˊεννας): each one makes myriads upon myriads of Glories, and each Ennead (ˊεννας) has a Monad (μονας) in it, and in each Monad (μονας) is a Space (τοπος) called: "Incorruptible" (αφθαρτος), that is to say: "The Holy Land"[1]. And a Source (πηγη) is in the Land of each of these Monads (μονας), and there are myriads upon myriads of Powers (δυναμις) receiving crowns upon their heads from the crown of the Triple-power (τριδυναμος). And in the midst of the Enneads (ˊεννας) and in the midst of the Monads (μονας) is the Immeasurable Deep (βαθος αμετρητος)[2]. Upon this All things are looking, (both) those of the Within, and those of the Without. And Twelve Fatherhoods are over it, thirty Powers (δυναμις) surrounding each:

α. The first Fatherhood is (of) boundless (απεραντος) aspect, and surrounding him are thirty Powers (δυναμις) which are boundless (απεραντος).

β. The second Fatherhood is (of) invisible (αˊορατος) aspect, and there are thirty invisible (αˊορατος) (Powers) surrounding him.

γ̄. The third Fatherhood is (of) uncontainable (αχωρητος) aspect, and there are thirty uncontainable (αχωρητος) (Powers) surrounding him.

δ̄. And the fourth Fatherhood is (of) ⟨unutterable⟩[3] aspect, and there are thirty ⟨unutterable⟩ Powers (δυναμις) surrounding him.

XXXIV
MS. f. 116ᵛ
C.S. p. 24

1. These Enneads are the three referred to on XXXIII. We are now, apparently, dealing with subdivisions of the place of the *Midst*, the topography of these spaces being after the same plan as before. The *Holy Land* represents the psychic principle of the creation. *Vide* notes 1 and 2, XXXI; also note 4, XXVIII.

2. This Deep was previously mentioned on XIX and XXX.

As observed in note 1, XIX, it is localized in the place of the   XXXIV
Midst. Surrounding the Pleroma, it is in contact with both the MS. f. 116ᵛ
noumenal or hidden world of the *Within*, and the phenomenal or C.S. p. 24
manifested world of the *Without*.

3. The Greek word standing in the text is α‘ορατος, which has
already been assigned to the second Fatherhood. Judging by
earlier categories and the usual sequence of the Greek adjectives
in the text, α‘ρητος is doubtless intended.

XXXV*
W. p. 97
C.S. p. 25

ε̄. The fifth Fatherhood (XXXV) is (of) all-powered (παντοδυναμος) aspect, and there are thirty all-powered (παντοδυναμος) (Powers) surrounding him.

ϛ̄. The sixth Fatherhood is (of) all-wise (πανσοφος) aspect, and there are thirty all-wise (πανσοφος) (Powers) surrounding him.

ζ̄. The seventh Fatherhood is (of) unknowable (αγνωστος) aspect, and there are thirty unknowable (αγνωστος) Powers (δυναμις) surrounding him.

η̄. The eighth Fatherhood is (of) still (ηρεμιο) aspect, and there are thirty still (ηρεμιος) Powers (δυναμις) surrounding him.

θ̄. The ninth Fatherhood is (of) unbegotten (αγεννητος) aspect, and there are thirty unbegotten (αγεννητος) Powers (δυναμις) surrounding him.

ι. The tenth Fatherhood is (of) unmoved (ασαλευτος) aspect, and there are thirty unmoved (ασαλευτος) Powers (δυναμις) surrounding him.

ῑᾱ. The eleventh Fatherhood is (of) all-mystery (πανμυστηριον) aspect, and there are thirty all-mystery (πανμυστηριον) Powers (δυναμις) surrounding him.

ῑβ̄. The twelfth Fatherhood is (of) triple-powered (τριδυναμος) aspect, and there are thirty triple-powered (τριδυναμος) Powers (δυναμις) surrounding him.

ε̄. And in the midst of the Immeasurable Deep (βαθος αμετρητος) there are Five Powers

---

* This—and the six following pages—are missing from the collection. The transcript of Woide-Schwartze—as emended by Dr Schmidt—is used.

(δυναμις), which are called by these unutterable (α῾ρητον) Names[1]:—

[α] The first is called: "Love" (αγαπη), from this all love (αγαπη) has come.

β̄. The second [is called]: "Hope" (῾ελπις), through this it is that all have hoped (῾ελπιзε) (XXXVI) in the Only-begotten (μονογενης) Son of God. XXXVI

[1]. The Immeasurable Deep contains all provision for the development and consummation of the universe. The Five Powers may be regarded as the Gifts of Divine Grace, by the aid of which the entities of the manifested cosmos will attain their appointed end.

XXXV
W. p. 97
C.S. p. 25

$\overline{\gamma}$. The third is called: "Faith" (πιστις), through this they have believed (πιστευε) the Mysteries (μυστηριον) of the Ineffable.

$\overline{\delta}$. The fourth is called: "Gnosis" (γνωσις), through this they knew the Primal Father through whom they came to be. And they knew the Mystery (μυστηριον) of the Silence, this which uttereth all things and is hidden—the Primordial Monad (μονας), through which All Things were made in non-substance (ανουσιος). This is the Mystery (μυστηριον): upon his Head, as it were the hair of a man, the three hundred and sixty-five Beings (ουσια) are a Crown: underneath his Feet is the Holy Pleroma ('ιερον πληρωμα) as it were footstools ('υποποδιον): This is the Door of God[1].

$\overline{\epsilon}$. The fifth (Power) is called: "Peace" (ιρηνη), through this was Peace (ιρηνη) given to all—to those of the Within and to those of the Without—for in this the Whole was founded.

This is the Immeasurable Deep (βαθος αμετρητον): the three hundred and sixty-five Fatherhoods are in this, and by means of these was the Year divided[2]. This is the Deep (βαθος) which encircles the Holy Pleroma ('ιερον πληρωμα). The Triple-powered One (τριδυναμος) is over it, with his branches (κλαδος) as it were trees. And over it is Mousanios (μουσανιος) with those that belong to him[3].

1. The appellation *Door* has a double significance. The un-manifested Deity is revealed to the creation through the Mono-genes, who is therefore called *the Door of God*; vide supra: "*the fourth (Power) is called Gnosis*". Cf. also § 7, *Excerpt. ex Theodot.*: "*Now since the Father was unknown, he willed to be known by the Aeons. And through his own* ἐνθύμησις (*heart's-desire*) *he knew himself, and the Spirit of Gnosis, in gnosis, brought forth the Monogenes. He then,*

who was begotten from gnosis, that is, from his Father's Enthymesis, pro- **XXXVI**
ceeds forth as Gnosis, that is, the Son, for the Father is known through the W. p. 99
Son". But the Monogenes is not only the medium of the Divine C.S. p. 26
revelation. In his capacity as the Triple-Power of Sonship, he
permeates the whole creation, conjoining the manifest and unmanifested worlds, and forming the link between. Cf. John x, 9:
*"I am the Door. By me if any man enter in, he shall be saved, and he shall
go in and out and shall find pasture"*.

2. The 365 Beings (*vide supra*), and the 365 Fatherhoods here
and on XXIII, are perhaps equations. A link with the Basilidian
cosmology is suggested by the association of the Fatherhoods with
the divisions of the Year. Hippolytus and Irenaeus, in their
accounts of the Basilidian Gnosis, speak of 365 Heavens in this
relation. According to Irenaeus, many Powers and Heavens were
produced in the cosmos, in downward order, there being a succession of descendants or reflections in every case; *"and so on"*, he
continues, *"after the same fashion, they declare that more and more
principalities and angels were formed and 365 Heavens. Wherefore the
Year contains the same number of days, in conformity with the number of
the Heavens"*. These Heavens were personifications, and Irenaeus
further explains the matter by saying that the world-creative
angels were the last of the emanations to number 365, and that the
government of this world is said to be divided amongst them
(Iren. I, xix, 1–2).

3. In note 2, V, the conjectured meaning of the name Mou-
sanios was given, and his affinity noted with 'Ρητός, the second
Ruler of the cosmos in the Basilidian system. The first Ruler,
Aphredōn—corresponding with the Ἄρρητος of Basilides—is
mentioned on the next folio. In our treatise, Aphredōn and
Mousanios are rulers in the place of the *Midst*.

XXXVII
W. p. 100
C.S. p. 27

(XXXVI) There also is Aphredōn (αφρηδων) (XXXVII) with his Twelve Righteous ones (χρς)[1]. In their midst there is a Rule (κανουν = κανων), for an offering of the praises and the hymns ('υμνος), the supplications and the prayers of the Mother of all things ('ολον), or (η) the Mother of the Universe[2]—that is to say, she who is called: "Manifest" (φανεριος)[3]—form (μορφη) is given them through the Twelve Righteous ones (χρηστος), and therefrom to the Pleroma (πληρωμα) of Sētheus (σηθευς) they are sent. Of these things they make record[4] in the Aeon (αιων) that is without, the same in which the Matter ('υλη) is[5].

This is the Deep (βαθος) from which the Triple-powered One (τριδυναμος) received glory when from the Indivisible he came[6]. And he received the Grace (χαρις) of the Unknowable, and therefrom a Sonship so great that the Pleroma (πληρωμα) endured not the excess of its Light and the shining that was in him. And the whole Pleroma (πληρωμα) was troubled: the Deep (βαθος) also moved, and all those that were in it, and they fled to the Aeon (αιων) of the Mother. And he gave commandment (κελευε), even the Mystery (μυστηριον), to cause the Veils (καταπετασμα) of the Aeons (αιων) to be drawn, until the Guardian (επισκοπος) re-established them. And the Guardian (επι-

XXXVIII σκοπος) re-established the Aeons (αιων), (XXXVIII) according (κατα) as has been written, saying: "He established the World (οικουμενη) that it shall not move". And again, saying: "The Earth was melted with all those that were upon it"[7].

XXXVII
W. p. 100
C.S. p. 27

1. Contraction of χρηστος (*vide infra*). The two great Rulers of the place of the *Midst*—Aphredōn and Mousanios—were first mentioned on V, the Twelve χρηστοί belonging to Aphredōn on XVI. Here the Twelve probably stand for the ideal patterns of

the types of life figured in the Twelve Zodiacal Signs. The import
of the present reference to Aphredōn is given *infra* (note 2).

2. This incident—which relates to the transmutation of the
Sophia's afflictions into the fundamental substances of the phenomenal world—was first referred to on **XXXI** (*vide* note 6).
There, the *Universal Womb*, and here, the *Mother of the Whole*,
denote the Sophia *outside* in the place of the *Midst*. The κανουν—
conjectured to be the standard of excellence for the creation—is
mentioned in both places. The present passage gives a few more
details of the happening, although the *Fruit of the Whole*, who is the
primary agent operating, is not mentioned. According to Valentinian doctrine, the transmutation of the Sophia's affliction was the
work of the second Christ, the Fruit of the Whole Pleroma, and
formed part of the process known as the *enformation in respect of
gnosis*. The sequence of events relating to the Sophia and the two
processes of her enformation—in so far as this can be gleaned from
the confused accounts of the Fathers—may be briefly recapitulated.
The deficient and shapeless substance to which the Sophia *within*
had given birth was excluded from the Pleroma, and banished to
the place of the *Midst*, thus becoming the Sophia *without*. The first
Christ—i.e. the Aeon *Christ & Holy Spirit*—dwelling within the
Pleroma, took pity on her forlorn and defective condition, and
extending himself beyond the Boundary, went to her aid in the
place of the *Midst*. His work of giving form and figure to her
shapelessness is described as the *enformation in respect of substance*
(μόρφωσις κατ' οὐσίαν), after which work the Christ left her to herself—filled, however, with a desire for better things—and himself
returned to the Pleroma (Iren. 1, i, 7). Finding herself hindered
by the Boundary from following after him who had given her life,
Sophia fell into a state of deep affliction (πάθος), after which she
turned herself to supplicate the Light that had forsaken her. In
answer to her prayers, there was sent forth to her, from the
Pleroma, the second Christ, Fruit of the Whole Pleroma (*ibid.* 8),
"*to be a Spouse for Sophia, and to set right her afflictions*". "*He there-
upon gave her enformation in respect of gnosis* (μόρφωσις κατὰ γνῶσιν),
*and having effected the healing of her afflictions, he set them apart from her,
by themselves, not however without care for them, for it was not possible to
do away with them. . .because they already had existence and virtual being.
But separating and placing them apart, he then commingled and consolidated them, and changed them from incorporeal afflictions, into incorporeal
matter* (ἀσώματον τὴν ὕλην), *thus conferring on them a fitness and innate
property to become structural compounds and corporealities*" (Iren. 1, i, 8).
The details of this occurrence—as presented in our treatise—
exhibit some variations. As pointed out in note 6, **XXXI**, it is the
praises, hymns, supplications and *prayers* of the Mother that are

[119]

XXXVII
W. p. 100
C.S. p. 27

perfected by the Fruit of the Whole and that correspond to the afflictions of the Sophia. There is a further point of resemblance to Valentinian speculations in the statement, *infra*, to the effect that *form* (μορφή) is given to the Mother's *supplications*, etc.— previously perfected by the Fruit of the Whole (*vide* XXXI)— through the agency of the Twelve χρηστοί of Aphredōn. This is an allusion to the creation of the world of discrete phenomena. In the passage from Iren. i, i, 8, quoted *supra*, after stating that the Christ, by his operations, had endowed the transmuted afflictions of the Sophia with the potentiality of becoming concrete substances, Irenaeus adds: "*on this account, they affirm that the Saviour virtually created the world*". In § 47, *Excerpt. ex Theodot.*, following a similar account of the transmuting and enabling operations, we read: "*In the first place, then, the Saviour was the universal Creator*". It is necessary, at this point, to note the characteristic doctrines of our Gnostics in regard to creative processes, the main features of which are re-enacted on each succeeding plane of the universe. It will be observed that in every case where we read of a creative functionary, there is associated with him a dodecad of some sort, whilst the details of the creative act are delegated to a being of secondary status, who again has with him an associated dodecad. Having satisfied the requirements of the monadic basis of the cosmogony by defining the First Cause as the *One Alone* (II and X)— whose Act is emanative, not creative (I)—the treatise introduces the Deity under his aspect as Father and Creator (XI), with the Twelve Deeps denoting his attributes (XIII)—this same phase being again presented on XXVI, as the Sētheus surrounded by Twelve Fatherhoods (XXI). On XXVI, the Monogenes is introduced as the organizer of the creation in relation to God the Father and Sētheus, Twelve Fatherhoods being in his Right-hand (XXIII). As previously observed (latter part of note 9, XIX), the Monogenes is the unitary aspect of the Triple Sonship; therefore, from this point onwards, the sequence of reflection becomes triplicate, creative and formative functions being predicated of the three manifestations of the Monogenes as Christ, and each manifestation having an associated dodecad. In regard to the delegation of creative details to secondary Powers, the sequence is as follows: in the World *within*, i.e. the Pleroma, to the Monogenes with Twelve Fatherhoods, and in the second place, to the Guardian, equalling the First Christ with Twelve Aspects. In the place of the *Midst*, the operating Powers are Aphredōn with Twelve χρηστοί, and the second Christ, called the Fruit of the Whole, who also has Twelve Aspects. In the World *without*, creative details are delegated by the Mother of the lower cosmos to the Forefather with Twelve χρηστοί, and to her First-begotten Son with Twelve Powers. In the Valentinian cosmogony, the sequence was on

[120]

similar, though less elaborate, lines, for—so far as can be judged
from extant sources—the great Forefather of the *Midst*, Aphredōn
—who in the scheme of our Gnostics is the prototype of the Forefather in the World *without*—has no place in that system.

3. Meaning, the *phenomenal* manifestation.

4. The Coptic term signifies *to make remembrance*. These processes
have to be re-enacted in detail on the next plane of the universe—
the Aeon that is without—all things in the world below being reflective of the forms and figures in the world above.

5. As here employed, ὕλη denotes the *material* or *stuff* of the
universe, and includes both psychic and gross physical matter.
Cf. note 3, XXVIII.

6. Meaning, the Immeasurable Deep, which is immediately
outside the Pleroma. It is not clear whether this passage refers to
the sending of the Spark of Light from the Indivisible, as recorded
on XXVIII—whereby the place of the *Midst* was illumined—or
to the coming forth of the second manifestation of the Christ after
his anointing, as related on XXXIII. Most probably the second
appearance is intended, as the Grace of God and the Sonship that
were then conferred on him are mentioned *infra*. His appearance
with the Glory of the Triple Sonship upon him causes a troubling
in the Pleroma and in the Deep outside. The restoration of tran-
quillity amongst the Aeons is effected by the Guardian of the
Pleroma. The subduing of the tumultuous movement that took
place in the Deep is again mentioned on XXXVIII.

7. Ps. xcii, 2 (Vulg.): "*He hath established the world, which shall not
be moved*". And Ps. lxxiv, 4 (Vulg.): "*The earth is melted and all that
dwell therein*". These passages are made to relate to the above-re-
corded events. The first—where the Coptic writer has retained the
οἰκουμένη (= *inhabited world*) of the Septuagintal Greek—has reference to the Pleroma, as the habitation of the Aeons. In the
second passage, the Coptic equivalent of γῆ = *earth* is used.
Hippolytus tells us that the Valentinians named the Sophia *outside*,
"*the Earth*", "*the Good Land*", etc., and that it was to her substance
—prior to her enformation by the Saviour—that they believed
Moses to refer in Gen. i, 2: "*Now the Earth was invisible and unfashioned*" (*Ref. Haer.* VI, 30). (Cf. also note 1, XXXI.) The final
clause of verse 4, Ps. lxxiv (Vulg.) runs thus: "*I have established the
pillars thereof* '. This is not utilized by the Gnostic writer, although
the reference to the *pillars* would have substantiated his view that
the passage related to the Sophia (*vide* § 47, *Excerpt. ex Theodot.*:
"*In the first place then, the Saviour was the universal Creator, but Sophia,
next, built a house for herself and strengthened it with seven Pillars*"). The
omission of the final clause is probably due to the fact that whereas the establishment of the Pleroma is recorded as having taken
place, the stabilization of the Mother's Aeon has yet to be effected.

And at that time (ⲧⲟⲧⲉ) the Triple-powered One (τριδυναμος) came forth, the Son(ship) being hidden within him, the Crown of establishment being on his Head, making myriads upon myriads of Glories. And ⟨they⟩ cried aloud, saying: ¹ "Make straight the way of the Lord, and let living creatures (ⲍⲱⲧⲛ) ² dwell in the Grace (χαρις) of God. And all your age (αιων) ³ shall be filled with the Grace (χαρις) of the Only-begotten (μονογενης) Son".

And he stood above the Immeasurable Deep (βαθος αμετρητος), even the Holy and All-perfect (παντελιος) Father, in whom is all the fullness, and from whose fullness we have received the Grace (χαρις) ⁴. Then (ⲧⲟⲧⲉ) the Aeon (αιων) was established, it ceased from moving, the Father established it, that it shall not move for ever.

And the Aeon (αιων) of the Mother awaited ⁵, being full of those things that were in it, till commandment (κελευσις) came forth through the Mystery (μυστηριον) hidden in the Primal Father—the One from whom the Mystery (μυστηριον) came forth—so that his Son should establish the Universe again in his Gnosis (γνωσις): this same in which the Universe is ⁶.

1. An adaptation of Luke iii, 4 and 6: " *The voice of one crying in the wilderness: Prepare ye the way of the Lord, make his paths straight. . . . And all flesh shall see the salvation of God*". These passages are made to relate to the Saviour's advent to the place of the *Midst*. *Vide* note 1, XXXIX.

2. Probably a contraction of ⲍⲱⲧⲓⲕόⲥ.

3. Or perhaps *life-time*, αιων here denoting a *period of time*. The word is used again with this meaning on LIX.

4. The reference is to the Monogenes as Father and Creator of the manifested cosmos.

5. The Coptic word equals *exspecto*, with reference, presumably, to the imminent *enformation in respect of gnosis*, which is to enable the Mother to bring forth an ordered creation. For although

the first Christ had given her *enformation in respect of substance*, XXXVIII
she had remained outside the Pleroma, a prey to ignorance, W. p. 102
perplexity, fear, and other afflictions. After healing and setting C.S. p. 28
apart her afflictions, and then transmuting them, the second
Christ—Fruit of the Whole Pleroma—had commingled them, and at
the same time conferred on them a natural disposition to become
concrete and corporeal substances (note 2, XXXVII). The inference is that by this commingling, the Saviour created the prot-
ideal substance of matter. Hippolytus (*Ref. Haer.* VI, 32) tells us
that the Sophia's afflictions became the fundamental substances
(ὑποστάτους οὐσίας) of the world. Finally, *grief* was made into
material substance, *perplexity* into daemonic substance, while her
fear and her *conversion* became the psychic substance and principle,
that is to say, of the last, i.e. the psychic element, there were two
distinct creations. In this way the Mother was provided with the
various material elements of her worlds, and thus her "*Aeon
awaited, being full of those things that were in it*". The pneumatic
principle required to complete the creation was arranged for in a
different manner. The Mother being herself of spiritual origin had
this element ready to hand, and when giving her the *enformation
in respect of gnosis*, the Saviour revealed to her all things concerning
the constitution of the universe (§ 45, *Excerpt. ex Theodot.*). Provided
with the requisite knowledge, and as the fruit of her vision of the
Saviour's angelic attendants, she was enabled to bring forth a
spiritual progeny (*vide* XL, and Iren. I, i, 8). These were the
feminine counterparts of the Angels. While the spiritual principle
possessed by the Mother was thus made available for the purposes
of her creation, it was, in itself, deficient and unformed, being of
feminine quality only. This was due to her own origin from a single
parent, i.e. the upper Sophia. The idea held by the Gnostics in
regard to generation was that the male parent supplied the *forma*,
and the female, the *materia*. Thus we find it recorded later
(XLIX–L) that the Mother appeals for aid in perfecting her
spiritual, but feminine progeny. (Cf. also § 40, *Excerpt. ex Theodot.*)

6. Cf. *Pistis Sophia*, p. 233 (Codex Askew, edit. Petermann), where,
in a discourse, the Saviour tells his disciples of the ultimate gnosis,
for the apprehension of which a man's knowledge of the mysteries
of the Kingdom of Light is not sufficient: "*he will not know the
Gnosis of the Whole, the cause wherefor all these things have come into
being, unless he knoweth the One Word of the Ineffable, which is Itself the
Gnosis of the Whole. And again, [I say unto you] plainly: I am the
Gnosis of the Whole*". The reference in our passage is to the
second process of "*enformation*", that "*in respect of gnosis*".

[123]

(XXXVIII) Then (τοτε) the Sētheus (σηθευς) sent a fashioning Word (λογος δημιουργος), (XXXIX) with whom there was a multitude of Powers (δυναμις) [1]. These were crowned upon their heads and their crowns cast forth rays (ακτιν). The effulgence of their bodies (σωμα) riseth [2] in the place (τοπος) to which they came, the word (λογος) which cometh from their mouth is life for evermore, and the light that cometh from their eyes to them it is repose (αναπαυσις). The movement of their hands is their swift flight to the place (τοπος) from whence they came, their inward looking is the inner knowledge (γνωσις) of themselves, their setting out unto themselves is their turning inwards once again. The outstretching of their hands is their establishment, and the hearing of their ears is the perception (αισθησις) in their heart. The uniting of their members (μελος) is the gathering in of the dispersed of Israel (ιηλ) [3], their consolidation is their fast-fixing in the Word (λογος). The number (ψηφος) in their fingers is the reckoning (αριθμος) or (η) numbering that came out, according (κατα) as has been written, saying: "Who numbereth the multitudes of stars and calleth them all by name" [4]. And the whole union of the fashioning Word (λογος δημιουργος) came about with those that had come from the movement that took place, and they

all were made one (XL), according (κατα) as has been written, saying: "All were made one in the One and Only One".

1. On this and the succeeding page, we learn a few details of the enforming operations of the Saviour. The λογος δημιουργος sent by the Sētheus—that is, by God the Father—is the Saviour, called Fruit of the Whole Pleroma, whose *enformation in respect of gnosis* enabled the Mother to found the lower cosmos. Irenaeus tells us that there was sent forth to her "*the Paraclete, that is, the*

Saviour, all power being conferred on him by the Father, who placed all things under his authority, the Aeons also doing likewise.... He, then, was sent forth to her with his accompanying Angels" (Iren. 1, i, 8). The company of Powers in our treatise equals the Angels. That the advent of the Saviour to the place of the *Midst* with a body-guard of Angels is the pre-figurement of his advent to earth, attended by the Angels who—according to the Gospel story—appeared at Bethlehem, is substantiated by the use of the heralding words of John the Baptist on XXXVIII. For although in the Gospels those words are anticipatory of the Saviour's baptism and not of his birth, the former event was regarded by the Gnostics as his true advent. Besides, quite apart from all connection with heretical views regarding the manner of union of the Divine Saviour with the Man Christ Jesus and the moment when this union took place, there is abundant evidence that until the fourth century there was no separate Feast of the Nativity celebrated in the Church. The earliest records point to a joint feast of Birth and Baptism being held on Jan. 6th. The separation of the two was effected in the fourth century in order to combat this very Gnostic doctrine that Jesus was not born divine, but became so at his baptism. Jan. 6th was retained as the Feast of the Epiphany and of the Baptism, while the Nativity was removed to Dec. 25th (*vide* "Christmas" and "Epiphany" in Hastings' *Ency. of Religion and Ethics*). To this day, however, one Eastern Church, that of the non-uniate Armenians, retains the old date of Jan. 6th for a joint celebration of the three Feasts, the Nativity, the Epiphany, and the Baptism. There is no mention of the Saviour's Baptism in our treatise, but his advent to earth, for the redemption, again accompanied by the Angels, is recorded on LVII.

XXXIX
W. p. 103
C.S. p. 29

2. The usual meaning of the Coptic word, i.e. *living*, would be meaningless here. Some years ago, I called the attention of the late Dr J. H. Walker to the term. He said that in his opinion it was a highly interesting use of the word with the meaning of *rising* or *rearing up*. Derived from the hieroglyphs, it is used in the demotic—with this meaning—in relation to the *Uraeus* on the royal diadem. *Vide* Griffith and Thompson, *Dem. Mag. Pap.* col. 1, 3 and col. IX, 16; also Brugsch, *Wörterbuch*, pp. 198–9; and Lepsius, *Todtenbuch*, c. 42, l. 9.

3. Cf. § 56, *Excerpt. ex Theodot.*: *"But Israel is an allegory for the spiritual [man] who shall see God"*. The Valentinians taught that at the final consummation, the elect souls (ἐκλεκτοί) on earth, i.e. the feminine spiritual seed, are to be united to the masculine Angels who appeared with the Saviour, and together with them to form spiritual unities. The uniting of the members probably refers to this by anticipation.

[125]

XXXIX
W. p. 103
C.S. p. 29

4. Ps. cxlvi, 4 (Vulg.): "*Who telleth the number of the stars, and calleth them by their names*". By calling the Name, the Gnostics understood creation by the *Word*. Cf. also Baruch, iii, 34–5: "*The stars shined in their courses and rejoiced: when he called them they said: 'Here we be'. And so with cheerfulness they showed light unto him that made them*".

Then (τοτε) the fashioning Word (λογος δημιουργος) became Mighty God, and Lord, and Saviour (σωτηρ), Christ (χρς), and King, and the Good (αγαθος), and Father and Mother. This is he whose work bore fruit[1]: he received honour, and he became Father of those who had believed (πιστευε). The same became Law (νομος) in the Formlessness (αφρηδωνια)[2], and Ruling Principle (δυνατος).

And the All-manifest (πανδηλος) came forth, being crowned, and bestowing (crowns) on those who had believed (πιστευε). And the Virgin (παρθενος) Mother ⟨conceived by⟩ the power of the Aeons (αιων)[3], and she gave order (ταξις) to her Worlds (κοσμος) in accordance with (κατα) the precept of the Within[4]. And therein she set the Spark (σπινθηρ) of Light, in accordance with (κατα) the pattern (τυπος) of the Monad (μονας)[5], and she placed the Covering (καλυπτος)[6] around.

1. The *work that bore fruit* is the process of *enformation in respect of gnosis*. The Valentinians called the Saviour the Spouse of the Sophia (Hippol. vi, 32). Cf. also the statement of Irenaeus, quoted *infra* (note 3), to the effect that after her vision of the Saviour and his attendant angels, the Mother brought forth fruit.

2. αφρηδωνια. A noun, formed in the same manner and bearing the same significance as the adjective αφρηδων = *unuttered* (*vide* note 2, V). A literal rendering would, of course, be *the Unutteredness*. But as pointed out in note 2, V, by *unuttered* the Gnostics intended *unmade*. Thus the *Aphredōnia* denotes a state or place where the formative Word has not yet been spoken. It is, in fact, the Aeon of the Mother, which *awaited, full of those things that were in it* (XXXVIII), until the enforming operation took place, and the unshaped and chaotic primaeval substance was brought under the Divine rule of form and order through the utterance of the fashioning Word. In the Basilidian cosmogony, we meet a similar notion. The universe below the Firmament was divided into the Ogdoad and the Hebdomad. Included in the

XL
W. p. 105
C.S. p. 30

latter was "*the Space of this world of ours*". This was designated the Ἀμορφία = the *Formlessness* (Hippol. VII, 22).

3. As pointed out by Dr Schmidt, Woide's transcript—from which this page of text is copied—is full of inaccuracies, due probably to the imperfect condition of the original. As transcribed by Woide, this sentence reads: "And the Virgin Mother *and* the power of the Aeons". In relation to the context, this is nonsense. The Coptic word for *and* is written ⲁⲩⲱ. The emendation I propose, i.e. ⲁⲥⲱ, is a phrase of three words, written in the Coptic manner as one, and meaning, *she did conceive*. This gives a sense which exactly accords with the narrative, and agrees with the Valentinian version of these events. The Valentinians related that when the Saviour came for the work of enformation, he was accompanied by a body-guard of angelic beings (*vide* note 1, XXXIX). Irenaeus states that after the Mother was freed from her afflictions, and had received the *enformation in respect of gnosis*, "*she gazed with rapture on the dazzling vision of the angels that were with him, and conceiving by them, brought forth fruit after her own art, a spiritual progeny, made in the likeness of the Saviour's body-guard*" (I, i, 8). Cf. also *ibid.* II, xlv: "*For [the Valentinians] say, in regard to nature and substance, three kinds (genera) were produced by the Mother. The first...is material. The second...is psychical. But that which she brought forth through her vision of those angels who are around the Christ, is spiritual*". Irenaeus (I, i, 9) goes on to say: "*There being now, according to them, three fundamental [substances]—that from the affliction, which is material, that from the conversion, which is psychical, and that which was of herself, which is spiritual—she next addressed herself to fashioning them. But, in truth, as regards the spiritual, she could not give fashion to this, because it corresponded to her own substance*". That is to say, it was of feminine quality only, and lacked the formative male principle. The spiritual beings, who appeared with the Saviour and on whom the Mother gazed, were *male* angels (cf. §§ 39, 40 and 44, *Excerpt. ex Theodot.*), and her vision was the *cause* of her conceiving seed; but the result was female, like herself (cf. note 5, XXXVIII). Hence it is to be argued that a further operation by the Saviour was required. This is described on L.

4. The *Within* is the Pleroma. Cf. § 45, *Excerpt. ex Theodot.*: "*Straightway then, the Saviour conferred on her enformation in respect of gnosis, and healed her afflictions, and showed her all that is in the Pleroma, from the Unbegotten Father even as far as herself*". Thus in arranging and organizing her universe, she was enabled to copy the perfect antitype.

5. Cf. XII, where the Monad is likened to a Spark of Light. The Spark placed by the Mother in her universe is the spiritual

principle which she conceived as the result of her vision of the   XL
angels (*vide* note 1, **XXXIX**, and *supra*, note 3). But being from   W. p. 105
her own substance, it was of feminine quality, and incomplete in   C.S. p. 30
nature.

6. καλυπτος, verbal adjective meaning *covered*. Here doing duty
for a noun, as previously on **IV**. A second reference to this *covering*
will be found on **L**.

(XL) And she appointed the Propator (προπατωρ)[1] after the pattern (τυπος) of the Indivisible, and the Twelve Righteous ones (χρς) surrounding him. Crowns were on their heads, and a Seal (σφραγις) of Glory (XLI) in their right hand. In their midst there was a ⟨Source⟩[2], and a triple-powered (τριδυναμος) aspect in the Source (πηγη), also a Rule (κανουν=κανων), which the Twelve Fathers surround, a Sonship being hidden among them.

And she set up the Autopator (αυτοπατωρ)[3], after the pattern (τυπος) of the uncharactered (αχαρακτηρ) Ennead ('εννας), and she gave him the authority (εξουσια) over everyone who is of (a) self alone father. And with all glory she crowned (στεφανου) him, and she gave to him of Love (αγαπη) and Peace (ιρηνη) and Truth (αληθια), and myriads of Powers (δυναμις), so that he shall gather in those that were scattered in the tumult that took place, at the time when, with rejoicing, the Triple-powered One (τριδυναμος) and Lord of the Universe came forth[4]—with whom is power to quicken and destroy.

And she set up the Protogenitor (προτογεννητωρ) Son[5], after the pattern (τυπος) of the Triple-Power (τριδυναμις)[6]. And she gave to him a nine-fold Ennead ('εννας), and she gave to him ten times five Decads (δεκας), so that he shall have power to complete the assemblage (αγων) committed to him.

1. The treatise now proceeds with an account of the creation of the lower cosmos, and apart from one or two interesting variants, the cosmology closely accords with that of Valentinus. The records of that system, however, differ in regard to the procedure of the Mother and the beings produced by her subsequent to her enformation by the Saviour. In Iren. 1, i, 9–10 and 13, and *Excerpt. ex Theodot.* §47, we learn of three entities connected with the lower cosmos: the Demiurge, the Cosmokrator and a psychical Christ.

As regards their positions in the lower cosmos, the three correspond
to the Propator, the Autopator, and the Protogenitor Son of our
treatise (*vide infra*). But the somewhat confused account given by
Irenaeus of their functions and operations is not entirely parallel.
The triple division postulated for the universe as a *whole*, is reflected in the part, i.e. the phenomenal world, where the Mother
takes the place of the Supreme Father. The three beings set up by
her have relationship to this triple division, and at the same time
reflect their prototypes in the world above. The multiplying of
states and spaces, with their related functionaries, which is a
feature of the highly evolved Gnostic systems—such as the one we
are considering—was perhaps due to the necessity felt by the
Gnostics of removing the Deity and other beings of high spiritual
rank from immediate contact with the phenomenal world. Thus
we get the delegated processes of creation (*vide* latter part of note 2,
XXXVII). Such speculations were not foreign to contemporary
thought. The theory that God employed angels to fashion the
world was current in Judaism. Similarly, in the Platonic cosmology
—from which Valentinus derived many of his notions—the details
of creation are the work of the lesser gods. In the system of our
treatise, this manner of operating holds good even when the scale
of beings with creative functions has descended as far as the
Mother of the lower cosmos. For although her position was outside the Pleroma, and her transmuted afflictions constituted the
materia of the universe, she was herself of spiritual origin and
nature, and only operated in the phenomenal world through
the beings she produced for this purpose. In § 47, *Excerpt. ex
Theodot.*, we read: "*In the first place, then, the Saviour was the universal
Creator, but Sophia next built a house for herself...and first of all she
produced a likeness of God the Father, through whom she built Heaven and
Earth....He, being the likeness of the Father, became the Father, and first
of all produced a psychic Christ, in the likeness of the Son*". This
passage continues with details of the creative activities of the
Demiurge, which follow the Genesis account of creation in certain
particulars, the statement that "*the Spirit of God brooded over the
waters*" being predicated of him. Our treatise shows some variation in detail, in respect both of the Demiurge or Forefather and
the psychic Christ, making the latter to be the Son of the Mother
directly, and further assigning to him a share in the work of
creation- he brooding operation being attributed to him instead
of to the Forefather (*vide* LIII). In our treatise, the Forefather,
with a surrounding of Twelve, is said to be after the pattern of the
Indivisible Deep. This has reference to the Twelve Fatherhoods
that surround that Deep (XXIX), and perhaps to the fact that
the Indivisible was the assembling place of the cosmos (XXIX–

XLI
W. p. 106
C.S. p. 31

XXX), the region of the Forefather being the world of differentiated phenomena. The grade of being to which he belongs is the *unbegotten* grade—he was fashioned by the Mother out of the psychic substance at her disposal. Irenaeus tells us that when the Mother failed in her attempt to give form to the spiritual substance—it being of the same feminine quality as herself (*vide* note 3, XL)—she applied herself to give shape to the psychic substance which had arisen from her *conversion* (*vide* note 5, XXXVIII): "*And she first formed out of the psychic substance him who is Father and King of all things, both of those which are of the same nature as himself—that is, the psychic substance, which they also call the Right-hand—and also that which was from the affliction, and the hylic substance, which they call the Left-hand*" (Iren. I, i, 9). He was thus overlord of the entire lower cosmos. In our treatise his immediate prototype is Aphredōn, the great Ruler and Forefather in the place of the *Midst* (*vide* XVI; cf. also latter part of note 2, V).

2. The word standing in Woide's transcript is αγαπη. It is clear from the context that this is a copyist's error.

3. As one of the three Beings set up in the lower cosmos, the Autopator corresponds in position to the Cosmokrator of the Valentinian cosmogony. References to the latter in the Patristic sources are few in number and not very clear. In I, i, 10, Irenaeus equates him with the Devil, and in regard to his origin says: "*the Devil, whom they also call the Cosmokrator, the demons, and all spirits of wickedness*" derived their origin from the *material* substance (ὑλικὴν οὐσίαν) formed out of the Mother's *grief*. In the same paragraph Irenaeus adds that the Cosmokrator had a knowledge of what was above himself because he is a *spirit of wickedness* (πνευματικὰ τῆς πονηρίας). On the face of it this is puzzling, and Irenaeus gives no indication as to how a *spirit*—whether wicked or otherwise—could be derived from a material substance. The Gnostic teacher Heracleon, while not designating the Devil as a material being, seems to have felt some difficulty about his nature. In frg. 45 he says: "*the Devil's substance is different from the holy rational substance*" (ἁγίων λογικῶν οὐσίαν) (*Texts and Studies*, vol. I, pt. 4, edit. Armitage Robinson). A partial explanation of the problem seems to be that in this particular instance πνεῦμα and πνευματικός are not used with the special sense of *spirit* or *spiritual*, but as denoting *air*, *breath*, etc. For later in the same paragraph (I, i, 10) Irenaeus states that the corporeal element *air* (ἀέρα) arose from the consolidation of the Mother's *grief* previously postulated by him as the originating source of the Devil and spirits of wickedness (*vide supra*). Also, the inference, that in this particular connection πνεῦμα is synonymous with ἀέρα, seems placed beyond doubt by Hippolytus. In an early passage (*Ref. Haer.* VI, 53), when naming the four

material elements made through the Mother, he agrees with
Iren. I, i, 10, and uses the term ἀέρα. But later on (*ibid.* x, 32–3),
where he speaks of the creation being formed of the four elements,
he employs πνεῦμα three times in place of ἀέρα, e.g. πῦρ καὶ πνεῦμα,
ὕδωρ καὶ γῆν = *fire and air, water and earth.* In I, i, 10, Irenaeus tells
us that *fire* was inherent in all the material elements of the world.
These notions may perhaps have come over from Judaism. In the
Kabbala, the origin of the devils is referred to the two *subtile* elements, *fire* and *air.* While it is clear from later statements (L and
LI) that the Autopator, like the Cosmokrator, is the ruling Power
in the material world, nothing is said in our treatise as to his nature
or the origin of his substance. The uncharactered Ennead, which
is the pattern after which he was constituted, is the Ennead in the
Indivisible Deep, which contained the ideal characteristics of
created things. On L–LI, some details of his activities are given.
These are not of a creative nature. His prototype in the greater
cosmos is Mousanios, the second Ruler in the place of the *Midst*
(*vide* latter part of note 2, V). The stress that—in the system of
our treatise—is laid upon the triple division and the three grades of
being postulated for the universe, necessitates the introduction at
this point in the cosmology of an entity who—in the lower cosmos
—shall represent the middle, or *self-alone begetting* grade (*vide*
note I, XXVIII), and to this, presumably, is due the Autopator's title. But beyond the fact that he is said to wield authority
over all that belong to this middle mode of generating, the nature
of his activities is left vague. When mentioned for the second time,
on L, his functions come more into line with those of the Cosmokrator of Valentinus, his sphere of action being there called the
Aeon of the Covering. This is the world of form, that is to say, the
material world, comprising both psychic and gross physical matter.
We learn that his activities are chiefly concerned with the psychic
element. It is in his capacity as ruler of this world that he is to be
correlated with the Valentinian Cosmokrator, whom Irenaeus
equates with the Devil. This equation is not made in our treatise,
nor has the Autopator any connection with the principle of evil,
except in so far as he rules over the world in which, so it is said:
Evil has manifested itself in Matter (XLIV–XLV). It is probable,
however, that Irenaeus did not altogether understand the beliefs
of the Valentinians in regard to the Devil. In *Ref. Haer.* VI, 33–4,
Hippolytus makes it quite clear that these Gnostics distinguished
two entities in this particular order of being, i.e. the Devil, Ruler
of the World, who owed his origin to the Mother's *grief*, and
Beelzebul (Βεελзεβούλ), Ruler of the demons, who was produced
from the Mother's *perplexity.* Irenaeus, as we have seen, *supra*,
refers the origin of both the Devil and the demons to *grief.* It was

[133]

Beelzebul, perhaps, who was the principle of evil, and Irenaeus may have confused the beliefs in regard to the two. The evil principle—as a personification—is not mentioned in our treatise, but there seems to be an allusion to his subversive activities on LI.

4. Referring to the incidents recorded on XXVIII and XXXVII.

5. The present page—which is missing from the Codex—is taken from Woide's transcript, and at first sight it might be thought that the title προτογεννητωρ = *First-begetter* is a mis-spelling of προτογενητος = *First-begotten*. But on XLII–XLIII, and LII—of which we possess the originals—προτογεννητωρ is repeated three times, and on LII, the First-begetter is also designated First-begotten. As will appear later, the double title denotes a double rôle. As the third of the great Beings produced for the organization of the lower cosmos, the First-begetter Son fills the place of the psychic Christ, son of the Demiurge postulated by the Valentinians (Iren. I, i, 13, and § 47, *Excerpt. ex Theodot.*). Cf. also note 1, *supra*. Our treatise, however, derives him from the Mother directly, not through the psychic Demiurge. Another point is to be noted. In our treatise, certain creative acts are attributed to this Being, in his rôle of *First-begetter*, that in the Valentinian cosmology are referred to the Demiurge. These variants give him a greater significance and importance in the system than is possessed by the somewhat indefinite psychic Christ of Valentinus. As in the case of the Autopator (note 3, *supra*), this additional significance may be due, in part, to the necessity felt by the originators of the system of laying emphasis on repetition and reflection throughout the successive states and spaces. As First-begotten Son of the Mother (LII), he represents the third or *begotten* grade of being, in which respect he has the Monogenes as his prototype, while his title of First-begetter has relation to his work of creation in the lower cosmos, in which connection he again reflects the Monogenes *through whom all things were made*. As regards his later association with the third manifestation of the Christ—the Saviour of the world—the First-begotten Son has, as his immediate antecedent, the Fruit of the Aeons, who was anointed by the Monogenes, and who represented the second manifestation of the Christ (*vide* notes 4 and 5, XXVII, and note 1, XXXIII). In both cases the idea seems to be that a body was formed of the elements of the region, to serve later as a vehicle for the particular manifestation of the Christ. According to the Valentinians, the anointing of the Saviour who represents the third and earthly manifestation took place after his baptism in Jordan, when the Name of the Son, i.e. the Power of the Monogenes, descended upon him (§ 26, *Excerpt. ex Theodot.*). The baptism itself—in the view of these Gnostics—implied *regeneration*, and was required by the Saviour to release

him from the deficiency inherent in his nature, owing to the origin
of his substance from the Mother (latter part of § 22, *Excerpt. ex
Theodot.*). But with the career of the Saviour in the world of men
our treatise is not at present concerned. On the next page (XLII),
and again on LII, we are told that the First-fruits and authority
of Sonship were bestowed on the First-begetter by the Mother,
meaning that he was constituted in the likeness of the Triple-
Power, and had authority to deal with the three principles in her
creation.

    6. Perhaps intended for τριδυναμος = *Triple-powered One.*

XLI

W. p. 106

C.S. p. 31

And she gave him the First-fruits (απαρχη) of the Sonship, whereby he was enabled to become triple-powered (τριδυναμος). And he received the promise of Sonship [1], through which the Universe was restored [2]. And he took upon him the assemblage (αγων) entrusted to him, and he raised up all the uncommingled ('ιλικρινες) Matter ('ηλη = 'υλη) [3], and he made it as a world (κοσμος) and an aeon (αιων) and a city (πολις), this same which is called, saying: "Incorruptible" (αφθαρσια), and "Jerusalem" ('ιερουσαλημ). Again it is called, saying: "The New Earth", and again, saying: "Self-complete" (αυτοτελης). And again it is called, saying: "Unruled" (αβασιλευτος) [4]. And this Earth, moreover, is a god-bearer and a life-giver [5]. This same it is for which the Mother prayed (αιτι) that it might be set up. For this she appointed precept and order (ταξις), and in this Earth placed Providence (προνοια) and Love (αγαπη). This is the Earth in relation to which it has been written, saying: "The Earth drinks the water of rain multitudes of times" [6], that is to say: it increases Light within it innumerable times from its going out to its coming in. This is the (Earth) in relation to which it has been written (of) the man: "endowed with senses" (αισθητος) [7], and he was moulded (τυπου) and made after the pattern (τυπος) of this Earth.

1. Can also be read: "*And he took the vow of Sonship*". There is perhaps an allusion here to his future association with the third manifestation of the Christ, the Redeemer of the world.

2. In the belief of our Gnostics, the restoration of the entire cosmos was wrought through the agency of the Triple-Power of Sonship operating in the three divisions.

3. 'υλη. As remarked in note 3, XXVIII, in our treatise this word stands for undifferentiated *stuff*. Both psychic and hylic substances were regarded by the Gnostics as *material*. By *uncommingled* or *pure* matter seems intended the psychic element un-

mixed with the grosser hylic in which Evil manifests itself   XLII
(*vide* XLIV–XLV).   MS. f. 118ᴿ

4. Literally: *without king*, and meaning *free*. All the foregoing   C.S. p. 32
are Valentinian designations for the psychic element in the
cosmos. Cf. note 1, XXXI, and note 1, XXXIV.

5. Cf. XXXI.

6. Heb. vi, 7: "*the Earth that drinketh in the rain which cometh often
upon it*".

7. Literally: the man *sensible*. From αἰσθάνομαι = *to perceive by
means of senses*. In the use of our Coptic writer, αἰσθητός appears
to stand for *sensible*, i.e. *endowed with senses*. The passage is difficult;
I give what appears to me to be the meaning. Examination of the
context shows that with the difference in position of one word, the
sentence in point is identical in construction with a preceding one:
"*This is the Earth in relation to which, etc.*", and with a succeeding
one: "*This is the Crown in relation to which, etc.*" (XLIII), all three
being contained in one paragraph. It was a habit with the Copts
thus to repeat the form of their sentences. Each sentence contains
a citation, but in the case of the one under consideration, the
source—perhaps some Gnostic text—is unknown. Hence some
uncertainty in translating. The theme of the discourse is the
psychic Earth, by which these Gnostics intended the psychic component of the cosmos. Some of their schools of philosophic thought
regarded the psyche, i.e. the *soul*, as the principle of sensation, that
is to say, the principle, in man, that apprehends by means of
senses. A passage in Irenaeus—dealing with Valentinian beliefs
concerning the constitution of man—seems to throw light on the
passage. After speaking of the three principles in the universe, i.e.
the pneumatic, the psychic, and the hylic, and forecasting the
destiny of each, Irenaeus continues: "[*They say that*] *the spiritual
[element] has been sent forth to be here united to the psychical and so be
given form, and be trained along with it in its sojourning [here]....For
the psychic [element] is trained by means of senses* (αἰσθητῶν παιδευ-
μάτων). *And on this account, so they say, the world was prepared*"
(Iren. I, i, 11). Also *ibid.* II, xxxi, 1: "*That which is spiritual was sent
forth imperfect, and required to descend into a soul, that in it it might obtain
form, and thus be perfected, and rendered fit for the reception of perfect
rationality*".

XLIII
MS. f. 118ᵛ
C.S. p. 33

(XLII) This same (Earth) it is that was made whole by the Protogenitor (πρωτογενητωρ) by his (XLIII) own power[1]. For the sake of this work the Father of the Universes[2]—the Endless One (αλεκτος = αληκτος)—sent a Crown, the Name[3] of these Universes being in it, whether (ειτε) boundless (απεραντος), or (ειτε) unutterable (α‘ρητος), or (ειτε) uncontainable (αχωρητος), or (ειτε) incorruptible (αφθαρτος), or (ειτε) unknowable (αγνωστος), or (ειτε) still (ηρεμος), or (ειτε) all-powered (παντοδυναμος), or (ειτε) indivisible. This is the Crown in relation to which it has been written, saying: "It was given to Solomon (σολομων) on the Day of the joy of his heart"[4].

And again, the Primordial Monad (μονας) sent[5] an ineffable Vesture, which is wholly light, wholly life, and wholly upraising (αναστασις), wholly love (αγαπη), wholly hope (‘ελπις), and wholly faith (πιστις), wholly wisdom (σοφια), wholly gnosis (γνωσις), wholly truth (αληθια), and wholly peace (ειρηνη). It is wholly all-manifest (παντηλως = πανδηλος), and wholly all-womb (πανμητωρ), wholly all-mystery (πανμυστηριον), wholly all-source (πανπηγη), and wholly all-perfect (παντελιος). It is wholly invisible (α‘ορατος), and wholly unknowable (αγνωστος), wholly boundless (απεραντος), and wholly unutterable (α‘ρητος). It is wholly depth (βαθος), wholly uncontainable (αχωρητος), and wholly fullness (πληρωμα).

XLIII
MS. f. 118ᵛ
C.S. p. 33

1. The Protogenitor Son was produced by the Mother in the likeness of the Monogenes of Triple-Power. As far as she was able she endowed him with similar powers and privileges (cf. *First-fruits of the Sonship of Triple-Power*, XLII and LII). His work seems to be the organization of the psychic element in the lower cosmos. The statement, that by his power he brings deliverance to this *Earth*, refers to his raising up the pure psychic *matter* (*vide* XLII), and freeing it from the grosser material elements of the world.

2. As stated in note 1, I, the implication of the Coptic term— XLIII
here translated *universes*—is *wholes* or *wholenesses*. The theme of the MS. f. 118ᵛ
present passage is illustrative of this meaning, the task of the C.S. p. 33
Protogenitor being to unify the scattered psychic elements of the
creation and form them into a *whole*, i.e. a *world*, an *aeon*, or a *city*
(cf. XLII). This work is crowned by the Father of the *Wholes*.
The reference, *infra*, to the crowning of King Solomon on the day
of his espousals seems intended to reflect the same idea, by presenting the state of union as the perfect state.

3. The *name* of the Universes is the distinguishing characteristic
of each.

4. Cf. Cant. iii, 11: "*Go forth ye daughters of Sion and see King
Solomon in the diadem wherewith his mother crowned him on the day of his
espousals, on the day of the joy of his heart*".

5. The pronoun of the 3rd pers. sing. masc. gen. stands here.
It can relate either to the Protogenitor or his work, both being
nouns of masc. gen. in Coptic. More probably it is the unified
Earth that is both crowned and endowed with potentialities
through the investing Power sent from above.

It is wholly silence (σιγη), wholly unmoved (ασα-λευτος), wholly uncreated (αγεννητος), and wholly all-still (πανηρεμος). It is wholly a monad (μονας), wholly an ennead ('εννας), and wholly a dodecad (δωδεκας), wholly an ogdoad ('ογδοας), wholly a decad (δεκας), and wholly a hebdomad ('εβδομας), wholly a hexad (εξας), wholly a pentad (πεντας), and wholly a tetrad (τετρας), wholly a triad (τριας), wholly a dyad (δυας), and wholly a unit (μονας). And all things are in it, and again, all things discovered themselves therein, and they knew themselves therein: and from its own ineffable Light it gave Light to them all. And there was given to (the Vesture) myriads upon myriads of powers (δυναμις), so that at one and the same time it should set up the universe. And it gathered its garments (ενδυμα) together, making them after the fashion of a veil (κατα-πετασμα) on every side surrounding it. And it spread itself over all, and raised up all, and divided (διακρινε) them all, in accordance (κατα) with order (ταξις), and in accordance (κατα) with precept, and in accordance (κατα) with forethought (προνοια).

(XLIV) Then (τοτε) that-which-is was separated from that-which-is-not, and that-which-is-not is the Evil (κακια) which appeared (XLV) in Matter ('υλη) ¹. And the Investing Power (δυναμις) separated those-who-are from those-who-are-not, and called those-who-are: "Eternal" (αιωνιος), and those-who-are-not: "Matter" ('υλη). And it separated in the midst those-who-are from those-who-are-not, and placed veils (καταπετασμα) between them. And it laid down purifying powers, so that they shall purify and cleanse (καθαριзε) themselves, and in this manner it gave precept to those-who-are ².

And it placed the Mother as head ³, and gave to her ten Aeons (αιων), there being a myriad Powers (δυναμις) in each aeon (αιων), and a monad (μονας) and an ennead ('εννας) in each aeon (αιων). And it placed within her a Universal Womb (πανμητωρ), and it gave to her a Power so that she shall lay the same hidden within it, and that none shall know of it ⁴. And it placed therein a great Rule (κανουν = κανων), with Three Powers (δυναμις) standing to it, an unbegotten (Power) (αγεννητος), an unmoved (Power) (ασαλευτος), and the great uncommingled (Power) ('ιλικρινες). And twelve other (Powers) were given to (the Rule), these being crowned and surrounding it. Again, seven others, Leaders (στρατηλατης), were given to it. These had the All-perfect (παντελιος) Seal (σφραγις), and (XLVI) on their heads a Crown with twelve adamantine (αδαμαντος) Stones therein, which are derived from Adamas (αδαμας), the Man of Light ⁵.

1. This is the only occurrence in the treatise of the word κακία. On several later occasions, however, we meet the inference that *evil* is inherent in *matter*, *vide* LI, LII, LIII and LIV. In these particular instances *matter* appears to be regarded as synony-

XLV
MS. f. 120ᵛ
C.S. p. 35

mous with evil, the intention being, of course, the gross hylic element, as distinguished from the psychic, which was also part of the totality of the *materia* of the world (cf. note 3, XXVIII). The views of our Gnostics and the Valentinians on the nature of evil were touched on in note 6, XIX. Their belief that evil was inherent in matter formed one of their principal points of divergence from orthodox Christian doctrine, which held that evil is not necessary in the constitution of things. There is no indication in our treatise to show how the association between evil and matter came about, or whether one is prior to the other. But in all probability, the views of the School coincided with those of Valentinus. In his system, the belief that evil is inherent in matter and that all the matter of the universe was produced from the substance and afflictions of the Sophia, involved the consequence that evil was antecedent to matter, and in the nature of the Sophia herself. This meant that evil was not, in itself, a positive thing, but of the nature of a *deficiency*, the matter which was produced from the substance and transmuted afflictions of the Mother necessarily sharing in the deficiency pertaining to its source. Hence we get the definitions: "*those-who-are-not* (are called) *Matter*", and "*that-which-is-not is the Evil which appeared in Matter*".

2. By the power of the Vesture, a separation was effected between the two grades of the *materia* of the universe, "*those-which-are*", i.e. the psychic entities, and *that-which-is*, i.e. the psychic substance—which had the potentiality of salvation—being set apart from all that was solely of the grosser hylic element—which is doomed to destruction—provision also being made for the purification of the former. In the system of Valentinus, this separation of the psychic and hylic substances is attributed to the Demiurge (*vide* Iren. I, i, 9, and § 48, *Excerpt. ex Theodot.*). The distinctions and divisions in quality and grade existing between the various substances of the cosmos have already received notice in the treatise. It will be useful, however, at this point, to review the manner in which the three principles and three regions are defined and delimited. In the world *Within*, there is one principle only, the *pneumatic*. In the place of the *Midst*, there are two, the *pneumatic* and the *psychic*. In the world *Without*, all three are present—*pneumatic*, *psychic* and *hylic*. Comparison of correlative passages in our treatise and Valentinian sources make it evident that besides these initial distinctions between the three principles, there was a further division into qualities or grades among the principles themselves. The pneumatic substance was of masculine or feminine quality (*vide* note 3, XXVIII, and latter part of note 5, XXXVIII). The psychic, being the mean between spirit and gross matter, was divided into the Right-hand and the

Left-hand, i.e. the good and the bad, according to whether the entities concerned made alliance with spiritual things above, or with material things below (cf. note 4, XXVIII). As to the hylic substance—the whole of which was doomed to destruction—it is clear, from what Irenaeus says about the composition of man's physical body as formed by the Demiurge, that this was also regarded as of two grades or qualities—*a moist and flowing matter* (κεχυμένου καὶ ῥευστοῦ τῆς ὕλης) which was invisible, and *a dry earth* (ξηρᾶς γῆς), the solid visible matter of the physical world (Iren. i, i, 10; cf. also, latter part of note 5, L).

XLV
MS. f. 120ᵛ
C.S. p. 35

3. After effecting a separation of the psychic and gross hylic elements (*vide supra*), the Investing Power confirms the various beings in their spheres of operation in the lower cosmos. The Mother—representing the pneumatic principle—is head in the world *Without*, thus corresponding in position to God the Father in the world *Within*.

4. That which was hidden in the παυμήτωρ is the feminine spiritual seed, conceived by the Mother after her vision of the Angels who appeared with the Saviour (*vide* note 3, XL). We meet here a slight variation from the Valentinian version. Irenaeus tells us that the Demiurge—whose principal work was the creation of mankind—was in ignorance of the existence of that seed of his Mother which she brought forth as the result of her contemplation of the Angels, and which was, like herself, of feminine spiritual nature. This seed she deposited in him "*without his knowing it*", so that by his instrumentality it might be infused into "*that psychic offspring that was engendered by himself, and be carried in this material body as in a womb, and there be made to grow and be fitted for the reception of perfect rationality* (τελείου [λόγου])" (Iren. i, i, 10). Being of psychic nature only, the Demiurge could have no personal cognizance of the spiritual seed deposited in his substance by the Mother. The Ophites held similar views in regard to the creation of mankind (Iren. i, xxviii). The reception of *perfect rationality*, for which the spiritual seed is to be prepared in the psychic body, relates to the ultimate destiny of the pneumatici, who, at the final consummation, are to be united to their syzygies, the male Angels, and thus become complete intelligible *Aeons* (αἰῶνες νοεροί) (§64, *Excerpt. ex Theodot.*).

5. These statements about the Seven Leaders and Adam are again reminiscent of Valentinian notions. The στρατηλάται belonging to the κανών are probably Powers presiding over the various orders in the creation. In the Valentinian story, the cradle of creation was the Hebdomad, the sevenfold realm of the Demiurge, who imagined that he created all things by himself, whereas in reality he made them through the power of the

[143]

XLV
MS. f. 120ᵛ
C.S. p. 35

Mother. Irenaeus says: "*He made also Seven Heavens, over which, they say, he, the Demiurge, is.... They say, further, that these Seven Heavens are intelligences, and suppose them to be Angels, and the Demiurge himself an Angel like unto God. Also that Paradise is above the third Heaven, and they say that a fourth Angel exercises power there, and that from this great one, Adam received light whilst in intercourse with him*" (I, i, 9).

And (the Investing Power) set up the Propator (προπατωρ) in the Aeons (αιων) of the Mother of all things
('ολων), granting him all the authority (εξουσια) of
Fatherhood, and giving to him powers to cause that he
be obeyed as ('ως) Father, and as ('ως) First Father of
all those that had come into existence¹. And it gave to
him, upon his head, a Crown of Twelve kinds (γενος),
and a Power (δυναμις) which was triple-powered (τριδυναμος) and all-powered (παντοδυναμος). It bestowed on him the Sonship, and gave to him myriads
upon myriads of glories, and it turned him to the
Pleroma (πληρωμα). It granted him authority (εξουσια) to make all things to quicken and to die², and it
gave to him a Power (δυναμις) from the Aeon (αιων)
called "Solmistos" (σολμιστος), concerning which the
Aeons (αιων) all enquire, saying: "From whence did
it appear?"³ And there were given to him and to the
Aeons (αιων) that belong to him, myriads upon myriads
of glories.

XLVI
MS. f. 122ᴿ
C.S. p. 36

1. The Forefather—counterpart of the Demiurge in the system
of Valentinus—was the first of the entities to be produced by the
Mother when organizing her creation (*vide* XL–XLI). He is now
confirmed in his sphere of action by the Investing Power. We learn
from Iren. I, i, 9 and 13, and Hippol. vi, 32, that when the three
kinds of substance—pneumatic, psychic and hylic—had been
made available for her use, the Mother first of all attempted to
give form and shape to the pneumatic substance, that is, the
spiritual seed conceived by her after her vision of the Saviour's
angels. This she failed to do, because it was of the same feminine
and deficient nature as herself, and lacking in the formative male
principle (cf. note 5, XXXVIII). She then turned her attention
to the psychic substance. With this she was able to deal, and it is
to be inferred—from her subsequent actions—that in shaping it,
she again had the future of her spiritual progeny in view. It is
clear—from Hippol. vi, 32, and Iren. I, i, 10—that after the transmutation, by the Saviour, of the Mother's afflictions, etc., there
were two separate creations of psychic substance, the one being
produced from her *fear* and the other from her *conversion*. It was

XLVI
MS. f. 122ᴿ
C.S. p. 36

out of the latter that she fashioned the Demiurge, who was to be her principal agent in the work of creation. *Vide* Iren. I, i, 10: "*the Demiurge they describe as owing his origin to conversion, but all other psychic substances they ascribe to fear*". Again, *ibid.* 9: "*She first formed out of psychic substance him who is Father and King of all things . . . [he then] formed all things which came into existence after him, being unwittingly moved thereto by his Mother*". We next learn that he first created Seven Heavens—that is, his own realm, the Hebdomad—and angels and archangels. Then that he fashioned the world, the elements of which had been produced from the Mother's afflictions (cf. note 5, XXXVIII). Following this, he made man, and it was at this point that the Mother's scheme for her formless spiritual progeny came into effect. The Demiurge had power over the psychic element of the creation, it being of the same order of nature as himself, and over the hylic which was below him. But of all that was of spiritual nature and higher than himself—including his Mother and her spiritual seed—he was without cognizance, and he believed himself to be God and Father of all. Taking advantage of his ignorance, the Mother deposited in him her spiritual seed, so that, being infused into the psychic substance that was to proceed from himself, it might, by his instrumentality, acquire form, and attain some measure of completeness in the souls he created (Iren. I, i, 10, and II, xxviii). The Gnostics held that the psychic substance was of a corporeal nature—a refined sort of matter—consequently, a soul had a definite bodily form. In this way the spiritual substance, on being united to the psychic, could "*assume shape, and being carried in this material body, as in a womb—the two elements being simultaneously subjected to the same discipline—it might be made to grow, and in time be fitted for the reception of perfect rationality*" (*ibid.* I, i, 10 and 11, and II, xxxi, 1). In I, i, 9–10, Irenaeus tells us that after having formed the world, the Demiurge "*fashioned the earthy [part of] man, taking him, not from the dry earth, but from an invisible substance of moist and flowing matter*", after which he breathed into him the psychic part of his nature. And finally he was enveloped all round with a covering of skin. This was the psychic man, formed by his inspiration, and who—without any knowledge on the part of his fashioner—"*was rendered a spiritual man through the simultaneous inspiration received from the Sophia*". And (*ibid.*): "*this then is the sort of man they conceive of, having indeed his soul from the Demiurge, the body from the earth, and the flesh from matter, but the spiritual man from the Mother*" (cf. also § 50, *Excerpt. ex Theodot.*). But the true nature and significance of the works of his hands were unknown to the Demiurge. Irenaeus says: "*He formed the heavens, yet was ignorant of the heavens. He fashioned man, yet knew not man. He brought to light the earth, yet had no acquaintance with the earth....He knew not even of the existence of his own Mother, but imagined that he himself was all things"* (I, i, 9). And (*ibid.* 10): "*as he was ignorant of his Mother, so also he knew not her offspring*". In this state of ignorance, Irenaeus says, the Demiurge remained until the coming of the Saviour, when he "*learned all things from him, and gladly, with all his powers, joined himself to him*" (*ibid.* 13). By the *Saviour* is here intended the psychic Christ, who—in this particular version of the story—was produced by the Demiurge as his own son, and whose body was later assumed by the Saviour of the world. This *son* was of the same psychic substance as his father, but, possessing the spiritual inspiration from the Sophia, was cognizant of spiritual matters, and thus wiser than his father (*vide* Iren. I, i, 13, and § 47, *Excerpt. ex Theodot.*). He corresponds to the Protogenitor Son of the Mother in the cosmology of our treatise. The above is the Valentinian version of the story. Although but few details are given, the germ of all these notions is to be traced in the matter of the present and three succeeding pages of the treatise; e.g. the Forefather is the first being to be produced in the lower cosmos (XLVII). He is given authority of Fatherhood in the Mother's Aeon and over the whole creation (XLVI, XLVIII and XLIX). The Powers necessary to produce living things are placed at his disposal (XLVI and XLVII). He fashions his own Aeon (the psychic realms), and is given angels and archangels (XLVIII). He has power in the material aeon (XLVI and XLVIII), although—in the system of this treatise—he is not the creator of the diversified kinds and species of that world. Again, his self-supposed autocracy and independence are expressed by his titles αὐτοθέλητος and αὐτοδόξαστος (XLVII). The manner in which the Forefather obtains knowledge of his true status, and a realization of his responsibility towards the spiritual souls of which he was—unwittingly—the father, is differently accounted for in our treatise. There is no evidence that he produced a son who instructed him—indeed such a being could have no place in this particular cosmogony—nor is it suggested that the counterpart of his son—the Protogenitor Son of the Mother—comes to his aid. We learn, however, that the Sonship is bestowed on him; this might bring about his enlightenment as to his own standing, and also make him cognizant of the third principle in the creation. At the same time, so we are told, he is himself *turned to the Pleroma* (XLVI). His subsequent care for the spiritual souls, and his collaboration with the Divine purpose, are particularized on XLIX. Returning to the teaching of the Valentinians on the subject of the Demiurge, we find that many more creative acts are attributed to him than to the Forefather in the system of our treatise. In § 47, *Excerpt. ex Theodot.*, we are told that through the Demiurge

XLVI
MS. f. 122ᴿ
C.S. p. 36

XLVI
MS. f. 122ᴿ
C.S. p. 36

"*the heavenly and the earthly things were made*". Also that of him it was said: "*The Spirit of God brooded over the waters*". Again, in § 48, that he made wild animals and the elements of the world (cf. also Iren. I, i, 10). It is also stated (*ibid.* 13–14) that besides the type of man originated—as we have seen above—with a spiritual soul, other types were created by the Demiurge. It must here be recalled that after the transmutation of the Mother's afflictions, there were two distinct creations of psychic substance—the one from her *conversion,* and the other from her *fear* (*vide* note 5, XXXVIII). From the first the Demiurge originated, and through him, and from his substance, the psychic man who was possessed of a spiritual soul (cf. also Hippol. VI, 34). From the second creation— that was from *fear*—were made "*the souls of irrational creatures, of wild animals, and of men*" (Iren. I, i, 10). Thus in regard to the creation of the human race, Irenaeus says: "*They conceive, then, of three kinds of men, spiritual, psychical, and hylical, corresponding to Cain, Abel, and Seth*". This category was adopted also by the Sethian School (Iren. I, xxviii, 5, and Hippol. V, 20). In our treatise, these creative acts—apart from the production of the psychic race of men originated with spiritual souls—are attributed to the Protogenitor (*vide* LIII).

2. Cf. § 50, *Excerpt. ex Theodot.*: "...*man*...*into whom he breathed, and gave him something of his own nature. He called this—in so far as it was invisible and incorporeal—the breath of Life*". § 58, *ibid.,* and a passage in Clem. Alex. (*Strom.* IV, 89, 4), make the Demiurge to be the originator of death. The meaning seems to be that the particular kinds of living beings produced by him were by nature subject to death.

3. The Aeon Solmistos must be the visible globe of matter, of which—according to the Valentinians—the Demiurge was the fashioner. The enquiry of the entities of the unseen psychical world: "*from whence did it appear?*" suggests the sudden appearance of a novel form of manifestation. In I, i, 9, when describing the operations of the Demiurge in fashioning the Earth, Irenaeus uses the term δεδειχέναι (δείκνυμι = *to display, to bring to light*). Also in § 48, *Excerpt. ex Theodot.,* we learn that in creating Light, the Demiurge "*made things manifest*". The word Solmistos may conceivably be compounded of σόλος = *spherical mass of mineral matter,* and μέγιστος, superlative of *great.*

(XLVI) The Power (δυναμις) moreover (μεν = μην), that was given to the Propator (προπατωρ) is called, saying: "First-manifest" (προτοφανης), because it is he (XLVII) who appeared first. And he is called, saying: "Unbegotten" (αγεννητος) ¹, because he was made of none. Again he is called, saying: "The Unspeakable", and "The Nameless One"². And again he is called, saying: "Self-alone-begotten" (αυτογενης), and again, "Self-alone-willed" (αυτοθελητος), because through his will he appeared. And he is called, saying: "Self-alone-glorified" (αυτοδοξαστος), because with his own glories he appeared, and again, saying: "Invisible", because he is hidden, and they see him not³.

And (the Investing Power) gave to him another Power, the same which made manifest the Spark from the Beginning, in the Self-same Place⁴: this which is called by the holy and All-perfect (παντελειος) Names, and which is: "The Prōtia" (πρωτια), that is to say, "The Foremost". And it is called, saying: "Pandia" (πανδια), that-which-*IS*-in-all, and again, saying: "Pangenia" (παγγενια), that-which-begetteth-all. Again it is called, saying: "Doxogenia" (δοξογενια), because it is the Begetter of Glory, and again, saying: "Doxophania" (δοξοφανια), because it is the Revealer of Glory. And again it is called, saying: "Doxokratia" ([δοξο]κρατια) ⁵, because it ruleth over Glory, and again, saying: "Arsenogenia"(αρσογενια = αρσενογενια), because it is the Begetter of Males. (XLVIII) And again it is called, saying: "Loia" (λωια), which interpreted is: "God-with-us", and again, saying: "Iouēl" (ιουηλ), which interpreted is: "God-unto-everlasting".

XLVII
MS. f. 122ᵛ
C.S. p. 37

1. He was not *begotten*, but fashioned from the psychic substance of the universe, by the Mother—*by herself alone* (*vide infra*, αυτο-γενης). The Valentinians named him 'Απάτωρ = *without male progenitor* (Iren. 1, i, 9).

2. He was in the likeness of the Supreme Father, of whom—according to his degree and grade—he reflects the attributes.

3. He was made of the invisible psychic substance.

4. The *Self-same Place* is the *Universal Womb* which is in the Indivisible (*vide* XVIII). It contained the Ennead of Powers that relate to all creative processes. The names of the Ennead are repeated below.

5. The word standing in the text is αρτοκρατια, but the interpretation which follows, and a comparison with the earlier list of names on XVIII, indicate that δοξοκρατια is intended.

And (δε) that which[1] called on these Powers (δυναμις) to appear, is named, saying: "Phania" (φανια), which interpreted is, "The Manifestation". And the Angel (αγγελος)[2] who appeared with them is by the Glories named: "Doxogenes" (δοξογενης), and "Doxophanes" (δοξοφανης), which interpreted is, "of-Glory-begotten", and "of-Glory-revealed", he being one of these Glories that stand around the great Power (δυναμις) who is called "Lord-of-Glory" (δοξοκρατωρ), because, when he was manifested, he ruled over the great Glories[3].

These are the powers (δυναμις) which were given to the Propator (προπατωρ) when he was placed in the Aeon (αιων) of the Mother. And myriads upon myriads of glories were given him, and angels (αγγελος) and archangels (αρχαγγελος) and ministers (λιτουργος), so that the things of Matter ('υλη) shall be serviceable (διακονι) to him. And authority (εξουσια) was given him over all things, and he made for himself a mighty Aeon (αιων), and in it he placed a great Pleroma (πληρωμα) and a great Sanctuary ('ιερον).

---

1. *The Investing Power. Vide* XLIII *et seq.*
2. The *Angel* is the Saviour. He was so called by the Valentinians, because, as Fruit of the Whole Pleroma, endowed with the powers of all the Aeons, he was sent forth as *Messenger* to the aid of the Mother (§ 35, *Excerpt. ex Theodot.*).
3. The *Lord of Glory* is the Monogenes. The *great Glories* are the Aeons of the Pleroma.

XLIX
MS. f. 124ᵛ
C.S. p. 39

(XLVIII) And all the Powers (δυναμις) that he had (XLIX) received he placed within it, and he rejoiced together with them, whilst regenerating his creation in accordance with (κατα) the bidding of the Father who is hidden in the Silence—the One who sent to him these riches. And the Crown of Fatherhood was bestowed on him, and he was appointed father of those that after him had come into existence ¹. Then (τοτε) did he cry aloud and say: "My children! with whom I am in travail until the Christ (χς) be formed (μορφη) in you". And again he cried out, saying: "I make ready, now (γαρ), a holy Virgin (παρθενος), to set beside (παρ'ιστα) one only Husband, Christ (χς)" ². But seeing now (αλλα επιδη) the Grace (χαρις) with which the Hidden Father had endowed him, the Propator (προπατωρ) himself desired to turn the Universe unto the Hidden Father— because (the Father's) Will is this, to cause the Universe to turn itself to him ³.

And when the Mother saw these wonders that to her Propator (προπατωρ) were given, with joy exceeding great did she rejoice, and because of this she said: "My heart is joyful and my tongue is glad"⁴. Then she cried out upon the Boundless (απεραντος) Power, the same that standeth with the Hidden Aeon (αιων) of the Father⁵, who is of the great Powers (δυναμις) of Glory, and who among the Glories is called: "Thrice-born

L

(τριγενιθλος)—that is to say, (L) the One who was brought forth three times—and again, saying: "Thrice-begotten" (τριγενης) ⁶: and yet again, saying: "Hermes" ('αρμης = ερμης?) ⁷.

XLIX
MS. f. 124ᵛ
C.S. p. 39

1. Irenaeus states that the Demiurge "*formed all that came into being after himself, being unwittingly moved thereto by his Mother*" (i, i, 9).
2. Cf. Gal. iv, 19: "*My little children, of whom I am in travail again, till the Christ be formed in you*". Also, II Cor. xi, 2: "*For I have*

espoused you to one husband, that I may present you as a chaste virgin to XLIX
Christ". The Valentinians held that at the beginning of his career, MS. f. 124ᵛ
the Demiurge was in ignorance of the existence of the spiritual C.S. p. 39
seed hidden in his substance by the Mother, and, through his
instrumentality, infused into the psychic substance out of which he
made the souls of men (*vide* note 1, XLVI). When, later, he learned
about this matter, he joined with all his powers in the work of
salvation. They further taught that he will continue to administer
the affairs of the world as long as is needful, more particularly
exercising a care over the Church (Iren. 1, i, 13). The Gnostics of
the School of Heracleon (*Fragments of Heracleon* (frg. 8), "Texts
and Studies", edit. Armitage Robinson), together with the Valentinians whose doctrines are recorded in the *Excerpt. ex Theodot.*,
regarded John the Baptist as typifying the Demiurge. The latter
school called the Demiurge "*the Friend of the Bridegroom*", who will
see his work accomplished when, at the final consummation, the
Mother, with the spiritual Seed, will pass through the Boundary
into the Pleroma, which is the *Bride-chamber*. In 1, i, 12, Irenaeus
says that when all the Seed shall have been brought to perfection,
the Mother will pass from the place of the *Midst* and enter the
Pleroma, where she will receive as her Spouse the Saviour, who
sprang from all the Aeons. The spiritual Seed will also enter with
her, after having laid aside their *psychic* bodies—i.e. the souls they
had from the Demiurge. They will then be bestowed as brides on the
Angels who came with the Saviour. Similar information is given
in §§ 63–5, *Excerpt. ex Theodot.*, where the matter is concluded as
follows: "*The Friend of the Bridegroom standing before the throne is
filled with joy at the voice of the Bridegroom, he has fullness of joy and
rest*". This has relation to the future state and dwelling-place of
the Demiurge, who, after the Mother and the Seed have entered
the Pleroma, will move up from the Hebdomad and take the place
vacated by the Mother, that is, at the Boundary, which is the antechamber of the Pleroma, this being the highest region to which a
purely psychic being can attain. With the above quotation from
the *Excerpt. ex Theodot.* must be compared John iii, 29: "*John
answered and said:...He that hath the Bride is the Bridegroom; but the
Friend of the Bridegroom, who standeth and heareth him, rejoiceth with joy
because of the Bridegroom's voice. This my joy therefore is fulfilled*".

3. On XLVI it is stated that after being endowed with the
power of Sonship, the Forefather was "*turned to the Pleroma*".
Understanding now the meaning of his creative work and the
purpose of the powers bestowed on him, he joins his will to the
Divine Will in an endeavour to convert the universe to God.
From the *Fragments of Heracleon* (frg. 6, "Texts and Studies", edit.
Armitage Robinson), we get a similar view of the nature and

XLIX
MS. f. 124ᵛ
C.S. p. 39

capacity of the Demiurge, who is represented as being ignorant and blind, but not ill-disposed to faith, and as ready to implore help for the spiritual souls he had created, but was himself unable to save.

4. Ps. xv, 9 (Vulg.): "*Therefore my heart hath been glad and my tongue hath rejoiced*".

5. The *Hidden* Aeon is the Pleroma. By the *Boundless Power* is here intended the Monogenes. The preliminary processes of creation, as relating to the spiritual Seed, are now completed so far as lay in the power of the Mother, working through her Forefather in whose psychic substance the Seed had acquired a certain form and shape. It will be recalled that this spiritual substance was, in itself, deficient, being of the Mother alone. There is little to be gleaned from Irenaeus as to how this state of things is to be remedied, but from the *Excerpt. ex Theodot.* (§§ 39–40) one may infer that the enforming male principle is sent by the Logos in response to the Mother's prayer for help. This agrees with what will be found on L of our treatise, and relates to some dispensation on behalf of the spiritual Seed only, which preceded the earthly manifestation of the Saviour.

6. τριγενιθλος and τριγενης. By the threefold generation and birth, the Gnostics understood the threefold dispensation of the Logos. It may be inferred from the *Excerpt. ex Theodot.* (§§ 59–61) that the Saviour was obliged to assume the first-fruits of all he came to redeem. This appears to mean that in each of the three regions of the cosmos, the redemptive manifestation was effected in a form and manner suited to the requirements of the entities of the particular region. The manner and significance of the triple manifestation is well set forth in the teachings of the Peratae, a school allied to the Ophite and Sethian groups, and having affinities with the Valentinians. To their mode of dividing the cosmos reference has already been made on XXVIII (*vide* note 1). Clement of Alexandria mentions the Peratae, and Theodoret records some of their doctrines, but the best source is the *Ref. Haer.* of Hippolytus (v, 12). These Gnostics held that the cosmos is one, triply divided, the first portion being *unbegotten* (τὸ πρῶτον ἀγέννητον), the second, *self-alone-begotten* (τὸ δεύτερον αὐτογενές) and the third, *begotten* (τὸ τρίτον γεννητόν) (*vide* note 1, XXVIII). "*Whence*", continues Hippolytus, "*they expressly declare that there are three Gods* (θεούς), *three Words* (λόγους), *three Minds* (νοῦς), *three Men* (ἀνθρώπους). *For to each portion of the cosmos of divided parts, they assign both Gods, and Words, and Minds, and Men and the rest. And they say that from above, from the unbegotten and the first segment of the cosmos, when the last part of the cosmos had been brought to completion, there came down—for causes to be declared later—in the time of Herod, a*

certain Man called Christ, with a triple nature, a triple body, and a triple   XLIX
power, having in himself all commixtures and powers from the three   MS. f. 124^v
divisions of the cosmos. . . . Therefore, he says, Christ was brought down   C.S. p. 39
from above, from the unbegotten, so that through his descent all things of
the three divisions should be saved". The belief in a plural manifestation of the Logos is an element in the Hermetic tradition, but
the particular development which the doctrine reached in the
minds of the Gnostics seems necessitated by their views regarding
the nature, constitution and needs of the cosmos. And in all probability, in framing their speculations, they were influenced by a
desire of adapting to their own particular purpose the normal
Christian mystical doctrine of the Triple Birth of Christ. It is
interesting to observe the forms under which this doctrine persists
at the present day, both in orthodox and unorthodox circles. In
the Catholic Church, the Threefold Birth is commemorated in
the custom, dating, according to Durandus (*Rationale Divin. Offic.*,
p. 419), from A.D. 142, of celebrating three Masses on Christmas
Day. These Masses, at midnight, at dawn, and in the morning,
are considered by liturgical writers to be mystically connected with
the Triple Birth of Christ; the first commemorating the eternal
generation of the Son in the bosom of the Father; the second, his
temporal birth on earth; the third, his spiritual birth in the heart
of man. (Cf. also *Summa Theol.* Thos. Aquin. III Q. LXXXIII, a. 2.)
Among the non-uniate Christian bodies of the East, an interesting
commemoration of this doctrine is observed in the beliefs of the
Ethiopic (Abyssinian) Church. The date of the coming of
Christianity to Ethiopia is not known, though there are indications that this occurred at an early period. The earliest definite
information concerns the first episcopal consecration in the already
existing Church. This was bestowed, in the fourth century, by the
Arian Bishop of Alexandria (Rufinus, *Historia Eccles.* 1–9, P.D.
XXI, 478–80). There is considerable evidence, however, to show
that as early as the first and second centuries there was frequent
intercourse and traffic between Ethiopia, and Syria and the Delta
of Egypt, and it is not unreasonable to suppose that Christianity
may have set foot in the country as early as that period (Art. by
Mgr E. T. Tisserant, "Äthiopien", in *Der Christliche Orient*, 1931,
pp. 18–21). If this was the case, the source of the Christian
missionary effort may well have been one or other of the many
sects that flourished in Syria and Alexandria at that date. The
Christianity of the Ethiopic Church is Monophysite, and there
are three schools within the Church, each having its own form of
the Monophysite doctrine. These three schools are the "Unionists",
the "Unctionists", and those who adhere to what is known as the
"Knife Faith". The Unionists are the recognized and official school,

[155]

XLIX
MS. f. 124ᵛ
C.S. p. 39

to which the native head of the Church and most of the clergy belong. The doctrine of the Triple Birth is taught by them in the following form: (*a*) Christ's eternal generation, by which he was the Only-begotten of the Father; (*b*) his birth from the Virgin's womb, whereby he was her First-born Son; (*c*) his spiritual generation at the baptism, by which he became the First-born of every creature. This particular interpretation of the third birth, which connects it with the Baptism in Jordan, suggests a link with the Advent doctrines of the Gnostics and certain other heretical Christian bodies. *Vide* note 1, XXXIX.

7. Only the last three letters of this word are legible. Woide's transcript gives ϩⲁⲣⲙⲏⲥ. In his revised translation of the Codex Brucianus (*Die Griech. Christl. Schrift*. Bd 1, Leipzig, 1905), Dr Carl Schmidt suggests that the word is intended for ϩⲉⲣⲙⲏⲥ. Woide's transcript is full of errors, and the ⲁ may be due to careless copying, or to the illegibility of the original. On the other hand, the Copts were notably inaccurate in their use of Greek vowels (*vide* note 2, V), and the scribe may have written ⲁ for ⲉ. The surmise that the word is intended for Hermes is supported by the fact that those Gnostic Schools that were in contact with Alexandrian thought certainly equated Hermes with Christ, also the titles *Thrice-born*, *Thrice-begotten* and *Triple-power*, occurring in our treatise, recall the well-known name of Hermes—*Thrice-greatest*. In the Greek magical papyri are found invocations and prayers to Hermes as the Logos, and Hippolytus, in the *Ref. Haer.*, points to the identification, by the Naassene School, of Hermes with the Logos and Christ. Commenting on the doctrines derived by the Gnostics from the Greeks, and by the latter from the Egyptians, Hippolytus thus quotes the Naassene teacher: "*For Hermes is Logos, . . . the utterer and fashioner of the things that have been, that are, and that will be . . .*" (Hippol. v, 7). Later, in the same chapter, the identification is made a second time.

[156]

And (the Boundless Power) itself besought the One who in all things is hidden, that he should send the Mother that which she needs¹. And the Hidden Father sent to her the Mystery (μυστηριον), this same which clothes all Aeons (αιων) and all Glories, with whom there is a Crown all-perfect (παντελης) and complete. And he laid it on the head of the great Invisible (Power) (α‘ορατος) which was hidden within her, which is incorruptible (αφθαρτος) and unbegotten (αγεννητος)². And the great Power that belongeth to (the Crown) is called: "Begetting-Males" (αρσενογενια)³. And through this the Aeons (αιων) shall all be filled with glory: and in this manner shall the Universe be crowned.

Then (the Investing-Power)⁴ set up the Aeonian (αιωνιος) Autopator (αυτοπατωρ) Father⁵, and gave to him the Aeon (αιων) of the Covering (καλυπτος)⁶, in which all things are found—the kinds (γενος) and the species, the similitudes, and the forms (μορφη), the modes, the varieties (διαφορα), and the four transmutations⁷, the number and the numbered, and the knower (νοι) and the known (νοι). And it appointed him to cause him to cover all those things that are in it, and so that (LI) he shall give to him that asks of him.

> 1. The Mother's *need* is that which shall complete her creation, i.e. the enforming *male* spiritual principle. This Mystery is sent to her by the Father, that is to say, there is a further manifestation and operation by the Monogenes, which precede the earthly manifestation of the Saviour. One may infer from passages in the *Excerpt. ex Theodot.* (§§ 2, 39 and 40), that after the creation of the bodies and souls of mankind, a σπέρμα ἀρρενικόν (male seed) was infused by the Logos into the souls of the ἐκλεκτοί (the *Chosen*). These latter are the feminine spiritual souls, offspring of the Mother *alone*. In § 40 it is stated that the Mother produced those of the Right-hand, i.e. the feminine spiritual seed, before seeking the Light, while the Seeds of the Church (σπέρματα ἐκκλησίας)—that is, the complete souls—were formed after, in consequence of an operation by *the Male* (ὁ ἄρρην).

L
MS. f. 126ᴿ
C.S. p. 40

LI

L
MS. f. 126ᴿ
C.S. p. 40

[157]

L
MS. f. 126ᴿ
C.S. p. 40

2. *Vide* XLV: "*And (the Investing Power) placed in her a Universal Womb, and it gave to her a Power so that she shall lay the same hidden within it, and that none shall know of it*". This *Power* was the spiritual Seed of feminine quality.

3. The *male* enforming principle. In § 68, *Excerpt. ex Theodot.*, it is said that while the spiritual souls remain the children of the *female alone*, they are *imperfect, helpless, foolish, feeble* and *ill-shapen*. But when the Seed has received enformation by the Saviour, it partakes of the nature of the male, and they become children of the Bride-chamber. The Gnostics claimed that they were themselves these perfected spiritual souls, and that they were superior to all others, inasmuch as a "*small particle*" from the Father of the Universe had been deposited in their souls. Also, that while still on earth they were acquainted with the Pleroma, because—though their souls were from the substance of the Demiurge—"*their indwelling man*" revealed to them the true Father (Iren. II, xxviii and xxix). Cf. also § 56, *Excerpt. ex Theodot.*: "*that which is spiritual is saved by its nature*".

4. The pronoun of the 3rd pers. fem. gen. stands here. It can relate either to the Investing Power or to the Mother. I believe the former to be intended, for the preliminary setting up of the Autopator by the Mother has already been recorded on XLI, and it would seem that, as in the case of the Mother herself, and the Forefather (*vide* XLV and XLVI), the Investing Power now brings about his establishment. Also, on LII, where the setting up of the Protogenitor Son is mentioned for the second time—this being more particularly the concern of the Mother—she is designated as the establishing Power.

5. αιωνιος and αυτοπατωρ. Both terms are used adjectivally. The Autopator was produced from the *self-alone-begotten* substance of the Mother, and is representative of the middle grade of generative modes (*vide* note 3, XLI; cf. also note 1, XXVIII). He is the ruler of the material world, i.e. the world of *form* (cf. *infra*, the *Aeon of the Covering*), and he thus equates with the Cosmokrator of the Valentinian cosmology. Irenaeus tells us that the Valentinians identified the Cosmokrator with the Devil, and called him a *spirit* of wickedness. They held also that he possessed a knowledge of what was above himself. As, however, the Church Father also states quite definitely that the Cosmokrator or Devil, and all the demons and other spirits of wickedness, owed their origin to the *material* substances formed from the Mother's *grief* and *perplexity*, πνεῦμα, as descriptive of the Cosmokrator, must be taken to signify *air, breath*, the element which—according to Irenaeus in the same passage—was formed from the consolidation of the Mother's *grief*. *Vide* Iren. I, i, 10, and note 3, XLI. In our treatise

[158]

nothing is said as to the particular element from which the Auto-   L
pator derived his being—all the underlying substances of the lower MS. f. 126ᴿ
cosmos were *self-alone-begotten* by the Mother (*vide* note 1, XXVIII). C.S. p. 40
But exact information on this subject is wanting also in the case
of the Forefather, although in regard to him the inference is clear.
As is the case with the Valentinian Cosmokrator, the Autopator has
a knowledge of what is above the world in which he is ruler, and
his particular function appears to be to assist the souls of men to
escape from their entanglement in the hylic elements of the world.
That his special concern is with these souls is perhaps confirmed
by the fact that the term αιωνιος is applied to him and to the psychic
component of the universe (*vide* XLV), and is not otherwise used
in the treatise. The rule of the Autopator Father over the Aeon of
the Covering indicates a more extended jurisdiction than is ordinarily understood by the *material* world. In the view of the Valentinians and our Gnostics, the term ὕλη covered all that was not of a
spiritual nature (*vide* note 3, XXVIII). Every other substance,
being *material*, could constitute bodily form. Hence the term:
Aeon of the Covering. Material substance was subjected to a primary
division into the psychic and hylic. These again were subdivided,
the psychic element into the Right-hand ("*those tending upwards*")
and the Left-hand ("*those tending downwards*"), and the hylic into the
"*invisible, moist and flowing matter*" (from which was formed man's
body in Paradise), and the "*dry earth*", the gross visible matter of
the world, from which was made man's fleshly body (*vide* Iren. 1, i,
9 and 10, also note 2, XLV). Included under the hylic category
were all the other constituents of the world.

6. Verbal adjective from καλύπτω, used as on IV and XL.

7. Probably the four primary elements of the earth are here intended. According to the Valentinians, these were produced from
the transmuted afflictions of the Sophia. In the system of our
treatise it is the *prayers, hymns, praises* and *supplications* of the Mother
that are thus transmuted (*vide* note 6, XXXI, and note 2, XXXVII).
Speaking of the tenets of those Gnostics whom he believed to be
followers of the School of Valentinus, Hippolytus says: "*They
declare that first of all the four elements—which they say are fire, water,
earth and air—were made through* (διά) *the Mother*" (VI, 53). Irenaeus
tells us that *earth* arose from her state of *consternation* (ἔκπληξις) (other
passages give ἀπορία = *perplexity*), *water* from the tears caused by
the agitation of her *fear*, *air* from the consolidation of her *grief*,
whilst *fire* was hidden in all these elements (*Adv. Haer.* 1, i, 10).

LI
MS. f. 126ᵛ
C.S. p. 41

And it bestowed on him ten powers (δυναμις), and nine enneads ('εννας), and a pentad (πεντας) of aeons (αιων). And luminaries (φωστηρ) were given him, and authority (εξουσια) was conferred on him over all the hidden things, so that he should freely give (χαριзε) ¹ to those who had striven (αγωνιзε). And they fled from the Matter ('υλη)² of the Aeon (αιων), leaving it behind them. And they hastened to the Aeon (αιων) of the Autopator (αυτοπατωρ), and laid hold of the promise assured them through him who spake and said ³: "Whoso shall leave father and mother, and brother and sister, and wife and child and possessions ('υπαρξις), and shall take up his Cross (στρος) and follow after me—shall receive the promises assured him ⁴. And I shall give to them the Mystery (μυστηριον) of my Father who is hidden ⁵, because they prized that which is theirs, and they fled from that which⁶ with violence constraineth them". And he gave to them of Praise and Joy, Gladness and Pleasure, Peace (ιρηνη) and Hope ('ελπις), Faith (πιστις) and Love (αγαπη), and the Truth (αληθια) unchangeable. This is the Ennead ('εννας) which was freely given

LII

(χαριзε) (LII) to those who fled from Matter ('υλη) ⁷. And they were made blessed (μακαριος) and perfect (τελιος), and they knew the true (αληθια) God. And they understood the Mystery (μυστηριον) that became Man—because for this he was manifested, till they saw *HIM* who is indeed invisible ⁸. Furthermore, because of this he wrote (λογρφη) his Word (λογος): until they knew him and fled to him: and they were deified, and perfected (τελιος).

LI
MS. f. 126ᵛ
C.S. p. 41

1. *Vide* the *Ennead, infra.*

2. Here, and *infra*, ὕλη is evidently synonymous with *evil.* Cf. note 1, XLV.

3. In these quotations from St Matthew's Gospel and the con-

text, we get the first reference—in the treatise—to the Redemption. The allusions to this subject do not give a very clear view of what our Gnostics believed in this regard, but certain points of contact can be found with Valentinian doctrine. We have seen—by reference to the Patristic records—that when the elements of the world were produced from the Mother's afflictions, there were two separate creations of the psychic substance—one from her *conversion* and the other from her *fear* (note 5, XXXVIII, and note 1, XLVI). From the former, the psychic Demiurge or Forefather was fashioned, and through him and from his substance the first race of mankind, into whose souls was first infused the feminine spiritual principle by the Mother, and later, the masculine enforming principle from the Logos. From points of detail in our treatise which agree with the Valentinian version of the story, one may infer that it is to this first spiritual race that reference is made on XLVI and XLIX. Of what was produced from the second creation of psychic substance—that originated from *fear*—we have, so far, heard nothing. Irenaeus (1, i, 9 and 10) gives us to understand that the souls of all other living creatures, including *men*, were made from this by the Demiurge. In the Valentinian cosmogony, he was—under the Mother—the sole creative agent in the lower cosmos. In our treatise, however, it seems as if his counterpart, the Forefather, is the fashioner of the world as a *whole*, and father of the first race of men, while the Protogenitor is concerned with the details of creation, and brings into existence the diversified races and species of living creatures, including the later types of mankind. As, however, we are told nothing of this until we reach LIII, we may conclude that the words of the Saviour, quoted *infra*, are addressed to the first race of men, who were originated with spiritual souls. The *Fragments* of the Gnostic teacher, Heracleon—a follower of Valentinus—supply more information than any of the other sources about the three races of men—the πνευματικοί, the ψυχικοί and the χοϊκοί—their mode of life in the world, and the manner of the redemption of the first two. The πνευματικοί—also called the ἐκλεκτοί = the *Chosen*, in contrast to the ψυχικοί, who were the κλητοί, i.e. the *Called* (*vide* Matt. xxii, 14)— are represented as having the spiritual germ of their souls imprisoned in matter, and owing to their intercourse with the wickedness in the world, their life is weak and corrupt. Thus in their first state they live in ignorance of God (frg. 19). Their spiritual nature is not, however, wholly dormant (frg. 25), being incorruptible, and of the same nature as God (frgs. 17 and 37). Thus they are secure of salvation, which does not depend on their own efforts (frgs. 19 and 37). The Saviour came to earth to rescue them, and teach them the true worship that should be offered to

LI
MS. f. 126ᵛ
C.S. p. 41

God (frgs. 17 and 19). It is these spiritual souls that at the final consummation will be given as brides to the Angels, when all together will enter the Pleroma for the great Marriage Feast (*Fragments of Heracleon*, in "Texts and Studies", vol. I, p. 4, edit. Armitage Robinson). (Cf. the words of the Forefather on XLIX of the treatise.) Irenaeus tells us that the Gnostics claimed that they were of this superior race. Their redemption consisted in an illumination of the mind, and a knowledge of the Mysteries, whereby they attained, whilst still on earth, to a perfect knowledge of God and the spiritual world. To bring them this gnosis the Saviour came to earth (Iren. I, i, 11, and *ibid.* II, xxviii and xxix). All this is in agreement with what we read, *supra*, about the escape of the souls from the Matter of the world, and *infra*, about the Mystery.

4. Matt. xix, 29: "*And everyone that hath left house, or brethren, or father, or mother, or wife, or children, or lands, for my name's sake, shall receive an hundredfold, and shall possess life everlasting*"; *ibid.* xvi, 24: "*If any man will come after me, let him deny himself and take up his cross and follow me*". Commenting on the latter passage, Irenaeus says the Gnostics understood this reference to the Cross to have been made by the Saviour in acknowledgment of the prototypal Stauros in the world above (Iren. III, xix, 4). The *Excerpt. ex Theodot.* also yield an interpretation of the passage. The Cross, which is the Sign of the Boundary of the Pleroma, effects, in the same way, a separation on earth between believers and unbelievers. Also Jesus, through the Sign upon his shoulders, raised up the spiritual seed and introduced them into the Pleroma, "*on which account, it is said: 'He that taketh not up his Cross and followeth me, is not my brother'*" (§ 42). The citing of these passages, bearing on the Saviour's work and teaching, is anticipatory, for his descent to earth has not yet been mentioned. The purpose is perhaps to mark the distinction in the manner of the redemption of the πνευματικοί and the rest of mankind who were to be saved. For on LIII–LIV, when the latter come on the scene, there is no mention of an impartation of the Mysteries, and emphasis seems to be laid on obedience to the law, and on the necessity for good conduct and for faith, which, in the case of the πνευματικοί, are not factors.

5. Cf. *Pistis Sophia* (Codex Askew.), edit. Petermann, p. 218: "[*Jesus saith unto them*]: *Now therefore, he who will receive the Mystery, renounceth the whole world, and the cares of all the Matter therein. . . . Amen, I say unto you: That Mystery is for you and for all who shall renounce the whole world and all the Matter that is in it*". Cf. also Matt. xiv, 11: "*to you it is given to know the Mysteries of the Kingdom of Heaven, but to them it is not given*". In the latter passage—in the belief of the Gnostics—the Saviour makes allusion to the two races

of men who shall be saved: the πνευματικοί, or *Chosen* race—whose redemption is brought about through a communication of the Mysteries—and the ψυχικοί, or *Called*, who could not receive the Mysteries, and whose salvation was dependent on making the good choice, and on faith and good works.

6. The dem. and rel. pro. translated "*that which*" can equally be rendered "*him who*". The reference is to the principle of Evil, whether personified as Beelzebul—in accordance with Valentinian speculations (*vide* latter part of note 3, XLI)—or meaning simply, "*the Evil which appeared in Matter*" (*vide* XLIV–XLV).

7. The Nine Gifts of Grace bestowed on striving souls, *vide supra*.

8. Cf. § 10, *Excerpt. ex Theodot.*: "*The Face of the Father is the Son, through whom the Father is known*". Also John xiv, 9: "*Jesus saith unto* [*Philip*]: *He that hath seen me, hath seen the Father*".

LI

MS. f. 126ᵛ
C.S. p. 41

Then the Mother set up her First-begotten (προτογενη-τος) Son[1], and gave to him the authority (εξουσια) of the Sonship. And she gave him hosts (στρατια) of Angels (αγγελος) and Archangels (αρχαγγελος), and Twelve Powers (δυναμις) to minister (διακονι) to him. And she bestowed on him a Vesture (ενδυμα) in which to accomplish all things[2]. And in it were all bodies (σωμα): the body (σωμα) of the fire, the body (σωμα) of the water, the body (σωμα) of the air (αηρ), the body (σωμα) of the earth, and the body (σωμα) of the wind[3], the body (σωμα) of the angels (αγγελος), the body (σωμα) of the archangels (αρχαγγελος), the body (σωμα) of the powers (δυναμις), the body (σωμα) of the rulers (δυνος), the body (σωμα) of the gods, and the body (σωμα) of the lords. And, in a word ('απλως), in it were all bodies (σωμα), so that there shall be naught to hinder him from going to the heights, or (η) descending to the depths (LIII) to the abyss.

LIII

1. The title, *First-begotten Son* (of the Mother), occurs only this once. It is used, perhaps, in view of his later connection with the person of the Redeemer of the world. For it is to be inferred that, as in the case of his correlative—the psychic Christ of Valentinus —he provides the vehicle prepared for the Saviour's use on earth (*vide* note 5, XLI). On the next page (LIII), where the creative activities of this Being are described, his earlier title, *First Begetter*, is once more employed.

2. The Vesture bestowed on the First-begotten Son confers omnipotence in the world of *form*, and gives him power to assume a suitable "body" for entry and use in every region and state in the universe. There is here some relationship of thought with the *Pistis Sophia* (Codex Askew.), where in caps. 10–15 the Saviour tells his disciples of a Vesture which conferred power over every region through which he passed on his descent to earth.

3. This word can also be translated *spirit*.

And this is the Protogenitor (προτογενητωρ), to whom those of the Within and those of the Without promised all he shall desire. And he it is who separated (διακρινε) all the Matter ('υλη), and in the way in which he spread himself over it—as it were a bird stretching forth its wings over its eggs—thus did the Protogenitor (προτογενητωρ) to Matter ('υλη), and he raised up myriads upon myriads of species (ειδος) or (η) races (γενος). When the Matter ('υλη) was grown warm, the multitude of powers (δυναμις) that belong to him[1] were set free, and they grew in the manner of the grass, and they were divided according to (κατα) races (γενος), and according to (κατα) species (ειδος)[2].

[3]And he gavè them the law (νομος) to love one another, and to honour God and to bless him, and to enquire after him: Who he is, and what he is. And that they should marvel at the place from whence they came, seeing it is strait and sad. And that they should not return to it again, but (αλλα) should follow after him who had given them the law (νομος). And he led them from the darkness of Matter ('υλη) which is their Mother, and he told them that the Light was come—for as yet they knew not of the Light, whether it was or not. (LIV) Then (τοτε) he gave them commandment not to injure one another, and he departed from them to the region (τοπος) of the Mother of the Universe, with the Propator (προπατωρ) and the Autopator (αυτοπατωρ), so that they should give precept to those who came from Matter ('υλη).

MS. f. 128ᵛ
C.S. p. 43

LIV

1. The use of the masc. pro. makes the multitude of powers set free by the brooding operation belong to the Protogenitor. This is perhaps a scribal error. The fem. pro. would make them the property of Matter, which seems more probable.
2. As already observed (note 1, XLI, and note 1, XLVI), according to our treatise, the Protogenitor performs certain of the

LIII
MS. f. 128ᵛ
C.S. p. 43

LIII
MS. f. 128ᵛ
C.S. p. 43

creative operations that in the Valentinian system are ascribed to the Forefather or Demiurge. According to § 47, *Excerpt. ex Theodot.*, the words of Gen. i, 2: "*the Spirit of God brooded over the waters*", were held to be illustrative of the action of the Demiurge. In our treatise, the brooding operation is performed by the Protogenitor. There has been some theorizing as to the meaning of the terms used in Gen. i, 2. Augustine (in *Gen. ad. lit.* 1) supposes that *water* signifies *formless matter*. Basil (in *Hom.* II, *in Hexam.*) states that the Spirit brooded over the element of *water*, fostering and quickening its nature and impressing vital power, even "*as a hen broods over her chickens*". Similar imagery occurs in Deut. xxxii, 11, of an eagle brooding over her young. This latter interpretation comes very close to the notion of our treatise regarding the action of the Protogenitor, who, by his energizing power, raises up all the species and races of the creation.

3. It is to be inferred that the race of mankind to whom the following admonitions of the Protogenitor are addressed are the ψυχικοί, i.e. the psychic race. These are the "*many who are called*", in contradistinction to the πνευματικοί, who are the "*few who are chosen*" (Matt. xxii, 14; cf. notes 3 and 4, LI). It has been conjectured, on substantial grounds, that the second creation of humanity—comprising the races of the ψυχικοί and χοϊκοί—which in the Valentinian system is attributed to the Demiurge, is the work of the Protogenitor in the system of our treatise (*vide* latter part of note 1, XLVI, and note 3, LI). To the race of the χοϊκοί, i.e. the *earthy*, who are doomed to destruction, there is no direct reference in our treatise. The ψυχικοί are the mean between the πνευματικοί and the χοϊκοί, of whom the fate in both cases is unalterable. The psychics were of two sorts, those who rose to salvation, and those who sank to destruction (*vide* LVII–LVIII). From the *Fragments of Heracleon* ("Texts and Studies", edit. Armitage Robinson), we learn that the ψυχικοί, like the πνευματικοί, are immersed in the matter of the world and are sick unto death. But their case is not hopeless; they are the *corruptible* that puts on *incorruption* (frg. 40). It was to set free the πνευματικοί and save such of the ψυχικοί as were salvable, that the Saviour came to earth (*ibid.* frg. 8). Irenaeus makes it clear that in the case of the latter class of souls there is a necessity for *faith* and a good life. In 1, i, 11, he says: "*Now psychic [men] are instructed in psychic [things]—these, who through works and a mere faith are established and have not the perfect gnosis. We, of the Church [Catholic], they say, are these [persons]. Wherefore they declare that it is necessary for us to be of good conversation, for otherwise it is impossible to be saved*". In the present passage of our treatise, there is no reference to a knowledge of the Mysteries, as was the case in regard to the πνευματικοί, on LI.

And the Mother of the Universe, and the Propator (προπατωρ), and the Autopator (αυτοπατωρ), and the Progenitor (προγενητωρ), and the Powers of the Mother's Aeon (αιων), upraised a mighty hymn ('υμνος), blessing the One and Only One, and saying unto him:

LIV
MS. f. 130ᴿ
C.S. p. 44

"Thou only art the Infinite (απεραντος). Thou only art the Deep (βαθος). Thou only art the Unknowable. And thou art He for whom all seek—and they find thee not—for none hath power to know thee without thy Will [1]: and none hath power to bless thee without thy Will. Thy Will alone became Space (τοπος) for thee, because it is not possible for any to be space (τοπος) for thee, in that of all, thou art the Space (τοπος) [2]. I pray thee to give order (ταξις) to those belonging to the World (κοσμος), and to give precept to my offspring in accordance with (κατα) thy Will. And cause not sorrow (λυπι) to my offspring—for never hath anyone been grieved (λυπι) through thee —(LV) and none hath understood thy counsel [3].

LV

---

1. Cf. Wisdom ix, 17: *"For who shall know thy Thought, except thou give wisdom"*.
2. Cf. I, VII and X of the treatise.
3. Cf. Wisdom ix, 13: *"For who among men is he that can know the counsel of God"*.

LIV
MS. f. 130ᴿ
C.S. p. 44

LV
MS. f. 130ᵛ
C.S. p. 45

Thou art he whom all things need, (both) those of the Within and those of the Without. For thou alone art uncontainable (αχωρητος), thou alone art invisible (ἀ‘ορατος), and thou alone art without substance (ανουσιος) ¹. Alone thou gavest character (χαρακτηρ) to all created things: thou mad'st them manifest in thee. Thou art the Maker (δημιουργος) of the things not yet revealed—these which thou alone dost know—as to us, we know them not. Thou showest them to us, thou alone, therefore we shall entreat (αιτι) thee on account of them, that thou shouldst reveal them, and we shall learn of them through thee alone. Alone thou didst present thyself to the mass of the hidden Worlds (κοσμος) until they knew thee². Thou didst grant to them to know thee, because thyself didst bear them in thy incorporeal (ασωματος) Body (σωμα) and didst create them: because thou didst beget the Man in thy self-alone-caused (αυτοφυης) Mind (νους), in the Thought (διανοια) and Idea that are complete. This is the Man of Mind (νους) begotten, to whom Thought (διανοια) gave form (μορφη)³. Thou art he who gavest all things to the Man, and in the manner of these vestures he wore (φορι) them. He put them on him in the manner of raiment, wrapping himself in the creation as it were a mantle. This is the Man that

LVI

All things pray (LVI) to know. At thy behest alone the Man appeared, and through him all learned to know thee, because thou didst beget him: and according to (κατα) thy Will thou wast revealed.

LV
MS. f. 130ᵛ
C.S. p. 45

1. For the significance of this word, *vide* note 2, I.
2. This is a reference to the creation of the *Universes*, i.e. the Aeons of the Pleroma. Cf. I of the treatise.
3. Reference to the creation of the Anthropos, *vide* II.

Thou art he to whom I pray—Father of every fatherhood, God of every god, and Lord of every lord—
the same whom I entreat that he shall give order
(ταξις) to my species (ειδος) and my offspring—these
that I have quickened¹ in thy Name and in thy
Power: O One and Only Source (μοναρχης)! the
only Changeless One! Give to me a power, and I
shall cause my offspring to learn of thee, because
thou art their Saviour (σωτηρ)".

And when the Mother ceased entreating the Infinite
(απεραντος) and Unknown One (αγνωστος)—who
filleth the Whole and preserveth all things—he
hearkened to her, and to those who were with her, who
belong to her. And he sent her a Power (δυναμις) from
the Man: this same whom all desire (επιθυμι) to see².
And forth from the Infinite (απεραντος) he came, even
the Infinite (απεραντος) Spark (σπινθηρ)³: at whom
the Aeons (αιων) marvelled, saying: "Where was he
hidden before he was made manifest from the Infinite
(απεραντος) Father—who from himself made manifest
the Whole—where was he hidden?"

1. In this passage the Coptic word has the meaning of *inciting, stirring up, arousing*, etc.; also in II Tim. i, 6, where it equals ἀναζωπυρεῖν,
and is translated: "*stir up* the Grace of God which is in thee". In the
Sahidic MS., "The Martyrdom of Jôôre" (Brit. Mus.), p. 155, the
word occurs with this same meaning: "they observed the *stirring* of
the air". The noun can equal πρόθυμος = *prime life* or *breath*.

2. This is a reference to the Monogenes. *Vide* XXI–XXII: "*the
Only-begotten who is hidden in (the Deep): this same for whom all seek*".
Also LI–LII: "*they understood the Mystery that became Man*".

3. In our treatise, the *Spark* is a name for the Monogenes in his
threefold manifestation as the Christ (*vide* note 3, XXVII). The
Spark shines forth three times: in the Pleroma or world *Within*
(XXVII), in the place of the *Midst* (XXVIII), and in the world
Without, as here recorded. The third shining is in respect of the
earthly dispensation, when the power of the Monogenes descended on the Man, Christ Jesus. In the belief of the Valentinians,
this descent of power took place after the baptism in Jordan.

LVII
MS. f. 132ᵛ
C.S. p. 47

¹And the Powers of the hidden Aeons (αιων) followed him till they came to that which is manifest, and issued forth from the Holy Pleroma ('ιερον πληρωμα) ². And he veiled himself in the powers (δυναμις) of those who came forth from that which is hidden. And he made them as a world (κοσμος), and he bore (φορι) it into the Holy Place ('ιερον), and the Powers (δυναμις) of the Pleroma (πληρωμα) saw him. And they³ (of the world) loved him, they praised him in unutterable hymns ('υμνος), unspeakable are they by tongue of flesh (σαρξ), they are wont to be conceived by the man out of his heart. And he took their hymn ('υμνος), and he made it as a veil (καταπετασμα) for their worlds (κοσμος), surrounding them in the manner of a defence⁴. And he came to the borders of the Mother of the Universe and he set himself up upon the All-containing Aeon (αιων παν'ολων). And the Universe was moved in the presence of the Lord of the whole Earth, and the Aeon (αιων) was troubled and remained still, as seeing him whom it knew not⁵.

⁶And the Lord of Glory sat (in judgment). He divided the Matter ('υλη), and he made it in two parts (μερος) and two places (χωρα), and he set bounds to each place (χωρα). And he made known to them that from one Father and one Mother they were come. And to those who fled to him and worshipped him, he gave the

LVIII   place (χωρα) on his Right-hand (LVIII), and freely bestowed (χαριзε) upon them immortality, and life for evermore.

LVII
MS. f. 132ᵛ
C.S. p. 47

1. The first paragraph on this page relates to the redemption of the spiritual seed (*vide* notes 3, 4 and 5, LI). The soteriological beliefs of our Gnostics are nowhere explicitly defined. The *Excerpt. ex Theodot.* afford some doctrinal resemblances, but the Eastern and Western forms of Valentinian doctrine are confused

together in the *Excerpta*, and it is only possible to indicate certain points of contact. From § 35, we learn that the Saviour—who was the Fruit of the Whole Pleroma—was sent forth from the Pleroma, accompanied, as before—when he appeared to the Sophia and gave her the *enformation in respect of gnosis*—by the male Angels who are destined ultimately to form unities with the feminine spiritual souls on earth (*vide* note 1, XXXIX, and note 3, XL). On coming down for the Redemption, he puts on a pneumatic body, formed —according to one account—by the Sophia, of her spiritual seed (§ 1), or, as stated in another place (§ 26), by uniting himself with the Sophia and pneumatic humanity. Further details are given in §§ 58 and 59, and some points can be related to our treatise. When descending, the Saviour united his own spiritual essence with that of the Sophia and clothed himself with the spiritual Seed. It is this *Seed* that he, figuratively—at the Crucifixion—bore up upon his shoulders and introduced into the Pleroma (§ 42). Besides this pneumatic body, with which he is said to have *adorned himself* (§ 41), he also *put on* the body of the psychical Christ, whom he found on coming to the region of the Mother and the Demiurge. This was a *sensible* (αἰσθητός) body, formed from the invisible psychic substance, which finally, "*by the operation of Divine contriving*", came into this sensible world (§§ 59, 60). On this body, compounded of the pneumatic and psychic elements (§ 61)—and called the *visible* in Jesus—the Name (ὄνομα) of the Son, i.e. the Power of the Monogenes (υἱὸς μονογενής) (§ 26), descended after the baptism in Jordan (§ 61). (Cf. Matt. iii, 17, and Mark i, 11 (Gk. text, Oxford, 1905): "*This is my Only Beloved Son*".) Returning to our treatise, we find (*vide* LVI) that the Spark of Light —who is here to be identified with the second manifestation of the Christ called *Fruit of the Whole* (*vide* note 3, XXVII, and note 1, XXXIII)—is sent from the Pleroma to the manifested world. He is followed by the Powers of the unmanifested world, i.e. the Angels. He clothes himself with the powers (δυνάμεις) that had come from the invisible world, meaning the *spiritual* Seed. These he forms into a *world* which he carries into the Pleroma. That it was the belief of our Gnostics that the Saviour also united himself with the First-begotten Son of the Mother is deducible from the fact that this Being is the equivalent of the psychical Christ of the Valentinians (*vide* notes 1 and 5, XLI). As we have several times had occasion to refer to the beliefs of the Ophite or Sethian School of Gnostics, it may be well to note here a point of difference between their Christology and that of the Valentinians. Their views as to the constitution of the body of the Saviour—in respect of the pneumatic and psychic components—were similar. But they held that in addition he assumed a *mundane* body. This was Jesus, who, *"being begotten of the Virgin Mary, through the operation of God, was wiser, purer, and more righteous than other men"* (Iren. i, xxviii, 6). At the resurrection the psychic body was raised from the dead and the *mundane* body resolved into its original elements (*ibid.* 7).

2. *The Powers of the hidden Aeons* are the male Angels who came with the Saviour when he appeared to the Mother and gave her *enformation in respect of gnosis*. From her vision of these Angels she conceived the feminine spiritual seed (*vide* notes 1, 3, XXXIX, and note 3, XL). Owing to their common nature, the Angels and the Seed are destined hereafter to form spiritual unities. *Vide* § 35, *Excerpt. ex Theodot.*: "*Jesus, our 'Light'* (meaning here the Fruit of the Pleroma)...*proceeded beyond the Boundary—for he was the Messenger* (ἄγγελος) *of the Pleroma—and took forth with him the Angels of the suffering Seed* (τοῦ διαφέροντος σπέρματος)... *to restore the Seed"*... § 35, *ibid.*, further informs us that the Angels pray for the Seed, i.e. their members (μέρους), because without these, they themselves cannot enter the Pleroma. This idea of the association of an Angel with every individual member of the spiritual Seed appears to be the Gnostic counterpart of the Christian doctrine of the Guardian Angels.

3. It is obvious—from the reference, *infra*, to a *tongue of flesh*—that the rel. pro. must relate to the spiritual race on earth, i.e. the powers that were made into a *world*, and not to the Powers of the Pleroma. Translation of the passage is uncertain; perhaps the text is corrupt.

4. Probably a reference to the *Veil* mentioned in § 38, *Excerpt. ex Theodot.* It covered the psychical realms in the lower cosmos. Through this Veil, the High Priest, i.e. Jesus, entered. It is further described in § 27 of the *Excerpta*, as the *second Veil* of the universe which divides off the intelligible world. Cf. also Heb. ix, 1–3. At this point in the treatise, reference to the redemption of pneumatic humanity is concluded.

5. Cf. Ps. lxxv, 9–10 (Vulg.): "*The earth trembled and was still, when God arose to judgement*". It is difficult to determine whether or not the present passage contains an allusion to the Crucifixion and subsequent events. The statement as to the Saviour being set up upon the Aeon, and the troubling that ensued at the sight, might be—mystically—so understood. Apart from this possible interpretation, there is nothing in any extant text, or in the Patristic sources, which in any way corresponds with the happenings here described. The Valentinians and schools doctrinally allied accepted the historical happening of the Crucifixion, to which, however, they gave their own mystical interpretation. The *Excerpt. ex Theodot.* once more provide the fuller details on this subject. At the time of the Passion, the constituent elements of the Saviour's

person were sundered. The Spirit that had descended on him in Jordan departed (§ 61). The pneumatic body received from the Sophia he committed to his Father on the Cross (§ 1). The pneumatic seed, which was consubstantial with himself, he took up with him upon the Cross, that is to say, he took it, figuratively, with him through the Boundary, into the Pleroma (§ 42). The body that was crucified was that of the psychical Christ (§ 62). Details of the Passion are nowhere hinted at in our text, but the statement that the Saviour sets himself up upon the Aeon, and that the world was troubled at the sight, may perhaps be a reference to that event. Dealing with the interpretations of the Gnostic teacher Heracleon, in his *Commentary* on John viii, 22, Origen says that the Jews had a traditional belief that the Saviour would not have his life taken from him, but would yield it up of himself. Cf. John x, 18: "*No man taketh [my life] away from me, but I lay it down of myself*". Also *ibid.* xii, 32: "*And I, if I be lifted up from the earth*", etc. The movement in the universe, and the troubling of the Aeon at the sight of One whom it knew not, may be compared with the events following the Crucifixion as related in the Gospel story, when "*the earth quaked, and the rocks were rent . . . and the centurion, and they that were with him, watching Jesus, having seen the earth quake, and the things that were done, were sore afraid, saying: Truly this was the Son of God*" (Matt. xxvii, 51–54).

6. We now get some particulars respecting the redemption of *psychic* humanity. There is a reference, in the first place, to one effect of the coming down of the Saviour to earth, that is, to the separation of the elements of psychic humanity into the Right-hand and the Left-hand. According to the Valentinians of the *Excerpt. ex Theodot.*, the instrument of this separation was the Cross. Vide § 42: "*The Cross* (σταυρός) *is the Sign of the Boundary* (ὅρος) *of the Pleroma. As Horos divides the lower world from the Pleroma, so the Stauros separates the faithful* (πιστῶν) *from the unfaithful* (ἀπίστους)". From this point onwards, the events related in our treatise are probably all post-resurrectional. The Valentinians held that the Saviour's mission was divided by the Passion into two periods, and together with the Ophite or Sethian School, they taught that the second period was a much longer one than the forty days allowed in the Acts (i, 3). In I, i, 5, and I, xxviii, 7, Irenaeus gives eighteen months as the length of the post-resurrectional period according to these schools, while in the *Pistis Sophia* we are told that, after he had risen from the dead, the Saviour remained on earth eleven years, conversing with, and instructing his disciples (cap. 1). Heracleon also taught that the Saviour's work was not ended by the Passion, and that he converted "*many more to faith*" after his Resurrection than before it (*Frags. of Heracleon* in "Texts and Studies", vol. 1,

LVII

MS. f. 132ᵛ

C.S. p. 47

LVII
MS. f. 132^v
C.S. p. 47

p. 4, edit. Armitage Robinson). These statements of Heracleon's are interesting and important in relation to what follows in our treatise concerning the redemption of the psychics, who were the *many who are called*, and whose salvation was dependent on *faith* and *good works*.

And the Right-hand he called, "The Place (χωρα) of Life", and the Left, "The Place (χωρα) of Death". The Right-hand place (χωρα) he called, "The Place (χωρα) of Light", and the Left, "The Place (χωρα) of Darkness". Again, he called the Right-hand place (χωρα), "The Place of Rest" (αναπαυσις), and the Left-hand place (χωρα), "The Place of Toil"[1]. And between them he set boundaries and veils (καταπετασμα), that they shall not see each other, and he placed watchers (φυλαξ) over their veils (καταπετασμα). And to those who worshipped him he gave many honours, exalting them above those who had gainsaid (αντιλεγε) and who withstood him. And he enlarged the Right-hand place (χωρα) to many places (χωρα)[2], and he made them order by order (ταξις ταξις), aeon by aeon (αιων αιων), world by world (κοσμος κοσμος), heaven by heaven, firmament by firmament (στερωμα στερωμα), height by height, space by space (τοπος τοπος), region by region, and country by country (χωρημα χωρημα). And he laid down laws (νομος) for them, and gave to them commandments, saying: "Abide ye in my Word, and I shall give you everlasting Life[3].

1. The simile of the Right-hand and Left-hand signifies a division in respect of both locality and quality. The same imagery is presented in the Gospel parable of the sheep and the goats, Matt. xxv, 33: "*And he shall set the sheep on his Right hand, but the goats on his Left*". Those on the Right are the psychics who make the good choice, "*allying themselves with truth and eternity*" (§ 56, *Excerpt. ex Theodot.*). "*Such men*", says Irenaeus, "*are instructed in psychic matters*" and "*are confirmed by their works, and by a mere faith, while they have not perfect gnosis*" (as had the pneumatics) (Iren. i, i, 11). Those on the Left are the other psychics, "*who make alliance with material things*", and are doomed to death and destruction (§ 56, *Excerpt. ex Theodot.*).

2. *Vide* John xiv, 2: "*In my Father's house are many mansions....
I go to prepare a place for you*".

LVIII
MS. f. 134ᴿ
C.S. p. 48

3. Cf. John viii, 31–2: "*Jesus said to those Jews who believed on him: If ye abide in my Word, ye shall be my disciples indeed*". Also *ibid.* x, 28: "*And I shall give unto them Life everlasting*". From the statements of Heracleon—in his *Commentary* on St John's Gospel—it is clear that the Valentinians regarded the Jews as symbolical of the psychic race. These men, in the days of their ignorance and former life, thought they knew God, but knew him not, and worshipped the Demiurge—identified by the Valentinians with the God of the Jews—instead of the Father of Truth. To bring them the knowledge of the true God, the Saviour came to earth (*Fragments of Heracleon*, 19, 20 and 21, in "Texts and Studies", vol. ɪ, p. 4, edit. Armitage Robinson).

(LVIII) And I shall send you powers (δυναμις), and shall
confirm you with mighty spirits (πνα): (LIX) and I
shall give you an authority (εξουσια) proper to you, and
none shall hinder (κωλυ) you in that which you desire.
And you shall possess aeons (αιων) and worlds (κοσμος)
and heavens, so that the intelligible (νοερον) spirits
(πνα) come and they dwell in them[1]. And you shall be
deified, and you shall know that you came forth from
God, and you shall see him that he is God within you:
and he shall dwell in your aeon (αιων)"[2]. These words
the Lord of all things spake to them, and he withdrew
(αναχωρι) from them and hid himself[3].

And they rejoiced, namely those that had been born
of Matter ('υλη), because they were remembered. And
they were glad, because they came from that which is
both strait and sad. And they besought the Hidden
Mystery (μυστηριον), saying: [4]"Give authority (εξουσια) to us, that we may make us aeons (αιων) and
worlds (κοσμος), according to (κατα) thy Word, O
Lord[5], which thou didst covenant with us thy servants.
For thou alone art Unchangeable, thou alone art the
Infinite (απεραντος), and thou alone art Uncontainable
(αχωρητος). Thou alone art Unbegotten (αγεννητος),
and Self-alone-begotten (αυτογενης) and the Self-alone-
Father (αυτοπατωρ). Thou alone art Unmoved (ασαλευτος) and Unknowable (αγνωστος). Thou alone art
the Silence (σιγη), and the Love (αγαπη), and the
Source (πηγη) of the Whole. Thou alone art Un-
material (ατ'υλη) and the only Spotless One—(LX)
unspeakable as to his generation (γενεα)[6], unimaginable (ατνοι) in his revelation.

1. By *intelligible spirits* is intended the spiritual Seed, which the
psychic and material body may, or may not, have indwelling in it.
Cf. Iren. I, i, 14: "*Again, subdividing the psychics themselves, they say*

that some are by nature good, and others by nature evil. The good are those who become recipients of the [spiritual] Seed, the evil by nature are those who are never able to receive that Seed". Also Hippol. VI, 34: *"From the material and diabolic substance, the Demiurge made the bodies of the souls. This is the saying: 'And God formed man, taking dust from the earth, and breathed into his face the breath of life, and man became a living soul'* (cf. note 1, XLVI). *This is, according to them, the inner man, the psychic, inhabiting the material body, which is material, corruptible, imperfect, formed from the diabolic substance. And the material man, according to them, is as it were an inn, or dwelling-place, sometimes of soul alone, sometimes of soul and demons, sometimes of soul and* λόγοι, *which are the* λόγοι *from above from the Joint Fruit of the Pleroma and the Sophia, in this world, and who inhabit the earthy [body] in company with the soul, when demons are not cohabiting with the soul".*

2. In a fragment of an Epistle of Valentinus, preserved in Clem. Alex. (*Strom.* II, 20, 114), the following occurs: *"But when the only Good Father visits the soul, it is hallowed and enlightened, and is called blessed, because one day it shall see God".*

3. Perhaps an allusion to the Saviour's Ascension. The Gnostics of the *Excerpt. ex Theodot.* and the Ophites held that he went up to the Heaven, which, in their cosmogony, was in the middle space. In both systems, it is the psychic Christ that is in question. In Iren. I, xxviii, 7, we learn that after his Resurrection, the Christ remained on earth eighteen months, instructing such of his disciples as he knew to be capable of understanding. After which he was taken up into Heaven, where he sat down at the Right-hand of his father, the Demiurge, that he might receive to himself the souls of men after they had laid aside their mundane flesh. Cf. § 62, *Excerpt. ex Theodot.*: *"Now* (after the Resurrection) *the psychical Christ sits down at the Right-hand of the Demiurge, as David says: 'Sit at my Right-hand'. Now he sits [there] until the consummation of all things 'that they may look on him whom they have pierced'. They pierced the visible, which was the flesh of the psychical Christ".* In the *Pistis Sophia*, the Ascension is mentioned, but the details of the incident show no relationship to the thought of our treatise, or to the above accounts in Irenaeus or the *Excerpt. ex Theodot.*

4. This prayer is addressed to the First Cause, i.e. the *hidden* Mystery, whose revelation to the cosmos is through the Monogenes. Cf. LI: *"They understood the Mystery that became Man—because for this he was manifested, till they saw HIM who is indeed invisible".*

5. Dr Schmidt notes that Woide, in his transcript at this point, makes the marginal addition of a phrase which reads: *"which thou didst covenant".* This is no longer to be seen in the MS., the disappearance being due to the margins having been cut down.

6. Cf. Is. liii, 8: *"Who shall declare his generation".*

Yea, hearken unto me, O Father Incorruptible (αφθαρτος) and Father Everlasting (αθανατος): God of the hidden things: the Only Light and Life! The Invisible alone, the Unutterable (α'ρητος) alone, the Undefiled (αμιαντος) alone, the Unconquerable(αδαμαντος) alone—from the Beginning the One Alone—and before thee there is none. Hearken to this our prayer, entreating him who in every place is hidden. Hear us, and send us incorporeal (ασωματος) spirits (πνα), that they may dwell with us. And they shall teach us of those things that thou didst promise us. And they shall dwell in us, we being to them as bodies (σωμα). Since thy Will it is that this should be—(thy Will) be done. And thou shalt give precept to our work and shalt establish it in accordance with (κατα) thy Will, and in accordance with (κατα) the precept of the hidden Aeons (αιων), and thou (Lord) shalt direct us, for we are thine."

And he hearkened to them, and he sent discerning (διακρινε) Powers (δυναμις), which know the precept of the hidden Aeons (αιων). He sent them forth in accordance with (κατα) the precept of the hidden things, and he instituted order (ταξις) in accordance with (κατα) the order (ταξις) on high, and in accordance with (κα) the hidden precept.

LXI
MS. f. 136ᵛ
C.S. p. 51

(LX) ¹And they began (αρχι) from below (LXI) upwards, so that the building shall fitly join together². And he made the air (αηρ) earth the dwelling-place of those that had come forth, that thereon they should await the confirming of those that were below them³. And next, the sojourning-place in very truth. Within this, the penitential (μετανοια) region⁴. Within this, the heavenly (αεροδιος)⁵ antitypes (αντιτυπος)⁶. And next, the penitential (μετανοια) dwelling change (παροικησις)⁷. Within this, the self-alone-begotten (αυτογενης) antitypes (αντιτυπος)⁸. There in that place they are cleansed in the Name of the Self-alone-begotten (αυτογενης), who is their God above⁹. And in that place were Powers appointed over the Source (πηγη) of the Living Waters, which straightway (?) were brought forth. These are the names of the Powers which are over the Living Water: Michar (μιχαρ) and Micheu (μιχευ), and through Barpharangēs (βαρφαραγγης)¹⁰ they are purified. And within these things¹¹ (are) the Aeons (αιων) of the Sophia (σοφια). Within these, the Truth (αληθια) in very deed. There is the Pistis Sophia (πιστ σοφια)¹², and the pre-living (προωντος)¹³ Jesus (ις), the Risen One¹⁴, and the heavenly ones (αεροδιος), and his Twelve Aeons (αιων)¹⁵. And in that region were placed Sellao (σελλαω), and Eleinos (ελεινος), Zōgenethlēs (ζωγενεθλης), Selmelke (σελμελχε), and the self-alone-begotten (αυτογενης) Aeons (αιων). And four luminaries (φωστηρ) were placed therein: Ēlēlēth (ηληληθ), David (δαυειδε), Oroiaēl (ωροιαηλ) | ⟨and Harmozēl⟩¹⁶.

LXI
MS. f. 136ᵛ
C.S. p. 51

1. This, the last page of extant MS., is a difficult one. There is no parallel in any known Gnostic source. It seems clear, however, from the references to purification and stages of progression, that we are concerned solely with the future of *psychic* humanity, the salvation of the spiritual race not being dependent on any conditions or circumstances either here or hereafter (cf. note 3, LI). In

his account of the origin, nature and divergent destinies of the two
races of mankind—the πνευματικοί and the ψυχικοί—Irenaeus tells
us that the Valentinian Gnostics claimed to be the pneumatics, the
Chosen race (ἐκλεκτοί), and thus, from the beginning, members of the
Ecclesia on high, while the ordinary Christians—who belonged to
the Church (Catholic)—were the psychic race, i.e. the *Called*
(κλητοί) (Iren. I, i, 11). Thus it is probable that in the present passage we have a Gnostic conception of the Church, on earth and in
the after-death state, in relation to psychic humanity. In regard
to some of the terms used, it will be recalled that the repetitive
character of certain Gnostic cosmogonies involved a triple partitioning of the spaces of the outer cosmos. In the Basilidian system,
the designations of the spaces outside the Pleroma accord with the
descriptions found in the present passage. Hippolytus, in the *Ref.
Haer.*, says that the Basilidian outer cosmos was divided into the
Formlessness—further defined as *"this space of ours"*, i.e. the *earth*;
the *Hebdomad*, or *aerial* region—extending from the earth to the
moon—and, thirdly, the *Ogdoad*, that is, the *aetherial* or heavenly
world, reaching up to the firmament which formed the boundary
of the Pleroma (Hippol. VII, 27, 24 and 23). But beyond this use
of similar descriptive terms there are no resemblances to our passage in the account of Hippolytus, and it is to Platonic thought that
we must turn for light on the subjects dealt with in the present
passage, which is concerned principally with after-death conditions. But while much of what follows seems to point to a source
in the Platonic speculations that exercised so strong an influence
on Christian and Gnostic doctrine of the day, there must also have
been, at that time, some continuity of thought with the Jewish
tradition, and, further, some contact with non-Jewish, non-
Christian beliefs regarding after-death conditions, such as are
found in the system of Zoroaster, and in the Greek doctrine of
Hades. In all these philosophies, a form of purification after death
is understood, although in many this purgation is wrought by fire.
In our treatise, *water* is the purifying agent, a fact which emphasizes
the link with a certain phase of Platonic thought (*vide infra*, note 3).

2. If the surmise is correct that this passage is descriptive of the
constitution of the Church, the *beginning below* must signify the
foundation on earth.

3. The *air earth*, or *aerial world*, is still in contact with this
earth. It marks the second stage in the soul's progress heaven-
wards. The term *sojourning-place* indicates that this abode in the
air is but a temporary one. By the *antitypes* of the *heavenly ones*
found there (*vide infra*) are perhaps intended the pattern souls,
who, by means of repentance and purification, shall attain to the
heavenly state. The heavenly ones (ἀερόδιοι) themselves are men-

LXI
MS. f. 136ᵛ
C.S. p. 51

tioned *infra*, in association with the Risen Jesus and the Pistis Sophia in the heaven world, i.e. in the place of the *Midst*. Many of the speculations here set forth regarding after-death conditions are reminiscent of Platonic thought on the one hand, and the teaching of Origen on the other. In the *Phaedo*, Plato deals at some length with the environment and changing circumstances to which souls are subjected after death (pp. 31 a–32 b). And in the *Laws* (x, 904 a–c) he says: "*All things that have soul change . . . and in changing move according to law and the order of destiny. . . . And when the soul becomes greatly different and divine, she also greatly changes her place, which is now altogether holy*". Again, a passage in the *Phaedo* has the following: "*Those who are remarkable for having led holy lives are released from the earthly prison, and go to their pure home, and dwell in the pure earth*". And, later, in the same passage, the imagery represents the purification of certain souls as taking place in the waters of the Lake Acheron: "*Those who appear to have lived neither well nor ill . . . go to the river Acheron, and are carried to the lake, where they dwell and are purified of their evil deeds . . . and are absolved, and receive the reward of their good deeds according to their deserts*" (pp. 110 b–114 d). The *air earth*, spoken of in our passage, which is the first resting-place of the souls coming out of earthly existence, seems to correspond with what Origen calls *the abode in the air*. This he believed to be still situated on the earth, and to be a place of instruction for the souls as well as a waiting-place. In his disquisition on the intermediate state, in *de Princ.* ii, he says: "*We are therefore to suppose that the saints will remain there until they understand the twofold mode of government in those things which are performed in the air*". By *twofold mode*, he explains himself to mean that while on earth we have the power to perceive objects and the diversity among them, but do not understand the reason of them, nor the principle upon which they are "*either created or diversely arranged*". Of this, "*the full understanding and comprehension will be granted after death*". Thus: "*we shall understand in a twofold manner what we saw on earth. Some such view, then, we must hold regarding this abode in the air. I think, therefore, that all the saints who depart from this life will remain in some place situated on the earth, which Holy Scripture calls Paradise, or in some place of instruction. . . . If anyone be pure in heart, and holy in mind, and more practised in perception, he will, by making more rapid progress, quickly ascend to a place in the air, and reach the Kingdom of Heaven, through those mansions, so to speak, in the various places which the Greeks have termed spheres, i.e. globes, but which Holy Scripture has called heavens . . . and thus he will in order pass through all gradations, following him who hath passed into the heavens, Jesus, the Son of God . . . and of this diversity of places he speaks, when he says: 'In my Father's House are many mansions'*" (Orig. *de Princ.* ii, 11).

4. μετανοια = *change of mind*; this, the original meaning of the term, is somewhat lost sight of in the English rendering.

5. αεροδιος. Probably ἀερο-δῖος = *divine air*.

6. αντιτυπος. As here used, the word denotes *impressions, patterns,* or *representations* of the real things in the world of reality above. The Gnostics believed that things here below, in the various grades of substance or matter, were stamped, as it were, with the patterns of things in the real world and gave back the image like a repercussion or echo. The heavenly beings—of whom these are the antitypes—are in the heaven world above (*vide infra*).

LXI
MS. f. 136ᵛ
C.S. p. 51

7. παροικησις, and μετανοια and αντιτυπος (*supra*). As here employed, παροικησις bears the meaning: *habitation-change*. (*Vide* L. and S. παρά, in Compos. IV = *alteration* or *change*, and οἴκησις = a *habitat* or *dwelling*). The term has the same import as μετενσωμάτωσις = *embodiment-change*, which occurs in the related passage from Plotinus, quoted *infra*. The three terms are noticed by Plotinus, in his treatise "Against the Gnostics", and the fact that in his context he deals with the subjects discussed in our passage is of importance. The matter has been dealt with at length by Dr Carl Schmidt, who expresses his belief that it was against the particular system of the Gnosis embodied in the present treatise that Plotinus was directing his remarks, and that he must have been dealing—if not with this very passage—with one similar in subject-matter. (*Plotin. Stellung z. Gnost. u. Kirchl. Christl.* C. Schmidt, *Text. u. Untersuch.* N.F. vol. IV, p. 61.) Comparison of the passages affords complete justification of Dr Schmidt's opinion. In the passage in point (*Plotin. opera*, II Enn. 9, 6), Plotinus first complains that the Gnostics neither regarded nor honoured "*the sensible construction of things, nor this visible earth, but said that there is a new earth prepared for them, into which they will ascend from hence*". Further, that they asserted that this *new earth* is the productive principle and pattern of the sensible world—after which he continues: "*And what must be said of the new hypostases* (ὑποστάσεις) *which they introduce—habitation-changes* (παροικήσεις), *and impressions* (on the soul) (ἀντιτύπους), *and changes of mind* (μετανοίας). *For if they declare these* (i.e. παροικήσεις) *to be what happen* (πάθη) *to the soul when it undergoes a change of mind* (μετάνοια), *and impressions* (ἀντιτύπους) *when it beholds the semblances only of real things but not as yet reality itself—this is a use of new-fangled terms for the purpose of introducing their particular school of philosophy. For as they do not adhere to the time-honoured [philosophy] of the Greeks, they devise cunningly in this way. The Greeks knew surely, and spoke without bombast of the way up from the cavern, and the advance, little by little, to a truer and truer vision. In short, part [of their teaching] has been taken from Plato, the rest—where they bring in something new in order to establish a special*

philosophy—these things are deviations from the truth. Since from that source (i.e. Plato) *come the suffering of penalties, the streams of water in the under-world, and the embodiment changes* (μετενσωματώσεις)". In this citation from Plotinus I have merely anglicized ὑπόστασις, since the meaning of this much-discussed term has no bearing on the relationship between the two passages. The three *hypostases*, however, appear to stand for *fundamental states* or *conditions* of soul life. Beside the verbal correspondences in the two passages, there are several instances of parallel imagery: (1) Ascent upwards from earth to the air world = ascent from the cavern. (2) Antitypes of heavenly things = semblances of real things. (3) Changes of (soul) habitat (παροίκησις) = changes of embodiment (μετενσωματώσεις). (4) Living waters for the purification of the souls (*vide infra*) = streams of water in the under-world. With reference to these *changes of embodiment* or *habitat*, cf. citation from Plato (*Laws*, x, 904 a–c) in note 3 (*supra*): "*All things that have soul change.... And when the soul becomes greatly different* (cf. μετάνοια) *and divine, she also greatly changes her place...*".

8. These antitypes are representations of the Aeons that belong to the Spaces of the *Self-alone-begotten*, i.e. to the place of the *Midst* (*vide* note 1, XXVIII). The Aeons themselves are mentioned *infra*, as being with the Sophia and other entities in the heavenly region.

9. Αὐτογενης is an appellation for the Christ, and initially, of course, for the Monogenes, who was *self-alone-begotten* by the Father (*vide* note 1, VII). The present reference is to the third Christ, whose psychic body was assumed by the Christ from the Pleroma, for the purpose of the earthly redemption. According to the Valentinians, this psychic Christ—also called Jesus by some of the schools—was the Son of the Demiurge. Our treatise makes him to be the Son of the Mother, and to be produced, like all her creations, from her *self-alone-begotten* substance.

10. *Michar, Micheu, Barpharanges.* I can find no satisfactory derivation or meaning for these names.

11. As observed in note 2, *supra*, the order of progression from a lower to a higher state is here pictured as a going inwards as well as upwards, and we now get a description of the heavenly or aetherial region, which reached up to the Boundary of the Pleroma. The manner in which our Gnostics divided the universe must once more be recalled. The cosmos, in its entirety, comprised the world *Within*, the place of the *Midst*, and the world *Without*. Both the first and the third regions were in contact with the middle space, which constituted the Boundary upwards and downwards. This place of the *Midst* was thus the highest region with which the lower world was in contact. It is the heavenly region here spoken

of. In the earlier part of the commentary, the Valentinian version LXI
of the Sophia's career was outlined, together with an account of MS. f. 136ᵛ
the coming into existence of all the regions outside the Pleroma, C.S. p. 51
following the banishment of her formless substance—called the
Sophia *outside*—from the Holy Place. According to the cosmogony
of our treatise, the place of the *Midst*—where the outside Sophia
dwelt—was peopled with her Aeons (*vide* latter part of note 4,
XII, XV, and *infra, the self-alone-begotten Aeons*). After her enformation by the Saviour, she proceeded with the creation of the lower
cosmos, operating through the Beings she produced for this end
(*vide* note 1, XLVI), while she herself remained in the place of the
Midst. Thereafter followed the creation of the various elements
and species of the world, including the different types of the human
race, and finally, the descent of the Saviour for the salvation of the
πνευματικοί and the ψυχικοί. Subsequent events—as pictured by the
Valentinians—can be learned from Iren. I, i, 12. At the end of the
world, when all the pneumatic Seed shall have been perfected, the
Mother will pass from the middle space and will enter the Pleroma, there to receive, as her Spouse, the Saviour who sprang
from all the Aeons. The πνευματικοί, divested of their souls (ψυχάς),
will be bestowed, as their brides, upon the Angels who came with
the Saviour and will also enter the Pleroma (*vide* note 2, LVII).
The Demiurge, who had hitherto dwelt below, in his own realm,
the Hebdomad, will then pass into the place of the Mother, i.e.
the Ogdoad. There also will repose for ever, in heaven, the *justified
souls* (δικαίων ψυχάς), that is to say, the psychics, now abandoned
by the pneumatic Seed associated with them during their earthly
existence. When these things have been accomplished, the fire that
lies hidden in all the grosser material elements of the world (*vide*
note 7, L) will blaze forth and burn, and, while consuming all
matter, will also itself be extinguished along with it. A substantially
similar account is found in Iren. II, xliv–xlv. The *Excerpt. ex
Theodot.* give a few more details. The πνευματικοί who have passed
from earthly life, repose, with the Mother, in the *abode of the Lord*,
in the Ogdoad, called the Lord's Rest, wearing their souls as garments, until the consummation. Afterwards they will put off their
souls, and becoming *complete intelligible Aeons*, through being united
to their syzygies, the Angels, will pass through the Boundary to the
presence of the Father. The rest of mankind who are saved, i.e.
psychic humanity—called the *faithful souls* (πισταί ψυχαί), are with
the Demiurge until the consummation, after which they will
ascend up and inhabit the Ogdoad, that is, the highest heavenly
world to which they can attain (§§ 63, 64). It is noticeable that,
in these passages, no distinction is made between the two classes
of souls—those who, from the first moment of their existence,

possessed the spiritual Seed—and those of the second creation, who, through allying themselves with Truth and Eternity, received the Seed during their lifetime on earth (cf. note 3, LI, and note 3, LIII). It is to be inferred that their ultimate destiny is the same; that is to say, in both cases the *spirits* are parted from the *souls*, the former then entering the Pleroma, and the latter remaining for ever in heaven. As for the other psychics—those who have chosen for the worse, and during their earthly life have not been united to intelligible spirits—these will not attain to an eternal abode, but will be destroyed with the third race (the χοϊκοί), and the gross material elements of the world with which they have allied themselves (Iren. I, i, 14, and *ibid.* II, xlv. Also § 56 *Excerpt. ex Theodot.*). The Gnostics regarded body, soul and spirit as three entirely distinct entities. The soul, moreover, coming as it did, in their view, under the category of ὕλη—though of a highly refined sort—could not possibly enter the world of pure spirit, which is the Pleroma. Hence their doctrine of the middle space, or heaven world, which must not be confused with the Catholic doctrine of the Intermediate Place, or Purgatorial realm. The heaven world of the Gnostics was to be the eternal abode of the just souls who were "saved", and whose highest attainment was a merely natural happiness, in conformity with their nature and capacity as psychic beings. That there was, besides, an antechamber to this heaven world, which is analogous to Purgatory, seems clear from the statements regarding the place of repentance and the purifying waters.

12. The occurrence here, of the double title, *Pistis* Sophia, is important. So far as is known, apart from this instance, it is found nowhere else outside the well-known Gnostic treatise—in the Askew Codex—which goes by that title. That this double title almost immediately follows the single name of Sophia (one line *supra*) suggests that there is a distinction between the two entities. The passage is concerned with the economy and conditions of existence in the space of the *Midst*. This we know was the dwelling-place of the Mother, i.e. the Sophia *outside*, and it was peopled with her Aeons and the beings she produced for the purpose of setting up and organizing the lower cosmos; i.e. the Propator, the Autopator, and her Protogenitor Son. The space of the *Midst* is the psychic world (*vide* notes 3 and 4, XXVIII, and note 1, XXXI), and the Aeons and other beings inhabiting and operating there were produced by the Mother out of the psychic substance. But though she dwelt in the psychic realms, the Mother herself was a spiritual, not a psychic being, and her true home was the spiritual world of the Pleroma, from which she had been cast out owing to the imperfection and deficiency of her feminine nature—a condition that was to be

[186]

remedied at the consummation of all things, when, united to her masculine counterpart, her Spouse and Saviour, the Christ who was the Fruit of the Whole Pleroma, with him she will enter the world of spiritual perfection. In the passage where the name *Pistis* Sophia is mentioned, we find her associated with the *pre-living risen Jesus*. This is a post-resurrectional designation for the psychic Christ—First-begotten Son of the Mother in our treatise, Son of the Demiurge in the Valentinian system—whose body was assumed by the Christ from the Pleroma, when he came forth for the redemption of the lower cosmos. We learn from the records of Ophite and Valentinian doctrine, that at the time of the Passion, the Christ abandoned the psychic body, which was left to be crucified on the Cross and finally raised again to life by a Ray of Power sent from on high (note 1, LVII). In no known system of the Gnosis is it ever suggested that the Christ from the Pleroma was reunited to the resurrected psychic Being, in fact, the reverse is distinctly implied (*vide* Iren. 1, xxviii, 7). It is further to be noted that, in our passage, with the Pistis Sophia and the pre-living risen Jesus are associated the beings belonging to the heavenly world. Heaven, in the sense of the Gnostics, was located in the middle space, immediately below and outside the Pleroma. It was a place of perfect natural happiness, and the highest region to which a psychic being could reach, since nothing but what is purely spiritual can enter the Pleroma. These various indications strongly suggest that in the *Pistis* Sophia we see a *third* manifestation of the *feminine* principle of the universe. The first of these manifestations was the Sophia *within*, who transgressed and was restored by the first Christ; the second, the Sophia *without*, fruit of the transgression of the first, who was to be restored by the second Christ, Fruit of the Whole Pleroma; and thirdly, the psychic Sophia, fruit of the afflictions of the second, who in her turn is associated with the third manifestation of the redeeming Power, i.e. the psychic Christ. Thus we have a threefold manifestation of the masculine and feminine principles, the ultimate union of which—in the view of the Gnostics—will constitute the perfect state. These conjectures, moreover, comport well with a comprehensive system, such as that of our treatise, in which the leading ideas, by reflection and re-enaction, are carried to a logical conclusion in every particular. There is but one source where one can look for support of this view of the *Pistis Sophia's* significance. That is in the treatise, contained in the Askew Codex, which goes under her name. It purports to contain the post-resurrectional teaching of the Saviour. After passing eleven years on earth, during which he instructed his disciples up to and concerning the 24th Mystery *without*, he is temporarily translated to

[187]

Heaven. On his return, he initiates them into the higher Mysteries, and further recounts his work of redemption on behalf of Pistis Sophia, whom he found *below* the 13th Aeon, where she was grieving and mourning because she was excluded from the 13th Aeon, her proper place in the height. The 13th Aeon was located in the *middle space*, and it is related that Pistis Sophia had fallen therefrom, because, having gazed into the Height and seen the Light of the Veil of the Treasury of Light that was above her, she had aspired to reach that region, and in abandoning her partner in the 13th Aeon, she had *ceased to perform the Mystery of her own Space*. It will be observed, that in this story we have a repetition of the adventure of the first Sophia within the Pleroma (cf. note 4, XII). On the appearance of the Saviour, Pistis Sophia sees in his Vesture the Mystery of her own Name, and the glory of the Mystery of the 13th Aeon to which she belonged. She then gives utterance to a series of thirteen "Repentances", which are prefaced by the words: "O Light of Lights, in whom I have had *faith* from the Beginning". Finally, after many adventures in chaos, she is led back by the Saviour into the 13th Aeon. It is to be noted that nowhere in the treatise is it suggested that Pistis Sophia attains to any higher region than that to which she was, from the beginning, adapted by nature. And in her final Song of Praise, she gives thanks to the Saviour for having returned her "*into the 13th Aeon, my dwelling-place*". All through the story, emphasis is laid again and again on the fact that her salvation was brought about through her *faith* in the Light, and to this fact is due her title of *Pistis*. And the title serves in another way to identify her with the psychic world and substance. When considering the nature, destiny and facilities for salvation offered to psychic humanity during earthly existence, it was noted that statements of Irenaeus and Heracleon make it clear that, in the case of the ψυχικοί, salvation was dependent solely on *faith* and the performance of good works following repentance (*vide* note 3, LIII). Further, in § 63, *Excerpt. ex Theodot.*, members of the psychic race are described as "the *faithful* souls" (πιστοί ψυχαί). In the case of spiritual beings, salvation was in no wise dependent upon *faith* (*vide* note 3, L, and notes 3 and 4, LI).

13. The term *pre-living* has reference to the Saviour's former existence on earth, for it is to his post-resurrectional, post-ascensional career that allusion is made in this passage (cf. note 3, LIX). The constituent elements of the Saviour's body must be remembered. On his descent to earth for the redemption of mankind, the Christ from the Pleroma assumed a body formed of the pneumatic and psychic substances which he found in the place of the *Midst*, which body, in the belief of Italic Valentinians, passed through Mary, "*as water through a conduit*" (Iren. i, i, 13). In the

view of others, he put on, in addition, an *earthly* body, which he
took in the Womb of the Virgin (*vide* note 1, LVII, note 5, XLI, and
Iren. 1, xxviii, 6). Upon this combination of the elements of the
cosmos, the Name (ὄνομα) of the Son, i.e. the Power of the Monogenes, descended at the baptism. At the time of the Crucifixion,
the Power of the Monogenes left him, and resigning into his Father's
Hands his pneumatic body, the Christ from the Pleroma departed, leaving the psychic—and with some—the earthly body, to
be crucified (cf. §§ 1 and 61, *Excerpt. ex Theodot.*) At the Resurrection a ray of spiritual power from the Christ above was sent
down into him, which raised from the dead the psychic body,
while the earthly body was resolved into its original elements.
Afterwards, Jesus tarried on earth, and "*knowledge descending into
him from above*", he taught the people, and instructed those of his
disciples who were capable of understanding the great mysteries.
Finally, he was received up into Heaven, where he will remain to
assist in the passage of the spiritual Seed into the Pleroma (Iren.
1, xxviii, 7). In none of the sources is there indication of a belief
that the post-resurrectional Jesus was reunited to the Christ from
the Pleroma, or that the Power of the Monogenes returned to him.
Irenaeus says that the Ophites drew attention to the fact that
neither before his Baptism, nor after his Resurrection, did he do
any mighty works. The inference, therefore, is that the post-
resurrectional Jesus, mentioned in our passage, is the psychic
Being with whom the Christ from the Pleroma united himself for
the purpose of the earthly redemption, and from whom he withdrew at the Crucifixion. There were, apparently, divergent opinions
in the schools as to the precise origin of the Being whose body the
Saviour from the Pleroma put on. The Valentinians of the
Excerpt. ex Theodot. called him the *psychic Christ*, Son of the psychic
Demiurge. Our Gnostics make the Mother to be directly re-
sponsible for his creation, and call him her First-begotten Son.
He was formed by her of the psychic substance which arose from
the transmutation of her afflictions (cf. note 5, XXXVIII, and
note 5, XLI).

14. The Coptic word translated *risen* is the same term as occurs
on XXXIX, in the sentence: "the effulgence of their bodies
riseth, etc." (*vide* note 2). This rendering, which was proposed by
the late Dr J. H. Walker, was there adopted, as making sense of
the passage, which the usual translation, *living*, fails to do. In the
present case also, *risen* provides the more fitting interpretation,
partly for the reason that the preceding word already bears the
sense of *living*—(προοωντος = πρὸ ὤν = *pre-living*)—and because the
term is used to designate the post-resurrectional Saviour. It is employed several times, in the same manner, at the beginning of

LXI
MS. f. 136ᵛ
C.S. p. 51

LXI
MS. f. 136ᵛ
C.S. p. 51

the Coptic Gnostic treatise entitled *First Book of Ieou* (*vide* Carl Schmidt's 1892 edition of the Codex Brucianus).

15. Meaning the Twelve Apostles, presumably. Cf. § 25, *Excerpt. ex Theodot.*: "*The Apostles, [Valentinus] says, took the place of the Dodecad of the Zodiac. For in the same way as [the world of] genera-tion is under their government, so is [the world of] re-generation under the Apostles*". The Ogdoad, i.e. the heavenly world, was within the compass of the Twelve Zodiacal Signs, that is to say, it extended from the Moon upwards to the Boundary or Firmament.

16. ⲛⲗⲏⲗⲏⲑ might perhaps be transliterated Lilith? ⲇⲁⲩⲉⲓⲇⲉ is David (*vide* XXIII), ⲱⲣⲟⲓⲁⲏⲗ is possibly Uriel. In the *Apoc. of John* (Cod. Berol.) the four luminaries are named Harmozēl, Ōroiaēl, Daueithe and Ēlēlēth, and are said to be manifested in connection with "*the Light which is Christ*" = "*the Autogenes God*". They are further designated Angels of Light, and are set over the 1st, 2nd, 3rd and 4th Aeons. Together with each Angel are three Aeons, con-stituting the Dodecad always associated with the manifestations of the Christ (*Iren. u. seine quelle in adv. haer.* German trans. p. 13, C. Schmidt, 1907). In the corresponding passage in Irenaeus, the order of names is the same as in the *Apoc. of John*, but Raguēl is there given in place of Ōroiaēl (I, xxvii, 1). That the order in which the names appear in our treatise is in the inverse to the other passages, is due to the fact that the cosmogonical details are here pictured as from below upwards. The extant MS. terminates with this folio, at the word *Ōroiaēl*. The sentence was doubtless completed on the next page, by the words: *and Harmozēl*.

Additional Notes and Corrections

P. 3, l. 11. (-ανουσιος) instead of (ανουσιος).

P. 3, l. 17. (-ανουσιος) instead of (ανουσιος).

P. 12, l. 4. (Members) instead of Members.

P. 12, l. 17. is instead of was.

P. 66, l. 8. (ἀ'ορατον) instead of (ἀ'ορατος).

P. 73, ll. 6–7. *literally*, a still, an inconceivable, and an infinite.

P. 86, note 9, l. 2. Phōsilampēs instead of Phōsilampes.

P. 90, ll. 2 and 15. Phōsilampēs instead of Phōsilampes.

P. 110, ll. 18–9, 21–2, 24–5. *literally*, a boundless, an unutterable, and an uncontainable—an invisible, an unbegotten,
and an unmoved—a still, an unknowable, and a triple-
powered.

P. 140, l. 2. unbegotten instead of uncreated.

P. 149, l. 12. (ἀ'ορατος) omitted after Invisible.

P. 175, l. 6. (χωρα) omitted after Place.

P. 175, l. 7. (χωρα) omitted after Place.

INDICES

I. COPTIC FORMS OF GREEK WORDS

ααα, ηηη, εεε, οοο, υυυ, ωωω, 94
ααα, ωωω, 108
αβασιλευτος (ἀβασίλευτος), 136
αγαθος (ἀγαθός), 36 *bis*, 38 *bis*, 127
αγαθον (ἀγαθός), 38, 89
αγαπη (ἀγάπη), 51, 70, 115 *bis*, 130, 136, 138, 160, 177
αγγελος (ἄγγελος), 89, 151 *bis*, 164 *bis*
αγεννητος (ἀγέννητος), 32, 58, 66, 73, 81, 104, 110, 114 *bis*, 140, 141, 149, 157, 177
-αγεννητος (ἀγέννητος), with prefix of condition, 33
ʽαγνον (ἀγνός), 51
αγνωστος (ἄγνωστος), 3, 17, 26, 32 *bis*, 38, 70, 101, 110, 114 *bis*, 138 *bis*, 169, 177
αγων (ἀγών), 102, 130, 136
αγωνιζε (ἀγωνίζεσθαι), 39, 40, 70, 160
αδαμας (ἀδάμας), 83
αδαμαντος (ἀδάμαντος), 141, 179
αει (ἀεί), 40
αεροδιος (ἀερο-δῖος), 180 *bis*
αηρ (ἀήρ), 164, 180
αθανασια (ἀθανασία), 58
αθανατος (ἀθάνατος), 102, 110, 179
αιδος (ἀΐδιος), 42
αισθανε (αἰσθάνεσθαι), 40
αισθησις (αἴσθησις), 124
αισθητος (αἰσθητός), 136
αιτι (αἰτεῖν), 136, 168
αιχμαλωτιζε (αἰχμαλωτίζειν), 97
χμαλωσια (αἰχμαλωσία), 97
αιων (αἰών), 26, 39, 42 *bis*, 54 *bis*, 56, 58 *bis*, 66, 84, 87, 94 *bis*, 97 *bis*, 102 *bis*, 104, 108, 110 *bis*, 118 *pass.*, 122 *pass.*, 127, 136, 141 *pass.*, 145 *pass.*, 151 *bis*, 152, 157 *pass.*, 160 *pass.*, 167, 169, 170 *pass.*, 175 *bis*, 177 *pass.*, 179 *bis*, 180 *bis*.
αιωνιος (αἰώνιος), 141, 157
αιων πανʽολων (αἰών πανόλα), 170

ακαταγνωστος (ἀκατάγνωστος), 3, 54, 56, 70, 73 *bis*, 81
ακτιν (ἀκτίς), 42, 83, 124
αλεκτος (ἄληκτος), 138
αληθια (ἀλήθεια), 54 *bis*, 58, 83, 101, 130, 138, 160 *bis*, 180
αλλα (ἀλλά), 39, 152, 165
αμετρητος (ἀμέτρητος), 3, 73, 90, 112, 114, 122; *vide* βαθος αμετρητος.
αμετρητον (ἀμέτρητος), 102, 116; *vide* βαθος αμετρητον
ʽαμην (ἀμήν), 108
αμιαντος (ἀμίαντος), 81, 179
αναγκαιον (ἀναγκαῖος), 22
αναπαυσις (ἀνάπαυσις), 36, 39, 51, 83, 124, 175
αναρχος (ἄν-αρχος), 51
αναστασις (ἀνάστασις), 51, 83, 110, 138
αναχωρι (ἀναχωρεῖν), 177
ανουσιος (ἀνούσιος), 3 *pass.*, 12 *bis*, 38, 51, 116, 168
-ανουσιος (ἀνούσιος), with prefix of condition, 3 *bis*
αντιλεγε (ἀντιλέγεσθαι), 175
αντιτυπος (ἀντίτυπος), 180 *bis*
αʽορατος (ἀόρατος), 3 *bis*, 26, 32 *bis*, 36 *bis*, 54 *bis*, 56, 73, 81, 84, 102 *pass.*, 104, 108, 110, 112 *bis*, 138, 149, 157, 168
αʽορατον (ἀόρατος), 66
απαρχη (ἀπαρχή), 136
απεραντος (ἀπέραντος), 3 *bis*, 26 *bis*, 36 *bis*, 42, 58, 73 *bis*, 81, 101, 108, 110, 112 *bis*, 138 *bis*, 152, 167, 169 *pass.*, 177
απεραντον (ἀπέραντος), 90
ʽαπλουν (ἁπλοῦς), 56, 73
ʽαπλως (ἁπλῶς), 164
αποʽρητος (ἀπόρρητος), 3
αποστολος (ἀπόστολος), 87
αʽρητος (ἄρρητος), 3, 26 *bis*, 58 *bis*, 73, 81, 90, 101, 110, 138 *bis*, 179

INDEX

ειρηνη (εἰρήνη), 138
ιρηνη (εἰρήνη), 116 *bis*, 130, 160
ειτε (εἶτε), 56 *pass.*, 138 *pass.*
'ελπις (ἐλπίς), 51, 115, 138, 160
ενδυμα (ἔνδυμα), 12, 40, 140, 164
'εννας (ἐννεάς), 17, 42, 51, 58, 70
   bis, 89, 102, 104 *pass.*, 110 *bis*,
   112 *bis*, 130 *bis*, 140, 141, 160 *bis*
εννοια (ἔννοια), 3, 12, 84, 91, 108
-ενωχλι (ενοχλεῖν), 90
εξας (ἑξάς), 140
εξουσια (ἐξουσία), 130, 145 *bis*,
   151, 160, 164, 177 *bis*
επιδη (ἐπειδή), 152
επιθυμει (ἐπιθυμεῖν), 26, 56 *bis*, 169
επινοια (ἐπίνοια), 3, 12 *bis*, 32
   bis, 66, 83, 108
επισκοπος (ἐπίσκοπος), 42, 58 *bis*,
   118 *bis*
ευνουσιος (ἐνούσιος?), 54

ζωγραφι (ζωγραφεῖν), 12, 94

η (ἤ), 12 *bis*, 38, 51 *bis*, 54, 83, 89,
   101, 104, 110, 118, 124, 164, 165
ηδη (ἠδέ), 84
ηρεμιο (ἠρέμιος), 114
ηρεμιος (ἠρέμιος), 73 *bis*, 81, 101, 114
ηρεμος (ἠρέμιος), 32 *bis*, 38, 110
   bis, 138
ερημος (ἠρέμιος), 17, 56
'υσυχια (ἡσυχία), 110

θελημα (θέλημα), 56, 102
θεωρι (θεωρεῖν), 38, 39

'ιερον (ἱερός), 58, 91, 151, 170
'ιερον πληρωμα (ἱερός πλήρωμα),
   17 *bis*, 56, 58, 94, 116 *bis*, 170

καθαριζε (καθαρίζειν), 141
κακια (κακία), 141
καλυπτος (καλυπτός), 22, 70, 83,
   127, 157
κανουν (κανών), 58, 104 *pass.*, 110
   pass., 118, 130, 141
καρπος (καρπός), 73, 104
κατα (κατά), 17, 26, 84, 87, 91,
   112, 118, 124 *bis*, 127 *bis*, 140
   pass., 152, 165 *bis*, 167, 168, 177,
   179 *pass.*

καταπετασμα (καταπέτασμα), 89,
   97, 101, 118, 140, 141, 170, 175
   bis
κατ'ικων (κατ'εἰκών), 42
κελευε (κελεύειν), 118
κελευσις (κέλευσις), 122
κεφαλη (κεφαλή), 58
κλαδος (κλάδος), 116
κοσμος (κόσμος), 22, 42 *pass.*, 54,
   56 *bis*, 83, 127, 136, 167, 168,
   170 *bis*, 175 *bis*, 177 *bis*
κωλυ (κωλύειν), 177

λιτουργος (λειτουργός), 151
λογικον (λογικός), 73
λογος (λόγος), 42 *bis*, 91 *pass.*, 124
   bis, 160
λογος δημιουργος (λόγος δημιουρ-
   γός), 91, 124 *bis*, 127
λογος μονογενης (λόγος μονογενής),
   70
λογος νοερον (λόγος νοερός), 12
λογρφη (λογογραφεῖν), 160
λμπι (λυπεῖν), 167 *bis*

μακαριος (μακάριος), 39, 160
μελος (μέλος), 3 *bis*, 12 *bis*, 17, 40,
   54, 56, 124
μεν (μέν), 97
μεν (μήν), 84 *pass.*, 149
μερος (μέρος), 170
μερος (μηρός), 22
μετανοια (μετάνοια), 180 *bis*
μητρα (μήτρα), 17
μητροπολις (μητρόπολις), 89
μοναρχης (μόν-αρχος), 169
μονας (μονάς), 17, 42, 54, 56, 58
   pass., 70, 89 *pass.*, 91 *bis*, 110,
   112 *pass.*, 116, 127, 138, 140
   bis, 141
μονογενης (μονογενής), 66 *pass.*,
   83, 87 *pass.*, 89 *bis*, 90 *bis*,
   91 *bis*, 94, 104, 108 *pass.*,
   110 *bis*, 122; *vide* λογος μονογενης
μορφη (μορφή), 40, 118, 152, 157,
   168
μυριαρχος (μυρί-αρχος), 22
μυστηριον (μυστήριον), 22 *bis*, 51,
   84 *bis*, 116 *pass.*, 118, 122 *bis*,
   157, 160 *bis*, 177

[197]

II. CONTRACTED WORDS

III. PROPER NAMES

IV. WORDS OF UNCERTAIN DERIVATION

V. SUBJECT INDEX

Text in roman: commentary in italic.

All-manifest, (the) 26, 127
All-mystery, (the) = the First
    Cause, 33, 38
    = the 3rd Deep of the Pleroma,
    51
All-perfect, (the) a designation of
    the Heavenly Man, 26
    Light, 33
    Father, 122
    Seal, 141
    Names, 149
All-power, (the) = the 10th Deep
    of the Pleroma, 54
All-powered, a designation of the
    Fruit of the Whole, 94
All-source, (the) = the First Cause,
    39
    = the 1st Deep of the Pleroma,
    51
All things, = the Aeons of the
    Pleroma, 40 bis, 54, 70, 73,
    91 bis, 112, 116, 168 (see
    also Aeons and Universes)
    = the outer Aeons, 110
All-wise, (the) = the First Cause,
    22, 39
    = the 2nd Deep of the Pleroma,
    51
Angel, (The) = the Saviour, 151
Angel, (The) = the Messenger of the
    Pleroma, 151
Angelic hierarchies, correlation with the
    Gnostic Aeons, 8
Angels, of the Monad, 89
    of the Propator (of the lower
    cosmos), 151
    of the Mother's First-begotten
    Son, 164
    the body of the, 164
Angels, (male), cause of the Mother's
    conception, 123, 127, 128
    the Saviour's body-guard of, 125,
    128
    future union of with the spiritual
    Seed, 125, 143, 153, 162, 171,
    172, 185
ἀνούσιος, significance of the term, 7–8
Anthropos, (the) = the Heavenly Man,
    Valentinian doctrine of, 14–15
    doctrine of in the Apocryphon of
    John, 15

in the Naassene cosmogony, 16,
    21, 23
    = the Primal Adam, 15–16
    likeness of the Divine Image, 15
    = the First Manifestation, 15
    syzygy of, 15, 23, 48
    = the Heavenly City, 15, 16, 40
    a bisexual being, 16, 21, 26
    prototype of the cosmos, 16
    manifesting in a series of pro-
    phetic figures, 16 (see also
    Man, (the Heavenly))
Antitypes, the heavenly, 180
ἀντίτυπος, significance of the term,
    183
Aphredōn, (great Ruler of the space
    of the Midst), 26, 58, 66,
    118
αφρηδων (adj.), 66, 81
Aphredōn, derivation and meaning of
    name, 27
    his significance, 27–31
    suggested affinity with the great
    Ruler in the Basilidian cosmo-
    gony, 28–29, 117
    prototype of the Propator of the
    lower cosmos, 30, 132
    great Ruler of the space of the
    Midst, 117, 118
Aphredōn Pēksos, proper name of
    the Indivisible, 66
αφρηδωνια, = the Formlessness,
    127
Aphredōnia, significance of the term,
    127
    correspondence in Basilidian cos-
    mogony, 127–28
Apocryphon of John, cited, 4–6, 8, 9,
    13, 14, 15, 18, 49, 59, 62, 63,
    77, 92, 94–95
    probable source of A. and present
    treatise, 20
Apostles, Twelve, of the Only-be-
    gotten, 87
Apostles, Twelve, reflections of the
    Dodecad of Aeons, of the Zodiac,
    and the divisions of the Year,
    87–88, 108, 190
Archangels, of the Monad, 89
    of the Propator (of the lower
    cosmos), 151

Books, (*The*) *of Ieou, cited*, 10, 70, 105
Boundary, (*the*) = *the Divine Image*, 8, 47
  in the Basilidian cosmogony, 28, 59
  = *the Stauros*, 46–47, 173
  is threefold, 47
  of the Pleroma, 172, 173
Brandis, Christian A., *cited*, 67–68
Burkitt, Prof. F. C., *on derivation and meaning of name Barbēlo*, 50

Called, (*Matt. xxii, 14*), = *psychic humanity*, 161, 163, 166, 174, 180–81 (*see also Psychic humanity*)
Character (χαρακτήρ), *imparted to created things*, 54, 83, 102, 110, 168
  (*uncharactered*), *attribute of the Monad*, 54
  attribute of the First Cause, 90
  attribute of the Ennead of the Indivisible, 102, 110, 130
Chariot, (*the*) *of the Only-begotten*, 89
Chosen, (*Matt. xxii, 14*), = *the spiritual souls*, 157, 161–62, 163, 180–81 (*see also Spiritual souls*)
Christ, (*the*) *the Prover*, 73
  = *the Fruit of the Whole*, 73
  = *the Logos*, 127
  the indwelling 152
  the Spouse of the Church, 152
Christ, (*the*) = *the Monogenes*, 13, 62
  = *the Guardian of the Pleroma*, 59, 63–64
  entitled "the Servant", 59, 63–64
  the Prover, 59, 63, 64, 74–75, 77
  triple manifestation of, 63–64, 74, 77–79, 95
  first manifestation of = *the Christ of the Pleroma*, 63, 64, 74, 75, 76, 77, 95, 99, 106, 119, 120, 123
  second manifestation of = *the Fruit of the Whole*, 63–64, 76–77, 96, 109, 110, 119, 120, 123

  third manifestation of = *the Saviour of the world*, 63, 64, 78, 134
  = *the Fruit of the Whole*, 63, 76–78, 95, 96, 110, 119–20, 123, 124–25
  triple generation and birth of, 64, 154–56
  = *the Spark of Light*, 94–95, 96, 110
  the Spouse of the Sophia, 119, 153, 185
  equated with Hermes, 156
Christ, (*the psychic*), *Valentinian doctrine of*, 130, 131, 134, 147, 164, 171, 173, 178, 184, 187, 189
  resurrection of, 178, 189
  post-resurrectional designations of, 187, 189
  association with Pistis Sophia, 187–88
Christ & Holy Spirit, (*a Valentinian Aeon*), 45, 55, 59, 63, 64, 74, 75, 77, 95, 119
Christhood, 110
Christmas Day, *the Three Masses of*, 155
Christology, *of the treatise*, 77–80
  of the Valentinians, 76–79
  of the Sethians, 78, 171–72
  of Origen, 79–80
  of the Peratae, 154–55
Church, (*the*) *care of the Demiurge for*, 153
  seeds of, 157
  Catholic C. = *psychic humanity*, 166, 181
  on earth and in the after-death state, 181–82
  (*Feasts of Birth, Epiphany and Baptism*)
  in the early C., 125
  in the non-uniate Armenian C., 125
  (*Commemoration of the Triple Birth*)
  in the Catholic C., 155
  in the Ethiopic C., 155–56
City, (*the Heavenly*), 12, 40
  = *the House of the Father, the Vesture of the Son, the*

Death, the Place of, 175
Death, the Demiurge originator of,
148
(after-death conditions) various views
on, 181–84
Decad, (a) in the Universal Womb,
70
Decad, (the) a duplication of the
Pentad, 5–6, 9–10, 15
the hidden and the manifested, 15,
18
Decads, (two) the hidden and the
manifested, 17
(ten) of the Pleroma, 58
(ten) of the Monad, 89
(ten) in the Universal Womb,
104
(fifty) of the Protogenitor of
the lower cosmos, 130
Deep, (the) of 365 Fatherhoods,
17
of the Universe = the First
Cause, 40
of Sētheus, 81
= the First Cause, 167
Deep, (a) containing three Fatherhoods, 70
Deep, the Indivisible 66 *et seq.*
the Immeasurable 73, 116, 118
Deep, the Twelfth = the Truth, equated
with the εἰκών and the μονάς,
54
the Indivisible 66, 101, 131
the Immeasurable 68, 73–74,
103, 111, 112–13, 115, 121
Deep, (the) = the First Cause, 41
of Sētheus, 81–82
Deeps, (Twelve) of the Pleroma:
1st the All-source, 2nd the
All-wise, 3rd the All-mystery, 4th the All-gnosis, 5th
the All-holy, 6th the Silence,
7th the Door of non-sub-
stance, 8th the Forefather
(Deep), 9th an All-father
(Deep), 10th the All-power
(Deep), 11th containing the
1st Invisible, 12th the Truth
covering all, 51, 54
(Twelve) surrounding the Indivisible, 101

Deeps, (Twelve) of the Pleroma, 6
representing the Divine perfections,
52–53
Demiurge, (the) of the lower cosmos,
130–32, 145–48
his psychic nature, 132, 143
creator of the Hebdomad, 143–44,
146
his state of ignorance, 143, 146–47
receives the spiritual Seed, 143, 146
originates the 1st race of psychic
humanity, 146, 148
his care for the Church, 153
St John the Baptist a type of, 153
future state of, 153, 185
Devil, (the) Valentinian notions of,
132–33
origin of, in the Kabbala, 133
identified with the Valentinian
Cosmokrator, 132–33, 158
distinguished from Beelzebul,
133–34
Dodecad, (the) of the Pleroma, 5, 6, 44
reflected in the 12 Fatherhoods, 87
reflected in the 12 Apostles, 88
reflected in the 12 Zodiacal Signs,
88
(a) associated with creative processes, 120
associated with the Christ, 120, 190
Door, (the) (of non-substance)
= the 7th Deep of the
Pleroma, 51
= the Mystery, 116
of God, 116
Door, (the) of non-substance, 52
= the Mystery, 52
of God, 52
= the Monogenes, 116–17
Doxogenes, (= of Glory-begotten),
151
Doxogenia, (= Begetting-Glory),
70, 149
Doxokratia, (= Ruling-Glory), 70,
149
Doxokrator, (= Lord-of-Glory),
151
Doxophanes, (= of Glory-re-
vealed), 151
Doxophania, (= Revealing-Glory),
70, 149

First Cause—continued
  through his Will produces Space,
    10
  known only through the Mono-
    genes, 13, 79, 90, 95, 116–17,
    178
  is self-alone-begotten, 34–35
  unity of nature of, 38
  Valentinian designations for, 41
  his revelation of Fatherhood, 43
  is unoriginated, 52
First-fruits, of the Sonship, 136
Five, Pentads, of the Pleroma, 58
  Powers, in the Immeasurable
    Deep: Love, Hope, Faith,
    Gnosis, Peace, 114, 115, 116
  Seals, 70
  Trees, 70
  the unbegotten F. 66
Five, Members of the Father, 5, 9,
    68–69
  Trees, mentioned in the Pistis
    Sophia and 2nd Book of Ieou,
    70–71
  Powers, in the Immeasurable
    Deep, 103, 115
Forefather (προπάτωρ), (the) of
    Light = the First Cause, 32
  = Aphredōn, the great Ruler
    of the Midst, 58
  (of the lower cosmos), 130, 145,
    149, 151, 152, 165, 167
  the Sonship conferred on, 145
Forefather (προπάτωρ), (the) Valen-
    tinian appellation for the First
    Cause, 41, 43
  (of the lower cosmos), 131–32
  a psychic being, 132, 145–46
  equated with the Valentinian
    Demiurge, 145–46
  creative operations of, 146–48,
    161, 166
  the Sonship conferred on, 147
  his care for the Church, 152–53
  his future state and abode, 185
Forefather Deep, (the)=the 8th
    Deep of the Pleroma, 51
Forethought (πρόνοια), of the
    Deity, 56
  and Afterthought (ἐπίνοια), 83
  = Providence, 136

Formlessness, = the chaotic prime-
    val substance, 127
Formlessness, the state of, 28, 29, 127–
    28
Four, extremities, of the body of
    the Heavenly Man, 22
  Gates, of the Pleroma, 58
  Monads, of the Pleroma, 58
  luminaries, in the space of the
    Midst, 180
Four, extremities, of the body of the
    Heavenly Man, 24, 59
  Gates, of the Pleroma, 24, 59
  afflictions, of the Sophia, 106–07,
    119, 159
  elements, of the material creation,
    133, 159
  luminaries, in the space of the
    Midst, 190 (see also Quadru-
    plicities)
Fruit, of himself alone = the First
    Cause, 38
  of the Whole = the Saviour,
    73
  of the Aeons = the Fruit of
    the Whole, 104
  the work that bore 127
Fruit of the Whole, (the) = the Joint
    Fruit of the Pleroma, 76–77,
    106–07, 119–20, 151, 171
  formation of by the Aeons, 76–77,
    95, 96, 110–11
  significance of his titles, 96
  = the Spark of Light, 96, 109,
    110
  anointed as Christ, 110–11
  the Spouse of the Sophia, 119, 153,
    185

Gamaliēl, a Guardian of the outer
    Aeons, 97
Gates, of the Pleroma, 22, 58
  of the Monad, 89
Gates, of the Pleroma, likened to the
    extremities of the Heavenly Man,
    24, 59
Generation, the Sophia's abortive at-
    tempt at, 45
  three modes of: unbegotten, self-
    alone-begotten, and begotten, 98
  Gnostic theories of, 123

Man, Valentinian and Ptolemaic appellation for the Deity, *43*
  (*the spiritual*) *akin to the mysteries, 85*
  (*the psychic*) *endowed with senses, 137*
  first creation of, 146
  feminine spiritual principle infused into, 146
  second creation of, 148
Manifest (φανερός), (the) = those who are not, 90
  = the phenomenal creation, 118, 151
Mankind, *three races of, 148, 161* (see also *Humanity*)
Marcosian doctrines, *4, 14, 34, 35, 87*
Marsanēs, a possessor of secret knowledge, 84
Marsanēs, *probable equation of with a Sethian prophet, 85*
Matter (ὕλη), in the space of the Midst, 97
  in the outer Aeon, 118
  comprising the psychic principle, 136
  the seat of Evil, 141
  = those-who-are-not, 141
  the things of to serve the Propator of the lower cosmos, 151
  renouncement of by the spiritual race, 160
  races and species of raised up, 165
  souls led from the darkness of, 165
  separation of into two grades, 170
  rejoicing of those born from, 177
Matter (ὕλη), *significance and use of the term, 98–99*
  two grades of, 99, 121, 136–37, 159
  the seat of Evil, 75–76, 141–42
  = *those-who-are-not, 142*
  separation of the two grades of, 142–43
Members (μέλος), (the) of the Father, their emanation, 3, 12

dwelling in the Father as their Space, 3
  made ἀνούσιος, 3, 12
  sealed with the Name of the Son, 12
  the Heavenly Man originates from, 12, 54
  their Praise made the outer Vesture of the Man, 12
  are incorporeal, 54
  are complete, 56
Members (μέλος), (*the Five*) *of the Father, 5, 6, 9, 68–69*
  = *the Pentad, 5–6, 9, 15*
  = *a First Man, 9, 15, 18*
  are complete and perfect, 68–69
μετάνοια, *significance and use of the term in the treatise, 183*
Michar, a Power over the Living Water, 180
Micheu, a Power over the Living Water, 180
Midst, (the) the entities of surround the Only-begotten, 91
Midst, (*the*) = *middle space of the cosmos, 29, 46, 68, 74, 78, 93, 97, 98, 111*
  two Rulers of, 29, 68, 117, 118
  dwelling place of the outside Sophia, 46, 68, 99, 119
  = *the Basilidian Boundary, 59*
  space of the outside Aeons and outside Worlds, 68
  the Immeasurable Deep contained in, 74, 105
  = *the Self-alone-begotten Spaces, 98*
  = *the psychical realms, 99, 186*
  the place of choice for psychic entities, 99–100
  the Saviour's advent to, 122, 125
  pneumatic and psychic principles in the space of, 142
  final abode of the Demiurge and psychic humanity, 153, 185–86
  = *the Gnostic Heaven, 178, 184–85*
Mind (νοῦς), God the source of, 36
  God prior to, 36, 38
  a designation of the Creator, 42

the Power of in the Heavenly
City, 40
of all the Aeons = the Monad,
54
of the 1st Ennead, 70
of All things, 108
of the lower cosmos) designated
"Manifest", 118, 145
the Aeon of, 118, 122, 151
of the Universe, (i.e. the lower
cosmos) 118, 165, 167, 170
establishes her Propator, Autopator and Protogenitor Son,
130
intercedes on behalf of her
creation, 136, 152, 167–
169
is established as head of the
lower cosmos, 141
receives the Mystery, 157
establishes her First-begotten
Son, 164
her hymn of Praise, 167
ther, (the) of all the Aeons, = the
Monad, 54
of the lower cosmos), equated with
the Sophia, 29–30, 54
transmutation of her afflictions
(πάθη), 106, 111, 119, 123,
128, 159
her Spouse the Saviour, Fruit of the
Whole, 119, 153, 185
her enformation (μόρφωσις) in
respect of substance (κατ' οὐσίαν), 119, 123
her enformation in respect of
gnosis (κατὰ γνῶσιν), 122–
23, 124, 127, 128
gives birth to the feminine spiritual
Seed, 123, 127, 128
produces three fundamental substances, 128
produces the Propator, the Autopator and the Protogenitor,
130–31, 132–33, 134–35
deposits the spiritual Seed in the
Universal Womb, 143
her future abode the Pleroma, 153,
185
receives the male spiritual principle
from the Logos, 154, 157, 158

Mother-city (μητρόπολις), of the
Only-begotten, 89
Mousanios, (2nd Ruler of the space
of the Midst), 26, 116
Mousanios, 2nd Ruler of the space of
the Midst, 26, 118, 133
derivation and significance of name,
27–30
suggested affinity with the 2nd
Ruler in the Basilidian cosmogony, 28–29, 117
prototype of the Autopator of the
lower cosmos, 133
Mysteries, the hidden 22
man's kinship with, 84
of the Ineffable, 116
Mystery, (the) man's knowledge of,
84
of the Silence, 116
= the Monogenes, 116
the Holy Pleroma under his
Feet, 116
= the Door of God, 116
causes the Veils of the Aeons
to be drawn, 118
is hidden in the Primal Father,
122
is sent to the Mother of the
lower cosmos, 157
of the Hidden Father, 160
that became Man, 160
Mystery, the All- = the 3rd Deep
of the Pleroma, 51
the Hidden 177

Naassenes, (the) doctrinal beliefs of,
14, 16, 21, 23, 37, 156
identified with the Sethians and
Ophites, 20
Name, the First Cause without, 38
the Stars called by, 124
(the) of the Son, 12
of God, 91, 169
of the Self-alone-begotten, (i.e.
the Saviour), 180
Name, power in the utterance of, 30, 126
(the) of the Son, 111, 134, 171
Nameless, a designation of the
Propator of the lower cosmos, 149
Names, all from God, 38, 56

(non-)substance—*continued*
the Door of, 51
All things, (= the Aeons)
made in, 116
*Substances, (primary) of the pheno-
menal world, 106–07*

Those-who-are, = the hidden and
eternal, 90, 141
Those-who-are-not, = the manifest and material, 90, 141
That-which-is and that-which-is-
not, = Good and Evil, 141
Thirty, Powers, in the Left-hand
of the Only-begotten, 87
Powers, surrounding Twelve
Fatherhoods in the Immea-
surable Deep, 112, 114
*Thirty, Aeons, of the Pleroma, 5, 47,
87*
Days, of the Month, 87
Powers, of the Only-begotten, 87
Thought (conceptive) (ἔννοια), 3,
12, 84, 91, 108
(ἐπίνοια), 3, 12, 32, 66, 108
(διάνοια), 168
Three, aspects, of the Guardian of
the Pleroma, 58
aspects, of the Indivisible Deep,
66
aspects, of the Twelve Fathers
in the Deep of Sētheus, 81
Enneads, outside the Indivisible with T. Fatherhoods in
each, 110
Fatherhoods, in the Indivisible Deep, 70
Guardians, in the space of the
Midst, 97
Powers, of the Only-begotten,
66
Powers, around a Trapeza, 73
Powers, in the Universal
Womb, 141
Three, (The) and One, 12
*Three, Beings, ruling in the Mother's
Aeon, 130–31*
*divisions, of the greater cosmos,
14, 29, 46, 93, 95, 98, 142*
*divisions, of the lower cosmos, 131,
133, 142, 181*

*Feasts, of the Birth, Epiphany,
and Baptism celebrated as one,
125*
generative modes, 98
kinds of substance, 128, 145
*manifestations, of the Monogenes,
63–64, 68, 74, 77–79, 94, 95,
111, 120, 154–55*
*manifestations, of the Spark of
Light, 95, 169*
*manifestations, of the feminine
principle of the universe, 187*
Masses, of Christmas Day, 155
*principles, of creation, 63, 128,
142*
*principles, of creation, (subdivi-
sions of), 98–99, 142–43, 159*
races, of mankind, 148, 161, 166
series of Aeons, 5
Three hundred and sixty-five,
Aeons, belonging to Adam,
58
Beings, forming the Crown of
the Mystery, 116
Fatherhoods, in the Immeasurable Deep, 17, 116
γένη, in the Crown of the
Indivisible, 101
Powers, in the Right-hand of
the Only-begotten, 87
*Three hundred and sixty-five, Beings,
117*
Fatherhoods, 60–61, 117
γένη, *in the Indivisible, 101*
Heavens, 117
Thrice-begotten (τριγενής), 152
Thrice-born (τριγένεθλος), 152
Time and Space, divisions of, 87
*Transmutation, of the Mother's afflic-
tions* (πάθη), *106–07, 111,
119–20, 123, 145, 148, 159*
Trapeza (τράπεζα), (a) in the
Immeasurable Deep, 70, 73
*Trapeza, (a) and other quadruplicities
associated with the Logos, 71*
Trees, (Five) in the 2nd Father-
hood of the Indivisible, 70
Trees, (Five), 70–71
Triad, (The) = the Gnostic Trinity,
14, 66
Triads, significance of, 63, 111

[226]

For EU product safety concerns, contact us at Calle de José Abascal, 56–1°,
28003 Madrid, Spain or eugpsr@cambridge.org.

www.ingramcontent.com/pod-product-compliance
Ingram Content Group UK Ltd.
Pitfield, Milton Keynes, MK11 3LW, UK
UKHW010049140625
459647UK00012BB/1714

* 9 7 8 1 1 0 7 6 5 0 9 6 1 *